A Wider Europe

The Process and Politics of European Union Enlargement

Michael J. Baun

ROWMAN & LITTLEFIELD PUBLISHERS, INC.
Lanham • Boulder • New York • Oxford

ROWMAN & LITTLEFIELD PUBLISHERS, INC.

Published in the United States of America
by Rowman & Littlefield Publishers, Inc.
4720 Boston Way, Lanham, Maryland 20706
http://www.rowmanlittlefield.com

12 Hid's Copse Road, Cumnor Hill, Oxford OX2 9JJ, England

British Cataloging in Publication Information Available

Library of Congress Cataloging-in-Publication Data

Baun, Michael J.
  A wider Europe : the process and politics of European Union enlargement / Michael J. Baun.
    p.   cm.—(Governance in Europe)
  Includes bibliographical references and index.
  ISBN 0-8476-9036-9 (cloth : alk. paper)—ISBN 0-8476-9037-7 (pbk. : alk. paper)
    1. European Union. I. Title. II. Series.

JN30 .B39 2000
341.242'2—dc21

                                                                                    00-028010

Printed in the United States of America

♾™ The paper used in this publication meets the minimum requirements of American
National Standard for Information Sciences—Permanence of Paper for Printed Library
Materials, ANSI/NISO Z39.48-1992.

Contents

Preface

The great experiment of European integration has entered another phase. The past fifty years have seen the economic and political integration of Western Europe. While this process remains incomplete and its ultimate goal uncertain (or at least highly contested), there is no denying that it has achieved a great deal; integration thus far has generated increased prosperity for Europeans and made war between the states of Western Europe unthinkable. Many of the achievements of European integration occurred during the era of the cold war, however, raising valid questions about whether the European Union (EU) would survive the disappearance of this simultaneously restrictive and supportive geopolitical context. With the EU's current efforts at eastward enlargement, we are beginning to find out.

The next phase of European integration concerns the extension of the EU's zone of democracy, prosperity, and stability into Central and Eastern Europe, an area of Europe that has previously known little of these things. It concerns transcending the geopolitical divisions of the cold war, as well as Europe's other historical and cultural cleavages, and achieving the unification of Europe. It concerns, in other words, the construction of a "wider Europe." The final end point of this next phase of European integration is also unknown, especially as it concerns the ultimate borders and membership of an enlarged EU. Perhaps as well, it is not so much the ultimate end as the process itself that is important.

For all of the achievements of European integration until now, this next phase of integration will likely be the historically decisive phase for the EU, determining its ultimate success or failure. This is because, ironically, enlargement has the potential to create new divisions in Europe as well as to unify it. How the EU enlarges, therefore, will determine whether the EU successfully completes its self-appointed mission to unite all of Europe. Enlargement also poses a challenge to the EU's institutions and policies. Thus, how the EU enlarges will also determine whether the

EU remains a cohesive and effective organization, and whether it will be able to make further progress toward its declared goal of "ever closer union."

Despite the undeniable challenge for the EU that eastward enlargement poses, this imperative must be faced, for an EU that refuses to enlarge would be a moral failure, under siege and insecure within a divided and conflictual Europe. While the success of an enlarged EU remains in doubt, there is no question that a narrow "fortress Europe" would ultimately fail. Exploring how the EU has faced this challenge of enlargement is the basic purpose of this book.

Before proceeding, a qualification. The focus of this book is the development of EU policy on enlargement. It admittedly does not give sufficient attention to what the applicant countries of Central and Eastern Europe have done to prepare for membership and to the impact of these efforts on their economies, societies, and domestic policies; this is a massive subject that requires a volume of its own. With this caveat, the author responds in advance to the inevitable criticism that this book is too one-sided in its attention to the EU side of the enlargement equation.

The author would like to make a second qualification as well. Writing about enlargement poses a difficult challenge, for this is a dynamic, ongoing process with a conclusion that remains highly uncertain. Unforeseen political and economic developments have the potential for altering the anticipated course of events. This book, therefore, as with any scholarly work on the EU and European integration, can only be a snapshot of the process at a particular point in time. It seeks to describe the enlargement process up to this moment, analyze its key dynamics and issues, and speculate—hazardous though this may be—about the direction the process is headed. Although the EU's Helsinki summit of December 1999 reached a number of critical strategic decisions about enlargement, thus providing a convenient stopping point (or "overlook") for surveying the progress of the enlargement process, it is entirely possible that developments after the time of writing (March 2000) may overtake or outdate some of the discussion in this book. This is a risk that is well worth taking, however.

While this book is the product of my own efforts, and I deserve any criticism for its faults, it could not have been completed without the help of a number of important people. I am deeply grateful for the assistance and advice of many individuals, including fellow academics and EU officials too numerous to name. My department chair, Dr. Jim Peterson, and Dean Thomas Dasher of the Valdosta State University College of Arts and Sciences were generous in providing me with release time from teaching to complete this book. I am also thankful to Colonel Vernon Pizer and the Marguerite Langdale Pizer Chair Foundation Account for funding that made research for this book possible. I also wish to thank Susan McEachern, executive editor at Rowman & Littlefield Publishing Group, for her patient support and unerring advice on preparation of the manuscript, and Professor Gary Marks, for including this book in his edited series "Governance in Europe." Special thanks also go to my wife, Julia, for her love and understanding, and to my son, Matthew, for inspiring me every day. It is to them that I dedicate this book.

Acronyms

CAP	Common Agricultural Policy
CDU/CSU	Christian Democratic Union/Christian Social Union
CEEC	Central and Eastern European country
CEFTA	Central European Free Trade Area
CEPS	Center for European Policy Studies
CFSP	Common Foreign and Security Policy
CIS	Commonwealth of Independent States
CMEA	Council for Mutual Economic Assistance
COREPER	Committee of Permanent Representatives
CSCE	Conference on Security and Cooperation in Europe
DG	Directorate-General
EBRD	European Bank for Reconstruction and Development
EC	European Community
ECJ	European Court of Justice
ECSC	European Coal and Steel Community
ECU	European Currency Unit
EEA	European Economic Area
EEC	European Economic Community
EFTA	European Free Trade Association
EIB	European Investment Bank
EMS	European Monetary System
EMU	Economic and Monetary Union
EP	European Parliament
EPU	European Political Union
ERDF	European Regional Development Fund
ERM	European Exchange-Rate Mechanism

ETF	European Training Foundation
EU	European Union
EUR	euro
EUROSTAT	European Union Statistics Office
G7	Group of Seven
G24	Group of Twenty-Four
GDP	gross domestic product
GDR	German Democratic Republic
GNP	gross national product
GSP	Generalized System of Preferences
IGC	intergovernmental conference
IMF	International Monetary Fund
ISPA	Instrument for Structural Policies for Pre-Accession
JHA	Justice and Home Affairs
MEP	Member of the European Parliament
MFN	Most Favored Nation
NATO	North Atlantic Treaty Organization
NGO	nongovernmental organization
OECD	Organization for Economic Cooperation and Development
OSCE	Organization for Security and Cooperation in Europe
PCA	Partnership and Cooperation Agreement
PHARE	Poland and Hungary Aid for Economic Reconstruction
QMV	qualified majority voting
SAPARD	Support for Agriculture and Rural Development
SEA	Single European Act
TACIS	Technical Assistance to the Commonwealth of Independent States
TEC	Treaty Establishing the European Community
TEMPUS	Trans-European Mobility Program for University Students
TEN	Trans-European Transportation and Energy Network
TEU	Treaty on European Union
VAT	value-added tax
WEU	Western European Union
WTO	World Trade Organization

Chronology of Main Events in the Eastern Enlargement Process

1987
June   Turkey applies for EC membership.

1989
July   G7 meeting in Paris asks Commission to coordinate multilateral aid to Poland and Hungary.
September–December   Central and Eastern Europe communist governments collapse. The Berlin Wall comes down on November 9.

1990
July   Cyprus and Malta apply for EC membership.
December   Commission receives mandate to negotiate Europe Agreements with Hungary, Poland, and Czechoslovakia.

1991
December   Maastricht European Council agrees to TEU. Europe Agreements signed with Hungary, Poland, and Czecho-slovakia.

1992
June   Lisbon European Council discusses prospects for EU enlargement.
December   Edinburgh European Council decides to begin accession negotiations with four EFTA applicants in early 1993.

1993

February	Europe Agreement signed with Romania.
March	Europe Agreement signed with Bulgaria.
June	Copenhagen European Council accepts Eastern enlargement in principle; promises future membership to CEECs meeting certain economic and political conditions.
July	Commission issues positive Opinions on the applications of Cyprus and Malta.
October	Europe Agreements signed with the Czech Republic and Slovakia.

1994

March	Hungary applies for EU membership.
April	Poland applies for EU membership.
June	Corfu European Council asks Commission to develop proposals for a pre-accession strategy for the CEECs; declares that Cyprus and Malta will be included in the next phase of enlargement.
December	Essen European Council approves the pre-accession strategy; key features are the enhanced Structured Relationship and Single Market White Paper.

1995

January	Accession of Austria, Sweden, and Finland to the EU.
March	Pact on Stability in Europe signed in Paris.
June	Europe Agreements signed with Latvia, Lithuania, and Estonia. Romania and Slovakia apply for EU membership. Cannes European Council approves Commission's White Paper; announces that accession negotiations with Cyprus and Malta will begin six months after conclusion of 1996 IGC.
October	Latvia applies for EU membership.
November	Estonia applies for EU membership.
December	Lithuania and Bulgaria apply for EU membership. Madrid European Council asks the Commission to prepare Opinions on the CEEC applications and submit reports on enlargement strategy and the impact of enlargement on EU policies and finances; announces that accession negotiations with CEECs will begin soon after conclusion of 1996 IGC, together with the beginning negotiations with Cyprus and Malta.

1996

January	The Czech Republic applies for EU membership.
March	IGC to review Maastricht Treaty begins in Turin, Italy.
June	Europe Agreement signed with Slovenia. Slovenia applies for EU membership.
October	Malta freezes its application for EU membership.

1997

June   Amsterdam European Council concludes IGC and reaches agreement on Amsterdam Treaty.

July   NATO's Madrid summit; Poland, Hungary, and the Czech Republic invited to join. Commission issues its Opinions on the CEEC applications and its enlargement strategy recommendations, along with its "Agenda 2000" proposals for policy and finance reform and 2000–2006 financial perspective.

December   Luxembourg European Council decides to begin accession process for ten CEECs and Cyprus in March 1998; accession negotiations with five best-prepared applicants and Cyprus to begin in March 1998; Turkey not included in the accession process, but invited to first European Conference in March 1998.

1998

March   First European Conference in London; boycotted by Turkey. Accession Partnerships for each of the CEECs adopted. Accession process formally launched; accession negotiations with Hungary, Poland, the Czech Republic, Estonia, Slovenia, and Cyprus officially begun.

September   Malta reactivates its membership application.

November   Commission's First Regular Progress Reports released. Substantive negotiations with the six first-group applicants are begun.

1999

March   War in Kosovo. Commission resigns following report of independent investigating committee. Berlin European Council reaches agreement on "Agenda 2000" reforms and financial perspective for 2000–2006; Romano Prodi chosen as next Commission president.

April   EU announces "Stability Pact" for Southeastern Europe; includes prospect of membership for Western Balkans states.

June   Cologne European Council decides to convene new IGC on institutional reform in early 2000; favors narrow IGC agenda.

July   Second European Conference; Turkey again boycotts.

August   Devastating earthquakes in Turkey.

October   Commission's Second Regular Progress Reports issued; recommends that "group" approach to accession negotiations be abandoned in favor of "regatta" approach. Revised Accession Partnerships issued. Report of Commission's Dehaene Committee calls for broader IGC agenda.

December   Helsinki European Council decides to open accession negotiations with all (twelve) applicant countries in early 2000; EU to be ready for enlargement after 2002; declares Turkey an official candidate for

EU membership; approves narrow agenda for 2000 IGC, with possibility for later expansion.

2000

February IGC on institutional reform begins. Accession negotiations begun with Slovakia, Latvia, Lithuania, Bulgaria, Romania, and Malta.

EU member states

Candidate states negotiating accession

Candidate state, not negotiating

Possible Dates of Accession

2003–2007	Cyprus
	Czech Republic
	Estonia
	Hungary
	Latvia
	Lithuania
	Malta
	Poland
	Slovakia
	Slovenia
2008–2010	Bulgaria
	Romania
2010–?	Turkey

FINLAND

SWEDEN

Helsinki

Stockholm

Tallinn

BALTIC
SEA

ESTONIA

LATVIA

Riga

Moscow

RUSSIA

Copenhagen

LITHUANIA

Vilnius

BELARUS

Minsk

Berlin

Warsaw

Kiev

POLAND

UKRAINE

Prague

CZECH REPUBLIC

SLOVAKIA

Bratislava

Moldova

Chisinau

Vienna

Budapest

AUSTRIA

HUNGARY

ROMANIA

SLOVENIA

Ljubljana

Zagreb

CROATIA

Bucharest

BLACK SEA

BOSNIA

Belgrade

Sarajevo

SERBIA

BULGARIA

ADRIATIC
SEA

MONTENEGRO

Sofia

Rome

Skopje

Ankara

Tirana

MACEDONIA

ALBANIA

TURKEY

GREECE

AEGEAN
SEA

Athens

SICILY

Nicosia

Valletta

IONIAN SEA

CYPRUS

LEBANON

MALTA

Beirut

Introduction

The end of the cold war provided Europe with an historic opportunity. For centuries many Europeans have dreamed of a united Europe, yet this has proven to be an elusive goal. The sudden collapse of Communism and the Soviet empire in Eastern Europe in 1989, however, has given Europe perhaps its best chance ever to realize this age-old dream in a peaceful and democratic fashion.

At the center of efforts to construct a united Europe is the European Union (EU).[1] The EU is a major reason that the countries of Western Europe have enjoyed peace and prosperity since the 1950s. With a gross domestic product (GDP) of over $8 trillion, the EU is today the world's largest integrated market and trading bloc, and the 370 million citizens of its fifteen member states enjoy some of the highest living standards in the world.[2] The EU also deserves considerable credit for the consolidation and spread of democracy in Western Europe and for the peaceful reconciliation of such former long-time enemies as Germany and France. Because of the EU, war among Western European states is now generally considered "unthinkable."

For many years, however, the eastward extension of the EU's zone of democracy and prosperity was prevented by the cold war and Europe's division into hostile political-military blocs. Not only was EU membership for the Communist states of Central and Eastern Europe impossible, but official ties between the EU and the Soviet bloc countries were not even established until the late 1980s. So while the EU grew from its original six member states in the 1950s to twelve by 1986, these member states were all Western European democracies. During the cold war period, therefore, while the EU expanded to the north (Denmark), west (Britain and Ireland), and south (Spain, Portugal, and Greece), its eastern boundary was effectively determined by the iron curtain. The 1989 revolution erased this geopolitical barrier to EU expansion, however, making enlargement into Central and Eastern Europe possible for the first time.

For the newly independent countries of Central and Eastern Europe, joining the EU immediately became a primary goal. EU membership offered these countries new economic opportunities and the hope of attaining Western levels of welfare and prosperity. It also offered them increased security and a way of permanently escaping the Russian sphere of influence. EU membership would also support the efforts of the former Communist countries to consolidate their new democracies and build stable civil societies. In historical terms, EU membership symbolized the return of these countries to the European political, economic, and cultural mainstream after more than forty years of enforced separation. For the Central and Eastern European countries (CEECs), therefore, EU membership meant "returning to Europe."

Within seven years of the fall of the Berlin Wall, ten CEECs had formally applied to join the EU. The first applications were submitted in the spring of 1994 by Hungary and Poland. Romania and Slovakia applied in June 1995, followed later that year by the three Baltic states—Latvia, Estonia, and Lithuania—as well as Bulgaria. The Czech Republic applied in January 1996, as did Slovenia five months later. In their bid to enter the EU, these countries joined the Mediterranean island states of Cyprus and Malta, both of whom had already applied in 1990. Also seeking EU membership was Turkey, which submitted its application in 1987.

The EU responded positively, but cautiously, to this demand for membership. At the Copenhagen summit in June 1993, the EU accepted eastward enlargement in principle, declaring that those CEECs that so desire, and that meet certain economic and political conditions, "shall become members of the European Union." Less than five years later, at the December 1997 Luxembourg summit, the EU decided to launch the accession process for the ten CEECs and Cyprus, Malta having temporarily suspended its application in late 1996. Turkey, on the other hand, was not recognized as an official candidate for membership and included in the accession process, mainly because of problems with its democracy and human rights record but also because many within the EU questioned Turkey's European identity and vocation.

After formally launching the accession process in March 1998, the EU began substantive entry negotiations the following November with the six best-prepared applicants—Poland, Hungary, the Czech Republic, Slovenia, Estonia, and Cyprus. The remaining five CEECs were promised that they could begin accession negotiations once the EU determined that they had made sufficient economic and political progress.

In the spring of 1999, however, the Kosovo war and the threat of widening conflict in the Balkans, coupled with fears that the EU's two-tiered accession strategy might create new divisions in Europe, forced a major rethinking of enlargement strategy. This led the EU to decide, at the December 1999 Helsinki summit, to begin accession negotiations with the five remaining CEECs and

Malta (which had since reactivated its application). The Kosovo war also led the EU to think beyond the next enlargement and consider its role and responsibilities in the "wider" Europe. At the Helsinki summit, therefore, the EU also agreed to designate Turkey as an official candidate for EU membership, promising that it could begin accession negotiations once it had met the necessary political conditions. The EU also held out the prospect of eventual membership for the troubled countries of the Western Balkans, making this possibility a key element of the EU-sponsored "Stability Pact for Southeastern Europe," which was launched in June 1999. From an initial focus on Central and Eastern Europe, therefore, by the end of the 1990s the enlargement process had taken on a more pronounced Southeastern Europe dimension.

As it begins the new century, therefore, the EU's historic process of the eastern enlargement[3] is well under way. Much remains uncertain, however, including the timetable for enlargement. It is probable that the first new member states, including the most advanced of the CEECs, will join the EU by 2005, possibly earlier. Others will follow. By the end of the next decade, an EU of twenty-seven or more member states is entirely possible. Also uncertain are the ultimate geographical limits of enlargement. In addition to Turkey, Ukraine and Moldova have expressed an interest in someday joining the EU. Membership for the Western Balkans states is also possible, though highly problematic. Beyond deciding whom to admit and when, another key challenge for the EU will be managing its relations with neighboring countries such as Russia, which are not, for the foreseeable future or perhaps ever, realistic candidates for EU membership yet whose interests are greatly affected by enlargement.

As it enters the new millennium, therefore, the EU faces the challenge of enlargement and a wider Europe. In the words of former European Commission President Jacques Santer, "Enlargement represents a historic turning point for Europe, an opportunity which it must seize for the sake of its security, its economy, its culture and its status in the world."[4] However, enlargement also poses a tremendous challenge for the EU and a certain amount of risk. For one thing, it requires substantial internal adjustment by the EU, including the reform of key common policies, such as the Common Agricultural Policy (CAP) and the Structural Funds, which together consume 80 percent of the EU's total budget. To prepare itself for enlargement, the EU must also reform its decision-making institutions and procedures so that a larger and more diverse EU can function effectively and democratically. The addition of more member states, each with distinctive traditions, interests, and views, will also change the EU's basic character and identity. Among many of the present member states, especially its six founding members, there is concern that enlargement will undermine the EU's cohesion and original sense of common purpose. Clearly, an enlarged EU will be a fundamentally different Union in many important ways.

Adding to the challenge of enlargement is the EU's parallel attempt to deepen integration among its member states, including the historic effort to create an Economic and Monetary Union (EMU). Both the end of the cold war and conflict in the Balkans have also spurred efforts to create a more effective Common Foreign and Security Policy (CFSP) for the EU, including the possibility of a common defense. In these and other ways, the EU is moving toward greater economic and political integration at the same time that it adds new members and increases its diversity. While in the long run the processes of "widening" and "deepening" may not be contradictory, and in fact may be mutually supportive, in the short term their conjuncture creates a number of problems and policy dilemmas for the EU.

BOOK PLAN

In this book, the EU's response to the historic challenge and opportunity of eastern enlargement is examined. Among the key questions it seeks to answer are the following: How has the EU responded to the demands of the CEECs for membership? What specific factors have determined or influenced EU policy toward these countries and its decision making on enlargement? How has the EU sought to integrate the CEECs and prepare them for membership, especially in view of their difficult transition from Communism to democracy and the market economy? How has the EU prepared itself for enlargement, in terms of reforming its policies, institutions, and finances, and has it done enough in this regard? When will enlargement occur, and which countries will eventually join the EU? Beyond the countries involved in the current accession process, what are the future geographical limits of EU enlargement, and what will determine these limits? And finally, what will be the impact of enlargement on the nature and functioning of the EU and on its role in a wider Europe?

To answer these questions, this book is organized into the following chapters. In chapter 1, the historic challenge of eastern enlargement is examined in the context of previous enlargements. This chapter also examines the reasons for enlargement, including the potential costs and benefits of enlargement for the EU and its fifteen member states. The chapter also describes the formal institutional mechanics of the enlargement process as established by EU law as well as the experience of previous enlargements. It concludes by considering the relevance of various EU theories for explaining and understanding decision making on enlargement.

The next three chapters analyze, in chronological-narrative fashion, the developments leading up to the historic Luxembourg summit of December 1997 and the decision to begin the accession process. Chapter 2 begins with the EU's initial response to the political upheavals in Central and Eastern Europe in 1989, including aid and assistance programs and the signing of bilateral Europe Agreements. It also discusses the early debate on eastern enlargement and the question of "widening" versus "deepening." The chapter concludes with the Copenhagen summit of June 1993, at which the EU opened the door to membership for the post-Communist countries by accepting eastward enlargement in principle.

Chapter 3 examines the development of the EU's "pre-accession strategy" for the CEECs after the Copenhagen summit, including the decisions of the December 1994 Essen summit. It also discusses the European Commission's May 1995 "White Paper" on preparing the post-Communist countries for integration into the EU's Single Market as well as the growing debate over enlargement strategy within the EU, including the questions of when and how to enlarge. Chapter 3 concludes with the important decisions on enlargement of the December 1995 Madrid summit.

Chapter 4 describes the events leading up to the December 1997 Luxembourg summit. It discusses the preparation and publication in July 1997 of the Commission's Opinions on the various applications as well as its "Agenda 2000" recommendations on policy reform and enlargement strategy. The chapter then examines the response to the Commission's recommendations on enlargement, and the EU's internal debate on the accession process in the run-up to the Luxembourg summit. It concludes with the historic decisions of the Luxembourg summit on launching the accession process.

Chapter 5 examines the beginning of the accession process and substantive negotiations with the more advanced applicants. After discussing the EU's Accession Partnerships for each of the applicants and the new instruments for pre-accession assistance, the chapter looks at the formal beginning of the accession process in late March 1998. It then examines the early stages of the accession process, including the Commission's "screening" exercise and the start of substantive negotiations with the more advanced applicants in November 1998.

Chapter 6 examines the developments leading up to the EU's historic change of enlargement strategy at the December 1999 Helsinki summit. The chapter begins by examining the efforts of the second-group applicants after Luxembourg to catch up to and join the accession negotiations. The Commission's first regular progress reports on each of the applicants in November 1998 are discussed, as are the decisions of the Vienna summit one month later. The chapter then examines the rethinking of EU enlargement strategy after the Kosovo war and the Commission's second regular progress reports in October 1999. The chapter concludes with a discussion of the Helsinki summit decisions and an analysis of the EU's change of policy toward Turkey.

Chapters 7 and 8 look at how the EU is preparing itself for enlargement. Chapter 7 examines the "Agenda 2000" reforms, especially the EU's efforts to reform its expensive agricultural and structural policies and its negotiations on the EU budget and finances. The chapter concludes with the Berlin summit of March 1999, at which a final deal on the "Agenda 2000" package—including a financial framework for 2000–2006 that encompasses the expected first new accessions—was reached.

Chapter 8 examines the issue of EU institutional reform in preparation for enlargement. After discussing both the necessity of reforming EU decision-making institutions and procedures and the features of various reform proposals, it examines the unsuccessful effort to negotiate such reforms at the 1996–97 intergovernmental conference (IGC) and Amsterdam summit. The chapter then examines the post-Amsterdam debate on EU institutional reform, including the October 1999 Dehaene committee proposals, and concludes with the Helsinki summit's decision to launch a new IGC on institutional reform in early 2000.

Chapter 9 analyzes the progress of the accession negotiations with the more advanced applicants from November 1998 to the expansion of negotiations in early 2000. It also discusses key problem areas and issues in the negotiations as well as the growing importance of domestic politics and public opinion for the accession negotiations and enlargement. The chapter concludes by looking at the European Parliament's (EP's) past and future role in enlargement and the accession process.

The conclusion examines the future prospects for enlargement and its impact on the EU. Among the key questions discussed are the eventual geographical limits of enlargement and the institutional architecture and political dynamics of an enlarged EU.

NOTES

1. The EU was established by the 1992 Treaty on European Union (Maastricht Treaty), which came into force in November 1993. Preceding the EU was the European Economic Community (EEC)—created by the 1957 Rome Treaty—which gradually came to be known as the European Community (EC). The EC itself was preceded by the European Coal and Steel Community (ECSC), established by the 1951 Paris Treaty. The EU encompasses the EC and two other "pillars" of intergovernmental cooperation: Common Foreign and Security Policy, and Justice and Home Affairs. In this book, usage of the terms "EC" and "EU" is determined by appropriateness to the historical period being discussed.

2. The GDP figure is for 1998 (source: EUROSTAT). In addition to its original six member states—Germany, France, Italy, the Netherlands, Belgium, and Luxembourg—the EU's current member states are Austria, Denmark, Finland, Greece, Ireland, Portugal, Spain, Sweden, and the United Kingdom (Britain).

3. In this book, the term "eastern enlargement" is used to include EU enlargement into not only Central and Eastern Europe but also Southeastern Europe and the Mediterranean (Cyprus and Malta).

4. Jacques Santer, European Commission Press Release IP/97/660, DOC 97/9, Brussels, 16 July 1997.

1

+

The Challenge
of Enlargement

Enlargement plays an important role in the EU's historical development. From six original members in the 1950s, the EU gradually expanded to fifteen member states by 1995. With twelve applicant countries currently negotiating accession, and with additional countries such as Turkey, the Western Balkans states, Ukraine, and Moldova also hopeful of someday joining the Union, enlargement is certain to be a dominant issue for the EU well into the future.

Enlargement affects the EU in many important ways. Through enlargement, the EU grows in population and territorial size. By adding new national interests, outlooks, and cultural traditions, enlargement makes the EU more diverse and its decision making more complex. The addition of new member states also changes its internal political balance and dynamics. At the same time, enlargement creates new problems and opportunities for its external relations and policy.

Along with "deepening" (the intensification of integration among the EU's member states), enlargement, or "widening," is a key dynamic of EU growth and development. Both processes are inherent to the EU's basic treaties, which commit the member states to achieving an "ever closer union" and invite the application for membership of "any European State" respecting certain democratic principles.[1] Although the processes of widening and deepening have sometimes come into conflict, they are not fundamentally contradictory or opposed. Historical experience, in fact, shows that they are generally complementary: widening has often led to further deepening, as the EU deals with new problems and seeks to maintain its functional efficiency, while deepening has usually made the EU more powerful and attractive for nonmembers, thus leading to new requests for accession and further widening.

The EU's openness to new member states has its limits, however. These limits are determined by the economic and political conditions that the EU sets for membership as well as by the requirement that potential members must be "European," a term that is not defined more precisely anywhere in the EU treaties. Perhaps most importantly, however, the limits to enlargement are determined by the political interests and goals of the EU member states, who must agree among themselves and achieve consensus on the entry of any new members. Within these (somewhat uncertain) limits, the EU proclaims itself open to all countries sharing its values and wishing to join.

PREVIOUS ENLARGEMENTS

Since its founding in 1958 as the EEC, the EU has experienced four "official" enlargements.[2] The first enlargement occurred in 1973, with the entry of Great Britain, Ireland, and Denmark into what was then the EC. The addition of these three countries to the EC's six founding member states (France, Germany, Italy, Belgium, the Netherlands, and Luxembourg) brought the total number of member states to nine. The second enlargement occurred in 1981 with Greece's accession, followed by the entry of Spain and Portugal in 1986. The accession of these three countries is often referred to collectively as the "Mediterranean" or "southern" enlargement. The fourth, and most recent, enlargement took place in 1995, with the entry of Austria, Sweden, and Finland into what was now the EU. This "northern" enlargement increased the total number of member states to fifteen. A fifth, "unofficial" or informal, enlargement occurred through German unification in 1990, which added the five new federal states (Länder) and sixteen million citizens of the former German Democratic Republic (GDR) to the EC.[3]

Each of these enlargements posed distinctive problems and challenges for the EU. The accession of Britain, Ireland, and Denmark made the achievement of internal consensus more difficult by adding two countries, Britain and Ireland, that valued their trans-Atlantic ties and were not always willing to subsume these to European interests, and by adding two member states, Britain and Denmark, that did not wholly accept the EC's political union goals. Britain's membership also generated conflict over national contributions to the EC budget that resulted in the controversial policy of the British rebate in 1984. The Mediterranean enlargement made the EC relatively poorer and more agricultural, necessitating increased intra-Community transfers from wealthy to poor countries and the first efforts to reform the CAP. Greece's membership also complicated the EC's relations with Turkey, Greece's traditional enemy and itself an applicant for membership in 1987. The accession of Austria, Sweden, and Finland added three relatively wealthy and established democracies to the EU. However, by expanding the EU's membership and shifting its geographical center of gravity to the north and east, this fourth enlargement also raised concerns about the EU's institutional efficiency and its internal political balance and cohesion.

Each of these enlargements generated debate about the relationship between widening and deepening. In all cases, enlargement was accompanied by concerns that a wider EU would be weaker and less cohesive, and that it would lose its original identity and sense of common purpose. In actuality, each enlargement was followed by further institutional and policy development, often in response to new problems that widening had created. Britain's accession in 1973, for instance, led to the creation of the European Regional Development Fund (ERDF) and a new regional policy, in large part to redistribute EC funds to London in compensation for the deleterious effects of the CAP on Britain's net budgetary position. The first enlargement was also followed by the creation of the European Council, the regular meeting of heads of state and government of the member states that has become the EU's top political body, and by agreement on the Single European Act (SEA), a treaty that launched the Single Market or "Europe 1992" project. The accession of Greece, Spain, and Portugal in the 1980s led to the rapid expansion of the Structural Funds and the creation of the Cohesion Fund, programs aimed at promoting social cohesion and assisting the EC's poorer regions and member states. Agreement on EMU was reached by an EC of twelve member states, while enlargement to fifteen was followed by the Amsterdam Treaty and ongoing efforts to improve the EU's capacity for action in the realms of social and employment policy, Justice and Home Affairs (JHA), and CFSP. In other words, widening has not precluded deepening, but seems to have gone hand in hand with it, perhaps even promoting it.

Previous enlargements have also raised the issue of changes to the EU's institutional architecture in response to the challenge of greater diversity. Since the first enlargement, there has been periodic discussion of creating a "multi-speed" or "variable geometry" design for the EU, which would allow some member states to move ahead with further integration without being held back by others who are less in favor of greater economic and political union. In fact, multi-speed arrangements have been an important part of the EU's development since the 1970s (and the entry of new member states that were less enthusiastic about integration). Examples include the European Monetary System (EMS) and the Schengen Agreement on removing internal border controls, both of which were initially established outside of formal EC structures, thereby allowing unwilling member states to not participate. Another such "parallel cooperation" arrangement is the Western European Union (WEU), an intergovernmental organization for defense and security cooperation in which not all EU member states are full members. The Maastricht Treaty gave special "opt outs" to Britain on EMU and social policy, while special exemptions for certain Maastricht chapters were also later granted to Denmark. The Amsterdam Treaty followed this precedent by allowing exemptions from the Schengen rules for Britain and Ireland once these rules were incorporated into the EU treaties. The EMU agreement also allows for differentiation, permitting only those member states that meet strict economic convergence criteria to join.

However, these multi-speed arrangements have not led to a permanently multi-tiered structure for the EU. Instead, they have been catalysts for further deepening, with most member states eventually joining so as not to be excluded or left behind. Also, most of the parallel cooperation arrangements initially set up outside of the EC, such as the EMS and Schengen, have eventually been integrated into the EU framework, or "communitized." This is also now happening with the WEU. As a result, a striking degree of uniformity in integration has been maintained, despite the dual processes of widening—which makes the EU more diverse—and deepening—which makes the terms of EU membership more demanding and complex.

All previous enlargements followed the "classical method" of enlargement.[4] This method stipulates that accession is conditional upon the candidate state's agreeing to fully accept and apply the *acquis communautaire*—the EU's ever-expanding body of rules, regulations, and standards—with only limited derogations and transitional arrangements permitted. No permanent exceptions or derogations are allowed. At best, the EU can agree to review a particularly unacceptable rule or policy after a certain amount of time, once the applicant is a full member. The nature and length of transitional arrangements have tended to vary, depending on the issue involved and the interests of both the member states and the applicant country. In the case of Spain and Portugal, transitional periods stretched to ten years for the export of "sensitive" Mediterranean agricultural products. The classical method of enlargement thus largely predetermines the outcome of the accession negotiations and places the main burden of adjustment on the applicant country. It also has the advantage of keeping the negotiations limited and insulating them from wider integration debates. These very features of the classical method are also potential disadvantages, however, especially when considering the unique problems and issues of eastern enlargement.

THE UNIQUE CHALLENGE OF EASTERN ENLARGEMENT

While all previous enlargements presented certain problems for the EU, none posed the sort of massive challenge that the current enlargement does. One obvious difference from previous enlargements is the greater number of countries attempting to join in the present enlargement wave. Altogether, twelve applicant countries—including ten from Central and Eastern Europe—have been accepted as candidates for membership by the EU and allowed to begin accession negotiations. One additional applicant, Turkey, has been accepted as an official candidate for EU membership but has not yet been admitted to the accession process. By comparison, previous enlargement rounds dealt with no more than four applicants simultaneously.[5] The number of prospective new members and the fact that all except Poland are relatively small countries—two, in fact, Cyprus and Malta, have populations under one million and could be deemed "microstates"—have profound implications for the structure and functioning of EU decision-making institutions. The addition of up to twelve new member states will also ensure a more diverse and heterogenous EU in terms of cultural values and economic and political interests, making agreement on common policies even more difficult.

Because of the number of prospective new member states and the fact that most of them are relatively small countries, reform of the EU's decision-making institutions and procedures is an indispensable precondition for further enlargement. The current EU of fifteen member states operates with institutions and procedures that were originally created for a community of six and that have been only slightly modified since. If a much larger and more diverse EU is to function effectively and not become paralyzed, these already overstressed (or "overstretched") institutions and procedures must be reformed. One necessary reform is the extended use of qualified majority voting (QMV) procedures in the Council of Ministers and a consequent reduction in the number of policy issues decided by unanimity. There must also be a reweighting of votes in the Council to the advantage of larger member states, so that the accession of additional smaller countries does not worsen the already existing bias toward small member states in Council voting. Also necessary is reform of the Commission, including a possible reduction in the number of commissioners, to prevent future Commissions from becoming too large and unwieldy. Beyond these minimal reforms, the EU could also prepare for enlargement by introducing more flexibility into its decision-making arrangements, thus allowing member states that favor greater integration in certain areas to proceed without being held back by others that are opposed.

Reforming the EU's institutions will not be easy, however, since this requires unanimous agreement among the fifteen member states, each of which possesses different institutional interests on the basis of such factors as size and underlying attitudes toward integration. Such differences prevented agreement on institutional reform at the June 1997 Amsterdam summit, but the member states are set to tackle this issue again in a new IGC launched in February 2000.

Another important difference from previous enlargements is the relatively poor economic condition of the current applicants. As a group, the ten CEECs have a per capita GDP that is only 40 percent of the EU average and less than half that of the EU's four poorest member states (Greece, Portugal, Ireland, and Spain).[6] While previous enlargements also admitted countries that were far below the EU's economic average, what is different about the current enlargement is the number of applicants and their combined population (greater than 100 million, compared to an EU population of 370 million), meaning that the economic impact of enlargement on the EU will be much greater. As a result, whereas the three-country Mediterranean enlargement had the effect of reducing the EC's per capita GDP by 6 percent, enlargement to twenty-six member states (excluding Malta) would lower this average (for a much larger EU) by 16 percent. By adding all ten CEECs, the EU would increase its total population by 28 percent but its total GDP by only 4 percent.[7]

Because of the economic situation and employment structure of the CEECs, substantial reform of key EU policies is another necessary precondition for enlargement. In particular, the CAP and Structural Funds must be reformed, since these two policies together account for 80 percent of the total EU budget. With more than 22 percent of their labor force employed in agriculture, compared to only 5 percent in the EU, the new member states from Central and Eastern Europe would be major recipients of CAP subsidies if admitted under current policies on an equal basis. At the same time, enlargement to twenty-six would more than double the EU population eligible for assistance under objective 1 of the Structural Funds, money that goes to regions where GDP per capita is below 75 percent of the EU average and that accounted for more than half of total Structural Funds spending in 1999.[8] In other words, extending the unreformed CAP and Structural Funds policies to new CEEC members would entail a sizable growth of expenditures and require a substantial increase of the EU budget. However, such an increase is firmly opposed by the current member states—especially wealthy net contributors to the budget, such as Germany and the Netherlands—many of whom are struggling with their own economic problems of slow growth and high unemployment. Also limiting spending on enlargement are the budgetary restrictions on member states imposed by EMU.[9]

As is the case with institutional reform, however, achieving policy and budgetary reform is politically very difficult. Member states that are large net beneficiaries of current EU policies, such as France in the case of the CAP, and poorer countries like Spain, Portugal, Greece, and Ireland in the case of the Structural and Cohesion Funds, oppose changes that could bring a sharp reduction in EU receipts. All member states must overcome domestic opposition from sectoral and regional interests that benefit from existing EU policies. Also complicating policy and budgetary reform is the reluctance of Britain to give up its previously negotiated rebate, thus helping to satisfy the desire of member states that are large net contributors for a reduction of their payments to the EU. Some steps toward policy and budgetary reform were taken by the member states with the March 1999 Berlin summit agreement (see chapter 7). It is likely, however, that further reforms will be necessary as the EU continues to enlarge.

In addition to the number of countries trying to join and the potential economic and budgetary impact of eastern enlargement, several other factors differentiate the current enlargement from previous ones and make it more challenging. One factor is that many of the applicant countries begin the accession process from a lower starting point than most previous applicants in terms of their political, legal, and administrative development. Most of the former Communist countries have little or no previous experience with democracy and hence face the difficult challenge of building and consolidating new democratic institutions and political cultures. Four decades of Communist rule have also left these countries inexperienced with the market economy and Western legal and administrative norms. Communist mismanagement has also left a terrible legacy of economic waste and environmental damage, which will take years to overcome. The enlargement process, therefore, must overcome a huge economic and political developmental gap between the EU and the applicant states. This gap not only poses a formidable challenge for the applicants as they seek to make the difficult transition to democracy and the market economy and to align their legislation and institutions with those of the EU, but also for the EU as it seeks to prepare both the candidate countries and itself for enlargement.

Moreover, the applicant countries are seeking to join an EU that itself is rapidly changing; as it enlarges, the EU is also engaged in further deepening. Most notable in this regard is the historic effort to create an EMU, including a common currency (the "euro") and a European Central Bank. The Maastricht and Amsterdam Treaties have also committed the member states to further cooperation in the areas of foreign and security policy, judicial and home affairs, and social and employment policy. This ongoing deepening poses a tremendous challenge for the applicant countries, since the EU they are attempting to join is something of a "moving target" (or as some have put it, a "moving target in the fog," since the final destination remains unclear). Thus, the acceding countries will have to accept a different and much larger *acquis communautaire* than existed at the time they applied. This parallel process of deepening and widening also poses a challenge for the EU, which must not only keep its focus on the goal of enlargement as it pursues further deepening but also find ways of rapidly integrating the applicants into a deepening EU while preserving the integrity and uniformity of the *acquis communautaire*.

Also different is the security dimension of the current enlargement. While enlargement is widely viewed as an important means of exporting security and stability eastward, and thus helping to create a peaceful and secure Europe, it also poses potential security risks for the EU. By enlarging, the EU risks importing instability by admitting countries with unresolved internal or external conflicts, such as ethnic tensions or border disputes with neighboring states.[10] An enlarged EU would also have more extensive borders with historically unstable areas of Europe, such as the Western Balkans, even as it seeks to stabilize these areas by integrating them into the EU orbit. Enlargement will also extend the EU into Russia's traditional sphere of influence and, with the accession of the Baltic states, into the area of the former Soviet Union itself, thereby expanding the EU's border with Russia and altering its security relations with Moscow. For all of these reasons, and because of its links to the (not exactly parallel) process of NATO's eastward expansion, it is not surprising that security and geopolitical considerations have played a large role in EU decision making on eastern enlargement.

Similar to all previous enlargements, eastern enlargement will also affect the EU's internal political dynamics and cohesion. By shifting the EU's geographical and political center of gravity further eastward, enlargement could increase Germany's influence in the EU and decrease that of France, thus causing problems for the vital Franco-German partnership that has been the traditional "motor" of European integration. Further enlargement could also accentuate existing political, economic, geographical, and cultural cleavages within the EU and possibly lead to the emergence of new ones. An EU of twenty-seven or more member states will inevitably be more diverse and less unified in outlook, thus making the achievement of consensus more difficult and inhibiting progress toward the original goal of an "ever closer union."

Eastern enlargement, therefore, presents the EU with an enormous challenge. Whereas in previous enlargements the burden of adjustment fell mainly on the applicant countries, the current enlargement process also requires the EU to make substantial adjustments, including changes to its policies, finances, and decision-making institutions. It is therefore an "adaptive" enlargement, in a way that previous "classical" enlargements were not.[11] The addition of new member states will make the EU more politically and culturally diverse, and possibly less coherent and effective as a result. Enlargement into Central and Eastern Europe will also pose new security risks and problems for the EU and create new headaches for its CFSP. Clearly, eastern enlargement will change the EU in many important ways.

WHY ENLARGE?

Given the enormous challenge posed by eastern enlargement and its potential costs and risks, a logical question is: Why enlarge? Would it not be easier instead for the EU to simply maintain its present size for the foreseeable future, especially as it seeks to deepen integration among its current member states?

One reason for further enlargement is that it offers the EU and its member states many potential benefits. According to former External Affairs Commissioner Hans van den Broek, "An enlarged EU will bring increased security, stability and prosperity to Europe."[12] In addition to these more tangible political and economic gains, the enlargement process is also driven by a strong sense of moral obligation and historical purpose.

A major benefit of enlargement is that it will make the EU more secure by spreading prosperity and stability to the countries of Eastern and Southeastern Europe. Among many EU leaders there is growing recognition that European security is indivisible, and that, in the words of former German Foreign Minister Hans-Dietrich Genscher, "If Eastern Europe fares badly, Western Europe, too . . . will not prosper."[13] Without the stabilizing effects of enlargement, instability in Eastern and Southeastern Europe could generate such security problems for the EU as increased inflows of refugees and asylum seekers, transborder environmental pollution, and increased international criminal activity and political terrorism. It would also likely require, at some point, military intervention by the West, as has recently been demonstrated by the conflicts in Bosnia and Kosovo. An unstable and nonintegrated Eastern Europe could also become a security vacuum that invites a future reassertion of power by a resurgent and more nationalistic Russia. Thus, the security benefits to the EU and its member states from enlargement are largely preventative and can be calculated in terms of the prospective costs of nonenlargement.

Enlargement also offers substantial economic opportunities for the EU and its member states.[14] The accession of all ten CEECs would expand the EU's internal market by some 100 million consumers, thus creating the possibility of increased sales for EU companies and efficiency gains from greater economies of scale. Also, the economically underdeveloped CEECs have a tremendous potential for future growth, thereby creating additional markets for EU producers of goods and services. Some indication of the potential market represented by Central and Eastern Europe is given by the rapid growth of EU exports to this region after 1989. Between 1989 and 1995, EU exports to the ten CEECs grew by 131 percent;[15] and between 1995 and 1997, they increased by another one-third.[16] Beyond providing an expanded market for their products, the CEECs present EU companies with a geographically proximate location for investment and low-cost production, thus enabling EU firms to improve their global competitiveness.

While the EU would undoubtedly enjoy many of these economic benefits even without enlargement—under arrangements that stop short of full membership for the CEECs, such as association or free-market agreements—enlargement will provide a more stable political and security context that ensures continued economic reform and progress in Central and Eastern Europe, thus providing Western companies and investors with the maximum opportunity for gain. In this manner, an economically developing Central and Eastern Europe could become the engine for growth of an enlarging EU.

The EU's role and weight as global actor would also be enhanced by enlargement. A wider EU would possess a larger internal market and a greater share of world trade, and thus have a larger voice in international commercial and economic affairs. An enlarged EU would also be more influential in international governmental organizations, such as the United Nations, the World Trade Organization (WTO), and the International Monetary Fund (IMF). By increasing the EU's membership and extending its borders, enlargement would also give the EU a greater regional role and responsibilities in Eastern Europe and the Mediterranean basin, an effect that would enhance its global importance and weight as well.

While enlargement would provide these political, security, and economic benefits to the EU as a whole, its individual member states would nevertheless enjoy them disproportionately. The security benefits of enlargement, for instance, would be most enjoyed by the member states that border the EU's eastern rim. Countries like Germany, Austria, Sweden, and Finland, because of their geographical locations, would be the most directly affected by instability to their east. For these countries, enlargement would also create a welcome buffer against Russia; it is more than just a coincidence that some of the member states most in favor of enlargement are those lying the shortest distance from Moscow. For Germany and other east-facing member states, enlargement automatically increases security by moving them from the EU's eastern border to its safe middle. These member states, therefore, have a strong and natural security interest in enlargement.

Because of their geographical locations, and close cultural and historical ties with the applicant countries in some cases, these same member states are also natural economic partners of the CEECs and therefore stand to gain the most economically from enlargement. By comparison, member states on the EU's western and southern rims are less likely to profit economically from enlargement. For poorer member states like Spain, Portugal, and Greece, this fact only compounds the threat that enlargement poses to their current receipts of EU financial aid, thus leading them to question whether enlargement is in their economic interests at all. Indeed, for these countries it may be more of a threat.

Despite the varying extent to which individual member states will enjoy the direct security and economic benefits of enlargement, all of the member states will enjoy these benefits at least indirectly. An insecure and unstable Eastern Europe would be in no member state's interest, and a prosperous Eastern Europe that fuels EU economic growth would ultimately benefit all. Nevertheless, the uneven distribution of the direct costs and benefits of enlargement helps explain why, among the fifteen member states, the prospect of enlargement is viewed with varying degrees of enthusiasm. In addition to different geographical positions and economic interests, also affecting member state views of enlargement are such factors as historical and cultural ties to the applicant countries and basic attitudes toward integration. As will be seen, these member state differences have played a key role in shaping EU policy on enlargement.

In addition to these more tangible economic and security benefits, there are also important moral and normative reasons for enlargement. Many within the EU feel a strong sense of moral obligation toward the former Communist countries, believing that the West's freedom and prosperity was somehow paid for by Eastern Europe's subjugation during the cold war. Now that the iron curtain is down, they feel an obligation to assist their eastern neighbors by integrating them into the EU and the Western zone of peace and prosperity. By doing so, some westerners may hope to assuage their feelings of guilt for Yalta and the cold war division of Europe.

Some within the EU also argue that enlargement is necessary to honor past promises to the countries of Central and Eastern Europe that they would be welcomed into the Western club once geopolitical conditions permitted. Now that conditions do permit it, according to former German Chancellor Helmut Kohl, the EU "should not . . . disappoint the trust that these countries have put in us."[17] The former German chancellor has also argued that by failing to enlarge, the EU would lose moral and political credibility and that this "would be a terrible loss that Europe would not quickly recover from."[18]

Among the member states, Germany, in particular, feels a special sense of moral obligation toward the CEECs. Many Germans remain grateful to the brave peoples of Poland, Hungary, and the former Czechoslovakia for their actions in 1989 that brought about the end of Communism and made German unification possible. Many are also motivated by the desire to atone for past aggression and atrocities committed against Germany's eastern neighbors by Hitler's Nazi regime. In large part because of such feelings of moral obligation, the German government has repeatedly proclaimed itself the primary "advocate" *(Anwalt)* of the CEECs on behalf of their efforts to join the EU and NATO.

Another normative factor motivating enlargement is what can be called the "idea of Europe." This is the view that Europe is a distinctive cultural and historical entity that belongs together and should strive toward unity. One implication of this view is that the EU, as the institutional manifestation of a united Europe, should embrace all members of the European family of nations, provided that they accept the EU's rules (the *acquis communautaire*) and respect basic democratic principles. This integrationist goal, in fact, finds institutional expression in article 49 of the Treaty on European Union (TEU) (see below). Despite the lack of agreement on the question of what is Europe or where Europe's proper borders lie, this ideal of European unity has been a powerful factor promoting EU enlargement since the end of the cold war.

In the end, it is difficult to assess the exact importance of these moral and normative factors in promoting EU enlargement. Such is the nature of subjective forces and the problem with relying upon them as explanatory factors in politics. Nonetheless, as the succeeding chapters of this book will show, such factors have played an important role in helping to overcome the barriers to enlargement raised by inertia, member state differences of interest, concern over enlargement's economic and financial costs, and the difficult task of adequately reforming EU policies and institutions. In seeking to answer the question "Why enlarge?" a limited focus on rational, materially based interests and motivations is not enough.

THE ENLARGEMENT PROCESS

The enlargement process is anchored in basic provisions of the EU treaties and established by the experience of previous enlargements. Decision making on enlargement also reflects the EU's unique nature as a complex multilevel polity, combining the principles of both "supranationalism"—the possession of a common authority, policies, and legal framework—and "intergovernmentalism"—cooperation on the basis of bargained agreement between independent states.

The basic legal provision for EU enlargement is article 49 of the consolidated version of the TEU, which states:

> Any European State which respects the principles set out in Article 6(1) may apply to become a Member of the Union. It shall address its application to the Council, which shall act unanimously after consulting the Commission and after receiving the assent of the European Parliament, which shall act by an absolute majority of its component members.

The conditions of admission and the adjustments to the Treaties on which the Union is founded that such admission entails shall be the subject of an agreement between the Member States and the applicant State. This agreement shall be submitted for ratification by all the contracting States in accordance with their respective constitutional requirements.[19]

The text of this provision differs only slightly from article 237 of the Rome Treaty. Reference to the need for assent of the EP was added by the 1986 SEA, and reference to the principles of article 6(1) was added by the 1997 Amsterdam Treaty. Article 6(1) declares: "The Union is founded on the principles of liberty, democracy, respect for human rights and fundamental freedoms, and the rule of law, principles which are common to the Member States."[20] Article 49 neither provides a definition of Europe nor attempts to define Europe's geographical boundaries. Beyond the respect for basic democratic and human rights principles, it also does not specify the political and economic conditions for membership. These conditions were first defined by the June 1993 Copenhagen summit, which in reference to the CEECs declared:

Membership requires that the candidate country has achieved stability of institutions guaranteeing democracy, the rule of law, human rights and respect for and protection of minorities, the existence of a functioning market economy as well as the capacity to cope with competitive pressure and market forces within the Union. Membership presupposes the candidate's ability to take on the obligations of membership including adherence to the aims of political, economic and monetary union.[21]

Nor, except in very sketchy fashion, do the EU treaties specify the formal procedures of the enlargement process. These procedures have evolved over the course of successive previous enlargements, however, and are by now well established.

The enlargement process begins with the formal application for membership of a nonmember state. As specified in article 49 of the TEU, this application is made to the Council of the European Union. The decision to apply is an autonomous decision of the applicant country, and the EU has not officially encouraged or solicited applications. In this regard, the decisions of the June 1993 Copenhagen summit, which promised eventual membership to the countries of Central and Eastern Europe, are somewhat exceptional because none of these countries had yet formally applied. The EU's actions in this instance, which will be discussed further in the next chapter, reflected the unique situation of the former Communist countries and geopolitical conditions in post–cold war Europe.

After formal application, the next major step is the Commission Opinion *(avis)*. The Opinion is a detailed analysis of the preparedness of the applicant country for membership, especially its ability to take on the *acquis communautaire*. It also identifies any problems for the EU that might result from the applicant country's membership. The Opinion is not a legal prerequisite for beginning accession negotiations but is meant to assist the Council in making its own decision on the application. However, it is customary for the Council to wait for the Commission to deliver its Opinion before deciding to open negotiations. Because it identifies the main issues to be dealt with in the accession negotiations, the Opinion can also exert an important shaping influence on the negotiations. Nevertheless, although it is influential, the Commission's Opinion is not always decisive. The Opinion on Greece's application, for example, which the Commission delivered in 1976, recommended a lengthy pre-accession period before Greece would be ready for membership. However, this recommendation was overruled by the Council in favor of political arguments for beginning accession negotiations to support Greece's fragile democracy.

The Opinion is usually requested by the Council soon after receiving an application. However, the amount of time taken by the Commission to prepare its Opinions has varied considerably—from four months (Norway in 1993) to three years (Turkey, 1987–89; Malta and Cyprus, 1990–93)—depending on the nature and complexity of the issues connected with a particular application. Also affecting the amount of time taken to prepare an Opinion is the speed with which the EU wishes to move in dealing with an application. A lengthy Opinion process can be a convenient means of holding off an unwanted applicant or delaying enlargement until the EU takes care of other pressing business.

To prepare the Opinion, the Commission's specialized services and departments work together with the government ministries of the member states and with other international organizations and experts. Once completed, the Opinion must be approved by the full college of commissioners by majority vote. The Opinion is then delivered to the Council.

After receiving the Commission's Opinion, the Council can decide by unanimity to open accession negotiations with the applicant state. This is a crucial decision since the opening of accession negotiations involves a substantial commitment of resources and effort by the EU and its member states. The decision to begin entry negotiations also launches a politically difficult process, as attention now shifts to concrete issues, problems, and interests. Beginning negotiations also implies a willingness to conclude them and thus a commitment to enlarge. Because of the importance and sensitive nature of this decision, it is usually made by the Council at the head of state and government level.

The accession negotiations are essentially an intergovernmental conference between the member states and the individual applicant country. They are therefore different from other EU negotiations with third parties, which are usually led by the Commission acting on a negotiating mandate granted by the Council. Before beginning the "Accession Conference," the Council adopts formal negotiating procedures. These procedures have become fairly standard: The Council is responsible for developing "common positions" on all problems posed by the accession negotiations. These common positions are decided by the Council by unanimity, on the basis of proposals submitted by the Commission. For matters related to CFSP and JHA—since these are intergovernmental pillars not involving a formal policy role for the Commission—the member state holding the EU presidency makes the basic proposals for common positions, although the other member states and the Commission are invited to submit proposals as well. Much of the actual work in preparing common positions is done by the Committee of Permanent Representatives (COREPER) of the member states or its equivalents for the EU's second and third pillars.

Negotiating sessions of the Accession Conference are normally held at the level of government ministers or ambassadors (for the member states, their permanent representatives in Brussels), and are chaired by the EU presidency. Before the conference begins, there is agreement on the specific chapters of the *acquis communautaire* (for instance, Agriculture, Free Movement of Persons, Competition Policy, and so on) that are to be negotiated. When there is more than one applicant country negotiating entry (as has usually been the case), the Accession Conferences are procedurally separate, although they inevitably are linked informally.

The outcome of accession negotiations is essentially predetermined: full acceptance of the *acquis communautaire* by the applicant country, with the possibility of only limited derogations or transition periods for particular aspects of EU legislation. In addition, new member states are expected to subscribe to the EU's evolving CFSP *(acquis politique)* and its long-term political union objective *(finalité politique)*. According to one experienced EU official, "The subject matter [of the accession negotiations] is not so much a future pact between the parties as the way in which one party will apply the rules of the other party's club."[22] The Accession Conference, therefore, is not a negotiation between equals, with the burden of adjustment being almost entirely on the applicant country. While in the case of eastern enlargement the EU must also make substantial adjustments, most of the necessary reforms to EU policies and institutions will be made prior to the accession of new member states, and the new members will have to accept these changes that are made without their participation or input.

The accession negotiations have two main phases. The first, the analytical or "exploratory" phase, involves an intensive screening of the *acquis communautaire* that is carried out by the Commission together with the applicant country. The purpose of this screening procedure is to determine the extent to which the applicant can apply EU laws and regulations and what adjustments by the applicant might be necessary. The second, "substantive" phase of the negotiations involves actual intergovernmental bargaining on the terms of entry and possible derogations and transitions. Once the substantive phase has begun, there is usually an attempt to set a target date for concluding the negotiations and ratifying the accession agreement.

The negotiations conclude with agreement between the EU and the applicant country on a Draft Treaty of Accession, which is submitted to both the Council and the EP. At this point, the Commission delivers another Opinion, in this case on the Accession Treaty. The Council must approve the treaty by unanimous vote, and the EP must give its assent by an absolute majority. Once these steps have occurred, the treaty is formally signed by the member states and the applicant country. The member states and the applicant country must then ratify the treaty, each according to its own constitutional rules and procedures. After final ratification, the treaty comes into effect on the appointed day of accession, on which date the applicant country officially becomes a member state of the EU.

The length of the entire enlargement process can vary considerably. In the case of the first enlargement, if one takes the initial application date of 1961 as the starting point, the enlargement process for Britain, Ireland, and Denmark took eleven years (less than six, however, using 1967—the date of their second applications—as the starting point). The enlargement process, from application to accession, took more than five years for Greece, and almost nine years for Spain and Portugal. By comparison, the enlargement process for the three newest member states was relatively short, taking more than five years for Austria yet less than four years for Sweden and less than three years for Finland.

Among the factors affecting the length of the enlargement process is the preparedness of the applicant country. Another is the nature and difficulty of the issues to be negotiated by the member states and the applicant. The internal negotiations among the member states that are a precondition for negotiations with the applicant country are also important. The EU's common positions in the accession negotiations must be decided by unanimity, creating the possibility of quite lengthy and difficult negotiations among the member states. Another factor affecting the current enlargement is that substantial internal reforms are a precondition for admitting new members, and these also are the subject of intense intergovernmental bargaining. It has often been the case, therefore, as it most certainly will be for the next accessions, that the biggest delays in the enlargement process come not from lack of preparedness by the applicant country or difficult negotiations between the member states and applicant but from negotiations among the member states themselves over common positions and internal EU issues.

EU THEORIES AND ENLARGEMENT

There have been few efforts to theorize about EU enlargement. This is all the more remarkable given the considerable extent to which European integration and the EU have been the subject of theoretical analysis and theory building. A brief look at some of the more prominent EU theories will help us to determine which of these is useful for understanding and explaining decision making on enlargement.

Various theories of EU integration and governance emphasize different actors and processes as well as different levels of decision making and types of decisions. Traditional "grand" theories of European integration seek to explain why and how integration takes place. They also tend to focus on "history-making" decisions (such as new treaties and treaty revisions) that determine the general pace and direction of integration.[23] *Neofunctionalism* explains integration in terms of functional and political "spillover" dynamics while stressing the important role of independently acting supranational institutions (that is, the Commission) and non-governmental (especially transnational) interests and actors.[24] *Intergovernmentalism,* by contrast, explains integration in terms of bargained agreements between sovereign nation-states, with national governments using integration and common institutions to enhance their own power and capacity for action. Intergovernmentalists believe that supranational institutions play mainly a facilitative role (for instance, by ensuring the "credibility of commitments") and are not independent actors in their own rights. In the intergovernmentalist model, nongovernmental interests also express themselves mainly through domestic politics and their influence on the bargaining positions of national governments.[25]

More recently, a new body of theories has emerged to explain EU politics and governance, focusing on "policy-setting" and "policy-shaping" decisions at the systemic or subsystemic level.[26] These new theoretical approaches include theories of multilevel governance, policy network analysis, and new institutionalism. Generally speaking, these theories argue that integration takes place in small (and accumulating) steps and decisions—through the daily operation and functioning of EU institutions, for instance—and not just through "big bang" events (such as IGCs and treaties). Theories of multilevel governance portray the EU as a complex multilevel polity, with important roles played by various actors at different levels of government and society, including supranational (EU) and subnational (regional and local) authorities. Policy network analysis examines how these various actors, including private and organized interests, form transnational networks of relationships that vary across policy sectors and that exercise an important influence on EU policy outcomes. Institutionalist theories argue that policy outcomes are also shaped by the institutional context, both formal and informal, of EU decision making.[27]

At first glance, decision making on enlargement would appear to fit the intergovernmentalist theoretical model. This is because of the central role of the member states, via the Council, and the centrality of intergovernmental negotiations in the enlargement process. The importance of member state interests and intergovernmental bargaining is further magnified by the requirement of unanimity for accession decisions. As a result, the member states are the most important actors in the enlargement process, and intergovernmental bargaining—both between the member states and the acceding country on terms of entry, and between the member states themselves on common positions—is the primary mode of decision making on enlargement. Enlargement decisions (that is, whom to admit and when) also have a "history-making" character, since they greatly affect the nature and functioning of the EU and its future orientation. The current enlargement, moreover, requires intergovernmental agreement on major policy and institutional reforms as well. For this reason, in line with intergovernmentalist assumptions, member state interests and intergovernmental bargaining are necessary focal points for examining decision making on EU enlargement.

Decision making on enlargement is much more complicated than a simple intergovernmentalist model would predict, however. For one thing, as both neofunctionalist and institutionalist theories would suggest, supranational EU institutions also play a key role in the enlargement process. A particularly important role is played by the Commission. Through its Opinion, the Commission can influence both the Council's decision to open accession negotiations and the substance of the negotiations themselves. The Commission also conducts the preliminary screening of the *acquis communautaire* with the applicant country, and it makes proposals for the EU's common positions in the negotiations. Although the Commission plays only a secondary role in the substantive negotiations, which are formally between the applicant and the fifteen member states, it can be asked by the Council to seek solutions with the applicant country in cases of serious disagreement between the applicant and the member states. The Commission also plays the role of "honest broker" in mediating among the member states in the formation of common positions, and it serves as an interlocutor of the applicant countries in the accession negotiations. In its traditional role as guardian of the treaties, the Commission also brings to the negotiations the perspective of an enlarged EU and a view of the EU's common interests after accession takes place. Once the negotiations are completed, the Commission also delivers its formal Opinion on the Accession Treaty.

The special circumstances of eastern enlargement have further enhanced the Commission's role in the enlargement process. The Commission was the main administrator of EU policy toward the former Communist states after 1989, including the Poland and Hungary: Aid for Economic Reconstruction (PHARE) aid program.[28] It also devised the model for the enhanced association agreements (Europe Agreements) that the EU negotiated with each of the CEECs after 1990, and it played a major role in developing the EU's pre-accession strategy to prepare the former Communist countries for membership. The Commission's recommendations, in both "Agenda 2000" and its regular progress reports for each of the applicants in 1998 and 1999, were also influential in EU decision making on enlargement strategy. The Commission has also played a central role in the EU's own preparations for enlargement, especially through its "Agenda 2000" proposals for reform of the CAP and Structural Funds and for the EU's future budgetary framework. The Commission's views have also been influential in the debate on institutional reform and preparations for the 2000 IGC.

Another important supranational actor in the enlargement process is the EP. Much of the EP's influence derives from the legal requirement of parliamentary assent to the accession of new member states. The EP must also give its approval to any changes to the Structural and Cohesion Funds, thereby giving the Parliament some leverage in the internal reform process that is an important precondition for further enlargement. The EP also exerts influence in the current enlargement process through the Joint Parliamentary Committees established with the national parliaments of each of the applicant countries. The EP also derives influence from its position as the EU's only directly elected institution, thus giving added weight to its resolutions on enlargement issues. Because of its democratic role within the EU, the EP also plays a vital role in securing public support for enlargement and the ratification of new accession treaties.

Beyond its neglect of the important (and independent) role of EU institutions, a simple intergovernmentalist model is also insufficient for explaining decision making on enlargement because it neglects or underemphasizes a number of other factors that affect intergovernmental bargaining in the EU. Many of these factors are typically emphasized by institutionalist theories of EU politics, including the institutional context of intergovernmental bargaining, the legacy of past decisions and policy commitments, and EU governance norms and values.[29]

The institutional context of intergovernmental bargaining includes not only the role of the Commission and the EP, which have already been mentioned, but also the institutional mechanics and operating procedures of the Council. For instance, there are the important roles of COREPER and Council voting rules and norms. Also exerting an important influence on decision making in the Council is the experience of regular interaction within an institutionalized setting. This experience tends to have a socializing effect on member state governments and their representatives, thus shaping their views and perceptions of national interest. According to Edwards,

> through constant interaction at a myriad of levels, from heads of state and government in the European Council to the most highly technical of Council working groups, member governments are a part of a complex network of institutions and procedures that makes up EU decision making. That interaction, indeed the institutional network itself, inevitably plays a part in determining government strategies and influencing the goals and objectives of governments both at the national as well as the European levels.[30]

In other words, such intergovernmental bodies as the European Council and the Council of Ministers are not simply interstate bodies but bodies at the supranational level;[31] and intergovernmental bargaining within the EU is not simply interstate bargaining (between isolated national governments) but supranational decision making. The participating governments recognize that they are making decisions not only for themselves on the basis of narrow national interests (if indeed these can even be neatly separated from broader EU interests) but also for the EU as a whole. Moreover, they recognize that the EU is an institutional arrangement in which they are closely integrated and into which they have all invested a considerable amount of political and emotional—to say nothing of financial—capital. Another key difference of supranational decision making from traditional interstate bargaining is a prior commitment to compromise and agreement, which in the EU has worked in the past to promote the progressive deepening and consolidation of integration.[32] This supranational context of intergovernmental bargaining inevitably affects decision making on enlargement by promoting compromise and ensuring that intergovernmental negotiations are guided by broader EU norms and systemic objectives.

Intergovernmental bargaining and decision making are also affected by the legacy of past decisions and policy commitments. According to "historical institutionalist" theory, political decisions and policy choices are often "path dependent," in that they are constrained, and to some extent even predetermined, by previous decisions and agreements. These constraints generate "sunk costs" and result in commitments that are difficult to alter or reverse.[33] In the case of enlargement, one type of path dependency is created by the voluminous and complex *acquis communautaire,* which new member states are required to accept and apply in full. Because this accumulation of rules and decisions represents a legacy of painful political compromise and adaptation, it cannot be easily undone or renegotiated. Strong vested interests (both institutional and sectoral) have also emerged to defend the institutional and policy status quo. Thus, past decisions and policy choices help to determine the terms of accession and impose constraints on intergovernmental bargaining in accession negotiations. They also limit the possibilities for the reform of EU institutions and policies in preparation for enlargement.

Also affecting intergovernmental bargaining and decision making are institutional norms and values. According to institutionalist theory, policy choices and decision making are often influenced by historically evolved "governance norms" that are embedded in, and reinforced by, institutional structures.[34] One important EU governance norm influencing enlargement is the classical method established by previous enlargements. The classical method of enlargement insists on the complete and full acceptance of the *acquis communautaire* by new member states and permits no permanent derogations or partial forms of membership. It thus limits the possibilities for flexible or creative forms of integration in response to unique situations or changing conditions.

Two other EU governance norms that have influenced decision making on enlargement are the key principles of cohesion and solidarity. As will be seen, these two principles have played a role not only in the accession process but also in negotiations among the member states on internal policy, budgetary, and institutional reform. Finally, one cannot overlook the important role of the integrationist ideals expressed in article 49 of the TEU; these imply a certain commitment to widening and an open door to all democratic European states wishing to join, and thus are an important normative factor pushing forward the enlargement process against the resistance of more materialist-based national and sectoral interests.[35]

In addition to these supranational, institutional, and normative factors, another important influence on intergovernmental bargaining and decision making is domestic politics, or the second level of Putnam's "two-level game."[36] Neorealist international relations theory, on which intergovernmentalism is largely based, views national interests as essentially given and immutable, and national governments as basically monolithic structures.[37] However, domestic interests and politics clearly play an important role in determining national government preferences in intergovernmental bargaining, often causing these preferences to change. Because of the influence of domestic lobbies and interests in determining national government positions, intergovernmental bargaining and decision making in the EU can perhaps be more accurately described as "conditional intergovernmentalism."[38] Also important is the partisan nature of government. As Helen Wallace reminds us, the EU's "member states" are actually "member governments," and the positions they defend as national interests are often nothing more than partisan preferences.[39] Thus, elections and changes of government may affect a member state's position in intergovernmental bargaining. Also important is whether a government is formed by a single party or is instead a multiparty coalition.

In the case of enlargement, economic sectoral and other organized interests may seek to influence government positions in the accession negotiations. Whether they are successful often depends on the relative strength of the interests concerned. It also depends on the nature of domestic political structures and processes, which determine the availability of channels of access to policy makers and the extent to which a government is vulnerable to interest group pressure. Public opinion (that is, the level of support for enlargement or for the accession of a particular candidate country) is another important factor influencing the decisions of member state governments to sign an accession treaty, and it can also play a significant role in the ratification of accession treaties.

Thus, decision making on enlargement reflects the EU's complex, multilevel character. While member state governments are clearly the main actors in the enlargement process and intergovernmental bargaining is its key dynamic, decision making on enlargement occurs within the EU's supranational institutional context, with an important role played by both the Commission and the EP. In this sense, decision making on enlargement is a supranational process. Normative factors also exert an important influence on enlargement decision making, as do domestic politics and public opinion. Any attempt to explain decision making on enlargement, therefore, must take these various factors into account. In the following chapters of this book, the role played by each of these factors in the EU's eastern enlargement will be examined.

NOTES

1. The EU's basic treaties are the Treaty Establishing the European Community (TEC), or the Rome Treaty, signed in 1957, and the Treaty on European Union (TEU), or the Maastricht Treaty, signed in 1992. The Rome Treaty was subsequently amended by the 1986 Single European Act (SEA), and both treaties were amended by the 1997 Amsterdam Treaty. The goal of "ever closer union" is set forth in the preamble of the Rome Treaty, which declares that the signatories to the treaty are "determined to lay the foundations of an ever closer union among the peoples of Europe." The treaty provisions inviting applications for membership from "any European state" are article 237 of the Rome Treaty, and article O of the Maastricht Treaty, amended by article 1(15) of the Amsterdam Treaty to include reference to respecting democratic principles. Article O is replaced by article 49 of the consolidated version of the TEU, which incorporates the amendments made by the Amsterdam

Treaty. For article 49, see *European Union Consolidated Treaties* (Luxembourg: Office for Official Publications of the European Communities, 1997), 31.

2. On previous EU enlargements, see Christopher Preston, *Enlargement and Integration in the European Union* (New York: Routledge, 1997); John Redmond and Glenda G. Rosenthal, eds., *The Expanding European Union: Past, Present, Future* (Boulder: Lynne Rienner, 1998); Thomas I. Pedersen, *European Union and the EFTA Countries: Enlargement and Integration* (London: Pinter, 1994); F. Nicholson and R. East, *From Six to Twelve: The Enlargement of the European Communities* (Harlow: Longman, 1987); and Loukas Tsoukalis, *The European Community and Its Mediterranean Enlargement* (London: Allen & Unwin, 1981).

3. On German unification as EU enlargement, see Andreas Falke, "An Unwelcome Enlargement? The European Community and German Unification," in *German Unification: Process and Outcomes,* ed. M. Donald Hancock and Helga A. Welsh (Boulder: Westview, 1994), 163–95.

4. For discussion of the "classical method" of enlargement and its implications for the EU, see Preston, *Enlargement and Integration.*

5. In both the EU's first and its most recent enlargements, Norway negotiated entry together with three other countries. In both instances, however, in 1972 and again in 1994, the Norwegian people voted down membership in a national referendum after the entry agreement had been negotiated and signed by the government.

6. Per capita GDP figures are for 1997 and are calculated for Purchasing Power Parity. The source of these figures is EUROSTAT, Economy and Finance 28/98; cited in Agence Europe, *Europe Weekly Selected Statistics,* no. 1068, 21 September 1998, 1.

7. The impact of enlargement on the EU is calculated by the European Commission and based on 1995 data. See European Commission, "Agenda 2000: For A Stronger and Wider Union," *Bulletin of the European Union,* supp. 5/97: 109–10. Malta is excluded from the calculation of per capita GDP after enlargement because its application was suspended at the time the calculations were made. Given Malta's tiny population of less than four hundred thousand, however, its inclusion would not affect these calculations appreciably.

8. European Commission, "General Budget of the European Union for the Financial Year 1999: The Figures" (Luxembourg: Office for Official Publications of the European Community, 1999), 19.

9. The Stability and Growth Pact, agreed to by EU leaders at Amsterdam in June 1997, requires euro-zone countries to keep budget deficits below 3 percent of GDP.

10. On eastern enlargement as a potential security risk for the EU, see Péter Balázs, "Strategies for the Eastern Enlargement of the EU: An Integration Theory Approach," in *The State of the European Union,* vol. 4, *Deepening and Widening,* ed. Pierre-Henri Laurent and Marc Maresceau (Boulder: Lynne Rienner, 1998), 70–73.

11. On the concept of "adaptive" enlargement and its contrast to "classical" enlargement, see Stuart Croft, John Redmond, G. Wyn Rees, and Mark Webber, *The Enlargement of Europe* (Manchester: Manchester University Press, 1999), 56; see also John Redmond and Glenda G. Rosenthal, "Introduction," in Redmond and Rosenthal, eds., *The Expanding European Union,* 4.

12. Graham Avery and Fraser Cameron, forward to *The Enlargement of the European Union* (Sheffield: Sheffield Academic Press, 1998), 9.

13. Hans-Dietrich Genscher, "A Spirit of Solidarity," *Financial Times,* 16–17 May 1992, 9.

14. For a study that argues that the economic gains to the EU of enlargement will outweigh the economic costs, see András Inotai, "Economy," in *Costs, Benefits and Chances of*

Eastern Enlargement for the European Union, ed. Bertelsmann Foundation Research Group on European Affairs (Gütersloh: Bertelsmann Foundation Publishers, 1998), 13–37.

15. Heather Grabbe and Kirsty Hughes, *Enlarging the EU Eastwards* (London: Royal Institute of International Affairs, 1998), 12.

16. In 1995, EU exports to the ten CEECs were valued at ECU 58.7 billion; in 1997, ECU 87.3 billion. Source is EUROSTAT, Eurostatistics 1/99; cited in Agence Europe, *Europe Weekly Selected Statistics,* no. 1099, 26 April 1999, 2.

17. Address by Chancellor Kohl to the Bundestag, *Bulletin,* no. 81, 15 October 1996 (Bonn: Presse- und Informationsamt der Bundesregierung), 871.

18. Address by Chancellor Kohl to the Bundestag, *Bulletin,* no. 103, 16 December 1996 (Bonn: Presse- und Informationsamt der Bundesregierung), 1117.

19. "Consolidated Version of the Treaty on European Union," in *European Union Consolidated Treaties,* 31. Former article O of the 1992 TEU.

20. "Consolidated Version of the TEU," 13. Ex article F(1) of the Amsterdam Treaty.

21. "European Council in Copenhagen, 21–22 June 1993: Presidency Conclusions," in *The European Councils: Conclusions of the Presidency, 1992–1994* (Brussels: European Commission, Directorate-General for Information, 1995), 86.

22. Graham Avery, "The European Union's Enlargement Negotiations," *Oxford International Review* (Summer 1994): 28.

23. On the distinction between different types of decisions and the implications for theorizing about the EU, see John Peterson and Elizabeth Bomberg, *Decision-Making in the European Union* (New York: St. Martin's, 1999), 4–30.

24. For classic statements of neofunctionalist theory, see Ernst Haas, *The Uniting of Europe: Political, Social, and Economic Forces 1950–57* (Stanford: Stanford University Press, 1958); and Leon Lindberg, *The Political Dynamics of European Integration* (Stanford: Stanford University Press, 1963). For more recent reformulations, see Jeppe Tranholm-Mikkelsen, "Neofunctionalism: Obstinate or Obsolete? A Reappraisal in the Light of the New Dynamism of the European Community," *Millennium* 20, no. 1 (1991): 1–22; and Anne-Marie Burley and Walter Mattli, "Europe Before the Court: A Political Theory of Legal Integration," *International Organization* 47, no. 1 (1993): 41–76.

25. For examples of intergovernmentalist theory, see Stanley Hoffmann, "Obstinate or Obsolete? The Fate of the Nation-State and the Case of Western Europe," *Daedalus* 95, no. 3 (1966): 862–915; Alan Milward, *The European Rescue of the Nation-State* (London: Routledge, 1992); and Andrew Moravcsik, "Preferences and Power in the European Community: A Liberal-Intergovernmentalist Approach," *Journal of Common Market Studies* 31, no. 4 (1993): 473–524.

26. Peterson and Bomberg, *Decision-Making in the European Union,* 16–28. The authors regard "history-making" decisions as taking place at the "super-systemic" level, because they transcend the EU's normal policy process (10).

27. For multilevel governance, see Gary Marks, "Structural Policy and Multilevel Governance in the EC," in *The State of the European Community,* vol. 2, *The Maastricht Debates and Beyond,* ed. Alan Cafruny and Glenda Rosenthal (Boulder: Lynne Rienner, 1993); Gary Marks, Liesbet Hooghe, and Kermit Blank, "European Integration from the 1980s: State-Centric versus Multi-Level Governance," *Journal of Common Market Studies* 34, no. 3 (1996): 341–78; and Beatte Kohler-Koch, "Catching Up with Change: The Transformation of Governance in the European Union," *Journal of European Public Policy* 3, no. 3 (1996): 359–80. For policy network analysis, see John Peterson, "Decisionmaking in the European

Union: Toward a Framework for Analysis," *Journal of European Public Policy* 2, no. 1 (1995): 69–93; and Jeremy Richardson, "Policymaking in the EU," in *European Union: Power and Policy-Making,* ed. Jeremy Richardson (London: Routledge, 1996), 3–23. For institutionalism, see Simon Bulmer, "The Governance of the European Union: A New Institutionalist Approach," *Journal of Public Policy* 13, no. 4 (1993): 351–80; Mark Pollack, "New Institutionalism and EU Governance: The Promise and Limits of Institutionalist Analysis," *Governance* 9, no. 4 (1996): 429–58; and Paul Pierson, "The Path to European Integration: An Historical Institutionalist Analysis," *Comparative Political Studies* 29, no. 2 (1996): 123–63. For a survey of EU governance theories, see Simon Hix, "The Study of the European Community: The Challenge of Comparative Politics," *West European Politics* 17, no. 1 (1994): 1–30; also Simon Hix, "The Study of the European Union II: The 'New Governance' Agenda and its Rival," *Journal of European Public Policy* 5, no. 1 (1998): 38–65.

28. For an analysis of the Commission's role in running the PHARE program, see Arne Niemann, "The PHARE Program and the Concept of Spillover: Neofunctionalism in the Making," *Journal of European Public Policy* 5, no. 3 (1998): 428–46. On the Commission's role in EU policy toward Central and Eastern Europe more generally, see Ulrich Sedelmeier and Helen Wallace, "Policies Toward Central and Eastern Europe," in *Policy-Making in the European Union,* 3rd ed., ed. Helen Wallace and William Wallace (Oxford: Oxford University Press, 1996), 353–87.

29. There are actually three main versions of institutionalist theory: (1) "rational choice institutionalism," which focuses on the impact of institutions on the choices of rational, interest-motivated actors; 2) "historical institutionalism," which views institutions as the product of historically unique origins and processes and often the result of the unintended consequences of purposeful actions; and (3) "sociological institutionalism," which focuses on the influence of culturally framed rules and norms that are embedded in institutions. This discussion draws on all three versions. For a brief review of these three institutionalisms, see Vivien A. Schmidt, introduction to "ECSA Review Forum: Approaches to the Study of European Politics," *ECSA Review* 12, no. 2 (Spring 1999): 2–3.

30. Geoffrey Edwards, "National Sovereignty vs. Integration? The Council of Ministers," in Richardson, ed., *European Union: Power and Policy-Making,* 127.

31. To paraphrase Wolfgang Wessels, "The EC Council: The Community's Decision-Making Center," in *The New European Community: Decisionmaking and Institutional Change,* ed. Robert O. Keohane and Stanley Hoffman (Boulder: Westview, 1991), 137.

32. Edwards, "National Sovereignty vs. Integration?" 128.

33. Pierson, "The Path to European Integration," 123–63.

34. Bulmer, "The Governance of the European Union." On the importance of norms and values in institutionalist theory more generally, see James March and Johann Olsen, *Rediscovering Institutions: The Organizational Basis of Politics* (New York: Free Press, 1989).

35. On the importance of normative factors in the enlargement process, see K. M. Fierke and Antje Wiener, "Constructing Institutional Interests: EU and NATO Enlargement," *Journal of European Public Policy* 6, no. 5 (December 1999): 721–42.

36. Robert D. Putnam, "Diplomacy and Domestic Politics: The Logic of Two-Level Games," *International Organization* 42, no. 3 (Summer 1988): 427–60. The first level is negotiations between national governments.

37. In his "liberal-intergovernmentalist" variant of intergovernmentalism, however, Moravcsik gives domestic politics an important role in determining national interests and preferences. See Moravcsik, "Preferences and Power in the European Community." On the

role of domestic politics in the EU, see Simon Bulmer, "Domestic Politics and European Policy-Making," *Journal of Common Market Studies* 21, no. 4 (1983): 349–63.

38. Sonia Mazey and Jeremy Richardson, "Agenda Setting, Lobbying and the 1996 IGC," in *The Politics of European Treaty Reform: The 1996 Intergovernmental Conference and Beyond*, ed. Geoffrey Edwards and Alfred Pijpers (London: Pinter, 1997), 233–35.

39. Helen Wallace, "Politics and Policy in the EU: The Challenge of Governance," in Wallace and Wallace, eds., *Policy-Making in the European Union*, 35.

2

+

Opening the Door

For more than three decades the EC existed within a divided Europe, a geopolitical situation that effectively defined the EC's eastern borders and limited EC membership to Western European countries. The cold war also limited the EC's interactions with the countries to its east. In fact, official relations between the EC and the Council for Mutual Economic Assistance (CMEA), the Soviet-bloc economic association, were not established until 1988. Because of the cold war the EC—as opposed to some of its member states—gave relatively little attention to the eastern half of Europe, focusing instead on its own internal affairs and the integration of Western Europe. The revolutionary changes of 1989 shattered this comfortable isolation, however, and thrust relations with Eastern Europe and the prospect of eastward enlargement onto the EC's agenda.

1989: INITIAL RESPONSES

In 1989 the EC was busily engaged in efforts at further deepening. It was in the midst of efforts to create a Single European Market for goods, services, capital, and labor by the end of 1992, a project that was formally launched with agreement on the SEA in 1986. The next step in economic integration was monetary union, and at the Madrid summit in June 1989, EC leaders approved the beginning of intergovernmental negotiations on EMU. They also agreed to set a firm date for launching these negotiations at the next regularly scheduled meeting of the European Council, planned for December in Strasbourg. Thus, by the fall of 1989 the process of European integration was back on track and picking up steam. In contrast to the mood of "Europessimism" that predominated earlier in the decade, there prevailed instead considerable optimism about the future of the EC and European integration.

It was precisely because of this progress toward greater integration that the revolutionary changes in Central and Eastern Europe were so unsettling for many within the EC. Despite the official rhetoric welcoming these changes, some EC leaders expressed concern that the crisis in the Soviet bloc could shift attention away from efforts at further deepening and thus undermine the integrationist momentum that had been achieved during the previous five years. These fears were only heightened by the fall of the Berlin Wall in November 1989 and the subsequent rapid movement toward German unification. The developments in Germany raised serious questions in the minds of some EC leaders about the German government's future commitment to EMU and further integration, and more generally about the future role in Europe of a united Germany.

In response to the political changes in Central and Eastern Europe, therefore, some EC leaders urged a continued focus on internal deepening, arguing that a more integrated EC would be better able to assist the new post-Communist democracies and would be a firmer foundation for a united Europe. According to Commission President Jacques Delors,

> in the face of these developments [in Central and Eastern Europe] the best response of the Community must be to step up its own drive toward integration: single market, social and human dimension, economic and monetary union, progress toward a common foreign policy along the path to political union. . . . In this way the dynamism of Community integration can amplify the dynamism of economic and political reforms in the countries of the other Europe and be a driving force in the changes between East and West.[1]

Delors also argued that further integration and the construction of a federal Europe was "the only acceptable and satisfactory solution to the German question," by which he meant the question of a united Germany's future place and role in Europe.[2]

Expressing similar views was French President François Mitterrand. At a speech to the EP in September 1989, Mitterrand declared that the political changes in Central and Eastern Europe must not be allowed to undermine Western political structures. Only by accelerating and strengthening the "political construction of Europe," he argued, could the EC "make a major contribution to positive developments in the East." Mitterrand also claimed that through increased integration, "not only will we equip ourselves with greater resources and move our Community to a higher plane but the Community will exert a greater attraction to the rest of Europe."[3]

Not everyone agreed that further deepening was the proper response to the changes in Central and Eastern Europe, however. One prominent dissenter was Britain's Prime Minister Margaret Thatcher. As early as September 1988, in her famous "anti-federalism" speech at the College of Europe in Bruges, Thatcher had called for a wider Europe that stretched from across the Atlantic to the Urals, arguing that a more tightly integrated EC would be less capable of responding to the needs and aspirations of the Eastern Europeans.[4]

Thatcher's view was not shared by many other EC leaders, however. Instead, most seemed to agree with Delors and Mitterrand that further deepening was necessary, both to strengthen the EC before it could take in new members from Central and Eastern Europe and to more firmly anchor a united Germany. As a result, at the Dublin summit in April 1990, EC leaders agreed to hold two parallel IGCs, the already-planned one on EMU and a newly conceived IGC on European Political Union (EPU) that would include discussions on creating a common foreign and defense policy. Both IGCs would be formally launched at the December 1990 Rome summit and would conclude one year later with agreement at Maastricht on the TEU. As the EC formulated its initial response to the demands for inclusion of the post-Communist democracies, therefore, it did so against the background of preoccupation with internal developments and a renewed commitment to further deepening.

ECONOMIC AND TECHNICAL ASSISTANCE

The EC first addressed the changes occurring in the Soviet bloc at its December 1988 summit in Rhodes. At this meeting, EC leaders announced their determination to assist the movement toward democracy and economic reform in Central and Eastern Europe.[5] At the Madrid summit six months later, the European Council took special note of developments in Poland and Hungary and declared its "common will" to support the efforts of those two countries to reform their economies.[6]

The EC's involvement with Central and Eastern Europe increased as a result of the July 1989 Group of Seven (G7) summit in Paris. At this meeting, Western leaders agreed to launch a coordinated effort to provide economic assistance to Poland and Hungary. In recognition of the EC's economic weight and geographical proximity to these countries, as well as its neutrality in security terms, the summit decided that the Commission should take the lead in coordinating the Western aid effort. Under the Commission's leadership, a multilateral aid program was developed that involved all twenty-four member countries of the Organization for Economic Cooperation and Development (OECD)—the "G24"—as well as various other international economic and financial organizations. While G24 assistance initially targeted Poland and Hungary, it was later extended to other CEECs as they introduced political and economic reforms.[7]

EC assistance to the post-Communist democracies took a variety of forms. The EC provided emergency food and medical aid to Poland and Romania in the early days of their political transitions. In cooperation with other Western governments and international financial organizations, the EC also contributed heavily to macroeconomic stabilization measures for the reforming countries, such as a $1 billion currency stabilization fund for Poland and balance-of-payments assistance for Hungary. The EC also provided loans to CEECs through the European Investment Bank (EIB) and facilities of the European Coal and Steel Community (ECSC). Individual member states also gave their own aid and participated in debt relief efforts within the Paris Club (of creditor governments) framework.[8]

The main program for providing EC aid to the CEECs was the PHARE program, which was established in December 1989.[9] The PHARE program provided direct grants aimed at promoting economic development and modernization in the transition countries, with a particular focus on projects in agriculture, the environment, education and training, health, and private sector development. After 1993, infrastructure development became a major focus of PHARE spending as well. PHARE assistance was initially used for the sole purpose of promoting market-oriented economic reforms, but in 1992, at the insistence of the EP, the Commission began linking assistance to the promotion of democracy and civil society as well. Under what was known as the PHARE "Democracy Program," the EC funded projects promoting parliamentary democracy, human rights, the rule of law, and the development of an independent media and trade unions, working mainly through nongovernmental organizations (NGOs).

The EC initially allocated ECU (European Currency Unit) 300 billion for PHARE assistance to Poland and Hungary in 1990, later adding ECU 200 billion as the program was expanded to other CEECs. The Commission's actual commitment of PHARE funds grew from ECU 495 billion in 1990 to ECU 774 million in 1991, and to slightly more than ECU 1 billion in 1992, a level at which it stabilized for the next several years.[10] By 1992, PHARE assistance was being provided to ten CEECs (eleven in 1993, after the breakup of Czechoslovakia). Responsibility for administering the PHARE program was given to the Commission, and for this purpose a new administrative service, DG IA, was set up within the Directorate-General responsible for external relations (DG I).

The EC also provided assistance to the successor states of the former Soviet Union beginning in late 1991, although this aid took the form of a separate grant program, Technical Assistance to the Commonwealth of Independent States (TACIS).[11] The three Baltic states (Latvia, Lithuania, and Estonia) were included in the PHARE program after they achieved independence from the Soviet Union in 1991, thus placing them in the same category as other CEECs. By developing separate aid programs for the CEECs and the Commonwealth of Independent States (CIS), the EC began the process of differentiating among the potential candidates for EC membership.

The PHARE program and other EC aid did not preclude the individual member states from providing their own assistance. As the member state with the greatest economic and political stake in Central and Eastern Europe, Germany in particular provided extensive assistance to the countries of this region. According to the OECD, through 1992 Germany contributed fully half of all international aid to the former Soviet bloc, and in the 1990–95 period it contributed nearly half of all EC bilateral assistance to Central and Eastern Europe.[12] By its own account, from 1989 through 1993 the German government spent a total of $24.2 billion on assistance to the former Soviet bloc in the form of grants, credits, export guarantees, and other types of aid.[13] Germany's interest in the countries to its east also made Bonn a key advocate of EC-level assistance and a major supporter of the PHARE program.

Another EC initiative to assist Central and Eastern Europe was the European Bank for Reconstruction and Development (EBRD). The EBRD originated as a French proposal that was approved by the European Council in December 1989.[14] After brief multilateral negotiations, the EBRD was established in May 1990 as a partnership of Western lenders and CEEC borrowers, with the EC and its member states subscribing a majority (51 percent) of the bank's ECU 10 billion capital. The EBRD's main objective was to promote investment and market-oriented economic reform in the CEECs, with most of its annual lending (60 percent) given to support the development of the private sector. The EBRD began its lending operations in April 1991 but soon became embroiled in scandal and controversy, leading to a major reorganization in 1993. Despite its problems, however, this EC-inspired institution has made significant contributions to economic reconstruction in the transition countries.

Two additional EC initiatives to assist Central and Eastern Europe were the Trans-European Mobility Program for University Students (TEMPUS) and the European Training Foundation (ETF). The former funded joint training projects linking universities and businesses in CEECs with counterparts in the EC. A key aim of the program was getting EC universities and firms to help upgrade university departments in the post-Communist countries. TEMPUS also promoted the exchange of teachers, students, and academic administrators between the EC and the CEECs. The ETF, on the other hand, provided assistance in adapting training systems in the CEECs to new market conditions, with a focus on vocational training, continuing education, and training in specific economic sectors. As with PHARE, both TEMPUS and the ETF were initiated in 1990 with Poland and Hungary but were later extended to other reforming countries.

While PHARE and other aid programs provided much-needed economic and technical assistance to the transition countries, what these countries most required was greater access to the EC market for their products. This access was granted only grudgingly by the EC, however, especially for those products of greatest importance to the CEECs, such as agricultural products, coal and steel, and textiles.

Official relations between the EC and the Soviet bloc had only first been established in June 1988, with the signing of a joint declaration by the EC and the CMEA.[15] This cleared the way for a series of bilateral trade and cooperation agreements between the EC and individual Soviet-bloc countries, beginning with Hungary in September 1988. In September 1989, a trade and cooperation agreement was signed with Poland, and in 1990 similar agreements were signed with Czechoslovakia, Romania, and Bulgaria.[16] After the breakup of the Soviet Union, trade and cooperation agreements were signed in 1992 with each of the Baltic states, and also that year with Albania. A trade and cooperation agreement with Slovenia was signed in 1993. These agreements were similar in providing for the gradual removal by the EC of quantitative restrictions on manufactured goods, although major exceptions were made for coal and steel, textiles, and agricultural products. The agreements also called for broader economic cooperation between the EC and the CEECs, and they established bilateral "joint committees" to study further cooperation and resolve disputes.[17]

While the trade and cooperation agreements represented a major advance at the time, they were quickly overtaken by the pace of events and the demands of the CEECs for greater economic and political integration with the EC. The EC responded to requests for greater market access by liberalizing quantitative restrictions on trade with Poland and Hungary in December 1989, effectively granting them Most Favored Nation (MFN) trading status and tariff-free access for manufactured products beginning in January 1990. The EC also extended trade concessions under the Generalized System of Preferences (GSP) to Poland and Hungary for certain industrial, textile, and agricultural products. Major exceptions to these GSP concessions were coal and steel products, and for Poland, fisheries products. Similar trade concessions were extended in October 1990 to Bulgaria and Czechoslovakia, and in January 1991 to Romania. In 1990, the EC decided to eliminate national quotas on coal and steel products for Poland, Hungary, and Czechoslovakia, and to raise quantitative limits for certain textile products as well.[18]

These trade concessions were adequate for the immediate economic needs of the reforming countries, but they hardly compensated for the collapse of intraregional trade within the old Soviet-bloc trading system after 1990. More comprehensive and far-reaching trade and economic agreements would be required as the post-Communist countries began reorienting their exports and economic relations toward the EC market. Also, these countries sought more than just aid and economic links to the EC. They wanted closer political ties, and eventually membership in the EC, as well.

THE EUROPE AGREEMENTS

One means of addressing the desire of the CEECs for closer economic and political integration with the EC was through the mechanism of "association." Association agreements would go beyond free trade arrangements and establish a special relationship between the CEECs and the EC. Association would not only promote more intensive economic integration of the EC and the CEECs but would also establish and institutionalize closer political links and create enhanced possibilities for social and cultural cooperation. More importantly for the CEECs, association could be an important stepping stone toward EC membership. According to

Czechoslovakia's Foreign Minister Jiri Dienstbier, association with the EC was more than just a matter of economic and financial assistance: "Rather, the principal objective is to integrate the economies and particularly the societies of Central Europe into an economic, social, cultural, and political environment that by its very nature is conducive to the adoption of European standards and norms."[19] In other words, association would prepare the CEECs for EC membership.

The legal provision for association agreements between the EC and nonmember countries is article 310 of the consolidated TEC (article 238 of the Rome Treaty), which enables the Community to conclude "with one or more States . . . agreements establishing an association involving reciprocal rights and obligations, common action and special procedures."[20] In the words of the European Court of Justice (ECJ), association agreements create "special privileged links with a nonmember country, which must, at least to a certain extent, take part in the Community system."[21] The EC had already signed association agreements with a number of nonmember countries, including Turkey (in 1963). Association agreements had also preceded accession for some current member states (Greece, Spain, and Portugal). While association agreements do not automatically lead to accession, some association agreements, including those with Turkey and Greece, have made explicit reference to accession as a future goal.[22]

The idea of offering the CEECs associated status first emerged in late 1989. An initial proposal along these lines was made in November by Prime Minister Thatcher, who referred to the EC's association agreement with Turkey as a possible model.[23] The association idea was also promoted by Germany's Chancellor Helmut Kohl, who in a speech in Poland shortly after the opening of the Berlin Wall urged the EC to go beyond the existing trade and cooperation agreements and build, over the medium and long term, "a much closer relationship" with the CEECs.[24] Two weeks later, in the November 28 speech announcing his "Ten-Point" plan for German confederation, Kohl mentioned the possibility of "specific forms of association which would lead the reformist countries of Central and Southeastern Europe to the European Community."[25]

At the Strasbourg summit in December 1989, EC leaders announced their readiness to examine "appropriate forms of association" with the CEECs, and they asked the Commission to develop proposals along these lines.[26] The Commission responded several weeks later by proposing a "new approach" to the development of EC relations with the CEECs that went beyond the existing trade and cooperation agreements and that would offer those countries fulfilling certain economic and political conditions the closest relations with the EC possible short of full membership.[27] The Commission's proposal was discussed in late January and early February 1990 by the Council of Ministers, which encouraged the Commission to further develop its ideas on this matter.[28] In April 1990, at the special European Council in Dublin, the Commission presented to the heads of state and government a paper providing the initial outlines of association agreements with the post-Communist countries. According to the Commission, these agreements would be offered to CEECs meeting certain preconditions, including evidence of their commitment to the rule of law, respect for human rights, the establishment of multiparty systems, free and fair elections, and economic liberalization with a view to introducing market economies.[29] The European Council welcomed the Commission's paper and pledged that the EC would "work to complete association negotiations with [the CEECs] as soon as possible."[30]

Four months later, the Commission sent a formal communication to the Council and the EP that contained its specific proposals for "Europe Agreements," so named by the Commission to distinguish them from association agreements with non-European countries (that is, those without a prospect of membership). According to the Commission's proposal, these agreements would build upon a common framework consisting of six elements: political dialogue, free trade and freedom of movement, economic cooperation, cultural cooperation, financial cooperation, and institutions of association to provide for consultation and joint decision making at different levels. There was also the promise of economic assistance to the associated countries in return for bringing their economies into line with EC laws and regulations. Within this common framework, the agreements would be "adapted to the circumstances of the country concerned." The Commission recommended beginning exploratory discussions on association agreements with Poland, Hungary, and Czechoslovakia, on the basis of their economic and political progress to date. The situation of other CEECs would be monitored closely, with the goal of opening talks with these countries once they had met the necessary conditions.[31]

On the crucial question of accession, the Commission's proposal carefully avoided any suggestion of an inherent link between association and membership. While noting that the governments of several CEECs had expressed an interest in eventually joining the EC, it emphasized that membership was not among the explicit objectives of the Europe Agreements. Instead, the Commission stressed that accession was a totally separate question that could only be addressed at a later date and through separate procedures. To emphasize this point, the Commission stated in its communication that the possibility of accession "would not be affected by the conclusion of association agreements."[32]

Indeed, for some within the Commission, the Europe Agreements were viewed as a useful means of forestalling eastward enlargement by offering the CEECs sufficient economic and political concessions to reduce their incentive to apply for membership. The targeted countries saw the Europe Agreements quite differently, however, viewing them as a stepping-stone to full membership. To support this interpretation, they pointed to previous association agreements with current member states—such as the agreements with Greece, Spain, and Portugal—as precedents. As if to underline this point, in June 1990 the Polish government handed the Commission a memorandum outlining a draft association agreement with the EC, to be followed within ten years by accession.[33]

In November 1990, the Commission presented the Council with its formal request for a mandate to negotiate Europe Agreements with Poland, Hungary, and

Czechoslovakia.[34] Final authorization for the Commission to begin negotiations was granted by the Council on December 18. The Council agreed that negotiations should begin immediately and proceed rapidly, with the intention of concluding the first Europe Agreements in time for them to take effect in January 1992.[35] The Commission received permission to open exploratory talks with Bulgaria and Romania in September 1991, and actual negotiations on Europe Agreements with these countries began in May of the following year.[36] Negotiations were also later begun with the governments of Slovenia and the three Baltic states.

The negotiations for the initial set of Europe Agreements took an entire year to conclude and were characterized by hard bargaining and conflict over specific products and sectors.[37] One reason for this difficulty was that the sectorally segmented structure of the negotiations and the EC's fragmented, open-to-access decision-making process allowed considerable influence to be exercised by producer lobbies and their government agents in the EC and individual member states. In the negotiations, therefore, narrow economic interests were often able to gain primacy over broader political considerations that favored a more generous treatment of the CEECs.[38] According to one observer, the Europe Agreement negotiations were "marked right to the end on the Community's side by hard-headed commercial protectionism at odds with the EC's political rhetoric about welcoming new democracies into the fold."[39] Quite naturally, this experience proved somewhat disillusioning for the CEECs.

While the EC had originally set the end of October 1991 as the deadline for concluding the negotiations, this goal proved impossible to meet, and the initial Europe Agreements with Poland, Hungary, and Czechoslovakia were not initialed until November 22.[40] The agreements were then formally signed in Brussels on December 16.[41] Because they are "mixed" agreements, including some provisions that are the responsibility of the EC and others that are the responsibility of the member states, the Europe Agreements required ratification by both national parliaments and the EP before they could take effect. Because of the need for ratification by each of the member states, the ratification process would take a while. In the meantime, the trade provisions of the Europe Agreements were implemented by special Interim Agreements, which did not require member state ratification, with the first such agreements taking effect in March 1992. Delays in the ratification process meant that the Europe Agreements with Poland and Hungary, the first to be fully ratified, did not finally take effect until February 1994. After the breakup of Czechoslovakia in January 1993, new Europe Agreements had to be negotiated with both the Czech Republic and Slovakia; these were signed in October 1993. The EC also signed Europe Agreements in 1993 with Bulgaria and Romania, with each of the three Baltic states in 1995, and with Slovenia in 1996. Once fully ratified, the Europe Agreements would serve as the legal basis for relations between the EC and the associated states until accession.

The ten Europe Agreements all had a similar structure but were tailored to the needs and conditions of individual CEECs.[42] The agreements called for the progressive establishment of free trade within ten years (six for Lithuania and Latvia, however, and immediately for Estonia), with the EC promising to lower its barriers to industrial imports even more quickly, within five to six years. In this sense, the Europe Agreements were asymmetrical in favor of the CEECs. However, special provisions were established in the agreements for the "sensitive" sectors of agriculture, textiles, and coal and steel. These provisions limited access to the EC market for products that made up a large percentage of the exports of the CEECs and in which these countries had the greatest comparative advantage in trade with the EC. In the first nine months of 1991, for instance, products in these sectors made up nearly 40 percent of Poland's total exports to the EC, despite the existence of heavy EC restrictions.[43] Altogether, in early 1993 some 40 percent of the total exports of Poland, Hungary, and Czechoslovakia to the EC were subject to some form of trade restraint under the Europe Agreements.[44] The Europe Agreements also provided the EC with commercial defense mechanisms, such as antidumping and safeguard clauses, which could be used by individual member states to stem the inflow of sensitive products.

The Europe Agreements also "protected" the EC by maintaining limits on the free movement of workers from the CEECs. However, the EC promised to improve the situation of workers from these countries already legally established in the EC. In the Europe Agreements, the CEECs agreed to the national treatment of EC-based enterprises after a transitional period. They also agreed to the free movement of capital and to allowing the repatriation of profits and investment returns.

The Europe Agreements also committed the CEECs to bringing their laws into line with EC legislation and to adopting EC rules on competition, public procurement, state aids, and intellectual property. In return, the EC agreed to provide economic, financial, and technical assistance. Thus, the Europe Agreements were conditional in that the EC made its trade concessions and economic assistance contingent upon "the actual accomplishment of economic, political, and legal reforms" by the CEECs. The Europe Agreements were also "flexible," in that they contained provisions for accelerated trade liberalization and increased EC assistance in response to progress with such reforms.

Also established by the Europe Agreements was a framework for political relations between the EC and CEECs. The so-called political dialogue institutionalized bilateral meetings at various governmental levels to discuss matters of common interest. It included the establishment of Association Councils, which were to meet at least once a year at the ministerial level to monitor implementation of the agreements. Also established were subministerial-level Association Committees and Parliamentary Association Committees (later renamed Joint Parliamentary Committees), the latter to provide a forum for interaction between the EP and the national parliaments of associated countries. Another key goal of the political dialogue was closer cooperation between the EC and the CEECs on foreign policy matters. The Europe Agreements also provided for increased cultural cooperation between the EC and the associated countries.

Except for the Baltic states, the EC did not offer to negotiate Europe Agreements with Russia and the other CIS states. Instead, it developed a separate type of Partnership and Cooperation Agreement (PCA) for these countries. The PCAs are contractual arrangements regulating economic, trade, and political relations between the EU and the CIS states. They also establish bilateral Cooperation Councils as a forum for regularized cooperation between the EU and the partner countries. The idea for the PCAs was developed by the Commission in the first half of 1992, and the Council authorized it to begin negotiations with Russia and other CIS states in October 1992.[45] The first PCAs were signed with Russia, Ukraine, and Moldova in 1994, and an agreement was signed with Belarus in 1995. The PCA with Ukraine came into force in 1996, while the agreement with Russia was not implemented until December 1997 due to EU objections to Russian conduct during the conflict in Chechnya. As was the case with the Europe Agreements, the trade provisions were initially implemented by Interim Agreements pending full ratification of the PCAs.

From the perspective of eastern enlargement, the main significance of the PCAs is that they are not Europe Agreements. By deciding to create a separate network of cooperation agreements with Russia and the other CIS states, the EU placed relations with these countries on a separate track from its development of ties with the CEECs and, thus, basically excluded them from the enlargement process.

REACTIONS TO THE EUROPE AGREEMENTS

The Europe Agreements marked a qualitative change in relations between the EC and the CEECs, establishing closer economic links and an institutional framework for political cooperation. Nevertheless, the governments of the CEECs were generally disappointed with the agreements, primarily due to their restrictiveness on trade and the movement of people and the absence of a clear link to accession. According to Vladimir Dlouhy, Czechoslovakia's economics minister, "When we started our political changes and then economic reforms, we had a lot of support from Western European political circles. But now, when we are really coming to the terms of that support, only cool-blooded economic facts are put on the table." Similarly, Poland's chief negotiator, Andrzej Olechowski, complained, "I think we were all disappointed by the format and the political climate of the talks. It soon turned into pure trade bargaining by the two sides across the table."[46]

What most disappointed the CEECs was the absence of any clear link in the Europe Agreements between association and accession. Obtaining a commitment on eventual membership had been a major goal of the CEECs, and in the negotiations they had pressed the EC to include an explicit reference to the prospect of accession in the agreements. Most of the member states, however, opposed the inclusion of any reference to membership in the agreements, with the notable exceptions of the German and British governments. In the end a compromise was reached, and in the Preambles of the Europe Agreements EC membership was recognized as a "final objective" of the CEECs.

This statement stopped far short of giving the CEECs the absolute commitment on future membership that they desired, however. At the same time, the EC stressed that future accession would not be automatic. According to Pablo Benavides, the Commission's chief negotiator for the agreements, the Europe Agreements were "not an entrance ticket," but rather "a kind of trial run [for CEECs to see] if they would like to become members later on."[47] However, Commission President Delors, an opponent of early enlargement, did concede that the agreements were the beginning of a process that could eventually lead to membership for the CEECs.[48] This was certainly the view of the CEECs. According to Polish Prime Minister Balcerowicz, "For us the [Europe] agreement is the beginning of the road to full EC membership."[49]

Still, the CEECs had hoped for a more specific road map for accession. According to Poland's Olechowski, this would have consisted of "a specific list of targets to be hit [for meeting EC standards and rules], followed by automatic entry [into EC]." Among other things, he argued, such an approach would provide valuable external support for difficult internal reforms in the transition countries, making them irreversible and protecting them against changes in domestic politics, such as an upsurge of antireform populism. By locking in reforms, the prospect of membership would also help close the book on authoritarianism in the CEECs. According to Olechowski: "The accent [of the Europe Agreements] should have been on helping us to go as quickly as possible to the *acquis communautaire*. What we wanted was a shield from wild politicians, but we really failed to achieve this."[50]

The Europe Agreements also drew considerable criticism from independent economists and policy experts, who argued that the restrictive provisions on trade and the movement of labor did not provide the CEECs with sufficient access to the EC market. Some experts also criticized the bilateral character of the agreements, which they argued not only gave the CEECs less leverage in their negotiations with the EC but also failed to promote the development of cooperation among the CEECs that a more multilateral approach would have promoted. Another common criticism was that the Europe Agreements were unclear about the steps that the associated countries must take to prepare for membership and that the agreements therefore did not provide a comprehensive strategy for the future integration of the CEECs. In short, it was argued that the Europe Agreements failed to provide the CEECs with the opportunities, support, and resources they needed to fully transform their economies and societies; instead, the Europe Agreements appeared to be aimed mainly at protecting the EC against the perceived economic threats posed by the CEECs.[51]

Some support for this criticism is provided by statistics measuring the trade effects of the Europe Agreements. After implementation of the Interim Agreements, the EU's trade surplus with the CEECs grew considerably, thus showing the EU's member states to be the primary beneficiaries of the agreements. By 1995, the EU's annual net surplus in trade with the ten CEECs had grown to more than $9 billion.[52] In June 1997, more than five years after the implementation of the first Interim Agreements, Czech Prime Minister Vaclav Klaus attacked the Europe Agreements, claiming that they were asymmetrical in the EU's favor and that they were largely to blame for the rising trade and current account deficits of the Czech Republic and other CEECs.[53] In a figure that supports Klaus's claim, a Hungarian expert, András Inotai, calculated that between 1992 and 1997 the ten CEECs amassed an ECU 64 billion deficit in trade with the EU, which was 83 percent of the EU's total trade surplus in that period.[54]

Defenders of the Europe Agreements, by contrast, have argued that the agreements constituted a fairly rapid response by the EC to new and unprecedented challenges and that they were the best deal that could be achieved under the circumstances and given the power of entrenched interests within the EC. They also point to the flexible and evolutionary character of the agreements, which permitted a deepening of relations with the CEECs once they were prepared for more integration. Supporters of the Europe Agreements also claim that the approach to membership taken by the agreements was a prudent one, given the economic, political, and environmental conditions in the CEECs and the difficult transitions they would have to make before they would be prepared for accession. They also argue that the EC was wise not to make promises to the CEECs at the time that it might have difficulty honoring later.[55] Indeed, until the declarations of the Copenhagen summit in June 1993, the EC's commitment to eastern enlargement was very much uncertain.

THE DEBATE OVER WIDENING

Despite the EC's reluctance to embrace the membership demands of the CEECs, in the early 1990s the issue of enlargement was on the EC's agenda. In addition to the post-Communist democracies, a number of other European countries wanted to join the EC, and by 1991 several either had applied for EC membership or were signaling their intention to do so. Among the applicants was Turkey, which formally applied to join the EC in 1987. Austria had applied for membership in 1989, and the Mediterranean island countries of Malta and Cyprus in 1990. Sweden added its name to the list of applicants in July 1991, followed by Finland, Switzerland, and Norway in 1992.

Each of these applications presented certain problems for the EC. Turkey had a large and growing population, a low level of economic development, questionable democratic institutions, and a poor record on human rights. Moreover, despite its secular government, Turkey was a predominantly Islamic country, leading many in the EC to question Turkey's identity as a European country and its European vocation. Turkey also had a bitter historical conflict with Greece, and since the admission of new members required the unanimous consent of current member states, this placed a tremendous political barrier in the way of Turkey's accession. These factors were all reflected in the Commission's strongly negative Opinion on Turkey's application that was given in late 1989.[56]

Cyprus's application was complicated by the island's division (since 1974) into separate Greek and Turkish communities and the fact that most member states did not want to admit a divided Cyprus or one whose political problems were unresolved. The Cyprus application—by the internationally recognized Greek Cypriot government in Nicosia—was strongly backed by Greece, however. A factor in the applications of both Cyprus and Malta was that both were very small countries and their accession would raise serious institutional and administrative issues for the EC. By comparison, the applications of Austria, Sweden, Finland, Norway, and Switzerland presented relatively few problems for the EC. These five members of the European Free Trade Association (EFTA) were all economically advanced and stable democracies. However, the fact that all but Norway were neutral countries posed a potential dilemma for the EC, with its ambitions to develop a common foreign and defense policy.

The EC initially responded to this sudden upsurge of interest in accession by trying to delay any serious discussion of enlargement until after the EC had achieved further deepening. In particular, it wanted to complete the intergovernmental negotiations on EMU and further political union that had begun in December 1990. As an alternative to full membership and a means of deferring enlargement, the EC offered the EFTA countries membership in an arrangement called the European Economic Area (EEA). The EEA would allow the EFTA countries to be a part of the Single Market, but they would not belong to EC institutions or have a voice in EC decision making. Although the arrangement was originally conceived with the EFTA countries in mind, some EC leaders also came to view the EEA as a possible model for integrating the CEECs if they continued with their economic reforms.[57]

Negotiations for the EEA began in 1990, and an agreement was signed in October 1991.[58] Well before this date, however, dissatisfaction with the EEA, especially the realization that it would only make them subject to EC rules and regulations that they had no voice in making, led several of the EFTA countries to decide to apply for full membership. Rather than being a means of deferring enlargement, therefore, the EEA may have actually accelerated it. Also playing a role in the decisions of some of the EFTA countries to apply were the geopolitical changes of 1989–91, which erased the neutrality objections of countries like Sweden and Finland to EC membership. By the time the EEA agreement was signed, even Delors—who originally conceived the EEA as a means of deferring enlargement—recognized the inevitability of further enlargement, declaring that the EEA was a "major step on the road to enlarging the Community."[59]

While many in the EC were now ready to consider membership for the EFTA countries, they were reluctant to discuss the possibility of eastern enlargement. By comparison with such highly developed democracies as Austria and Sweden, the post-Communist countries were poor and just beginning a lengthy and difficult process of economic and political reform. It was obvious to most EC leaders that many years of hard effort would be required for the transition countries to achieve the capacity to withstand competition in the Single Market and to develop the administrative and legal structures that would enable them to adopt and apply the *acquis communautaire*. In Delors's own view, it would be fifteen to twenty years before the CEECs were ready for membership.[60]

To prepare the CEECs for eventual membership, the Commission urged them to cooperate more among themselves, for instance through the creation of intraregional free trade arrangements. The Commission also discussed a number of arrangements that might satisfy the desire of the CEECs for increased political links to the EC and thus help reduce their interest in early accession. One idea was to offer the CEECs some type of partial membership in the EC. The best-known proposal along these lines was the idea of "affiliated membership" suggested by External Affairs Commissioner Frans Andriessen in the spring of 1991. According to Andriessen, as affiliated members the CEECs would have the right to take part in Council meetings on certain issues, but they would not have formal voting rights. Andriessen argued that this arrangement would help integrate the CEECs and give them some degree of "political security." In promoting the idea of affiliated membership, Andriessen declared that "creative thinking" was required to reconcile the conflicting demands of a wider Europe and the goal of deepening. According to Andriessen, the EC needed "to define the arrangements whereby the Community could offer the benefits of membership and the gains for stability, without wrecking its drive towards integration."[61]

Andriessen's proposal and others like it were not warmly received by the CEECs, however. What these countries wanted was full membership, and they viewed affiliated membership, or other such partial membership schemes, only as a means for postponing eastern enlargement. Andriessen's proposal also did not command much support among the member states, some of whom—especially Ireland and the Benelux countries—feared that partial membership would dilute the EC's institutional structures and blur the boundaries between members and nonmembers. Some member states that were more in favor of eastern enlargement, including Germany and Denmark, also opposed the idea of affiliated or associate membership status for the CEECs, mainly because they shared the suspicion of these countries that this was a way of delaying enlargement indefinitely.[62] Andriessen's proposal was also criticized within the Commission by those who questioned the precedent of allowing countries to join only parts of the EC and by others who felt that—based on the experience of the EFTA countries and the EEA—such ideas might only whet the appetites of the CEECs for full membership.[63]

Among the member states there were divergent views on the possibility of eastern enlargement. The French government was particularly reluctant to offer the CEECs a firm prospect of membership. In the wake of German unification, French authorities were afraid that eastern enlargement—by shifting the EU's political center of gravity eastward and adding countries with close political and economic ties to Germany—would only further enhance Germany's influence within the EC relative to that of France. This growing imbalance in influence and power, it was felt, might undermine the vital Franco-German partnership, which was both the traditional engine of European integration and a key pillar of French foreign policy. French elites also worried that further enlargement would weaken the EC's institutional coherence and effectiveness, thereby diminishing the EC's capacity to be an influential global actor and turning it into nothing more than a loose intergovernmental organization or a glorified free trade area.[64]

As an alternative to enlargement, President Mitterrand proposed the idea of a "European Confederation."[65] This arrangement would exist parallel to the EC yet would be organizationally separate from it. The European Confederation would embrace all European states, including Russia, and would provide a multilateral forum for the discussion of pan-European political, economic, and technical issues. According to Mitterrand, the European Confederation would promote stability and security in Central and Eastern Europe, while satisfying the desire of the post-Communist countries for closer political ties to the West.

Mitterrand's proposal for a European Confederation was discussed by European governments at a June 1991 conference in Prague. In the end, however, this idea was rejected by the CEECs, who felt that the European Confederation would only be a second-class "waiting area" for countries to be excluded from the EC. For similar reasons, the proposal was also viewed skeptically by Germany. At the Prague conference, Mitterrand only reinforced suspicions about the true motivations behind his proposal when he declared that it would be "decades and decades" before any of the CEECs would be able to join the EC.[66]

France was not the only member state that was skeptical about eastern enlargement. The governments of the three Benelux countries—Belgium, the Netherlands, and Luxembourg—shared French concerns about the impact of enlargement on the EC's institutional coherence and effectiveness as well as on its historical identity and sense of purpose. Also unenthusiastic about the prospect of eastern enlargement were Spain and other poorer member states, which viewed the accession of the even poorer CEECs as a threat to their generous shares of EC financial assistance.

Other member states, however, viewed the prospect of eastern enlargement more favorably. One such country was Germany, whose geographical position made it highly vulnerable to political and social upheaval in the former Soviet bloc, thus giving it a strong security interest in extending the EC's stabilizing influence eastward. As Chancellor Kohl stated frequently, a united Germany did not want its border with Poland to remain the eastern border of the EC for long; instead, it wanted to be surrounded on all sides by friendly countries with which it was closely integrated both economically and politically. Because of its central geographical location and historical ties to many of the CEECs, Germany also stood to be among the main economic beneficiaries of eastern enlargement.

The Kohl government also claimed that Germany had a special moral obligation to promote the integration of the CEECs, deriving from its historical record of aggression against the countries to its east as well as its special debt of thanks to the peoples of Poland, Hungary, and Czechoslovakia for making unification possible through their actions in 1989. The German government, therefore, regularly insisted that it would be the primary advocate of the CEECs on behalf of their efforts to join the EU and NATO. Enlargement was also a key element of Germany's policy of historical reconciliation (*Versöhnung*) with its immediate eastern neighbors, especially Poland, with which Bonn sought to establish a special relationship matching the one it had forged with France after 1945.[67]

The German government also rejected the notion that enlargement would hinder or preclude further integration. Almost alone among the member states, it proclaimed that widening and deepening were not contradictory, but that instead it was possible to do both together.[68] For all of these reasons, the German government insisted from the very beginning on giving the CEECs a firm prospect of EC membership.

Another early supporter of eastern enlargement was Denmark, mainly because of its close historical and cultural (and potential economic) ties to the post-Communist states along the Baltic rim: Poland, Estonia, Latvia, and Lithuania. Denmark also strongly supported the admission of Sweden and Finland into the EC, and beginning in 1995 these three countries would form an important "Nordic bloc" pushing for eastward enlargement and inclusion of the Baltic states. Also supporting enlargement was the British government, mainly because it felt that a wider and more diverse EC would be less prone to deepening and developing in a federal direction.

TOWARD A NEW STRATEGY

Faced with increasing demands for membership, the EC could no longer defer serious discussion of further enlargement. As a result, in the second half of 1991, with the IGCs on EMU and EPU underway and moving toward their Maastricht conclusion, the Commission increasingly focused on this issue and a new strategy on enlargement began to emerge.

In July 1991, following the formal application for membership by Sweden, the Commission met to discuss its enlargement strategy and the implications of enlargement for the EC.[69] Discussions continued into the fall. By this point, there was general support within the Commission for the idea that future enlargements should take place in successive "waves." The first wave would consist of the highly developed EFTA countries, which would be followed by other groups of applicants.[70]

A political boost for enlargement was needed from the member states, however, and this came in late November. On the eve of the Maastricht summit, President Mitterrand suggested that if the IGC negotiations ended successfully and an agreement was reached on EMU, the European Council might formally ask the Commission to begin examining the enlargement issue.[71] Indeed, this is what happened. While the December 9–10 Maastricht summit focused on concluding the negotiations on EMU and political union, EC leaders did find time to discuss enlargement. Thus, in its "Presidency Conclusions" for the summit, the European Council declared that accession negotiations with the EFTA applicants could begin once the EC had completed work on its financial perspective for 1993–99 and related issues, meaning probably sometime after the end of 1992. The European Council also asked the Commission to further study the enlargement issue, including the implications of enlargement for the EU's future development.[72]

In May 1992, the Commission completed and approved its report, entitled "Europe and the Challenge of Enlargement."[73] The report's conclusions indicated a shift of EC policy on enlargement toward acceptance of the prospect of a wider Europe and eventual membership for the post-Communist countries.

The Commission's report noted that, in addition to the applications of several EFTA countries and of Turkey, Malta, and Cyprus, some CEECs had expressed an interest in joining the EC. The report thus addressed the issues raised by the prospect of a wider EC of twenty or more members. Of primary importance, according to the Commission, was that enlargement must be done in a way that did not weaken, but rather strengthened, the EC: "The accession of new members will increase [the EC's] diversity and heterogeneity. But widening must not be at the expense of deepening. Enlargement must not be a dilution of the community's achievements. On this point there should be absolute clarity, on the part of the member states and of the applicants."[74]

The Commission's report carefully differentiated among three categories of candidate countries: those countries that were immediately eligible for membership due to their high level of economic development (Austria, Sweden, and other EFTA members); the three Mediterranean applicants (Turkey, Cyprus, and Malta); and the CEECs with aspirations to apply and for whom accession was only a distant possibility. Regarding the latter group of countries, the report declared that

> the integration of these new democracies into the European family presents a historic opportunity. In the past, the enlargement of the Community took place in a divided continent; in [the] future, it can contribute to the unification of the whole of Europe. The Community has never been a closed club, and cannot now refuse the historic challenge to assume its continental responsibilities and contribute to the development of a political and economic order for the whole of Europe.[75]

Although the Commission's report recognized that accession was only a distant possibility for the CEECs, it called for going beyond the existing Europe Agreements and strengthening the political links between the EC and these countries to create a new form of "partnership." The report declared that new mechanisms should be created to bind the CEECs to the EC politically. These mechanisms would build on the existing "architecture" of European organizations and would constitute a new "European political area." Several possible formulas for this new political area were mentioned, including Mitterrand's European Confederation idea, and—echoing Andriessen's affiliated membership proposal—the possibility that the CEECs could become "partner members" in specific EC policies, a status that would allow them to participate, but not vote, in Council meetings on issues that concerned them.[76]

The Commission's report also called for greater economic and technical cooperation between the EC and the CEECs to help prepare the potential applicants for meeting EC standards and regulations. It also mentioned the possibility of accelerated trade liberalization by the EC and measures to improve the free movement of workers. The Commission also welcomed the efforts at cooperation undertaken by the three "Visegrad" countries (Poland, Hungary, and Czechoslovakia), and it encouraged the formation of a free trade area among the CEECs and other forms of intraregional cooperation as a way of preparing for eventual membership.[77]

The Commission's report was released against the background of growing political support for enlargement. In May 1992, Germany's outgoing foreign minister, Hans-Dietrich Genscher, expressed the views of many EC leaders when he declared that "in Maastricht we agreed on the timetable for deepening the Community. Now we must agree on the timetable for enlargement."[78] Later that month, President Mitterrand and Chancellor Kohl concluded a bilateral summit by jointly announcing that accession negotiations with the EFTA applicants should begin as soon as possible.[79]

Meeting in Lisbon on June 26–27, the European Council endorsed the Commission's report on enlargement and reaffirmed the EC's intention to open accession negotiations with the EFTA applicants as soon as possible. EC leaders also declared their desire to intensify relations with the CEECs and to assist them in preparing for possible accession. They asked the Commission to evaluate the progress made by the post-Communist countries in their economic and political reforms and to report on this progress to the next scheduled European Council in December.[80]

The Commission's new report, "Towards a Closer Association with the Countries of Central and Eastern Europe," was finalized in the late fall. In it the Commission assessed the economic and political progress made by the CEECs and proposed new ways for reinforcing their relationship with the EC. The report did not recommend making a firm commitment to the CEECs on accession, nor did it specify the conditions of membership. It did, however, propose that the EC accept "the goal of eventual membership in the European Union for the countries of central and eastern Europe when they are able to satisfy the conditions required." The Commission was recommending, in other words, that the EC accept the idea of eastern enlargement in principle.[81]

Meeting at Edinburgh on December 11–12, 1992, the European Council decided to begin negotiations with the EFTA applicants early in the next year.

However, the summit was too preoccupied with other pressing issues—reaching agreement on the EC's budgetary package, on opt outs from the Maastricht Treaty for Denmark, and on the location of various EU institutions—to fully discuss the Commission's report on enlargement. Instead, the heads of state and government requested the Council to study and debate the Commission's recommendations. They also declared that at its next regular meeting, scheduled for Copenhagen in June 1993, the European Council would "reach decisions on the various components of the Commission's report in order to prepare the Associate countries for accession to the Union."[82] This statement was the first official indication by the EC that the CEECs could eventually become members.

THE COPENHAGEN SUMMIT

Continuing its work on enlargement strategy, the Commission approved a new report on policy toward the CEECs in May 1993.[83] In its report, the Commission proposed specific measures for deepening the association relationship with the CEECs, including improved access to the EC market, increased economic and technical assistance, and intensified political links. It also recommended that the associated CEECs become eligible for accession once they met certain economic and political conditions, providing that the EC was able to safely absorb the new members. After being discussed by the Council, the Commission's report was presented to EC leaders at the June 21–22 Copenhagen summit.

Meeting in Copenhagen, the European Council announced a historic turning point in EC policy toward Central and Eastern Europe. The European Council endorsed the conclusions of the Commission's report, announcing that it "agreed that the associated countries in Central and Eastern Europe *shall* become members of the European Union" (my emphasis). According to the European Council, "accession will take place as soon as an associated country is able to assume the obligations of membership by satisfying the economic and political conditions required." These conditions included the achievement of stable institutions that guaranteed "democracy, the rule of law, human rights and respect for and protection of minorities, the existence of a functioning market economy as well as the capacity to cope with competitive pressure and market forces within the Union." Also, "membership presupposes the candidate's ability to take on the obligations of membership including adherence to the aims of political, economic and monetary union."[84]

To these conditions—henceforth known as the "Copenhagen conditions"—the European Council added one more: "the Union's capacity to absorb new members while maintaining the momentum of European integration."[85] By including this condition, the European Council effectively linked future enlargement to the EC's ongoing efforts at internal deepening and institutional reform. In the end, this condition could prove to be the biggest hurdle to membership for the CEECs.

At Copenhagen, the European Council also agreed that "future cooperation with the associated countries shall be geared to the objective of membership," thus establishing an explicit link between cooperation and accession that did not exist in the Europe Agreements. To this end, the European Council proposed the creation of a new "structured relationship" with the CEECs, which it defined as a "multilateral framework for strengthened dialogue and consultation on matters of common interest." The structured relationship would consist of meetings between the Council and its counterparts (government ministers) from the CEECs on policy matters falling under each of the three pillars of EU activity: EC areas (transportation, energy, the environment, science and technology), CFSP, and JHA (immigration, asylum, combating organized crime). Separate procedures were also established for meetings of foreign ministers under CFSP. The European Council also proposed regular high-level meetings of the Commission president and EU presidency with their counterparts from the CEECs, and joint meetings of the heads of state and government when appropriate.[86]

The Copenhagen summit also decided to accelerate efforts to open the EC market to the CEECs, moving faster in this regard than was originally envisioned in the Europe Agreements. Customs duties would be reduced and quotas raised across all products, including (although to a lesser degree) the sensitive sectors of coal and steel, textiles, and agriculture. The EC also committed itself to increased and more effective economic assistance for the CEECs, including reorienting a portion of the PHARE budget (up to 15 percent) to infrastructure projects. The European Council also agreed to assist the associated countries in their efforts to approximate EC laws by providing training in EC law and procedure, and it decided to open additional EC programs to participation by the CEECs.[87]

The Copenhagen summit also indicated the probable geographical limits of EU enlargement. By declaring that accession was possible only for those CEECs with whom the EC "had concluded or plans to conclude" Europe Agreements, the European Council effectively excluded from its enlargement plans Russia and the other CIS states with whom the EC was developing a separate network of PCAs. On the other hand, the European Council declared that it was the EC's objective to conclude Europe Agreements with the three Baltic states "as soon as the necessary conditions have been met."[88] Much less clear after Copenhagen were the EC's future relations with the troubled countries of the Western Balkans, although negotiations on a Europe Agreement with Slovenia—the former Yugoslav republic that was the most advanced in economic and political terms and the most oriented historically and culturally toward Western Europe—were begun in the fall of 1993.

By accepting eastward enlargement in principle, the Copenhagen decisions of the European Council represented a major turning point for EC strategy toward Central and Eastern Europe. A number of factors contributed to this change of strategy, including pressure on the EC exerted by the CEECs themselves. In a series of joint memoranda in 1992 and 1993, the Visegrad governments repeated their demand for full membership. In a memorandum presented to the Commission in

September 1992, the governments of Poland, Hungary, and Czechoslovakia asked the EC for an explicit list of conditions for membership and a timetable for negotiations. They also proposed beginning accession negotiations in 1996, so that the three countries could become members by 2000.[89] And in an October 1992 memorandum, the three Visegrad governments declared that

> our three countries are convinced that stable democracy, respect for human rights and continued policy of economic reforms will make accession possible. We call upon the Communities and the member states to respond to our efforts by clearly stating the integration of our economies and societies, leading to membership of the Communities is the aim of the Communities themselves. This simple, but historic statement would provide the anchor which we need.[90]

This pressure from the CEECs was important for highlighting the gap between EC rhetoric about welcoming the post-Communist democracies into the EC fold and the substance of actual policy, thus embarrassing the EC into responding. Also through such pressure, the CEECs exploited the feelings of moral obligation toward Central and Eastern Europe held by many within the EC.

Also contributing to the change in EC strategy was the criticism of independent economists and policy experts, many of whom argued that existing policies toward Central and Eastern Europe—especially the Europe Agreements—were inadequate and shortsighted. Such criticism was important because, among other reasons, it provided the CEECs and their supporters in the EC with ideas and arguments for their efforts to change EC policy.[91]

Pressure for a change in strategy was also exerted by the governments of several member states. The German government, in particular, consistently argued that the post-Communist countries must be given a firm prospect of membership. During a visit to Warsaw in February 1992, German Foreign Minister Genscher declared that Poland, Hungary, and Czechoslovakia should become full EC members "as soon as possible."[92] The following month, he declared that these countries should be admitted to the EC by the end of the decade.[93] Also favoring a more open policy toward the CEECs were the British and Danish governments. These two governments held the EC's rotating presidency for the last half of 1992 and the first half of 1993, respectively, with the British government in particular using its term in office to promote improved relations with the CEECs.[94] Even among the member states that were less enthusiastic about enlargement, there was a growing acceptance of the need to better integrate the CEECs. One reason for doing so was to maintain Germany's future commitment to the EC. As Delors put it, "If the rest of the Community wants Germany to remain firmly anchored inside the EC, Eastern Europe cannot be left outside it."[95]

Within the Commission, strong pressure for a change in strategy came from the two commissioners heading the departments that were responsible for policy toward the CEECs, Hans van den Broek of DG IA and Leon Brittan of DG I. Another key advocate of policy change was the Commission's special interdepartmental Task

Force on Central and Eastern Europe. Together with sympathetic member states, the governments of the CEECs, and independent experts, these segments of the Commission forged an "advocacy coalition," which successfully pushed for the adoption of a new EC strategy toward Central and Eastern Europe.[96]

Certain external factors also played a role in bringing about this change in strategy. The tragic developments in the former Yugoslavia after 1991, especially in Bosnia, convinced many Europeans that the EC needed to play a more activist role in Central and Eastern Europe to preclude such instability from emerging there. Also important was the evidence of decreased popular support for difficult economic reforms within the CEECs, especially the reelection of former Communists in some countries in 1992 and 1993. In response to these developments, supporters of enlargement argued that by offering the CEECs a firm prospect of membership, the EC could promote stability in these countries and encourage continued economic and political reforms. Also pressing the EC to do more to integrate the post-Communist countries was the U.S. government. In other words, broader political and security considerations were beginning to supersede narrow economic concerns in shaping EC policy toward Central and Eastern Europe.

NOTES

1. "Address by Mr. Jacques Delors to the Council of Europe," *Bulletin of the European Communities* 9–1989: 95.
2. "Address by Mr. Jacques Delors at the College of Europe in Bruges," *Bulletin of the European Communities* 10–1989: 117.
3. "Address by President Mitterrand," *Bulletin of the European Communities* 10–1989: 85–86.
4. Margaret Thatcher, *The Downing Street Years* (New York: HarperCollins, 1993), 744.
5. "Presidency Conclusions," *Bulletin of the European Communities* 12–1988.
6. "Presidency Conclusions" of the European Council in Madrid, 26–27 June 1989, *Bulletin of the European Communities* 6–1989: 12 and 14.
7. On the Paris G7 meeting, see *Bulletin of the European Communities* 7/8–1989: 8–9. The G24 countries were the twelve EC member states: Sweden, Austria, Finland, Norway, Switzerland, Iceland, the United States, Canada, Japan, Australia, New Zealand, and Turkey. Among the international organizations participating in the G24 effort were the IMF, World Bank, OECD, EFTA, and EBRD. G24 assistance was extended to Czechoslovakia, the German Democratic Republic, Yugoslavia, and Bulgaria in July 1990, to Romania in 1991, to Albania and the Baltic states in 1992, and to the former Yugoslav republic of Slovenia in 1993.
8. For more details on EC assistance to Central and Eastern Europe, see Heinz Kramer, "The European Community's Response to the 'New Eastern Europe,'" *Journal of Common Market Studies* 31, no. 2 (June 1993): 224–25.
9. For the legislation establishing the PHARE program, see Council Regulation 3906/89 (18 December 1989), in *Official Journal,* L 375, 23 December 1989. For a more detailed discussion of the PHARE program, see Alan Mayhew, *Recreating Europe: The Euro-*

pean Union's Policy Towards Central and Eastern Europe (Cambridge: Cambridge University Press, 1998), 138–50.

10. European Commission, "The Phare Programme Annual Report 1995," COM (96) 360 final, Brussels, 23 July 1996, 44.

11. Similar to PHARE, TACIS distributed grants to finance the provision of expert advice for transformation projects and the development of democratic societies and market economies in the CIS countries. In its first five years of operation (1991–95), TACIS provided nearly ECU 2.3 billion to finance more than 2,200 projects in twelve countries of the former Soviet Union and Mongolia. See European Commission, "The Tacis Programme Annual Report 1995," Brussels 22.07.1996, COM (96) 345 final. The legislation for a reformed TACIS program, providing more than EUR 3.2 billion for the 2000–2006 period, was approved in December 1999. On the objectives and basic principles of the reformed TACIS program, see Agence Europe, *Europe Daily Bulletin,* no. 7373, 30 December 1998, 5–6; and Agence Europe, *Europe Daily Bulletin,* no. 7628, 7 January 2000, 6.

12. "Deutschland ist einer der größten Zahler," *Frankfurter Allgemeine Zeitung,* 1 October 1994, 1; cited in Jeffrey J. Anderson, "Hard Interests, Soft Power, and Germany's Changing Role in Europe," in *Tamed Power: Germany in Europe,* ed. Peter J. Katzenstein (Ithaca: Cornell University Press, 1997), 93, fn. 28. The EU figure is from the European Commission, cited in Mayhew, *Recreating Europe,* 157.

13. This includes the German share in multilateral efforts by such organizations as the EBRD and IMF. "The Stabilization of Central and Eastern Europe," *Focus On* . . . (New York: German Information Center, April 1994), 1.

14. *Bulletin of the European Communities* 12-1989: 13. On the EBRD, see Stephen Weber, "Origins of the European Bank for Reconstruction and Development," *International Organization* 48, no. 1 (1994): 1–38.

15. On the EC–CMEA joint declaration, see John Pinder, *The European Community and Eastern Europe* (London: Pinter Publishers, 1991), 23–25.

16. *Bulletin of the European Communities* 5–1990: 69–71.

17. On the trade and cooperation agreements, see Pinder, *European Community and Eastern Europe,* 25–30.

18. *Bulletin of the European Communities* 11–1989: 57; 12–1989: 86. For a summary of EC trade measures toward Eastern Europe after 1989, see Ulrich Sedelmeier and Helen Wallace, "Policies Towards Central and Eastern Europe," in *Policy-Making in the European Union,* 3rd ed., ed. Helen Wallace and William Wallace (Oxford: Oxford University Press, 1996), 360.

19. Jiri Dienstbier, "Central Europe's Security," *Foreign Policy,* no. 83 (Summer 1991): 127.

20. "Consolidated Version of the Treaty Establishing the European Community," in *European Union Consolidated Treaties* (Luxembourg: Office for Official Publications of the European Communities, 1997), 163.

21. Case 12/86, 1987 ECR 3719. The European Court of Justice is the EU's highest court and is responsible for deciding disputes about the interpretation of EU law among the EU's institutions and its member states.

22. On association agreements and their links to accession, see David Phinnemore, *Association: Stepping-Stone or Alternative to EU Membership?* (Sheffield, Eng.: Sheffield Academic Press, 1999).

23. *Financial Times,* 15 November 1989, 1; cited in Sedelmeier and Wallace, "Policies Towards Central and Eastern Europe," 367.

24. Speech of Chancellor Helmut Kohl at the Catholic University in Lublin, 13 November 1989, reprinted in *Bulletin,* no. 128, 16 November 1989 (Bonn: Presse- und Informationsamt der Bundesregierung), 1092–93.

25. "A Ten-Point Program for Overcoming the Division of Germany and Europe" (Official Translation) in *Statements and Speeches,* vol. 12, no. 25 (New York: German Information Center, 1989), 6.

26. "Conclusions of the Presidency," European Council in Strasbourg, 8–9 December 1989, *Bulletin of the European Communities* 12–1989: 12.

27. European Commission, "The Development of the European Community's Relations with the Countries of Central and Eastern Europe," SEC (90) 194 final, 1 February 1990.

28. *Bulletin of the European Communities,* 1/2–1990: 71.

29. European Commission, "The Development of the Community's Relations with the Countries of Central and Eastern Europe," SEC (90) 717 final, 18 April 1990.

30. Special Meeting of the European Council in Dublin, 28 April 1990, "Conclusions of the Presidency," *Bulletin of the European Communities* 4–1990: 9.

31. European Commission, "Association Agreements with the Countries of Central and Eastern Europe: A General Outline," COM (90) 398 final, 27 August 1990.

32. European Commission, "Association Agreements with the Countries of Central and Eastern Europe," 3.

33. *Bulletin of the European Communities* 6–1990: 93.

34. *Bulletin of the European Communities* 11–1990: 72.

35. *Bulletin of the European Communities* 12–1990: 112; Pinder, *European Community and Eastern Europe,* 59–60.

36. *Bulletin of the European Communities* 9–1991: 46; 5–1992: 82.

37. On the Europe Agreement negotiations, see Wolfgang H. Reinicke, *Building a New Europe: The Challenge of System Transformation and Systemic Reform* (Washington: Brookings Institution, 1992), 93–95.

38. Sedelmeier and Wallace, "Policies Towards Central and Eastern Europe," 371–72.

39. David Buchan, "Central Europeans Sign Trade Accords with EC," *Financial Times,* 17 December 1991, 2.

40. *Bulletin of the European Communities* 11–1991: 67.

41. *Bulletin of the European Communities* 12–1991: 95–96.

42. For details of the Europe Agreements, see Mayhew, *Recreating Europe,* 41–131; see also *Bulletin of the European Communities* 12–1991: 95–96.

43. Anthony Robinson and Martin Wolf, "Europe's Reluctant Empire-Builders," *Financial Times,* 2 December 1991, 15.

44. "Eastern Europe: The Old World's New World" (Survey), *Economist,* 13 March 1993, 20.

45. *Bulletin of the European Communities* 10–1992: 74.

46. Cited in Robinson and Wolf, "Europe's Reluctant Empire-Builders," 15.

47. Andrew Hill and Christopher Bobinski, "EC Paves Way for Free Trade with E Europe," *Financial Times,* 23–24 November 1991, 2.

48. Hill and Bobinski, "EC Paves Way," 2.

49. Quoted in Reinicke, *Building a New Europe,* 97.

50. Robinson and Wolf, "Europe's Reluctant Empire-Builders," 15.

51. On expert criticism of the Europe Agreements, see Sedelmeier and Wallace, "Policies Towards Central and Eastern Europe," 371; see also Anna Michalski and Helen Wallace, *The*

European Community: The Challenge of Enlargement (London: Royal Institute of International Affairs, 1992), 139–40.

52. Heather Grabbe and Kirsty Hughes, *Enlarging the EU Eastwards* (London: Royal Institute of International Affairs, 1998), 18. On the negative economic impact of the Europe Agreements on the CEECs, see also Richard Stevenson, "East Europe Says Barriers to Trade Hurt its Economies," *New York Times,* 25 January 1993, A1.

53. Anthony Robinson and Robert Anderson, "Czech Premier Attacks EU Association Agreements," *Financial Times,* 18 June 1997, 3.

54. Cited in Attila Ágh, "Europeanization of Policy-Making in East Central Europe: The Hungarian Approach to EU Accession," *Journal of European Public Policy* 6, no. 5 (December 1999): 852, n. 3.

55. Michalski and Wallace, *European Community,* 139.

56. European Commission, "Opinion on Turkey's Request for Accession to the Community," SEC (89) 2290 final, 18 December 1989. On Turkey's relationship to the EU and its application for membership, see Christopher Preston, *Enlargement and Integration in the European Union* (London: Routledge, 1997), 213–19.

57. On the motivations behind the EEA, see Edward Mortimer, "Into the EC Swim," *Financial Times,* 23 October 1991, 16.

58. Because of a ruling by the ECJ, however, a final EEA agreement was not signed until May 1992. On the EEA idea and negotiations, see Michalski and Wallace, *European Community,* 130–36. On the EFTA enlargement, see Thomas Pedersen, *European Union and the EFTA Countries: Enlargement and Integration* (London: Pinter, 1994); also Preston, *Enlargement and Integration,* 87–109.

59. Quoted in David Buchan, "Delors Says EFTA Deal Will Lead to Larger EC," *Financial Times,* 24 October 1991, 18. See also Alan Riding, "Europeans in Accord to Create Vastly Expanded Trading Bloc," *New York Times,* 23 October 1991, A1.

60. Charles Grant, *Delors: Inside the House that Jacques Built* (London: Nicholas Brealey, 1994), 143.

61. Frans Andriessen, "Towards a Community of Twenty-Four?" Speech to the 69th Assembly of Eurochambers, Brussels, 19 April 1991.

62. "European Stability: EU's Enlargement with the Central and East European Countries" (summary) (Copenhagen: Danish Institute of International Affairs, n.d.), 6. See also Lykke Friis and Anna Murphy, "EU Governance and Central and Eastern Europe: Where are the Boundaries?" (paper presented at the 5th Biennial Conference of the European Community Studies Association, Seattle, Wash., 29 May–1 June 1997), 16–17.

63. "Into the Unknown," *Economist,* 13 July 1991, 4; and David Buchan, "EC May Admit New Members if Union is Agreed," *Financial Times,* 25 November 1991, 16.

64. On French views on enlargement, see Michael Sutton, "France and the European Union's Enlargement Eastward," *The World Today* 50 (August–September 1994): 153–56. See also Ronald Tiersky, "France in the New Europe," *Foreign Affairs* 71, no. 2 (Spring 1992): 131–46; and Philip H. Gordon, *France, Germany, and the Western Alliance* (Boulder: Westview, 1995), 46–53.

65. Mitterrand first made the European Confederation proposal on December 31, 1989. On the proposal, see Ernst Weidenfeld, "Mitterrands Europäische Konföderation: Eine Idee im Spannungsfeld der Realitäten," *Europa-Archiv* 46, no. 17 (1991): 513–18; see also D. Vernet, "The Dilemma of French Foreign Policy," *International Affairs* 68, no. 4 (1992): 655–64.

66. Cited in Sutton, "France and the European Union's Enlargement Eastward," 153–54.

67. On the importance of Germany's relations with Poland in the post–cold war era, see Elizabeth Pond, *The Rebirth of Europe* (Washington: Brookings Institution, 1999); and Roland Freudenstein, "Poland, Germany, and the EU," *International Affairs* 74, no. 1 (January 1998): 41–54.

68. See, for instance, Hans-Dietrich Genscher, "A Spirit of Solidarity," *Financial Times,* 16–17 May 1992, 9.

69. David Buchan, "Commission Discusses Larger EC," *Financial Times,* 25 July 1991, 2.

70. Buchan, "EC May Admit New Members," 1.

71. Buchan, "EC May Admit New Members," 1.

72. Maastricht European Council, "Conclusions of the Presidency," *Bulletin of the European Communities* 12–1991: 8.

73. European Commission, "Europe and the Challenge of Enlargement," added to the "Presidency Conclusions" of the European Council in Lisbon, 26–27 June 1992, in *The European Councils: Conclusions of the Presidency 1992–1994* (Brussels: European Commission, Directorate-General for Information, 1995), 24–29.

74. European Commission, "Europe and the Challenge of Enlargement," 24.

75. European Commission, "Europe and the Challenge of Enlargement," 24.

76. European Commission, "Europe and the Challenge of Enlargement," 28–29.

77. European Commission, "Europe and the Challenge of Enlargement," 29.

78. "Farewell Address by Hans-Dietrich Genscher, Minister for Foreign Affairs of the Federal Republic of Germany, at a Reception for the Diplomatic Corps, Bonn, 15 May 1992," in *Statements and Speeches,* vol. 15, no. 10 (New York: German Information Center, 1992), 2.

79. Ian Davidson, "France and Germany Back EC Expansion," *Financial Times,* 23–24 May 1992, 2.

80. "European Council in Lisbon, 26–27 June 1992: Presidency Conclusions" ("Lisbon Presidency Conclusions"), in *European Councils,* 6–7. For an analysis of the Lisbon European Council and its decisions on enlargement, see Michalski and Wallace, *European Community,* 47–49.

81. European Commission, "Towards a Closer Association with the Countries of Central and Eastern Europe," SEC (92) 2301 final, 2 December 1992.

82. *European Council in Edinburgh, 11–12 December 1992: Conclusions of the Presidency* (Luxembourg: Office for Official Publications of the European Communities, n.d.), 94.

83. European Commission, "Towards a Closer Association with the Countries of Central and Eastern Europe," SEC (93) 648 final, 18 May 1993.

84. "European Council in Copenhagen, 21–22 June 1993: Presidency Conclusions" ("Copenhagen Presidency Conclusions"), in *European Councils,* 86.

85. "Copenhagen Presidency Conclusions," 86.

86. "Copenhagen Presidency Conclusions," 86 and 92.

87. "Copenhagen Presidency Conclusions," 86–87 and 92–94.

88. "Copenhagen Presidency Conclusions," 86–87.

89. "Memorandum of the Governments of the Czech and Slovak Federal Republic, the Republic of Hungary, and the Republic of Poland on Strengthening their Integration with the European Community and on the Perspective of Accession," 11 September 1992; cited in Agence Europe, *Europe Daily Bulletin,* no. 5813, 12 September 1992.

90. Quoted in Michalski and Wallace, *European Community,* 114.

91. Sedelmeier and Wallace, "Policies Towards Central and Eastern Europe," 373–74.

92. Christopher Bobinski, "Genscher Proposes States to Join EC," *Financial Times,* 5 February 1992, 2.

93. Andrew Fisher, "Genscher Expects EC to Expand," *Financial Times,* 23 March 1992, 3. Genscher's statement was supported by the declaration of another top Foreign Ministry official, Ursula Seiler-Albring, that the Visegrad countries had a "realistic possibility of joining [the EU] around the year 2000." Craig R. Whitney, "Germany Focuses on German Unity; European Unity Will Wait," *New York Times,* 13 May 1992, A4.

94. Philip Stephens, "Major Seeking to Draw Visegrad Countries to EC," *Financial Times,* 23–24 May 1992, 2.

95. Quote cited in Jackie Gower, "EC Relations with Central and Eastern Europe," in *The European Community and the Challenge of the Future,* 2nd ed., ed. Juliet Lodge (New York: St. Martin's, 1993), 289.

96. Gerda Falkner, "Enlarging the European Union," in *European Union: Power and Policy-Making,* ed. Jeremy Richardson (London: Routledge, 1996), 244, n. 9. An advocacy coalition is "composed of people from various organisations who share a set of normative and causal beliefs and who often act in concert. At any particular point in time, each coalition adopts a strategy(s) envisaging one or more institutional innovations which it feels will further its objective." Paul Sabatier, "An Advocacy Coalition Framework of Policy Change and the Role of Policy-Oriented Learning Therein," *Policy Sciences* 21 (1988): 133. See also P. A. Sabatier and H. C. Jenkins-Smith, eds., *Policy Change and Learning: An Advocacy Coalition Approach* (Boulder: Westview, 1993).

3

+

The Pre-Accession Strategy

The decisions of the Copenhagen summit opened the door to EU membership for the countries of Central and Eastern Europe. However, although at Copenhagen the European Council accepted eastern enlargement in principle, it provided no detailed road map or timetable for accession. Moreover, the conditions for membership that it established were quite vague and subject to interpretation. There remained much work to do, therefore, to bridge the gap between the general promise of membership and the actual beginning of accession negotiations. The next step in the enlargement process would be the development of a comprehensive pre-accession strategy for the CEECs, to guide and assist their preparations for membership. The EU would also have to begin confronting the implications of further enlargement for its own policies and institutions.

BEYOND COPENHAGEN

In the initial months following the Copenhagen summit, there was little visible progress on policy toward Central and Eastern Europe. Instead, the EC was absorbed with the difficult struggle to secure ratification of the Maastricht Treaty, which was finally accomplished in October. The TEU took effect on November 1, 1993, thereby establishing the EU. The EU was also rocked by an exchange-rate crisis in July and August 1993, which threatened to destroy the European Exchange-Rate Mechanism (ERM) and derail plans for EMU. Also absorbing the EU's attention were the ongoing accession negotiations with Austria, Sweden, Norway, and Finland.[1]

By the end of 1993, the EU was coming under renewed pressure to integrate the CEECs. A major reason for this pressure was political developments in Russia, where the ultranationalist politician Vladimir Zhirinovsky enjoyed surprising success in parliamentary elections in December. Zhirinovsky's success raised new concerns about the prospects for democracy in Russia, and increased fears in the CEECs and among Western governments that a more nationalist Russia might seek to reclaim its empire in Central and Eastern Europe. In response to developments in Russia, the CEECs renewed their demands for closer ties with the West, including NATO and EU membership. Increased pressure also came from the U.S. government, with President Clinton urging the EU to do more to integrate the post-Communist democracies while attending a NATO summit in January 1994.

Responding to this pressure, in late January 1994 the Commission launched a wide-ranging review of EU policy toward the CEECs. According to Commission President Delors, it was now time to think in terms of a "Greater Europe."[2] The Commission's review focused on the impact of EU agricultural policies on trade with the CEECs, reform of the PHARE program to target more aid on infrastructure spending, and the need for the CEECs to harmonize their competition and state aid policies with EU regulations in these areas.[3]

The EU also discussed ways to enhance the political and security integration of the CEECs. In early March, EU foreign ministers approved a plan for greater foreign policy cooperation with the associated CEECs. This cooperation would include yearly meetings among the EU presidency, the Commission, and the heads of state or government of the associated countries as well as special Council meetings involving the foreign ministers of the CEECs. Also included were regular meetings at the subministerial level as well as meetings of experts and special working groups to discuss common foreign and security policy issues. The Council's plan also allowed for formal cooperation between the EU and CEECs at international conferences. It also provided the CEECs the opportunity to associate themselves with EU statements on individual foreign policy issues and created the possibility of joint foreign policy actions by the EU and the associated countries.[4]

In the spring of 1994, the first formal applications for membership by the CEECs were made. On March 31, 1994, Hungary presented its application to the EU, followed on April 5 by Poland. For both of these applications, on April 18 the Council decided to implement the procedures laid down in Article O of the TEU, which provides for consultation of the Commission. Lined up behind Poland and Hungary were eight other CEECs that either had signed or were negotiating Europe Agreements and were preparing to file their own applications. These CEECs would join Turkey, Cyprus, and Malta, which had already applied, as prospective candidates for the next wave of EU enlargement.

The first formal applications by the CEECs only increased the pressure on the EU to develop a strategy to prepare the post-Communist states for accession. Progress in developing such a strategy was hindered, however, by the emergence of a growing cleavage between northern and southern member states that reflected both economic and geopolitical concerns. This cleavage was fully in evidence by early 1994, as the EU neared the end of accession negotiations with the four EFTA applicants and contemplated new policy initiatives to prepare the CEECs for eventual membership. Specifically, France and other southern member states were concerned that enlargement to the north and east, and the EU's growing focus on Central and Eastern Europe, would lead the EU to neglect its southern or Mediterranean flank. To counterbalance what it saw as the EU's increasing northward and eastward tilt, the French government demanded a new EU Mediterranean policy. Relatively poor southern member states, such as Greece and Spain, were also worried about a shift in EU aid flows to Central and Eastern Europe and a reduction in their own aid shares as a result.

Tensions along north-south lines surfaced in the later stages of entry talks with the EFTA countries. Accession negotiations with Sweden, Finland, Norway, and Austria were finally concluded and entry agreements initialed on March 30, opening the way for assent by the EP and ratification by the applicant countries. Toward the end of the negotiations, however, France and other southern member states—particularly Greece, which held the EU presidency—became upset with the vigorous manner in which the German government pushed the pace of the negotiations. They also objected to the heavy-handed tactics used by Germany to bring the negotiations to a close. This episode produced renewed tensions in Franco-German relations, which also reflected French concern about the new assertiveness of German foreign policy after unification and sensitivity to Bonn's enthusiasm for enlargement more generally.[5]

These tensions were soon assuaged, however, by agreement on a new "strategic bargain" that sought to balance northern and southern interests with the EU. Essentially, France and other southern member states accepted the need for eastern enlargement, while the German government endorsed the idea of a new EU Mediterranean policy. This new Mediterranean policy would provide economic aid and market access for nonmember states of the Mediterranean rim and would aim at achieving greater stability and security in the Mediterranean region. With agreement on this new strategic bargain, the way was opened for progress in defining a comprehensive pre-accession strategy for the CEECs.[6]

This new strategic consensus was reflected in the decisions of the EU summit at Corfu on June 24–25. At Corfu, the European Council asked the Commission to make specific proposals for further implementing the Europe Agreements and the decisions of the Copenhagen European Council. More significantly, it asked the Commission to develop a strategy for preparing the CEECs for accession. The Corfu summit also discussed the applications of Malta and Cyprus, both of which had received positive evaluations from the Commission the previous summer. With the Greek government in particular pushing for action on Cyprus's application, the European Council declared that the next phase of enlargement would include these two countries. In keeping with the north-south strategic bargain, the Corfu summit also asked the Commission and Council to examine ways of strengthening the EU's Mediterranean policy.[7]

At Corfu, the European Council also began confronting the internal reforms the EU would need to make to prepare for further enlargement. Noting that institutional reform was a necessary precondition for further enlargement, the European Council instructed the intergovernmental "Reflection Group" preparing for the 1996 IGC—which was mandated by the Maastricht Treaty to review the operation of the TEU—to consider reforms "necessary to facilitate the work of the Institutions and guarantee their effective operation in the perspective of enlargement."[8]

TOWARD A PRE-ACCESSION STRATEGY

Over the next six months, the EU worked on developing its pre-accession strategy for the CEECs. While this effort was spearheaded by the Commission, it was also greatly promoted by the German government, which held the EU presidency in the second half of 1994. Upon assuming the presidency, the Kohl government declared that progress on integrating the CEECs was a key goal of its term in office.[9]

After Corfu, the Commission responded quickly to the European Council's request for proposals for a pre-accession strategy. Only three weeks after the summit, the Commission produced a new Communication entitled "The Europe Agreements and Beyond," which outlined the major components of such a strategy. In its report, the Commission declared: "The goal for the period before accession should be the progressive integration of the political and economic systems, as well as the foreign and security policies of the associated countries and the Union, together with increasing cooperation in the fields of justice and home affairs, so as to create an increasingly unified area." Hinting at a differentiated approach to accession for the individual CEECs, the Commission added that "the needs and capacities of each partner will determine the pace of their progress towards membership."[10]

The Commission's report named the already-existing "structured relationship" and the Europe Agreements as the primary instruments for the new pre-accession strategy, claiming that together they provided a "framework for diverse forms of cooperation" that was both "flexible and dynamic, permitting the intensification of cooperation and integration." The multilateral structured relationship, it argued, had the dual benefit of promoting a closer working relationship and habits of cooperation between the EU and CEECs, while encouraging cooperation in resolving common or trans-European problems. However, the Commission called for expansion of the structured relationship beyond joint meetings with the Council to include other EU institutions, for instance, the EP. It also argued that second- and third-pillar issues (CFSP and JHA, respectively) should be included in the EU's multilateral dialogue with the CEECs. In reference to the Baltic states and Slovenia, the Commission also declared that additional countries could be included within the structured relationship once they had concluded Europe Agreements with the EU.[11]

The main focus of the Commission's proposed strategy was integrating the CEECs into the Single Market. The Commission urged the associated countries to approximate national laws and standards to those of the EU, particularly in the areas of competition and state aids policies. It also urged the CEECs to cooperate more among themselves in preparing for accession, citing approvingly the Central European Free Trade Area (CEFTA) and other intraregional economic initiatives.[12] The report's main innovation, however, was the Commission's proposal to "prepare a White Paper setting out a program for meeting the obligations of the internal market which can be followed by each associated country and monitored by the Union." The Commission suggested that this paper could be accompanied by a study of the impact of enlargement on the EU's common policies, especially the CAP.[13]

In a more detailed follow-up Communication two weeks later, the Commission proposed specific measures for implementing its pre-accession strategy. These included measures aimed at the following: (1) expanding and enhancing the structured relationship, including specific suggestions for future meetings between EU institutions and the associated states; (2) promoting the progressive adoption of EU laws and regulations by the CEECs, especially in the areas of competition and state aids policies; (3) enhancing trade opportunities for the CEECs, including the modification of EU antidumping and safeguard measures and rules of origin; (4) promoting macroeconomic and structural changes in the CEECs; and (5) improving the effectiveness of EU financial assistance for the CEECs, including the reorientation of PHARE aid toward infrastructure spending and increased lending for structural adjustment reforms. The Commission also announced that it would review options for EU agricultural policy in a wider Europe.[14]

Under the leadership of the German EU presidency, the member states endorsed the main elements of the Commission's pre-accession strategy in the fall. At a meeting in early October, the Council agreed to the Commission's proposal for a White Paper that would detail the measures the CEECs needed to adopt to prepare themselves for membership in the Single Market. It also agreed in principle to an enhanced structured relationship that would be multilateral in nature and would complement existing bilateral meetings held under the Europe Agreements. In the enhanced structured relationship, representatives of the CEECs would be allowed to participate in extended meetings of the Council of Ministers and European Council. Not all member states favored this arrangement, however, and in securing this agreement the German presidency had to overcome the fears of some member state governments that Bonn was trying to give the CEECs EU membership "through the backdoor."[15]

On the basis of these agreements, the Kohl government hoped to win final approval of a comprehensive pre-accession strategy at the Essen summit in December. In the weeks before the summit, however, disputes erupted over a number of issues. There was disagreement over a package of trade and market-access concessions that the EU planned to offer the CEECs, with the governments of France, Spain, and Portugal opposing plans to progressively reduce the use of antidumping and safeguard measures against imports from the associated states. There was also disagreement over the respective levels of financial aid to be allocated for the pre-accession strategy and the new Mediterranean policy, and over the future balance between the EU's eastern and Mediterranean policies more generally. Another problem was the Commission's delay in submitting proposals for changing the EU's "rules of origin" for CEEC products. Also threatening to cause problems was increased attention to the prospective financial cost of enlargement, with the Commission now estimating that eastern enlargement would require a doubling of EU spending on the CAP and Structural Funds if the present policies were extended to new CEEC members. In response to these estimates, the British government demanded an immediate and full debate on CAP reform as a precondition for enlargement, but such a debate was strongly opposed by the French government.[16]

Because of these disagreements, work on the pre-accession strategy moved slowly, leading the German government to lower its expectations of what could be achieved at Essen. Bonn even reconsidered its plans to invite government leaders of the CEECs to attend the summit. In the end, however, sufficient agreement on pre-accession measures was made to permit Chancellor Kohl to go forward with his invitations. For Kohl, the presence of these leaders at the summit was an important symbolic gesture, because it would send the CEECs the message that the EU was "not a closed shop." According to Kohl, "We want to show that these countries will be welcome if they want to join [the EU] and if their domestic and economic situations permit that."[17]

THE ESSEN SUMMIT

The Essen summit on December 9–10, 1994, was a major step forward in the process of eastern enlargement. In Essen, EU leaders formally approved a comprehensive pre-accession strategy for the CEECs. Following the Commission's original proposals, this strategy had two key parts: an enhanced structured relationship and a White Paper drawn up by the Commission that would provide a "route plan" for progressively integrating the CEECs into the Single Market. The pre-accession strategy also included the promise of increased EU financial and technical assistance for the CEECs.[18]

The enhanced structured relationship was aimed at integrating the CEECs politically and promoting cooperation between the EU and the associated countries in addressing problems of common interest. It also aimed at socializing the CEECs into the complex process of EU policy formation and decision making. The European Council agreed that the structured relationship would cover each of the three pillars of EU activity: "Community areas, especially those with a trans-European dimension (including energy, transport, science and technology, etc.), Common Foreign and Security Policy as well as Home and Judicial Affairs."[19]

As a framework for the structured relationship, the EU established a schedule of regular multilateral meetings that would be held alongside the bilateral meetings of the Association Councils established by the Europe Agreements. This schedule consisted of the following:

- Annual meetings of the heads of state and government, held at the margins of a European Council meeting;
- Semiannual meetings of foreign ministers for the discussion of general relations, "in particular the status and progress of the integration process";
- Annual meetings of "Ministers responsible for internal market developments, in particular Finance, Economic, and Agricultural Ministers";
- Annual meetings of transport, telecommunications, research, and environment ministers;
- Semiannual meetings on JHA;
- Annual meetings on cultural affairs and education.[20]

The ministerial meetings would generally be held in conjunction with corresponding Council meetings, although additional meetings were also possible. The EU also stressed the need for careful preparation of these meetings to ensure their effectiveness, a response to criticism that previous structured dialogue meetings were poorly planned and prepared.[21] In an effort to enhance the associated countries' sense of inclusion, the EU also announced that there would be more meetings of the CEECs with the full fifteen member states, rather than the previous reliance on meetings with the EU *troika* (the current, preceding, and succeeding EU presidencies) and the Commission.

The main focus of the pre-accession strategy, however, was on preparing the CEECs for integration into the Single Market. The EU promised that the Commission would prepare a White Paper by spring of 1995, which would outline the measures these countries would need to adopt to align their commercial laws and regulations with those of the EU. Specifically, the White Paper would identify the relevant aspects of the *acquis communautaire* in particular sectors necessary for the effective functioning of the Single Market, which the associated countries would therefore be required to adopt. The EU also promised to provide financial aid— mainly through the PHARE program—to assist the CEECs in transforming their economies, as well as necessary technical and legal assistance. The EU warned, however, that "the major tasks fall to the associated countries, which will have to put into place legislative and regulatory systems, standards and certification methods compatible with those of the EU."[22]

To improve market access and trade opportunities for the CEECs, the EU promised that it would provide more warning and clarity in the application of commercial defense instruments such as antidumping and safeguard measures. The EU also pledged to reduce its barriers to textiles imports from the CEECs and to modify its policies on the cumulation of rules of origin to benefit CEEC producers. The EU also promised to progressively reduce its use of commercial defense measures if the CEECs adopted EU rules on competition and state aids policy. In the agriculture sector, the EU promised that it would review the impact of the CAP on the CEECs and that the Commission would prepare "a study on alternative strategies for the development of relations in the field of agriculture between the EU and the associated countries with a view to a future accession of these countries."[23]

Also approved as part of the pre-accession strategy was a set of flanking measures, including new EU policies to promote foreign investment in the CEECs. There were also policies to promote cooperation between the EU and CEECs in the areas of CFSP and JHA, the environment, Trans-European Transportation and Energy Networks (TENs), and culture, education, and training. The pre-accession strategy also called for revamping the PHARE program to better enable it to support economic reform in the CEECs. In particular, there would be a reorientation of PHARE spending toward infrastructure development and away from technical assistance. The EU also stressed the importance of intraregional cooperation and good neighborly relations among the CEECs as a precondition for accession and therefore called attention to the ongoing negotiations for a "Pact on Stability in Europe" (see the next section).[24]

The pre-accession strategy approved at Essen was one-sided in that it focused on what the CEECs needed to do to prepare for membership while saying nothing about the internal reforms the EU needed to make as a precondition for enlargement. However, in its "Presidency Conclusions" for the Essen summit, the European Council addressed the issue of institutional reform by reaffirming that "the institutional conditions for ensuring the proper functioning of the Union must be created at the 1996 Intergovernmental Conference, which for that reason must take place before accession negotiations begin."[25] The European Council also asked "the Commission to submit as soon as possible the detailed analysis desired by the Council of the effects of enlargement in the context of the Union's current policies and their future development," a reference to the impact of enlargement on the CAP and the Structural Funds.[26] There was no discussion of a timetable for enlargement at Essen, except for the agreement that negotiations could not begin until after conclusion of the 1996 IGC.

While the primary focus of the Essen summit was on Central and Eastern Europe, the European Council also discussed new initiatives on Mediterranean policy. In Essen, EU leaders approved a Council report on the EU's future Mediterranean policy, which called for the creation of a "Euro-Mediterranean Partnership" to promote peace, stability, prosperity, and cooperation in the region. This goal would be achieved through political dialogue, the progressive establishment of free trade, and increased EU financial assistance to participating countries. The European Council also endorsed the proposal for convening a Euro-Mediterranean Ministerial Conference in the second half of 1995, under the Spanish EU presidency.[27] It also stressed the need "to maintain an appropriate balance in the geographical allocation of Community expenditure and commitments," thus confirming an earlier

Council decision that spending on Mediterranean policy over the next five years would rise, although it would not necessarily keep pace with the increased spending on Central and Eastern Europe.[28] However, it was decided at Essen that final decisions on the amount of financial aid to each region would not be made until the European Council in June 1995.

In an important symbolic gesture, the government leaders of the six CEECs that had already signed Europe Agreements with the EU—Poland, Hungary, the Czech Republic, Slovakia, Bulgaria, and Romania—attended the Essen summit's closing session.[29] In the "Presidency Conclusions" for the summit, the European Council also requested the Commission to do everything necessary to ensure that Europe Agreements with the three Baltic states and Slovenia would be concluded in the first half of 1995 so that these countries could be included in the pre-accession process.[30]

Because it represented a major step forward in the process of eastern enlargement, the Essen summit was hailed in the media as a victory for Chancellor Kohl and German policy on enlargement.[31] After the summit, however, Kohl preferred to emphasize the difficult task facing the CEECs in preparing their economies and societies for accession. Along with other EU leaders, Kohl stressed that the pre-accession process did not constitute membership negotiations, and he declared that it was "important not to awaken any false expectations" among the associated countries about early accession. Kohl and other EU leaders also emphasized that the CEECs would not be dealt with as a group, but that instead accession negotiations would proceed with individual applicants on a case-by-case basis, depending upon their progress in meeting EU standards.[32]

THE PACT ON STABILITY
AND THE WESTERN EUROPEAN UNION

An important part of the pre-accession strategy approved in Essen was the emphasis on "good neighborly relations," which the European Council declared in its "Presidency Conclusions" were a basic precondition for accession.[33] This emphasis reflected the EU's concern that the accession of new member states should not bring into the EU any new conflicts or instability. The EU thus sought to minimize the security risks of enlargement by encouraging prospective member states to resolve outstanding conflicts with neighboring countries over such issues as borders and the rights of ethnic minorities.

To achieve this objective, in 1994–95 the EU sponsored negotiations for the "Pact on Stability in Europe." The pact was basically an attempt to use preventative diplomacy to encourage the CEECs to resolve potentially dangerous disputes among themselves, with assistance from the EU and other international actors.

The idea for the Pact on Stability originally came from French Prime Minister Eduoard Balladur in the spring of 1993. By proposing the pact, Balladur sought to make a distinctive French contribution to the EU's eastern policy and thereby reverse the general perception of French defensiveness regarding this part of Europe. He also sought to demonstrate that the EU could play the lead role in managing regional security problems, thereby restoring the EU's image as an external actor that had been damaged by its embarrassing failure to stop the conflicts in the former Yugoslavia after 1991.

The CEECs reacted suspiciously at first to Balladur's proposal, believing that it was yet another French attempt, like Mitterrand's European Confederation proposal before it, to divert them from their ultimate goal of EU membership. For much the same reason, the German government was also skeptical. There was also concern among some Western governments that the pact would overlap too much with the responsibilities of the Organization for Security and Cooperation in Europe (OSCE) (at that time still the Conference on Security and Cooperation in Europe).[34]

Despite these reservations, the Balladur proposal was endorsed by the European Council at Copenhagen in June 1993. In doing so, EU leaders noted that the pact initiative would provide the EU with an early opportunity to use the new "joint action" procedures for the CFSP that were agreed to at Maastricht.[35] Indeed, enthusiasm for the pact idea grew as it became viewed as a means of demonstrating the effectiveness of the CFSP. Thus, after receiving a study of the pact idea conducted by EU foreign ministers, at the December 1993 Brussels summit the European Council formally decided to begin the diplomatic process that would lead to the signing of a Pact on Stability in Europe.[36]

Negotiations for the pact were launched at an inaugural conference in Paris in May 1994.[37] Attending the conference were representatives of the EU and of the governments of the six associated CEECs (Poland, Hungary, the Czech Republic, Slovakia, Romania, and Bulgaria). Also represented were the governments of the three Baltic states and Slovenia, the Russian and U.S. governments, and relevant international organizations.

Negotiations continued over the next ten months at two multilateral round tables, one for the Baltic states and one for the other CEECs. Within this multilateral framework, bilateral negotiations were conducted between the CEECs, and between them and other Eastern European states, with assistance provided by the EU, the United States, and various international organizations. The negotiations concluded less than one year later at a final conference in Paris in March 1995, where the Pact on Stability in Europe was signed.

Attached to the main document of the pact were some ninety-two "good neighborliness and cooperation agreements and arrangements" between various CEECs, and between individual CEECs and various EU member states and nonmember states (such as Russia, Belarus, Ukraine, and Turkey). All participants in the pact pledged to use only peaceful means to settle disputes. For its part, the EU agreed to provide supportive "flanking measures," including PHARE-financed projects dealing with particular minorities and cross-border cooperation, some of which had already been launched under the PHARE Democracy Program. Responsibility for further developing and guaranteeing the pact was given to the OSCE.[38]

In the end, the Pact on Stability was a success for the CFSP and a positive step in the EU's efforts to become an important external actor. By helping to resolve potentially dangerous bilateral disputes, the pact promoted stability and security in Central and Eastern Europe. It also helped to create the political and security preconditions for the EU's eastern enlargement by minimizing the security risks to the EU of taking in new member states.

The EU also sought to promote security and stability in Central and Eastern Europe by associating the CEECs with the WEU. While the WEU—an intergovernmental organization for European defense and security cooperation that was originally created in 1948—was formally separate from the EU, all ten of its full members were also EU member states, giving the two organizations close links.[39] Thus, giving the CEECs associate status in the WEU would not only promote stability and security in Eastern Europe and give the CEECs a much-desired political and security link to the West, but it would also link these countries more closely to the EU and, through increased cooperation on defense and foreign policy matters with the EU member states, help prepare them for eventual accession.

The idea of giving the CEECs associate status in the WEU was discussed within the Commission as early as 1991 and was also strongly pushed by the French and German governments. The WEU moved in this direction with its June 1992 Petersberg Declaration, which mentioned the possibility of "associate status" for the CEECs.[40] Two years later, in its June 1994 Kirchberg Declaration, the WEU announced the creation of "associate partnership status" for CEECs that had signed Europe Agreements with the EU. Associate partnership status would allow the CEECs participate without a vote in the WEU's Permanent Council as well as in working group meetings and WEU Ministerial Councils. It also meant that the CEECs would receive regular information about the WEU's activities, and that they could establish liaison agreements with the WEU's Planning Cell. As associate partners, the CEECs could also associate themselves with WEU decisions and take part in WEU operations in some instances.[41] Upon their admission to the North Atlantic Treaty Organization (NATO), Poland, Hungary, and the Czech Republic became "associate members" of the WEU in March 1999, giving them a vote, but not a veto, in the WEU Council.[42]

The Pact for Stability and the association of the CEECs with the WEU prepared the grounds for enlargement by promoting stability and security in Central and Eastern Europe. They also prepared the CEECs for accession by promoting habits of cooperation and helping to socialize them into Western and European organizations. The greatest challenge facing the CEECs as they sought to join the EU, however, was adoption of the EU's voluminous and complex *acquis communautaire*, particularly the rules and regulations governing the Single Market.

THE WHITE PAPER

The main element of the pre-accession strategy approved at Essen was the White Paper. This document would provide a detailed road map for integrating the CEEC economies into the Single Market. In Essen, the European Council requested the Commission to prepare and deliver this White Paper in time for its next regularly scheduled meeting in June 1995.

Preparation of the White Paper posed a dilemma for the Commission, since in presenting the CEECs with a road map to accession it wanted to strike just the right balance. According to one senior EU official, there was the "danger of sending the wrong signal to [the CEECs], either if we are too lax or too tough."[43] Being too tough might discourage the CEECs or lead them to believe that the EU really did not want them as members. Being too lax, however, would not give them sufficient incentive to carry out difficult reforms.

Another issue was whether to emphasize adherence to EU social and environmental legislation in the White Paper or to focus more narrowly on Single Market rules. The latter approach was favored by Commission officials responsible for the Single Market, who argued that social and environmental policy should not be dealt with in future accession negotiations with the CEECs because they were so far behind the EU in these areas. The commissioners responsible for social and environmental policy, however, strongly pressed for including social and environmental legislation in the White Paper, arguing for full application of the *acquis communautaire* and against giving opt outs in these areas to the applicant countries.[44] In the end, a more narrowly defined approach for the White Paper was approved.

Despite these issues, the Commission completed and approved the final version of the White Paper by early May. The four-hundred-plus page document consisted of two parts: (1) an overview of the purpose, context, and nature of the alignment process in political terms; and (2) a detailed "Annex," which presented a sector-by-sector analysis of key EU legislation and the necessary administrative and legal measures for the CEECs to adopt. The stated purpose of the White Paper was "to provide a guide to assist the associated countries in preparing themselves for operating under the requirements of the European Union's internal market."[45]

More specifically, the White Paper did three things. First, it identified the key legislation, or elements of the *acquis communautaire,* to be adopted by the CEECs in each of twenty-three economic sectors in order for the expanded Single Market to function properly. It suggested the proper sequence for adopting these measures within each sector, although it did not attempt to prioritize among sectors. Instead, the White Paper declared that each country must decide on its own sectoral priorities and programs for reform, in accordance with specific national interests and conditions.[46]

Second, the White Paper emphasized that the simple transposition of EU legislation by the CEECs would not be enough. Also needed was the creation of a legal and administrative infrastructure to ensure the proper implementation and enforcement of Single Market laws. This was especially important in the areas of certification and testing to ensure that products from CEECs met minimum EU standards and to maintain a level playing field within the Single Market. The White Paper thus described the administrative and legal structures that CEECs would have to put in place before they could join the EU.[47]

Third, the White Paper outlined the various forms of financial and technical assistance the EU would provide the CEECs to help them in reforming and aligning their economies. This aid included the creation of a new technical assistance information exchange office that would be managed by the Commission and supported by the PHARE program. The White Paper also repeated the Essen summit's suggestion that the EU might waive antidumping and other commercial defense measures as a reward to the CEECs for progress in adopting economic reforms.[48]

The Commission also took pains in the White Paper to clearly distinguish the alignment process from formal accession to the EU. While alignment focused on the adoption of key or selected legislation, accession, the White Paper stressed, would "involve acceptance of the *acquis communautaire* as a whole." Nor would the pre-accession process "prejudge any aspect of [accession] negotiations, including possible transitional arrangements." The Commission also declared that the White Paper had no legal force, and that it did not "change the contractual relationship between the Union and [the CEECs]," which remained based on the Europe Agreements.[49]

The White Paper did not mention any timetable for accession. Nor did it provide any specific, quantifiable targets for the CEECs to hit in their alignment process or a sequence of priorities for them to achieve. Instead, the focus was on qualitative changes rather than on precise indicators of economic reform. This led some critics to remark that the White Paper was "a road map without kilometer marks."[50]

These and other shortcomings of the White Paper were also criticized by the CEECs. Without a firm timetable, they argued, it would be difficult to mobilize popular support for difficult economic and social reforms. They also complained about the generality of the White Paper and its lack of differentiation between the needs of individual CEECs. Government officials from some CEECs argued— with some justification—that the White Paper exercise was simply a clever way to mark time, a means for delaying enlargement while the EU decided how to confront its own difficult internal reforms.[51] Such criticism was firmly rejected by the EU, however. According to Commissioner van den Broek, the White Paper was "not an obstacle [to EU membership]," but was instead "a tool" for use in achieving this goal.[52]

The White Paper was also criticized (but not by the CEECs) for its narrowly defined approach and exclusion of most social and environmental legislation. While admitting that "most Community legislation could be considered as being relevant to the Single Market," the Commission nevertheless decided in the White Paper to focus only on those measures "which directly affect the free movement of goods, services, persons, or capital," while exempting from consideration legislation (such as most environmental legislation) "which only indirectly affects the operation of the Internal Market by, for example, affecting the competitive position of firms."[53] In the area of environmental policy, therefore, the White Paper considered only "product-related environmental standards." In this manner, the environmental policy aspects of the *acquis communautaire* were essentially put on the back burner, leaving them to be dealt with later in the accession process.[54]

THE CANNES SUMMIT

The White Paper was formally approved by the European Council at its June 26–27 meeting in Cannes. At Cannes, the European Council also asked the Commission to report to the next scheduled European Council (in December 1995) on progress in implementing the White Paper and on the various studies and analyses it had requested at Essen. In reviewing the pre-accession process in the first half of 1995, the European Council declared that the measures taken thus far, and the progress achieved, confirmed "the validity of the chosen course and the desirability of continuing along it."[55]

In Cannes, the European Council also noted the ongoing work of the "Reflection Group" of national government representatives that was preparing for the 1996 IGC, reaffirming that it would "elaborate options" on institutional reform questions "in the run-up to enlargement." The European Council also decided that the associated countries should be not be isolated from the IGC, declaring that "the necessary procedures should be established to ensure that they are kept fully informed of developments in the discussions at the Intergovernmental Conference, bearing in mind their status as future members of the Union."[56]

In a move with significant implications for enlargement, the Cannes summit also reaffirmed an agreement reached three months earlier regarding entry negotiations with Cyprus and Malta. Since receiving positive evaluations of their applications by the Commission in 1993, the governments of both countries were pressuring the EU to begin entry negotiations before it became embroiled in the process of eastern enlargement. The Greek government was also pushing for the early admission of Cyprus and was withholding its approval of an EU customs union agreement with Turkey as leverage. In March 1995, the French EU presidency brokered a political compromise. Greece agreed to allow new financial aid for Turkey, thus unblocking the customs union agreement, in return for agreement by other member states to begin accession negotiations with Cyprus and Malta six months after conclusion of the IGC.[57] The Cannes summit confirmed this deal while also calling for implementation of the customs union agreement with Turkey and welcoming closer EU ties with that country.[58]

Seeking to achieve the geographical balance in EU policy desired by France and other southern member states, the Cannes summit also approved the Council's report on EU Mediterranean policy and the objectives to be achieved at the Euro-Mediterranean Ministerial Conference to be held in November in Barcelona. The European Council also agreed on the specific aid amounts for the pre-accession strategy and Mediterranean policy, deciding to provide the CEECs with a total of ECU 6.7 million in financial assistance for the period of 1995–99, while approving ECU 4.7 million in aid for the Mediterranean countries.[59]

The final session of the European Council at Cannes was attended by the government leaders of the same six CEECs that were represented at Essen. Joining them this time, however, were the leaders of the three Baltic states and Cyprus and Malta. The Baltic states had each signed Europe Agreements with the EU just before the summit, thus allowing them to join the pre-accession process.[60] Europe Agreement negotiations also continued between the EU and Slovenia, although because of a dispute with Italy over property restitution and the right of foreigners to purchase property a final agreement would not be signed until one year later.[61]

The list of formal applicants for admission also continued to grow. By the Cannes summit, the number had grown to four, with the applications of Romania on June 22 and Slovakia on June 27. In the coming months, formal applications would be filed by Latvia (October 1995), Estonia (November 1995), and Lithuania and Bulgaria (December 1995).[62] The formal applications of the Czech Republic in January 1996 and Slovenia in June 1996 brought the total number of CEEC applicants to ten.

DEBATING ENLARGEMENT STRATEGY

Following the Cannes summit, attention increasingly focused on the issue of a timetable for eastern enlargement. During a visit to Warsaw in early July 1995, Chancellor Kohl promised that Poland, and by implication Hungary and the Czech Republic, would enter the EU by 2000. Speaking at a press conference on July 7, Kohl declared that, while a formal entry agreement for Poland may not yet be ratified by this date by all fifteen member states, "a negotiated settlement must be ready which can then be ratified."[63] He thus became the first EU leader to publicly announce a date for eastern enlargement.

Kohl's statement surprised nearly everyone, including his own aides, and Bonn later backtracked to say that the chancellor meant only that Poland, Hungary, and the Czech Republic should be formally assured by this date of EU entry, not that they would actually be members by then.[64] However, German officials also admitted that Kohl's remarks were purposefully designed "to set markers" in the approaching debate about enlargement and the future of Europe. According to one official, "We [the German government] have to make clear to other members of the EU what it is that we want."[65]

Attention was also focusing on the internal adjustments the EU would have to make in preparation for enlargement. Before the EU could take in new member states, it would have to reform key common policies, such as the CAP and Structural Funds, which together consumed about 80 percent of the EU budget. The EU would also have to reform its decision-making institutions and procedures so that a larger Union could function effectively. Enlargement would also affect the EU's financing system, with Germany and other net contributors to the EU budget concerned that they would pay a disproportionate share of the costs of admitting new member states. As the EU's largest net contributor (about 30 percent of the total), the German government in particular argued that a rebalancing of national contributions was a necessary precondition for enlargement. According to German Finance Minister Theo Waigel, "A one-sided and exaggerated burden for one member-state is no longer acceptable." Waigel argued, therefore, that reform of the EU's financing system was "urgently necessary" before the next enlargement, adding that Bonn rejected any new EU taxes or borrowing as a way to pay for enlargement.[66]

The interconnectedness of these various issues prompted the German government to call, in September 1995, for a four-year reform agenda that would address necessary changes to the CAP and Structural Funds as well as the EU's financing system. According to Bonn, this reform process should parallel the discussion of institutional reform in the 1996 IGC and the ongoing preparations for EMU. The goal would be to prepare the EU for the launching of EMU in 1999 and for further enlargement shortly thereafter.[67]

Enlargement was discussed by EU leaders at an informal brainstorming summit in Majorca on September 22–23, 1995. While no definitive conclusions were reached at this meeting, member state leaders agreed on a tentative strategy for enlargement: The upcoming IGC would wrestle with the issue of institutional reform. Following conclusion of the IGC, the Commission would put forward proposals for the EU's post-1999 budget package and financial framework, which would incorporate assumptions about enlargement and its impact on the CAP and Structural Funds. While no final decision was made on a timetable for accession negotiations, it was becoming increasingly apparent that negotiations with at least some of the CEECs would have to begin along with the launching of talks with Cyprus and Malta. This meant beginning accession negotiations soon after conclusion of the IGC, probably in early 1998.[68]

Two main strategies for the accession negotiations were discussed at this time. The first of these was the "big bang" approach, in which negotiations would begin simultaneously with all of the applicant countries, letting the order of accession be determined by the progress of the individual applicants in making economic and political reforms. This approach raised technical questions about the Commission's capacity to issue Opinions on so many applications simultaneously, however, and about the Council's capacity to conduct so many negotiations at once.[69]

The second option was to differentiate among the applicant countries according to certain objective criteria and to negotiate with them in distinctive groups or "waves." This strategy, its proponents claimed, would recognize the different levels of preparedness of the CEECs for EU membership. One argument against this approach, however, was that giving priority to some applicants could send negative signals to the others, thus eroding their confidence and undermining their reform efforts. It was also argued that a differentiated approach could exacerbate tensions among the applicant countries and result in new lines being drawn in Eastern Europe between EU "ins" and "outs." Also arguing against a differentiated approach were the special ties of some member states to particular applicant countries—such as Finland and Sweden to the Baltic states, and France to Romania—and their consequent reluctance to endorse a strategy that would discriminate against these countries. France and other southern member states also desired an enlargement that was geographically balanced and did not ignore southeastern Europe.[70]

These member state differences were apparent in a dispute over enlargement strategy that flared in December, on the eve of the Madrid summit. The dispute was ignited by the German government's announcement that it favored beginning accession negotiations with only three CEECs—Poland, Hungary, and the Czech Republic. According to Bonn, negotiations with these three countries should begin six months after conclusion of the IGC, to coincide with the beginning of accession talks with Cyprus and Malta. The German government also argued that the accession of these countries should take place fairly quickly, with lengthy transitional periods for certain policies to give the EU time to make necessary internal adjustments.[71]

The German government justified its stance by arguing that the EU needed to set a firm time frame for beginning accession negotiations in order to give clear signals to the CEECs, to support their difficult economic reforms, and to prevent a political vacuum from emerging in Central Europe. By advocating a limited first-wave enlargement, Bonn also sought to minimize the financial costs of enlargement and its impact on EU policies and institutions. Another factor was the Kohl government's preference for admitting only those CEECs that were either members of NATO or likely to soon become so (as, it appeared by now, was the case for Poland, Hungary, and the Czech Republic). The German government was especially concerned that EU membership for the Baltic states would only encourage their demand for Western security guarantees—through membership in NATO or the WEU—which the West could not give them without antagonizing Russia.[72]

The German announcement only angered other member states, however. In particular, the Nordic member states—Denmark, Sweden, and Finland—were upset about the possibility of the Baltic states being excluded from the next enlargement wave, arguing that this would amount to consigning them to the Russian sphere of influence. They argued instead that all the applicant countries should be treated equally, and that objective entry criteria, rather than the foreign policy interests of powerful member states like Germany, should determine which countries were allowed to begin accession negotiations. Taking a similar position was the French government, because it did not want to see Romania excluded from consideration and because it favored a more geographically balanced enlargement. The Nordic countries and the British government also objected to the German strategy on the grounds that it would minimize pressure for necessary internal reforms, and they argued instead for immediate and vigorous efforts to reform EU policies, especially the CAP.[73]

THE MADRID SUMMIT

The dispute ignited by the German government's announcement did not prevent the Madrid summit on December 15–16 from making important decisions about enlargement. At Madrid, the European Council decided to ask the Commission to prepare Opinions on the applications of all ten CEECs and to forward these to the Council "as soon as possible after the conclusion of the Intergovernmental Conference." It also asked the Commission to prepare a "composite paper on enlargement" and to pursue further its analysis of the impact of enlargement on EU policies, especially the CAP and Structural Funds. The European Council also asked the Commission to conduct a detailed analysis of the EU's financing system and to submit "immediately after the conclusion of the Intergovernmental Conference, a Communication on the future financial framework of the Union as from 31 December 1999, having regard to the prospect of enlargement."[74] These various reports and analyses would form the basis of the Commission's "Agenda 2000" document, which would be issued in July 1997.

The Madrid European Council also declared that, following the conclusion of the IGC and taking into account the Opinions and reports of the Commission,

> the Council will at the earliest opportunity, take the necessary decisions for launching the accession negotiations. The European Council hopes that the preliminary stage of negotiations will coincide with the start of negotiations with Cyprus and Malta.[75]

In other words, the EU now hoped to begin the preparatory phase of accession negotiations with at least some of the CEECs six months after the end of the 1996 IGC. As this was widely projected to be sometime in the middle of 1997, it meant that accession negotiations could begin in early 1998.

While the decision to set a time frame for beginning accession negotiations marked a victory for the German government, the Nordic member states and France were successful in their demands that negotiations should not be preemptively limited to a select group of countries, but that instead all applicants should be treated equally. Thus, the Madrid European Council announced that the EU would determine which countries it would begin accession negotiations with on the basis of objective criteria for membership and that "the applicant countries [would be] treated on an equal basis."[76] For now, at least, the principle of equal treatment applied, but the possibility for later differentiation remained.

Although the German government was only partially successful in asserting its views at Madrid, after the summit a satisfied Chancellor Kohl was able to declare that the EU had "set the switches" (*die Weichen gestellt*) for eastern enlargement. Kohl announced that while the German government accepted the principle of equal treatment, it also insisted upon dealing with each applicant country individually, and it rejected the possibility of a politically bargained "package deal" (*Paketlösung*) that would link the applications of different CEECs.[77]

The CEECs, by contrast, and in particular the governments of the more advanced applicants (Poland, Hungary, and the Czech Republic), were not as happy with the Madrid outcome. They argued that the Madrid promise on beginning entry negotiations was too vague. What they wanted instead were a more precise commitment and dates for accession negotiations. They also wanted the EU to name the individual countries that would be included in the negotiations.[78] For these decisions, however, they would have to wait a while longer.

NOTES

1. Switzerland, another EFTA, had also applied for EU membership in May 1992, but its application was effectively withdrawn after Swiss voters rejected the EEA in a December 1992 referendum.

2. Lionel Barber, "Delors Calls for Closer Ties to Eastern Europe," *Financial Times,* 29–30 January 1994, 2.

3. Lionel Barber, "EU Seeks Faster Integration of East Bloc," *Financial Times,* 7 March 1994, 1. See also Ulrich Sedelmeier and Helen Wallace, "Policies Towards Central and Eastern Europe," in *Policy-Making in the European Union,* ed. Helen Wallace and William Wallace (Oxford: Oxford University Press, 1996), 378.

4. Barber, "EU Seeks Faster Integration," 1; *Bulletin of the European Union* 3–1994: 68.

5. Quentin Peel, "French-German Strains Show," *Financial Times,* 17 March 1994, 14; David Buchan, Quentin Peel, and Lionel Barber, "Franco-German Row Downplayed," *Financial Times,* 18 March 1994, 16. The entry treaties were formally signed at the June European Council at Corfu. Before the treaties could take effect, they first had to be ratified in national referendums in each of the applicant countries. The Austrians overwhelmingly voted for accession in June, and Sweden and Finland ratified the treaties in fall referendums. In Norway, however, membership was narrowly rejected in a November 29 vote. Thus, on January 1, 1995, Austria, Sweden, and Finland formally entered the EU, bringing its total membership to fifteen countries.

6. Sedelmeier and Wallace, "Policies Towards Central and Eastern Europe," 378.

7. "European Council at Corfu, 24–25 June 1994: Presidency Conclusions" ("Corfu Presidency Conclusions"), in *The European Councils: Conclusions of the Presidency 1992–1994* (Brussels: European Commission, Directorate-General for Information, 1995), 130–31. For the Commission's Opinions on Cyprus and Malta, see "Commission Opinion on the Application of the Republic of Cyprus for Membership," COM (93) 313 final, Brussels, 30 June 1993; and "Commission Opinion on the Application of Malta for Membership," COM (93) 312 final, Brussels, 30 June 1993.

8. "Corfu Presidency Conclusions," 136.

9. Klaus Kinkel, "Germany in Europe: The Aims of the German Presidency of the European Union," in *Statements and Speeches,* vol. 17, no. 7 (New York: German Information Center), 3–4.

10. European Commission, "The Europe Agreements and Beyond: A Strategy to Prepare the Countries of Central and Eastern Europe for Accession," COM (94) 320 final, Brussels, 13 July 1994, 1.

11. European Commission, "The Europe Agreements and Beyond," 1–4.

12. The CEFTA was established in 1992 by Poland, Hungary, and Czechoslovakia to promote economic cooperation and free trade as a way of preparing for EU membership. In 2000, its members were Poland, Hungary, the Czech Republic, Slovakia, Slovenia, Romania, and Bulgaria.

13. European Commission, "The Europe Agreements and Beyond," 4–5, quote on 5.

14. European Commission, "Follow Up to Commission Communication on 'The Europe Agreements and Beyond: A Strategy to Prepare the Countries of Central and Eastern Europe for Accession,'" COM (94) 361 final, Brussels, 27 July 1994.

15. David Gardner, "EU Begins Move to Expand Eastwards," *Financial Times,* 5 October, 1994, 1; Sedelmeier and Wallace, "Policies Towards Central and Eastern Europe," 380.

16. Lionel Barber, "EU's Outstretched Hand to the East Begins to Waver," *Financial Times,* 23 November 1994, 3; Lionel Barber, "EU to Tackle Blueprint for Enlargement," *Financial Times,* 28 November 1994, 2; Lionel Barber, "Union Tries to Agree Line on Enlargement," *Financial Times,* 29 November 1994, 2.

17. Lionel Barber, "Kohl Invites Eastern States to EU Summit," *Financial Times,* 1 December 1994, 2.

18. The pre-accession strategy is contained in the "Report from the Council to the Essen European Council on a Strategy to Prepare for the Accession of the Associated CCEE" ("Pre-Accession Strategy"), attached to the "Presidency Conclusions" of the Essen European Council as annex 4. See "European Council in Essen, 9–10 December 1994: Presidency Conclusions" ("Essen Presidency Conclusions"), in *European Councils,* 155–62. See also "Essen Presidency Conclusions," 145–46. For a summary of the pre-accession strategy that emerged from the decisions of the Essen summit, see European Commission, *The European Union's Pre-Accession Strategy for the Associated Countries of Central Europe* (Brussels: European Commission, 1996).

19. "Pre-Accession Strategy," 156.

20. "Pre-Accession Strategy," 156.

21. "Pre-Accession Strategy," 156.

22. "Pre-Accession Strategy," 156–58, quote on 158.

23. "Pre-Accession Strategy," 157–58.

24. "Pre-Accession Strategy," 158–62.

25. "Essen Presidency Conclusions," 145.

26. "Essen Presidency Conclusions," 146.

27. "Council Report for the European Council in Essen Concerning the Future Mediterranean Policy," attached to the "Presidency Conclusions" as annex 5, 163–64. See also "Essen Presidency Conclusions," 146–47.

28. Barber, "Kohl Invites Eastern States to EU Summit," 2.

29. Craig R. Whitney, "European Union to Open Talks on Expanding East," *New York Times,* 11 December 1994, A8; Lionel Barber, "Europe Recovers its Sense of Direction," *Financial Times,* 12 December 1994, 2.

30. "Essen Presidency Conclusions," 146.

31. Lionel Barber, "Kohl Wins EU Debate Over Plans for New Members," *Financial Times*, 12 December 1994, 1.

32. Christopher Parkes, "Hungarians and Czechs Set Their Eyes on 2000," *Financial Times*, 12 December 1994, 2; Whitney, "European Union to Open Talks," A8. For the full text of Chancellor Kohl's post-summit remarks, see "Erklärung des Bundeskanzlers vor der Presse," *Bulletin*, no. 118 (Bonn: Presse- und Informationsamt der Bundesregierung, 19 December 1994), 1086–88.

33. "Essen Presidency Conclusions," 146.

34. Philip H. Gordon, *France, Germany, and the Western Alliance* (Boulder: Westview, 1995), 49.

35. "Copenhagen Presidency Conclusions," 87.

36. "European Council in Brussels, 10–11 December 1993: Presidency Conclusions," in *European Councils*, 115.

37. The text of the "Concluding Document" from the inaugural conference for a Pact on Stability in Europe is reprinted in *Bulletin of the European Union* 5–1994: 100–101.

38. For the text of the "Political Declaration" adopted at the final conference on the Pact on Stability in Europe and a list of the good neighborliness and cooperation agreements and arrangements, see *Bulletin of the European Union*, 3–1995: 112–16.

39. The WEU's ten full members are Britain, France, Germany, Italy, Belgium, the Netherlands, Luxembourg, Spain, Portugal, and Greece. Although its membership is composed of EU member states, the WEU is formally separate from the EU. However, the Maastricht Treaty, in article J.4(2), established a formal link between these two institutions for the first time, designating the WEU as an "integral part of the development of the Union" and giving it responsibility to "elaborate and implement decisions of the Council which have defense implications." The 1997 Amsterdam Treaty provides for the eventual formal merger of the WEU into the EU. This possibility has been discussed in order to give the EU a distinctive European Security and Defense Identity within NATO. At the June 1999 Cologne summit, the EU decided to complete the merger of these two organizations. On the WEU and its relationship to the EU, see Joseph I. Coffey, "WEU After the Second Maastricht," in *The State of the European Union*, vol. 4, *Deepening and Widening*, ed. Pierre-Henri Laurent and Marc Maresceau (Boulder: Lynne Rienner, 1998), 113–32; Peter van Ham, "The EU and WEU: From Cooperation to Common Defence?" in *The Politics of European Treaty Reform: The 1996 Intergovernmental Conference and Beyond*, ed. Geoffrey Edwards and Alfred Pijpers (London: Pinter, 1997), 306–25; and Stuart Croft, John Redmond, G. Wyn Rees, and Mark Webber, *The Enlargement of Europe* (Manchester: Manchester University Press, 1999), 89–111.

40. For the relevant sections of the Petersberg Declaration, see WEU Council of Ministers, *Petersberg Declaration*, 9 June 1992, sec. III, pt. A.

41. WEU Council of Ministers, *Kirchberg Declaration*, 9 May 1994, pt. 2.

42. "Declaration on the New Associate Members of WEU: The Czech Republic, Hungary and Poland," in "Conclusions of the Ministerial Meeting of the Western European Union Council, in Bremen on 10 May and 11 May [1999]," reprinted in Agence Europe, *Europe Documents*, no. 2138, 15 May 1999, 5.

43. Unnamed official quoted in Lionel Barber, "EU Considers Where to Place Welcome Mat," *Financial Times*, 16 March 1995, 2.

44. Barber, "EU Considers Where to Place Welcome Mat," 2.

45. European Commission, "White Paper: Preparation of the Associated Countries of Central and Eastern Europe for Integration into the Internal Market of the Union," COM

(95) 163 final, Brussels, 3 May 1995; "Annex," COM (95) 163 final, Brussels, 10 May 1995, 2. Quote is on page 2 of the overview.

46. European Commission, "White Paper," 2 and 4.

47. European Commission, "White Paper," 2 and 4.

48. European Commission, "White Paper," 2, 5, and 32–36. On the possibility of waiving commercial defense measures, see page 38.

49. European Commission, "White Paper," 2 and 5.

50. Christopher Preston, *Enlargement and Integration in the European Union* (London: Routledge, 1997), 203.

51. Barber, "EU Considers Where to Place Welcome Mat," 2.

52. Lionel Barber, "East Europe's Reform Route to EU," *Financial Times,* 4 May 1995, 2.

53. European Commission, "White Paper," Annex, 1.

54. For the section dealing with relevant environmental legislation, see European Commission, "White Paper," Annex, 214–57. For criticism of the White Paper from an environmental perspective, see Brian Slocock, "'Whatever Happened to the Environment?': Environmental Issues in the Eastern Enlargement of the European Union," in *Back to Europe: Central and Eastern Europe and the European Union,* ed. Karen Henderson (London: UCL Press, 1999), 158–59.

55. "Cannes European Council, 26–27 June 1995: Presidency Conclusions" ("Cannes Presidency Conclusions"), in *The European Councils: Conclusions of the Presidency 1995* (Brussels: European Commission, 1995), 10. See also part B of the "Presidency Conclusions," "Preparation of the Associated Countries of Central and Eastern Europe for Integration into the Internal Market of the European Union," 16–17; and "Implementation of the Strategy, in the First Half of 1995, to Prepare for Accession," 18–21. Quote is on page 18.

56. "Cannes Presidency Conclusions," 13–14.

57. *Bulletin of the European Union* 3–1995.

58. "Cannes Presidency Conclusions," 6 and 10.

59. "Cannes Presidency Conclusions," 23–34 (pt. B: "Euro-Mediterranean Conference in Barcelona: Position of the European Union"), and 36.

60. "Baltic States Sign EU Accords," *Financial Times,* 13 June 1995, 2. See also *Bulletin of the European Union* 6–1995: 113.

61. *Bulletin of the European Union,* 6–1995, 113. The restitution issue concerned the nationalized property of Italians who left formerly Italian-controlled areas of Slovenia (and Croatia) after World War II. On the dispute with Italy, see Irena Brinar, "Slovenia: From Yugoslavia to the European Union," in Henderson, ed., *Back to Europe,* 246–50.

62. *Bulletin of the European Union,* 6–1995: 110–11; 10–1995: 83; 11–1995: 74; and 12–1995: 125.

63. "Erklärung vor der Presse in Warschau," *Bulletin,* no. 58, 14 July 1995 (Bonn: Presse- und Informationsamt der Bundesregierung), 575; Michael Lindemann, "Kohl Suggests Poland Could Join EU by 2000," *Financial Times,* 8–9 July 1995, 22.

64. "Just Do It," *Economist,* 15 July 1995, 35–36.

65. Lindemann, "Kohl Suggests Poland Could Join EU by 2000," 22.

66. Andrew Fisher, "Bonn Pushes EU Budget Reform," *Financial Times,* 6 April 1995, 1.

67. Quentin Peel, "Germans Seek 4-Year Agenda on EU Reform," *Financial Times,* 13 September 1995, 3.

68. Lionel Barber, "EMU Turmoil Hits EU's Majorca Summit," *Financial Times,* 22 September 1995, 2; Lionel Barber, "Hard Work Ahead to Solve EU Puzzle," *Financial Times,* 25 September 1995, 15.

69. *Enlarging the Union: The Intergovernmental Conference of the European Union 1996*, Federal Trust Papers, no. 5 (London: Federal Trust, 1996), 14.

70. Barber, "EMU Turmoil," 2. On the discussion of both of these options at the Madrid summit, see *Enlarging the Union,* 14.

71. Lionel Barber, "Kohl Draws Line Across Europe," *Financial Times,* 14 December 1995, 1.

72. Barber, "Kohl Draws Line Across Europe," 1.

73. Lionel Barber, "Union Struggles to Regain its Sense of Direction," *Financial Times,* 15 December 1995, 2.

74. "Madrid European Council, 15–16 December 1995: Presidency Conclusions" ("Madrid Presidency Conclusions"), in *European Councils* (1995), 48.

75. "Madrid Presidency Conclusions," 44.

76. "Madrid Presidency Conclusions," 48.

77. "Beitrittsverhandlungen sollen bereits in zwei Jahren beginnen," *Süddeutsche Zeitung,* 18 December 1995, 1.

78. Caroline Southey, "Compromise on Expansion," *Financial Times,* 18 December 1995, 2.

4

The Road to Luxembourg

Following the Madrid summit, the EU's attention shifted from enlargement to other pressing issues. One of these was the IGC set to begin in March 1996, which was to consider modifications to the Maastricht Treaty and other institutional reforms. EMU was also high on the agenda, with many important decisions remaining to be made, including which countries would qualify to be a part of the "euro-zone" once EMU was officially launched in January 1999. Further decisions on enlargement would await completion by the Commission of its Opinions and the various enlargement studies that had been requested by the European Council in Madrid. These Opinions and reports were due to be submitted to the European Council soon after the June 1997 Amsterdam summit.

Well before this point, however, the number of countries seeking to join the EU was reduced by one. In October 1996, Malta's newly elected Labor government announced that it was freezing that country's EU application. Instead of accession, the new Maltese government declared that it wanted to pursue a free trade agreement with the EU. This decision (which would eventually be reversed in 1998 with the return to power of a conservative Nationalist government) was significant because it temporarily eased the pressure on the EU to make institutional reforms to accommodate another microstate as a member.

Another factor affecting the EU's decision making on enlargement was NATO enlargement. By the end of 1996 NATO had decided to expand eastward, announcing that it would decide which former Communist countries to admit at its Madrid summit in July 1997. Within NATO, opinions diverged over which countries should be invited to join. While the U.S. government favored admitting only Poland, Hungary, and the Czech Republic, France and other NATO members also pushed for the inclusion of Romania and Slovenia. In the end, American preferences prevailed, however, and the Madrid summit decided to invite only the three Central European countries to join NATO in 1999.[1]

Despite the obviously close links between NATO and the EU, due to overlapping memberships—eleven EU member states also belong to NATO—and the complementarity of their functions—NATO provides military security, while the EU provides the economic and political bases for security—they are nevertheless formally separate and different organizations. Not only are their memberships not identical, but they also have fundamentally different purposes and institutional logics. Despite early talk of "parallelism" in the two enlargements, therefore, and despite U.S. pressure on the EU to link the two enlargements by expanding faster and including countries (such as the Baltic states) that would not soon be admitted to NATO, NATO and EU enlargement have proceeded along different tracks and at different speeds.[2] Nevertheless, NATO's decisions on whom to admit and when would inevitably influence the EU's decision making on its own enlargement.

THE COMMISSION'S OPINIONS

Further decisions on EU enlargement would await completion by the Commission of its Opinions on the various applications. The Commission began work on the Opinions in early 1996.[3] The Opinions (*avis* in French) were largely technical assessments of the capacity of each applicant to become an EU member. They were intended as an aid to the European Council, which would make the final political decisions about the opening of accession negotiations with individual candidate countries. The Commission's views could be ignored by national leaders, as in 1980 when, for political reasons (the desire to support Greek democracy), the European Council overrode a negative Opinion on Greece and chose to begin accession negotiations with Athens. In the case of eastern enlargement, however, because of divisions among the member states on the desirability and extent of enlargement, the Commission's Opinions were likely to play an important role in the European Council's decisions. Another (convenient) benefit of the Opinion exercise was that it enabled the member states to postpone serious discussion of enlargement for a while and focus their attention instead on the IGC, EMU, and other pressing issues.

The main purpose of the Opinions was to assess the capacity of individual applicants to assume the obligations of EU membership. Mainly, the Opinions assessed the compatibility of the laws, regulations, and policies of the applicant countries with the *acquis communautaire,* as well as their administrative and legal capacities to apply EU legislation. The Commission also needed to take account in its Opinions of the additional political and economic conditions defined by the Copenhagen European Council in 1993: the existence of stable democratic institutions and the rule of law; respect for human rights and the protection of minorities; the possession of a functioning market economy and the ability to cope with market forces and competitive pressures within the EU; and adherence to the aims of political, economic, and monetary union.

In preparing its Opinions on the CEEC applications, the Commission faced a number of unique challenges. One problem confronting the Commission was the production of Opinions on so many applications simultaneously. The Commission initially considered the possibility of issuing a single combined Opinion on the ten applicants—as had been done in 1967 with the applications of the United Kingdom, Ireland, Denmark, and Norway—but soon decided instead to prepare ten separate documents, "to emphasize the fact that the applications were considered on their individual merits rather than as a group." The Commission also decided that each of the Opinions would be self-contained, "without comparisons with other candidates or references to other Opinions."[4]

Another problem in preparing the Opinions was the absence of sufficient detailed information on particular countries, as well as the reliability and comparability of statistics. Also posing a problem was that political and economic conditions were changing rapidly in some CEECs, making it difficult to assess what was essentially a moving target. Therefore, to acquire the necessary factual information and to supplement information gathered from other sources,[5] the Commission decided to rely heavily on information provided by the applicants themselves. It thus prepared an extremely detailed (150-page) questionnaire, asking for specific economic, statistical, and legislative information and covering all the main areas of the *acquis communautaire*. To assess their adherence to the political conditions specified at Copenhagen, the applicants were also invited to make observations about the political situation in their country and to provide summaries of their constitutional and institutional structures and memberships in international organizations.[6]

The questionnaires were sent to each of the CEECs in late April 1996, with the request that they reply within three months. Replies from all ten countries were received by the end of July. A first assessment of the replies was made by the Commission in September, and a series of supplementary questions was sent to the applicants in the fall. In early 1997, as it became more apparent that the IGC would conclude with the Amsterdam European Council in June, the applicants were told that additional information or updates of their previous questionnaire replies must be submitted by May. A round of "pre-Opinion" visits to the applicant countries was then conducted by Hans van den Broek, the commissioner in charge of enlargement. Final conclusions for the Opinions were not drawn up until the very end of the process, in late June and early July.[7]

The Commission formally presented its Opinions[8] on July 16, one month after the Amsterdam summit, as part of the "Agenda 2000" report. The "Agenda 2000" report also contained the Commission's proposals for reforming the CAP and Structural Funds, the proposed EU financial perspective for 2000–2006, and the Commission's recommendations on enlargement strategy.[9]

The Opinions on the CEEC applicants differed from previous Opinions in that they did not evaluate the preparedness of the applicants for membership at the moment but rather in a medium-term perspective of five years' time (2002). By doing so, the Opinions took into account the transitional status of the CEECs as well as the anticipated length of accession negotiations. The speculative nature of these projections, however, subjected the Commission to criticism from the individual applicants that they could make more progress in adopting the *acquis communautaire* over this time period than expected by the Commission.

By focusing on the medium term, the Commission assumed that accession negotiations could be launched with applicants that were not yet prepared for actual membership. A major exception to this medium-term perspective, however, was the political criteria for membership announced at Copenhagen. As the case of Slovakia would show, these criteria would have to be substantially fulfilled in the immediate term before the Commission would even recommend the beginning of accession negotiations with an applicant country.

The ten Opinions all have a similar structure.[10] After a brief preface recounting the formal application for admission and providing the general political background and context of the Opinion (including the decisions of the European Councils in Copenhagen in 1993 and Madrid in 1995), there is a short discussion of the progress of bilateral relations since 1990, covering the Europe Agreements, the pre-accession strategy, and the development of trade relations. The main body of the Opinion consists of four parts: (1) an evaluation of adherence to the political criteria for membership (democracy and rule of law, respect for human rights, and the protection of minorities); (2) an evaluation of adherence to the economic criteria for membership (general economic situation and the economy in perspective of membership); (3) an evaluation of ability to assume the obligations of membership (compliance with and adoption of the *acquis communautaire*); and (4) an evaluation of administrative capacity to apply the *acquis communautaire*. Each Opinion concludes with a "Summary and Conclusions," in which the Commission's final recommendations concerning the preparedness of the applicant for accession negotiations are made.

Regarding the political criteria for membership, the Commission identified problems in all countries with establishing the rule of law and human and minority rights. Only Slovakia, however, received an overall negative evaluation in this area from the Commission. In making this evaluation, the Commission referred to problems with treatment of the parliamentary opposition by the government of Prime Minister Vladimir Meciar; the government's lack of respect for other constitutional institutions, including the presidency; and the lack of independence of the judiciary. Because of this negative evaluation, the Commission recommended that Slovakia not be included in the group of applicants with which the EU should open accession negotiations, even though Slovakia met the economic criteria for beginning negotiations.

Regarding the economic criteria for membership, the Commission found that six countries (Poland, Hungary, the Czech Republic, Estonia, Slovenia, and Slovakia) either qualified as functioning market economies or came close to doing so. It was also concluded that two countries (Poland and Hungary) should be able to withstand competitive pressures within the EU in the medium term should present trends continue, while three others (the Czech Republic, Slovakia, and Slovenia) should also meet this criterion if they strengthened their reform efforts. A sixth country, Estonia, was judged to be close to this latter group.

The section analyzing the abilities of the applicant countries to assume the obligations of membership made up by far the largest part of the Opinions. After evaluating the situation in each policy area (Single Market, telecommunications, agriculture, regional policy, environment, and so on), the Commission concluded by attempting to answer the question of whether the country concerned could be expected to satisfy the obligations of membership in the medium term. Because of the speculative nature of this question, the answer was generally qualified. Moreover, the Commission declined to make any overall evaluation of the applicants in this section, making relative comparison of the ten applicants difficult.

Regarding administrative capacity, the Commission concluded that while all applicants needed to make improvements, Hungary was the closest to having the institutional ability to administer the *acquis communautaire,* while Romania and Bulgaria were the furthest from this goal. The Commission displayed less certainty in its evaluations of legal and judicial systems, however, generally leaving it open as to when the applicants would be able to effectively apply the *acquis communautaire.*

In the conclusions of its Opinions, the Commission recommended that, in light of its evaluations of the various applicant countries, "negotiations for accession should be opened with" five CEECs: Poland, Hungary, the Czech Republic, Slovenia, and Estonia. This recommendation was supposedly based on an objective evaluation of adherence to the Copenhagen political and economic conditions as well as the capacity of the applicant countries to take on and apply the *acquis communautaire.* Additional political considerations also clearly influenced the Commission's recommendations, however, as will be discussed below. The Commission also recommended that accession negotiations be opened with the remaining countries—Bulgaria, Romania, Slovakia, Latvia, and Lithuania—"as soon as they have made sufficient progress in satisfying the conditions defined by the European Council in Copenhagen." Therefore, although it differentiated among the applicants regarding their preparedness for accession negotiations, the Commission did not submit a negative Opinion for any of the ten CEECs.

"AGENDA 2000"

The ten Opinions were presented as part of the Commission's "Agenda 2000" report. In addition to the Opinions, this 1,200-page document consisted of three main parts: (1) an analysis of existing EU policies, particularly the CAP and the Structural and Cohesion Funds, and proposals for their reform; (2) a paper on enlargement, which included a review of the Opinions and a proposed strategy for beginning accession negotiations; and (3) a proposed budgetary and financial framework for the EU for the 2000–2006 period.[11] The overriding goal of "Agenda 2000" was to prepare the EU for enlargement.

In the section on enlargement strategy, after reviewing the general conclusions of its Opinions on the applicant countries and discussing the impact of enlargement on various EU policies, the Commission recommended beginning negotiations with five CEECs: Hungary, Poland, the Czech Republic, Slovenia, and Estonia. It also recommended that negotiations with these countries should begin together with the accession negotiations with Cyprus, which, as the Commission noted, the European Council had agreed to begin six months after conclusion of the IGC. For the remaining five CEEC applicants (Lithuania, Latvia, Slovakia, Romania, and Bulgaria), the Commission recommended an annual review of economic and political progress and the provision of special financial assistance to help with their reforms. Once it determined that any of these countries was ready to begin accession negotiations, the Commission would recommend to the European Council that negotiations be launched with that country as well.[12]

In its "Agenda 2000" recommendations, therefore, the Commission opted for an "accession in waves" strategy that differentiated among the applicants on the basis of an objective assessment of their preparedness for negotiations and membership. Given the pressure exerted by some applicants and member states for a common start to the negotiations (with all applicants together), this was a politically courageous decision by the Commission.[13] At the same time, however, by calling for an annual review of the applicants not chosen to begin negotiations, with the possibility that these countries could begin negotiations once they were deemed ready, the Commission also sought to keep the accession process open and inclusive. This would encourage non-first-wave countries to continue with their reform efforts and would prevent the distinction between "ins" and "outs" from hardening into permanent new divisions in Central and Eastern Europe. As Commission President Jacques Santer declared in presenting the "Agenda 2000" proposals, "This is not a process of excluding other countries. It is a process of inclusion which will be pursued permanently."[14]

To help prepare the CEECs for membership, the Commission proposed developing a "reinforced pre-accession strategy." This would consist of additional financial support beyond the existing PHARE aid, with two new pre-accession aid instruments targeted at the specific objectives of agriculture reform (ECU 500 million per year) and infrastructure development (ECU 1 billion per year). The structural aid instrument would also have the purpose of familiarizing prospective members with the operation and arrangements of the EU's Structural Funds.[15]

The main instrument of the enhanced pre-accession strategy, however, would be the bilateral "Accession Partnerships." These would be developed by the Commission for each applicant, in consultation with the country's government. The Accession Partnerships would identify specific priorities for reform in each country, to which the applicants would make precise commitments. Future aid would then be conditional upon the achievement of specified objectives and the general progress of reforms. The Commission also recommended abandoning the multilateral structured relationship (in place since the Copenhagen summit and a key part of the existing pre-accession strategy) in favor of bilateral contacts between the EU and individual applicant countries, with ad hoc multilateral meetings as necessary. This recommendation was, in part, a response to the wishes of the applicants, who generally favored one-on-one contacts with the EU over multilateral sessions. The Commission also recommended increased participation by the applicant countries in various EU educational, cultural, and technological programs as part of the enhanced pre-accession strategy.[16]

The Commission's enlargement report also addressed the problematic issue of Turkey. While the Commission reaffirmed Turkey's eligibility for EU membership, it noted continued economic and political problems affecting Ankara's application. It therefore suggested a separate strategy for Turkey and referred to proposals for the future development of bilateral relations made in an earlier Communication.[17]

The Commission's report on enlargement strategy also endorsed the Franco-German proposal for a standing "European Conference," which would consist of the member states and all associated countries that were prospective EU members and would provide an inclusive framework for cooperation on foreign policy and external and internal security matters.[18] Although this was not explicitly stated, the European Conference might also provide a useful means of integrating Turkey, in the likely event that Ankara was not included in the accession process by the European Council.

In addition to its report on enlargement strategy, "Agenda 2000" also contained the Commission's analysis of key EU policies and their future development. In particular, "Agenda 2000" focused on the CAP and the Structural and Cohesion Funds, two policy sectors that together consumed a great majority (80 percent) of the EU budget. While it was widely agreed that these policies needed to be reformed as a precondition for admitting relatively poor and heavily agricultural CEECs, the Commission argued that reform was necessary in any case because of pressure on the CAP from future rounds of global trade talks and the need for EU budgetary and financing reform. One reason for presenting the reform proposals in this way was to protect the enlargement process from being undermined by domestic politics, by de-linking it as much as possible from the painful and politically difficult restructuring of these programs. In this manner, it was hoped, resentment over the loss of EU subsidies would not turn into opposition to enlargement.

Regarding the CAP, the Commission proposed reducing support prices paid to farmers for grain, beef, dairy, and other products by up to a third, thereby forcing European farmers to be more competitive in world markets. It also proposed shifting EU assistance from price subsidies to direct income payments, with a limit on the amount of aid that individual farmers could receive. The Commission also favored incorporating agriculture policy into a more coherent rural aid policy by integrating it with environmental and structural policies and allowing member states greater freedom in deciding how to allocate aid (in keeping with the "subsidiarity" principle[19]). Despite these reforms, the Commission claimed that new CEEC members would require a lengthy transition period before they could be fully integrated into the CAP and benefit fully from its subsidies. During this transition period, the new member states would receive assistance to help them modernize their agricultural sectors.[20]

The Commission's proposals for reforming the Structural Funds were equally far-reaching. The Commission proposed consolidating structural operations by reducing the present seven "Objectives" for structural spending to three and tightening up the eligibility requirements for assistance. Altogether, the Commission's plans would reduce the percentage of the EU population receiving structural assistance from its 1997 level of around 50 percent to between 35 and 40 percent. The Commission also proposed shifting funding away from projects in poor regions and toward the broader struggle against unemployment. National governments would also be given more control over the use of Structural Funds. However, the Commission recommended maintaining Cohesion Fund assistance to the poorest member states in its present form, at least for the time being. According to the Commission's plan, by 2006 the percentage of structural assistance going to new member states (projected to join in 2002) would grow to around one-third of the EU total.[21]

The third part of "Agenda 2000" was the Commission's proposed financial framework for the 2000–2006 period in the perspective of enlargement. In presenting this framework, the Commission argued that enlargement could be accomplished without any increased budgetary contributions from the member states. Instead, EU spending would be kept within the 1.27 percent of gross national product (GNP) limit established by the European Council in Edinburgh in 1992. The Commission's financial perspective included spending on agricultural and structural assistance for new members and pre-accession aid for CEECs not included in the first enlargement wave. The Commission also argued that, while the next enlargement would "inevitably provoke a deterioration in the budgetary positions of all the current Member States," it should not "lead to major changes in [their] relative budgetary positions" nor to increased national contributions. Nevertheless, the Commission warned that further enlargement, beyond the first wave of six countries, would probably require raising the EU spending ceiling and reforming more fundamentally the financing system.[22]

The Commission's proposals for reform of the CAP and the Structural Funds and its proposed financial perspective for 2000–2006—collectively known as the "Agenda 2000" reforms—would be the subject of intensive debate and intergovernmental negotiations over the next two years, before a final agreement was reached at the March 1999 Berlin summit. Because of their importance for the enlargement process, the debate over the "Agenda 2000" reforms is discussed more extensively in chapter 7.

THE RECOMMENDATIONS ON ENLARGEMENT

While the Commission's "Agenda 2000" proposals for policy reform and the EU's future financial perspective would eventually become the focus of widespread debate and intensive intergovernmental negotiations, in the immediate term attention focused mainly on the Commission's recommendations on enlargement strategy, and in particular its recommendation that the EU begin negotiations with only five CEECs. The Commission's recommendations were just that. Final decisions on the opening of accession negotiations—when and with whom—would be made by the European Council at the December 1997 summit in Luxembourg.[23] However, because of the divergent views of the member states on enlargement, the Commission's recommendations on this matter were likely to carry some weight.

In making its recommendations, the Commission was influenced by a number of factors. To begin with, it was aware of the divergent views of the member states. The Commission knew, for instance, that while the German government favored beginning negotiations with only a small group of Central European countries, other member states preferred a common start to negotiations for all of the applicants. According to the "regatta" or "starting line model," all applicants would begin accession negotiations together, but negotiations with the better prepared applicants would then be allowed to proceed at a faster pace. Supporters of this strategy argued that it would respect the principle of equal and nondiscriminatory treatment of the applicants while permitting differentiation on the basis of objective (rather than political) criteria. The common-start strategy was particularly favored by the Nordic member states, who sought to ensure that the Baltic states were not excluded from the first wave of the next enlargement. Other member states supported this strategy because it would inevitably slow the enlargement process and thus be a means of delaying eastern enlargement.

In formulating its recommendations, the Commission was also aware of NATO's impending decision to include only three Central European countries—Poland, Hungary, and the Czech Republic—in its next wave of expansion. NATO's decision was accompanied by pressure on the EU from the U.S. government to admit countries, such as the Baltic states, that would not be invited to join NATO, thus providing them with some consolation for being excluded by NATO. There was also increased pressure on the EU from the CEECs not invited to join NATO, since these countries now placed an even higher value on EU membership as a means of integrating with the West and gaining security from Russia. At the same time, however, NATO's decision gave the EU an opportunity to act strategically in its own decisions on enlargement and to differentiate itself from NATO by pursuing a broader and more geographically balanced enlargement strategy.

Another factor for the Commission to take into consideration was the disappointing outcome of the 1996–97 IGC on institutional reform and the Amsterdam Agreement that enlargement beyond twenty members would require the launching of yet another IGC to negotiate further institutional reforms (see chapter 8). A limited enlargement of five or fewer countries, therefore, would avoid triggering such a conference. On the other hand, a recommendation to begin negotiations with more than five countries could be a means for the Commission to increase pressure on the member states to reach an agreement on institutional reform.

The issue of enlargement strategy was the subject of considerable debate within the Commission. This debate came to a head in early July. By this point, there was general agreement that differentiation among the CEEC applicants was necessary, and that an "enlargement in waves" strategy was preferable to a common start. Disagreement remained, however, over the number of countries to be included in the first group to begin negotiations. The main proponents of a broader first wave were Commissioner van den Broek and the Nordic (Finnish, Swedish, and Danish) commissioners. President Santer was among those who favored limiting the first wave to a smaller number of countries. On July 10, after a week of intense debate, the full Commission met to approve van den Broek's proposal for opening negotiations with five CEECs and Cyprus. Key to this agreement was the intervention of two important commissioners, Britain's Leon Brittan (trade) and Germany's Martin Bangemann (industry), both of whom argued that the two countries that were the main subjects of debate, Estonia and Slovenia, were prepared for accession negotiations based on an objective assessment of their economic performance and that to exclude them would amount to political discrimination. There was also agreement within the Commission that simply opening accession negotiations with six countries would not necessarily trigger a new IGC on institutional reform, since this action involved no commitment on a date for entry.[24]

In recommending that the EU begin negotiations with five CEECs, the Commission claimed that its decision was based solely on objective performance and adherence to specified economic and political criteria by the applicants. Political considerations also played a large role, however. These considerations included the need to compromise between the extreme positions of beginning negotiations with just three CEECs (Poland, Hungary, and the Czech Republic) and a common start to negotiations with all applicants. Also affecting the Commission's recommendations were geopolitical considerations, with the Commission favoring a geographically balanced enlargement that would not be limited to just Central Europe but would also include a country from the north (Estonia) and one from the south (Slovenia).[25]

Also influencing the Commission was NATO's recent enlargement decision. By recommending that the EU open accession negotiations with five CEECs rather than just the three NATO entrants, the Commission hoped to limit the effects of any "double-rejection shock" for those countries not chosen for the first wave of either EU or NATO enlargement. In particular, the decision to include Estonia in the first wave would send a clear signal to the Baltic states that their prospects for membership were good and that these countries—which were unlikely to be invited to join NATO anytime soon because of Moscow's strong opposition— would not once again be abandoned by the West. The inclusion of Slovenia, on the other hand, was viewed as a positive signal to the Balkans and an opening to south-eastern Europe.[26]

By recommending a broader and more geographically balanced first wave, the Commission also sought to differentiate the EU from NATO. At the same time, however, the Commission had to counter suggestions that it was responding to U.S. pressure to include the Baltic states or other countries not selected for NATO expansion as a form of compensation or a consolation prize for not being invited to join NATO.[27] For countries like Slovenia, however, the importance of EU membership only grew after their exclusion from NATO expansion.[28]

REACTIONS

Reactions to the Commission's "Agenda 2000" recommendations varied among the applicant countries. The governments of the five CEECs named to the negotiating group naturally were quite happy and relieved. For Poland, Hungary, and the Czech Republic, the Commission's recommendations were expected and merely confirmed their status as front-runners for accession. Estonia and Slovenia were more enthusiastically grateful. The governments of these countries welcomed the Commission's positive evaluations of their progress and claimed that this would give them fresh impetus for making further reforms. All five of the first-group countries also expressed, somewhat optimistically, the hope that accession negotiations could be concluded in rapid fashion.[29]

The five applicants not chosen to begin negotiations voiced their strong disappointment, along with criticism of the Commission's recommendations. Perhaps the strongest reaction came from the governments of Latvia and Lithuania, who were stung by not being included with Estonia in the negotiating group. The Lithuanian prime minister, Gediminas Vagnorious, warned EU leaders that any delay in admitting his country might encourage nationalist forces in Moscow to try and reassert Russian influence over the Baltic region. He also criticized the Commission for using "obsolete" economic data in its analysis and for failing to take account of recent legislative and economic developments in his country. Such oversights led him to question whether the Commission had indeed made its decisions solely on objective grounds.[30] Similar criticisms were voiced by the Latvian government. In both countries, there was strong suspicion that the Commission's recommendations had been influenced by political considerations. The governments of both countries also complained that the Commission's strategy unfairly split the Baltic states and would cause problems in relations among them. In the months preceding the Luxembourg summit, the governments of both countries launched an intensive campaign to convince EU leaders to overrule the Commission's recommendations and include them in the accession negotiations with Estonia.[31]

Also critical of the Commission's recommendations were Romania and Bulgaria. Following publication of the recommendations, the Romanian prime minister criticized the Commission's decision to proceed with enlargement in waves, arguing that this would create new divisions in Europe and undermine popular support for reforms in the excluded (non-first-wave) countries. Instead, he demanded that Romania be included in accession negotiations as a "symbolic political gesture" and a reward for the difficult reforms that it had made.[32] The Romanian government also argued that the Commission's strategy would distort trade relations between the CEECs and harm foreign investment into the region. Speaking at a conference in November, Romanian President Emil Constantinescu demanded a clearer road map for accession, arguing that the absence of precise economic criteria for membership led him to suspect that it was political, not economic, factors that had kept his country out of the Commission's first group.[33]

The Bulgarian government's reaction to the Commission's recommendations was comparatively mild. Nevertheless, it expressed concerns about the security implications of the Commission's strategy, with Prime Minister Alexander Boshkov arguing that the double exclusion of some CEECs from both the EU and NATO could give rise to a geopolitical vacuum in Eastern Europe that someone (clearly he was referring to Russia) would inevitably try to fill.[34]

Also more restrained in its criticism was Slovakia. Prime Minister Meciar at first admitted that it was his government's own fault for not convincing the Commission that Slovakia deserved EU membership.[35] However, Slovak authorities later mounted a strong effort to rebut the Commission's report on the political situation in Slovakia by pointing out factual errors and inaccuracies in its analysis. Meciar also promised that through reforms and new elections, "Slovakia [would be] able to remove the obstacles [to EU membership] within its political system within a year."[36]

The criticism of the second-group countries was firmly rejected by the Commission. In an article published in the *Financial Times* in September, van den Broek, the primary author of the Commission's strategy, argued that the EU was not seeking to draw any new dividing lines in Europe. There were no "ins and outs" in the Commission's scheme, he declared, but rather "ins and pre-ins." Van den Broek defended the information-gathering and analysis processes of the Commission, claiming that "all member states accept the fairness and essential accuracy of the Commission's work." He went on to say that this analysis showed "beyond a shadow of a doubt that some applicants are more advanced than others." Hence, differentiation was necessary, but "differentiation in no way implies discrimination." Van den Broek also rejected calls for a common start to accession negotiations, arguing that this would only give momentary political satisfaction. He argued that negotiations with all applicants, regardless of their levels of preparedness, would soon become bogged down, leading to delays in enlargement and growing disenchantment with the EU.[37]

The Commission's strategy was also supported by the first-group countries. Hungary's prime minister, Gyula Horn, argued that a common start for accession negotiations would be unfair to the more advanced countries by not rewarding them for their hard efforts and progress and would therefore be "demoralizing."[38] Also reluctant to endorse a common start was the Estonian government. In the fall of 1997, it gave only ambivalent support to the efforts of Latvia and Lithuania to gain a place in the negotiations, mainly because it worried that disagreement over how to deal with the Baltic states could lead the EU to decide in favor of a smaller first wave that excluded Estonia.[39]

THE DEBATE ON ENLARGEMENT

The Commission's recommendations on enlargement strategy were not final. It would be the governments of the member states that would make the final decisions on when to begin accession negotiations and with whom. These decisions would be made by the European Council at the Luxembourg summit in December.

In the months and weeks preceding Luxembourg, the debate on enlargement intensified, with member state views on this issue remaining considerably divided.[40] The two Scandinavian member states, Denmark and Sweden, continued to push for a common start to accession negotiations with all applicant countries, with the exception perhaps of Slovakia because of its poor human rights record. While it had formerly advocated such an approach, Finland broke ranks with its Nordic neighbors after the Commission named Estonia to its first-wave group, and now favored a more differentiated strategy. The Finnish government justified this shift by arguing that a common start would fail to reward Estonia for its bold market-oriented reforms. Denmark and Sweden, however, wanted inclusion of their own "client" states, Lithuania and Latvia, respectively.

Also advocating a common start to accession negotiations were Greece and the other Mediterranean member states. The Greek government favored this approach because, for regional security reasons, it did not want to see Bulgaria and Romania indefinitely excluded from the enlargement process and becoming the victims of "double-rejection shock." Athens also felt that a common start would make the proposed European Conference unnecessary, thereby avoiding the need to invite Turkey. Other Mediterranean member states, led by Spain, saw a common start to accession negotiations as a way to delay enlargement. They also thought a broader accession process would force the wealthy member states to reconsider their opposition to increasing the EU budget to pay for enlargement. Thus, the common-start strategy was supported by, in the words of one EU diplomat, an "unholy alliance" linking the Mediterranean and Scandinavian member states.[41]

The German government, however, continued to favor a more limited first-wave enlargement, mainly because it thought that this approach would be cheaper, and because it would allow the more rapid accession of its three immediate eastern neighbors. According to Foreign Minister Klaus Kinkel, a common start would slow down the enlargement process by allowing "the slowest ships to set the pace."[42] Also supporting a more differentiated approach was the British government, both for budgetary reasons and because it wished to see the integrity of the Single Market preserved. The French government had also come around to this view. Although it had initially supported the "regatta" approach, both as a means of slowing enlargement and because it wanted to be seen as presenting a broader strategic vision for the EU and Europe, the French government soon came to regard a common start as too unwieldy and impractical.

The member states discussed their different views at a series of Council meetings in September and October.[43] These meetings also revealed that enlargement could be threatened by its links to other issues. One of these issues was EU institutional reform, with the Belgian, French, and Italian governments now insisting that institutional and decision-making reform must precede any further enlargement, not simply enlargement beyond twenty member states as specified in the Amsterdam Treaty. This demand raised the possibility that some member states might hold enlargement hostage to progress on institutional reform.[44]

Also posing a threat to enlargement was the dispute over EU finances. Germany and other wealthier member states were demanding that enlargement should not lead to increased EU spending, and they insisted upon maintaining the Edinburgh budget ceiling of 1.27 percent of GNP. The German and Dutch governments were also demanding an improvement in their net contributor status and a rebalancing of member state budgetary contributions. These demands greatly upset Spain and other poorer member states, which argued that budgetary increases were necessary to pay for eastern enlargement. Otherwise, enlargement could only be paid for by reducing the Structural and Cohesion Funds assistance these countries received from the EU. North-south tensions were further exacerbated by a German government suggestion that countries joining EMU (including, it now appeared increasingly likely, Spain, Portugal, and Ireland) should no longer be eligible for Cohesion Fund assistance. Infuriated by this suggestion, the Spanish government threatened to veto any decisions on enlargement taken in Luxembourg.[45]

Gradually, however, a consensus emerged behind the Commission's strategy of beginning accession negotiations with the five CEECs and Cyprus (the "five plus one" strategy), and the focus shifted instead to the question of how to ensure that the enlargement process would be inclusive and nondiscriminatory. With this question in mind, Germany's Kinkel proposed what he called the "stadium model" *(Stadion-Modell)* for accession negotiations. According to Kinkel, while not all applicants would begin accession negotiations at first, those applicants not initially chosen could later join the negotiations once they were sufficiently prepared, and then catch up with, and even pass, the applicants who had begun negotiations earlier.[46]

By the end of November, the Swedish and Danish governments had given up their demand for a common start and were pushing instead for firm guarantees that applicants left out of the first group would be reviewed annually by the EU, with the possibility of joining negotiations once they were prepared. The Danish government also proposed that all applicant countries, with the possible exception of Slovakia, should be included in a common first phase of the accession process—the "screening phase," in which the EU would carefully examine to what extent the various candidates complied with the *acquis communautaire*. The Commission countered that this idea could slow down accession negotiations by at least twelve months. One Commission official, terming the Danish proposal for a common screening phase a "de facto postponement of the negotiations," claimed that it was merely "a transparent ploy to help the two [excluded] Baltic states catch up with the front-runners."[47] While voicing support for the Danish proposal, Germany's Kinkel stressed that "legally-binding accession negotiations" should only begin with the five CEECs judged ready for this by the Commission and with Cyprus.[48]

Eventually, the member states settled on a formula for the accession negotiations that was proposed by the Luxembourg EU presidency. As described by two Commission insiders:

> This formula sought to define different layers of the "overall enlargement process": a "multilateral framework" bringing together member states and all countries aspiring to membership, including Turkey (10 plus 1 plus 1), in the European Conference; a "single accession process" with all the applicant countries of Central and Eastern Europe and Cyprus (10 plus 1) who would benefit from the reinforced preaccession strategy; and a phase of accession negotiations, which certain candidates would enter in 1998 (5 plus 1) and others at a later stage.[49]

Final agreement on this "process" formula was threatened at the last minute, however, by the Greek government's objections to inviting Turkey to attend the European Conference or including it in the enlargement process at all. Greece's opposition to Turkey's participation in the European Conference was also originally supported by the German government, but Bonn later relented.[50] In the end, Greece did not block a decision on enlargement at the Luxembourg summit, but the disagreement over Turkey affected the outcome and conclusions of the summit.

The EU also decided not to exclude Slovakia from the accession process, despite its political and human rights problems. It was generally felt that excluding Slovakia would do more harm than good. Besides, the Commission had determined that Slovakia was fairly advanced when it came to meeting the other criteria for membership, and it was felt that political changes could quickly put Slovakia in the first-wave group. Also arguing for Slovakia's inclusion in the accession process was the Czech Republic, which maintained close economic and cultural ties to Slovakia after the 1993 split, and the governments of other neighboring countries, such as Austria and Hungary.

THE LUXEMBOURG SUMMIT

Meeting in Luxembourg on December 12–13, 1997, the European Council formally decided to begin the accession process for the ten CEECs and Cyprus. In the "Presidency Conclusions" for the summit, the European Council underlined the historic significance of this decision by declaring that "with the launch of the enlargement process we see the dawn of a new era, finally putting an end to the divisions of the past [in Europe]."[51]

In Luxembourg, the European Council decided on a multilayered enlargement process. To provide an inclusive framework for enlargement, it "decided to set up a European Conference which will bring together the Member States of the European Union and the European States aspiring to accede to it and sharing its values and internal and external objectives." The summit's "Presidency Conclusions" described this Conference as a "multilateral forum for political consultation, intended to address questions of general concern to the participants and to broaden and deepen their cooperation on foreign and security policy, justice and home affairs, and other areas of common concern, particularly economic matters and regional cooperation." It was decided that the European Conference would meet annually at the heads of state and government and foreign ministers levels, with the first meeting to be in London in March 1998. The European Council also announced that it would invite the ten CEEC applicants and Cyprus—as well as Turkey—to attend the initial European Conference.[52]

Embedded within this broader framework were the accession process and negotiations. The Luxembourg European Council decided that the accession process would be formally launched on March 30, 1998, at a meeting of the foreign ministers of the EU member states and the ten CEECs and Cyprus. It was also decided that the accession process would have a "single framework" that would include all eleven candidate countries. To emphasize the nondiscriminatory nature of the accession process, the European Council pointed out "that all these States are destined to join the European Union on the basis of the same criteria and that they are participating in the accession process on an equal footing."[53]

However, accession negotiations would be initiated with only a smaller group of applicants. Following the Commission's recommendations, the European Council decided "to convene bilateral intergovernmental conferences in the spring of 1998 to begin negotiations with Cyprus, Hungary, Poland, Estonia, the Czech Republic and Slovenia on the conditions of their entry into the Union and the ensuing treaty adjustments." Parallel to the accession negotiations with the first group (or "five plus one") countries, "the preparation of negotiations with Romania, Slovakia, Latvia, Lithuania and Bulgaria will be speeded up in particular through an analytical examination of the Union acquis." The European Council also decided that, beginning in late 1998, the Commission would make annual reports on the progress of each CEEC applicant toward meeting the Copenhagen criteria and adopting the *acquis communautaire*. On the basis of these reports, the European Council could decide to open accession negotiations with additional countries.[54]

The Luxembourg European Council also agreed that the CEECs would benefit from an enhanced pre-accession strategy and increased pre-accession aid in order to prepare them for membership. The centerpiece of the enhanced pre-accession strategy would be the bilateral Accession Partnerships, which the European Council instructed the Commission to prepare for each country by March 1998. Responding to criticism that the non-first-wave applicants required more financial aid than envisioned by the Commission in its "Agenda 2000" report, the

European Council also endorsed the idea of a special "catch-up facility" for these countries, although the amount of this fund was left undetermined.[55]

Regarding the difficult issue of Cyprus, the European Council declared its hope that accession negotiations would "contribute positively to the search for a political solution" to the island's problems, and it urged the government of Cyprus to include representatives of the Turkish Cypriot community in the country's negotiating delegation.[56]

The Luxembourg European Council also welcomed the Commission's "Agenda 2000" report on reforming the CAP and the Structural Funds and its proposals for the EU's future financial framework, declaring these submissions to be a good basis for intergovernmental negotiations. It also invited the Commission to submit more detailed legislative proposals on these questions. While confirming the need to adjust EU policies in advance of enlargement, the European Council also stressed the "imperative of budgetary discipline and efficient expenditure." EU leaders also noted that institutional reform was an important prerequisite for enlargement.[57]

The decisions of the Luxembourg European Council were generally welcomed by the applicant countries, including those not in the first-wave or negotiating group. Although his government would have preferred to be in the negotiating group, Latvian Prime Minister Guntars Krasts termed the Luxembourg decisions on enlargement "a formula that we fully accept."[58]

The Luxembourg summit was clouded, however, by the dispute over Turkey. The Turkish government wanted to be treated by the EU as an official candidate for membership, on an equal basis with such "slow-track" applicants as Bulgaria and Romania. However, both Greece and Germany—and probably other member states as well—were opposed to Turkey's participation in the enlargement process. While Turkey's questionable democracy, its poor human rights record, and its role in the Cyprus conflict were generally cited as the reasons for this opposition, economic and cultural reasons were also a factor. Turkey had a large and relatively poor population and, despite its secular government, was a predominantly Muslim country, leading many within the EU to question Turkey's European identity. As Chancellor Kohl explained it, "a dramatic change in the number of Turks in Germany would not be tolerable to German public opinion nor to those in the rest of the EU."[59]

In Luxembourg, therefore, it was decided not to give Turkey equal treatment with the other applicant countries. While the European Council confirmed Turkey's eligibility for membership, it nevertheless declared that Turkey would not be allowed to join the accession process because it did not yet meet the necessary political and economic conditions for doing so. The European Council sought to assuage Turkey by inviting it to attend the inaugural meeting of the European Conference; indeed, with the single-framework accession process agreed in Luxembourg providing an inclusive framework for the applicant countries, integrating Turkey was now the European Conference's chief purpose. However, the EU also attached a number of conditions to this invitation, requiring Turkey to respect international legal rulings on territorial disputes with Greece and to demonstrate a commitment to peace, security, and good neighborliness and respect for other countries' sovereignty.[60]

The European Council also pledged to draw up a special strategy for Turkey, "to prepare Turkey for accession by bringing it closer to the European Union in every field." This strategy would include enhancement of the Customs Union agreement with Turkey, increased financial cooperation, the approximation by Turkey of EU laws and adoption of the *acquis communautaire,* and Turkey's participation in certain EU programs and agencies. The European Council also declared that stronger links between the EU and Turkey depended on the latter's improving its human rights performance and protection of minorities, establishing satisfactory and stable relations with Greece, and supporting the achievement of a political settlement in Cyprus.[61]

With the historic decisions of the Luxembourg summit, the EU reaffirmed its commitment to enlargement and set the stage for the formal beginning of the accession process. The Luxembourg decisions established a two-tiered enlargement strategy that divided applicants into two distinctive groups: those who were allowed to begin accession negotiations and those who were not. Although it was embedded within an inclusive overall accession process, this two-group strategy was criticized by the non-negotiating countries and others as unfair and potentially divisive. For the non-negotiating countries, joining the accession negotiations as quickly as possible became a top priority. The enlargement strategy adopted at Luxembourg was also controversial for its exclusion of Turkey, a decision that led to an immediate deterioration of EU–Turkey relations.

NOTES

1. Craig R. Whitney, "3 Former Members of Eastern Bloc Invited into NATO," *New York Times,* 9 July 1997, A1. On NATO's enlargement debate, see Philip H. Gordon, ed., *NATO's Transformation: The Changing Shape of the Atlantic Alliance* (Lanham, Md.: Rowman & Littlefield, 1997); Jonathan Eyal, "NATO's Enlargement: Anatomy of a Decision," *International Affairs* 73, no. 4 (October 1997): 695–719; and James Goldgeier, "NATO Enlargement: Anatomy of a Decision," *Washington Quarterly* 21, no. 1 (Winter 1998): 85–102.

2. On the discussion of "parallelism," see James Sperling, "The Enlargements of the EU and NATO: Constructing a Two-Tiered or Two-Speed European Security Order?" (paper presented at the Conference on Globalization and its Implications for the Future of Europe and the United States, 12 March 1999, EU Center of the University System of Georgia, Atlanta, Ga.), 2. On the relationship between EU and NATO enlargement more generally, see *Two Tiers or Two Speeds? The European Security Order and the Enlargement of the European Union and NATO,* ed. James Sperling (Manchester: Manchester University Press, 2000). On NATO (and U.S.) efforts to link EU and NATO enlargement, see Lionel Barber, "NATO Holds Talks with EU on Push for New Members," *Financial Times,* 15 November 1996, 14; Hugh Carnegy, "Baltics May Have to Take 'Second Best'," *Financial Times,* 22 November 1996, 2; Lionel Barber, "EU and NATO Discover Togetherness," *Financial Times,* 9 December 1996, 13; and Lionel Barber, "Clinton Urges EU Enlargement," *Financial Times,* 29 May 1997, 1. See also Ronald D. Asmus and Robert C. Nurick, "NATO Enlargement and the Baltic States," in Gordon, ed., *NATO's Transformation,* 155–76.

3. On preparation of the Commission's Opinions, see Graham Avery and Fraser Cameron, *The Enlargement of the European Union* (Sheffield, Eng.: Sheffield Academic Press, 1998), 34–53; Alan Mayhew, *Recreating Europe: The European Union's Policy Towards Central and Eastern Europe* (Cambridge: Cambridge University Press, 1998), 174–76; and Heather Grabbe and Kirsty Hughes, *Enlarging the EU Eastwards* (London: Royal Institute of International Affairs, 1998), 41–54.

4. Avery and Cameron, *Enlargement of the European Union,* 35.

5. These sources included information gleaned from bilateral relations and dialogue with the CEECs (that is, via the Association Councils and reports from the Commission's delegations in the CEECs), information and analyses from international organizations (for example, the OSCE, Council of Europe, IMF, World Bank, EBRD, and OECD) and non-governmental organizations, and independent academic and policy experts.

6. Avery and Cameron, *Enlargement of the European Union,* 35–38. An extract from the questionnaire is provided on pages 37–38.

7. Avery and Cameron, *Enlargement of the European Union,* 39–43.

8. European Commission, "Commission Opinion on Hungary's Application for Membership of the European Union," COM (97) 2001 final; "Commission Opinion on Poland's Application for Membership of the European Union," COM (97) 2002 final; "Commission Opinion on Romania's Application for Membership of the European Union," COM (97) 2003 final; "Commission Opinion on Slovakia's Application for Membership of the European Union," COM (97) 2004 final; "Commission Opinion on Latvia's Application for Membership of the European Union," COM (97) 2005 final; "Commission Opinion on Estonia's Application for Membership of the European Union," COM (97) 2006 final; "Commission Opinion on Lithuania's Application for Membership of the European Union," COM (97) 2007 final; "Commission Opinion on Bulgaria's Application for Membership of the European Union," COM (97) 2008 final; "Commission Opinion on the Czech Republic's Application for Membership of the European Union," COM (97) 2009 final; and "Commission Opinion on Slovenia's Application for Membership of the European Union," COM (97) 2010 final. The ten Opinions are published as supplements 6–15 of the *Bulletin of the European Union* (1997).

9. European Commission, "Agenda 2000: For A Stronger and Wider Union," *Bulletin of the European Union,* supp. 5/97; Lionel Barber and Neil Buckley, "Brussels Unveils Plans for Reforms in an Enlarged EU," *Financial Times,* 17 July 1997, 12; Lionel Barber, "No Turning Back From Brave New Europe," *Financial Times,* 17 July 1997, 3.

10. For details, see the individual Opinions listed in note 8.

11. European Commission, "Agenda 2000."

12. European Commission, "Agenda 2000," 39–59.

13. Avery and Cameron, *Enlargement of the European Union,* 43.

14. Barber, "Brussels Unveils Plans for Reforms in an Enlarged EU," 12.

15. European Commission, "Agenda 2000," 52–53.

16. European Commission, "Agenda 2000," 53.

17. European Commission, "Agenda 2000," 56–57. The earlier communication is European Commission, COM (97) 394.

18. European Commission, "Agenda 2000," 55. The European Conference idea was originally proposed by the French government in 1996, and it later gained German support. See Christopher Bobinski and David Owen, "Chirac Wants 'Sister Poland' in EU by 2000," *Financial Times,* 13 September 1996, 3; and Andrew Gowers, "Germany Seeks EU Expansion Dialogue," *Financial Times,* 25 November 1996, 3. Also see Klaus Kinkel, "Ost-

Erweiterung der Europäischen Union: Chance und Herausforderung," speech on 12 November 1996 in Hamburg; and German Foreign Ministry, "MOE-Botschafterkonferenz," 22 May 1996, available on the Internet at www.auswaertiges-amt.government. de/de/int_kont/ p960522.htm.

19. This is the principle that decisions should be made at the level of government as close to the people as possible. The subsidiarity principle is anchored in article 5 of the consolidated TEC, which states: "In areas which do not fall within its exclusive competence, the Community shall take action . . . only if and insofar as the objectives of the proposed action cannot be sufficiently achieved by the Member States and can therefore, by reason of the scale or effects of the proposed action, be better achieved by the Community." *European Union Consolidated Treaties* (Luxembourg: Office for Official Publications of the European Communities, 1997), 44.

20. European Commission, "Agenda 2000," 29–33.

21. European Commission, "Agenda 2000," 21–26.

22. European Commission, "Agenda 2000," 61–69; quotes are on page 68.

23. As agreed by the European Council in Amsterdam. See "Presidency Conclusions" of the Amsterdam European Council, available on the Internet at http://ue.eu.int/amsterdam/en/conclusions/main.htm.

24. Lionel Barber, "EU Enlargement Takes in Five Eastern States," *Financial Times*, 11 July 1997, 2. On the debate within the Commission on enlargement strategy, see also Barber, "Estonia and Slovenia to Enter Talks on Joining EU," 1; and Lionel Barber, "Santer Calms First Wave Row," *Financial Times*, 10 July 1997, 2.

25. On the influence of geopolitical considerations on the Commission's recommendations, see Avery and Cameron, *Enlargement of the European Union*, 42–43. See also Mayhew, *Recreating Europe*, 176; and Grabbe and Hughes, *Enlarging the EU Eastwards*, 58.

26. Avery and Cameron, *Enlargement of the European Union*, 42–43; Mayhew, *Recreating Europe*, 176; and Grabbe and Hughes, *Enlarging the EU Eastwards*, 58.

27. Barber, "Estonia and Slovenia to Enter Talks on Joining EU," 1; "Geduckt in der Furche," *Der Spiegel*, 30 June 1997, 38.

28. Bruce Clark, "Slovenia Looks to EU Pact for Consolation," *Financial Times*, 10 July 1997, 2.

29. Kevin Done, "Promise to East Rings Hollow," *Financial Times*, 17 July 1997, 3.

30. John Thornhill, "Lithuania Presses EU for Accession," *Financial Times*, 18 July 1997, 3.

31. Thomas Urban, "Die Balten wollen mehr als warme Worte," *Frankfurter Rundschau*, 16 October 1997; Hannes Gamillscheg, "Lettland und Litauen wollen nicht abgehängt werden," *Frankfurter Rundschau*, 21 October 1997. On the reactions of the Baltic states to the Commission's recommendations, see Graeme P. Herd, "The Baltic States and EU Enlargement," in *Back to Europe: Central and Eastern Europe and the European Union*, ed. Karen Anderson (London: UCL Press, 1999), 263–65.

32. Done, "Promise to East Rings Hollow"; and Anatol Lieven, "Romania Presses Its Case," *Financial Times*, 30 September 1997, 3.

33. "EU Urged to Introduce Progress Reports," *Financial Times*, 10 November 1997, 3.

34. "EU Urged to Introduce Progress Reports," 3.

35. Gordon Cramb, "EU Keeps Door Open to New Members," *Financial Times*, 28 June 1997, 3.

36. Robert Anderson and Kevin Done, "Slovakia Struggles to Rebut EU Criticism," *Financial Times*, 16 October 1997, 3. On Slovakia's reaction to the Commission's recommendations, also see Karen Henderson, "Slovakia and the Democratic Criteria for EU Accession," in *Back to Europe*, ed. Henderson, 221–40.

37. Hans van den Broek, "No New Dividing Lines," *Financial Times*, 22 September 1997, 16.

38. Avery and Cameron, *Enlargement of the European Union*, 125.

39. Urban, "Die Balten wollen mehr als warme Worte"; Gamillscheg, "Lettland und Litauen wollen nicht abgehängt werden."

40. On member state views on enlargement strategy, see Grabbe and Hughes, *Enlarging the EU Eastwards*, 57; and Avery and Cameron, *Enlargement of the European Union*, 129.

41. Lionel Barber, "EU Under Pressure Over Terms for Membership Talks," *Financial Times*, 25 November 1997, 18.

42. "European Union Still Undecided on Procedures for Expansion," *Week in Germany*, 31 October 1997, 2.

43. On these meetings, see Lionel Barber, "Row Threatens EU Enlargement Plans," *Financial Times*, 15 September 1997, 2; "EU Streitet über Ost-Erweiterung," *Süddeutsche Zeitung*, 27 October 1997; and Lionel Barber, "Spa Town May Not Soothe EU Nerves," *Financial Times*, 24 October 1997, 2.

44. Lionel Barber and Michael Smith, "EU States in Revolt Over Cost of Admitting Poorer Members," *Financial Times*, 16 September 1997, 16.

45. David White, "France Tries to Ward Off EU Clash," *Financial Times*, 3 December 1997, 3; and "EU streitet vor dem Gipfel über Finanzierung der Ost-Erweiterung," *Süddeutsche Zeitung*, 8 December 1997, 21.

46. "Bonn ist Anwalt der Balten," *Süddeutsche Zeitung*, 18 October 1997; and Thomas Urban, "Neues Konzept für die Erweiterung," *Süddeutsche Zeitung*, 20 October 1997.

47. Lionel Barber, "EU May Mollify Rejected Applicants," *Financial Times*, 8 December 1997, 2.

48. "EU spricht zunächst mit sechs Bewerbern," *Süddeutsche Zeitung*, 9 December 1997, 8.

49. Avery and Cameron, *Enlargement of the European Union*, 130–31.

50. Michael Smith, "EU Olive Branch for Turkey Amid Worries on Cyprus," *Financial Times*, 27 October 1997, 2; Knut Pries, "Bonn macht für Ankara einen Platz in der Europa-Konferenz frei," *Frankfurter Rundschau*, 11 November 1997; Lionel Barber, "Greece Threatens to Block Meeting," *Financial Times*, 9 December 1997, 2.

51. "Presidency Conclusions of the Luxembourg European Council" ("Luxembourg Presidency Conclusions"), introduction, available on the Internet at http://europa.eu.int/council/off/conclu/dec97.htm#intro.

52. "Luxembourg Presidency Conclusions," paras. 4–9.

53. "Luxembourg Presidency Conclusions," paras. 10–11.

54. "Luxembourg Presidency Conclusions," paras. 27 and 29.

55. "Luxembourg Presidency Conclusions," paras. 13–22.

56. "Luxembourg Presidency Conclusions," para. 28.

57. "Luxembourg Presidency Conclusions," paras. 37–38 and 3.

58. Cited in Avery and Cameron, *Enlargement of the European Union*, 139.

59. Cited in Edward Mortimer, "Pyrrhic Victory," *Financial Times*, 17 December 1997, 16. See also Edward Mortimer, "Turkey's PM Demands an Upgrade From 'Third Class,'" *Financial Times*, 11 December 1997, 2; Emma Tucker, "Turkey Dispute Hangs Over Expansion Talks," *Financial Times*, 13–14 December 1997, 2; and Lionel Barber, "Germany Wins the Day at EU Summit," *Financial Times*, 15 December 1997, 2.

60. "Luxembourg Presidency Conclusions," paras. 31 and 5–6.

61. "Luxembourg Presidency Conclusions," paras. 31–36.

5

Beginning the
Accession Process

In accordance with the Luxembourg decisions, the accession process for the ten CEECs and Cyprus formally began on March 30, 1998. The following day, the Accession Conferences with each of the five first-group applicants were formally launched. For both groups of applicants, the initial step in the accession process was the analytical "screening" of the various chapters of the *acquis communautaire* that was conducted by the Commission. Substantive negotiations between the EU and the more advanced applicants was then begun in November 1998. Before beginning the accession process, the EU finalized its Accession Partnerships for each of the CEECs, and it prepared new pre-accession assistance for them as well. Casting a cloud over the launching of the accession process, however, was the crisis in EU relations with Turkey.

THE CRISIS IN EU–TURKEY RELATIONS

While the other applicants were generally satisfied with the outcome of the Luxembourg summit, Turkey was not. The Turkish government responded harshly to the EU's Luxembourg decisions and accused the EU of treating it unfairly. Ankara was stung by the EU's refusal to consider Turkey a candidate for EU membership on a par with the other applicants and to include it in the accession process. It also rejected as "unacceptable" the conditions attached to Turkey's participation in the European Conference and indicated that it would not attend. The Turkish government also broke off formal political dialogue with the EU, declaring that it would no longer discuss with Brussels such issues as human rights, relations with Greece, and the Cyprus conflict. However, it did not follow through on threats to break the Customs Union or withdraw its application for EU membership. Some Turkish politicians even threatened a veto of NATO expansion unless Turkey was included in the EU's enlargement process, but this course of action was quickly rejected by more moderate voices in the government. The Turkish government also criticized the EU's decision to open accession negotiations with Cyprus, claiming that this was incompatible with the island's international status.[1]

In the days and weeks following the Luxembourg summit, the EU's relations with Turkey only worsened. While on a visit to Washington in late December, Turkish Prime Minister Mesut Yilmaz attacked Chancellor Kohl personally, accusing him of religious discrimination against Turkey and of wanting to keep the EU a "Christian club."[2] In early March 1998, Yilmaz charged Germany with pursuing a policy of *lebensraum* in Central and Eastern Europe, referring to Nazi Germany's policy of aggressive expansion in the 1930s. This statement provoked a furious reaction from the German government, which accused Yilmaz of "inexcusable defamation of Germany and European policy."[3] Turkey also leveled criticism at the Greek government, accusing it of blocking EU relations with Turkey and suggesting that the EU suspend Greece's veto whenever addressing issues related to Turkey.[4]

The EU's deteriorating relations with Turkey generated concern that Ankara might try to sabotage efforts to reach a political settlement for Cyprus. Fueling this concern was Ankara's announcement in January 1998 of steps to integrate the Turkish Cypriot government more closely with Turkey, including the establishment of joint diplomatic missions in third countries. Such steps, it was feared, could harden the island's division and be a prelude to the full annexation of northern Cyprus by Turkey.[5] Ankara also pressured Turkish Cypriot leaders not to join the Cyprus delegation for accession negotiations, thus creating another potential problem for Cyprus's accession bid, and indeed for the entire enlargement process.

As the date for the European Conference approached, the British EU presidency and the Commission launched a last-minute effort to persuade Turkey to attend. This included the EU's offer of a broader Customs Union agreement and increased cooperation in such areas as agriculture, industry, and services.[6] This diplomatic effort was rejected by the Turkish government, however, which in the end decided to boycott the European Conference.

Turkey's absence emptied the inaugural meeting of the European Conference of much of its significance. Attending the March 12 meeting in London were the heads of state and government of the fifteen EU member states and the eleven candidate countries. At the meeting, European leaders discussed such issues as cooperation in fighting organized crime and drug trafficking, and in cleaning up the environment. The European Conference was mainly of symbolic importance, however, with EU leaders proclaiming that it represented the end of the Yalta division of Europe. In reference to the absent invitee, the meeting's host, British Prime Minister Tony Blair, made certain to emphasize that "the door will remain open to Turkey."[7]

THE ACCESSION PARTNERSHIPS AND PRE-ACCESSION AID

Toward the end of March, the EU finalized and approved its Accession Partnerships for each of the CEECs. The idea for the Accession Partnerships was originally proposed by the Commission in its "Agenda 2000" report. According to this proposal, the Accession Partnerships would be drawn up by the Commission, in consultation with the government of each applicant country. They would involve precise commitments by the applicants with regard to specific political and economic reforms, focusing on the goals of democracy, macroeconomic stabilization, and nuclear safety. They would also include National Programs for the Adoption of the *acquis communautaire* within a precise timetable, focusing on the priority areas identified by the Commission in its Opinions. The Accession Partnerships would also provide a single framework for EU financial aid; in the future, aid would be granted to each applicant on the basis of annual financial agreements and would be conditional on achieving the objectives identified in the Accession Partnerships and on general progress made. The Accession Partnerships would also provide the basis for the Commission's annual reports on the economic and political progress of the CEECs. On the basis of these annual progress reports, the Accession Partnerships would be updated and revised.[8]

Even though the Commission's proposal was not formally endorsed by the European Council until the Luxembourg summit, the Commission began its work on the Accession Partnerships in the second half of 1997. By early 1998 this work was largely completed, and the final texts of the individual Accession Partnerships were adopted by the Commission on March 25.[9] The Accession Partnerships were then sent to the Council for approval so that they could be presented to the CEEC governments at the March 30 meeting officially launching the accession process.

Each of the ten Accession Partnerships followed a similar format, setting out both short- and medium-term "priorities" and "intermediate objectives." The short-term priorities and objectives were those that the Commission believed "realistic to expect [can] be completed or taken substantially forward by the end of 1998." The medium-term priorities were those expected by the Commission "to take more than a year to complete, although work may and should be done on them during 1998."[10]

The objectives listed in the Accession Partnerships reflected the various chapters of the *acquis communautaire* and covered "areas such as meeting the political criteria for membership, economic reform, reinforcement of institutional and administrative capacity, preparation for membership of the internal market, justice and home affairs, agriculture, environment, transport, employment and social affairs, regional policy and cohesion." While some of these objectives were common to all applicants, the texts of the individual Accession Partnerships reflected the "specific situation and needs" of each country.[11]

Each Accession Partnership also specified the main instruments for EU financial and technical aid and emphasized the conditionality of future assistance. It also set out the procedures for monitoring and reviewing the implementation of the Accession Partnership, mainly through the institutional framework established by the Europe Agreements (Association Councils and Committees). Each Accession Partnership was also accompanied by an annex listing specific "Recommendations for Action" to address issues identified in the Commission's Opinion.[12]

Among the notable short-term priorities and objectives mentioned in the various Accession Partnerships were the following: Poland, the adoption by June 30, 1998, and start of implementation of a viable restructuring program for the steel sector; Lithuania, the establishment of a long-term comprehensive energy strategy, including a decommissioning plan for the Ignalina nuclear power plant; Latvia (and Estonia), the taking of measures to facilitate the naturalization process and to better integrate noncitizens, including stateless children, and enhanced language training for non-Latvian (non-Estonian) speakers; Slovakia, the holding of free and fair presidential, parliamentary, and local elections in 1998, ensuring effective opposition participation in parliamentary oversight committees and supervisory boards, and the adoption of legislative provisions on minority language use and related implementing measures; Romania (and Bulgaria), the implementation of measures to combat corruption and organized crime and improve border management; and Bulgaria, the adoption of a long-term strategy that respects international nuclear safety standards and includes realistic closure commitments for certain nuclear power units.[13]

The Accession Partnerships were not entirely well received by the CEECs. The governments of these countries were unhappy that the Accession Partnerships were essentially dictated to them by the Commission. They also criticized the haste with which the Accession Partnerships were put together, giving the applicant countries little opportunity for input and discussion. They also criticized the linking of future financial aid to the progress of reforms. Nevertheless, the CEECs believed that the Accession Partnerships would be difficult for the EU to enforce, because of their generality and lack of detail. However, according to one official from an applicant country, the conditionality of the Accession Partnerships "shows that the honeymoon is over" for the countries seeking to join the EU.[14]

To help them prepare for membership, the EU was also providing special assistance to the applicant countries as part of its enhanced pre-accession strategy. In "Agenda 2000," the Commission had proposed the creation of two new pre-accession instruments for agricultural and structural aid. These new instruments would augment aid given under the PHARE program and would be used, respectively, for promoting the restructuring and modernization of agriculture in the CEECs and for aligning the infrastructural standards of these countries with those of the EU. By concentrating on transport and the environment, the pre-accession structural aid would have the same focus as the Cohesion Fund assistance given by the EU to its poorest member states. The structural aid instrument would also prepare the applicants for membership by familiarizing them with the EU's Structural Funds arrangements. The Commission proposed coordinating the aid provided by the new pre-accession instruments and the traditional PHARE aid within the single framework of the Accession Partnerships.[15]

The Commission's proposal for the new pre-accession aid instruments was endorsed by the Luxembourg European Council, along with the proposal for a special "catch-up" fund for those applicants "with the greatest need" (that is, those not selected to begin negotiations).[16] In March 1998, the Commission presented the Council with detailed legislative proposals for the new aid instruments, together with its proposal for a third instrument for coordinating the various sources of pre-accession aid. For the agricultural instrument—Support for Agriculture and Rural Development (SAPARD)—the Commission proposed spending ECU 520 million per year for the ten CEECs, or a total of ECU 3.64 billion for the 2000-2006 period. Use of the money, which would come from the EU's normal agricultural budget, would be guided by a "Rural Development Program" for each applicant, drawn up by the Commission in cooperation with each country. For the new Instrument for Structural Policies for Pre-Accession (ISPA), the Commission proposed spending ECU 1.04 billion per year for the ten CEECs, or a total of ECU 7.28 billion for seven years. Use of the aid would be guided by the priorities mentioned in the Accession Partnerships. Aid given under both instruments would be allocated among the applicants on the basis of such factors as population, per capita GDP, and territorial size.[17] After some debate, the three pre-accession aid instruments were approved by the Council in early November 1998.[18] Final approval came in March 1999, with agreement on the "Agenda 2000" financial and budgetary package for 2000-2006 (see chapter 7).

THE ACCESSION PROCESS BEGINS

After the European Conference, the focus shifted to the formal beginning of the accession process in late March. The opening of accession negotiations with the first group countries was threatened, however, by a last-minute dispute between France and Greece over Cyprus. The French government did not want to pursue accession talks with Cyprus in the absence of a political settlement for the island, yet Greece threatened to block the entire enlargement process if Cyprus was not included in the accession negotiations. A compromise was reached, however. France and other member states agreed to allow Cyprus to begin accession negotiations, but the Cypriot government was put on notice that it could not expect automatic entry into the EU and was told that it must work toward achieving a political settlement for the island. It was also agreed that the Commission would make regular reports to the Council on the progress of settlement talks, implying that accession negotiations with Cyprus could be suspended if progress was insufficient.[19]

The accession process was formally launched on March 30, 1998, with a celebratory meeting in London of the foreign ministers of the fifteen member states and the eleven candidate countries. At the meeting, the ten CEECs were presented with their individual Accession Partnerships. EU representatives also stressed that accession required the full acceptance and effective application of the *acquis communautaire*. Speaking at the meeting, British Foreign Minister Robin Cook summed up the historic importance of the event, declaring that "by enlarging the EU we are finally overcoming the cruel and unnatural division of our continent. We are creating the conditions that will help prevent a return to the terrible suffering and destruction Europe has known this century."[20]

On the following day in Brussels, the Accession Conferences between the EU and each of the first-group countries—Poland, Hungary, the Czech Republic, Estonia, Slovenia, and Cyprus—officially began. In keeping with the Luxembourg summit decisions, the other five applicants—Latvia, Lithuania, Slovakia, Romania, and Bulgaria—were assured that they would have the opportunity to begin accession negotiations at a later date, once the EU decided that they were sufficiently prepared. They were also told that the order of beginning accession negotiations did not necessarily determine the order of eventual accession; in other words, the second-group countries not only might catch up with the negotiating countries, but they could also pass them.

At the March 31 meeting, British Foreign Minister Cook, the president-in-office of the Council, laid down the ground rules for the accession negotiations. He stressed that membership involved acceptance of the entire *acquis communautaire*, as well as introduction of the administrative and institutional structures necessary to ensure that EU laws and regulations are effectively applied and enforced. He also emphasized that any derogations from the *acquis communautaire* that might be granted would be only limited and temporary. Cook also informed the representatives of the six applicant countries that separate intergovernmental negotiations with each of them would be conducted on the basis of the same principles and criteria, but that the pace of negotiations and the date of their conclusion would depend solely on how well prepared the country in question was.[21]

The beginning of the accession process seemed to bolster public enthusiasm for EU membership in the applicant countries. According to a *Eurobarometer* survey conducted by the Commission in November 1997, the percentage of those who would vote "yes" in a referendum on accession had increased in most of the candidate countries, compared with results from surveys conducted in the previous year.[22] A separate survey conducted in Poland, and made public two weeks before the beginning of accession negotiations, indicated that 64 percent of Poles would vote in favor of membership in a referendum, while only 9 percent would vote against it. The survey also revealed, however, that many Poles felt that their country would have difficulty coping with the competitive challenges of EU membership, with many worried in particular about the ability of small local businesses to compete with larger EU companies. It also revealed different views on EU membership among persons in different socioeconomic groups; while young people and white-collar managers were mostly in favor of EU membership, farmers were the most skeptical.[23] The Polish findings mirrored survey results from other applicant countries and indicated a cautiously optimistic stance toward EU membership among Central and Eastern Europeans as the difficult accession process got under way.[24]

THE SCREENING PROCESS

The first phase of the accession process for all applicants was the analytical examination, or "screening," of the thirty-one chapters of the *acquis communautaire*.[25] This exercise was carried out by the Commission, together with the applicant countries. The objective of the screening process was to determine the extent to which the applicant was in compliance with EU laws and regulations and what adjustments might be necessary. The screening process also identified potential problems that might need to be dealt with in the accession negotiations, perhaps through the granting of temporary derogations or transitional arrangements for the applicant countries.

The screening process for all eleven applicants formally began with a general informational meeting in Brussels on April 3, 1998. After this point, the screening proceeded separately with each applicant group.[26]

For the first-group countries, the screening was conducted by the Commission's special Enlargement Task Force. This unit consisted of experts from the Commission's various administrative departments and services. Named as the initial head of the Enlargement Task Force was veteran EU official Klaus van der Pas. The Commission also appointed an individual negotiator for each applicant in the first group.

The screening for the first group countries proceeded as follows: After multilateral sessions introducing each chapter of the *acquis communautaire*, analytical examination of the chapter was carried out with each applicant individually. In the bilateral meetings, the applicants were asked

- whether they can accept the relevant chapters of the *acquis*;
- whether they intend to request transitional arrangements in the chapter under review;
- whether they have already adopted the laws necessary to comply with the *acquis*; if not, when they intend to adopt such laws;
- whether they possess the administrative structures and other capacity needed to implement and enforce EU laws properly;
- if not, when these structures will be put in place.[27]

After the bilateral screening of each chapter, the Commission submitted individual reports for each country to the Council. These reports contained the Commission's analysis of the problems identified and the information supplied by the applicants for each chapter as well as the Commission's views on problems likely to arise in the negotiations on each chapter. The reports would be used by the Council in deciding whether to begin substantive negotiations on specific chapters; they would also serve as the basis for the EU's common positions for the negotiations. These decisions would need to be taken once applicant countries had presented to the Council their formal negotiating positions on a given chapter.

The screening for the second-group countries was conducted by the Commission's DG IA,[28] and was carried out multilaterally, with all five applicants together. After multilateral meetings on all thirty-one chapters of the *acquis communautaire* were completed, the Commission would hold bilateral sessions with each of the applicant countries. In these sessions, the applicants would be given the opportunity to indicate which aspects of the *acquis communautaire* they had already transposed into national legislation, and to explain their timetable for implementing the remainder. The bilateral sessions would also help identify any problems for the applicants in applying EU rules. Unlike its procedure with the first group, the Commission announced that it would not issue reports on the screening of the second group until after completion of the entire screening exercise.[29]

In the screening for both groups, representatives of the Council presidency were also present at meetings dealing with the EU's intergovernmental second (CFSP) and third (JHA) pillars, and representatives of the individual member states were present for the screening of third pillar matters.

After the initial informational meeting, the screening for both groups began in late April. For the first group, the initial chapters of the *acquis communautaire* to be screened were those that were considered to be relatively "easy," with screening of the more sensitive or difficult chapters (such as agriculture and the environment) saved for later.

By late July, screening of the first eleven chapters of the *acquis communautaire* had been completed. These were the chapters on science and research, telecommunications and information technology, education and training, culture and audiovisual policy, industrial policy, small and medium-sized enterprises, CFSP, company law, consumer protection, fisheries, and statistics. After a summer pause, the screening process resumed in September with the chapter on free movement of goods. Later that month, screening of the agriculture chapter also began. This was expected to be among the most challenging areas of EU legislation for the applicants to adopt and implement, especially for heavily agricultural countries like Poland.[30]

By the end of the year, a total of twenty-two chapters, more than two-thirds of the *acquis communautaire*, had been screened for the first-group countries, including the chapters on transport, energy, external relations, customs union, competition policy, social policy and employment, free movement of capital, and economic and monetary union.[31]

In early December, Task Force Director van der Pas reviewed the progress of screening for the first group. He declared that the screening exercise had demonstrated that, while the applicants have no difficulty accepting the *acquis communau-*

taire, they continue to have problems implementing it. He stressed that the ability of the applicants to effectively implement EU legislation would become a greater priority as the accession process moved forward and began tackling more difficult areas of the *acquis communautaire*, such as agriculture, the free movement of persons, the Structural Funds (regional policy), and environmental policy. He also argued that the pace of accession negotiations, the substantive phase of which had begun in November (see below), should match the ability of the applicants to implement the *acquis communautaire*.[32]

Screening for the first group continued in January 1999 with the difficult chapter on environmental policy. In late February, the screening of EU legislation in the area of JHA was begun. By early July, the screening process for the first-group countries was concluded.[33]

For the second-group countries, the multilateral ("educational and explanatory") phase of the screening process began in late April 1998, with an examination of the relevant chapters of the EU's Single Market legislation. The multilateral phase of the screening process continued throughout the summer and fall and was completed in early 1999.[34]

In January 1999, the progress of screening for the second-group countries was reviewed by François Lamoureux, deputy director-general of DG IA. He concluded that the screening process thus far had shown that there was not much difference between the candidates of the first and second groups in their adoption of the *acquis communautaire*. Most of the second-group countries, he claimed, were doing their best to catch up with the first group and join the accession negotiations.[35] For these countries, joining the accession negotiations was an immediate and important goal.

In March 1999, the bilateral meetings between the Commission and individual applicants of the second group began. This bilateral phase of the screening process was completed by the middle of July for all chapters of the *acquis communautaire* except agriculture, which was dealt with beginning in September.[36]

BEGINNING SUBSTANTIVE NEGOTIATIONS

By early summer 1998, the screening process was well under way and the EU was contemplating the next step in the accession process: the launching of substantive negotiations with the first-group countries. Rather than waiting until the screening process was completed for all thirty-one chapters of the *acquis communautaire*, the possibility was discussed of beginning negotiations on those chapters for which screening had already concluded. This option was favored by the applicants. According to a Polish government official, "We [the applicants] all want to get on with talks as we feel that we're merely shuffling papers around while soon our citizens will want to see signs of progress."[37] Some member states, however, including France and Spain, were not anxious to begin concrete negotiations. Disagreement on this issue surfaced at the June Cardiff summit, preventing the European Council from issuing a call in its "Presidency Conclusions" for the applicants to prepare position papers on the screened chapters in preparation for substantive negotiations.[38]

After the Cardiff summit, however, the Austrian government, which was preparing to assume the EU presidency for the second half of 1998, announced its intention to "begin real accession negotiations with the six countries of the first group sometime in autumn." It thus encouraged these countries to submit their negotiating positions on the already screened chapters, including any requests for transitional derogations.[39] At a meeting on July 13, the Council accepted in principle the idea of beginning concrete negotiations in the fall.[40] In response, the first-group countries stepped up their preparations for negotiations. Meeting in Ljubljana, Slovenia, in the middle of July, the six applicants agreed to submit position papers on at least the first seven of the screened chapters in September.[41]

The first country to submit its negotiating positions to the Council and Commission was Poland (on September 1), followed by Cyprus and Hungary (September 7), Estonia (September 9), and the Czech Republic and Slovenia (September 15). While Hungary presented position papers on eleven chapters and Estonia on twelve, the other four applicants submitted position papers on only the first seven of the screened chapters: science and research, telecommunications, education and training, culture and audiovisual policy, industrial policy, small and medium-sized enterprises; and CFSP. The individual position papers contained relatively few requests for derogations, with most requests for transitional arrangements being for the telecommunications and culture and audiovisual policy chapters. With the first batch of position papers now in hand, the member states asked the Commission to begin drafting common positions for the EU, on the basis of which the Council would decide whether to open substantive negotiations on some or all of the first seven chapters.[42]

The Austrian presidency favored opening substantive negotiations in early November. Some member states, however, particularly France and Spain, were reluctant to agree to this date. In September, the French government sought to delay the beginning of negotiations by requesting that the Commission draw up a full "political assessment" of the accession process, including an analysis of the Cyprus situation. According to France's minister for European affairs, Pierre Moscovici, the accession process should be "under political control," not on "automatic pilot." The French government also demanded that the Commission provide full details of the position papers submitted by the applicants, including any potential problems foreseen in adopting specific EU rules and standards.[43]

The French requests were viewed by the Commission as an attempt to postpone the beginning of substantive negotiations and to delay enlargement. Commission officials claimed that the French government wanted to use the political assessment to say that "it would not be very smart to go ahead with the next phase [of enlargement]," and that it wanted the details of the position papers only "to get all the dirt to delay the [accession] process." According to one Commission official, "The Commission has been working too efficiently for the tastes of some member states."[44] The French government, however, angrily denied any suggestions that it wanted to delay enlargement. Instead, it claimed that it was merely trying to get its fellow member states to focus on the real problems created by enlargement. According to one French official:

> Our partners are behaving like ostriches. They pretend there is no problem. We see the problems and know we have to overcome them. We are trying to make people focus on this. But every time we raise these questions, people suggest we are against enlargement. That is rubbish. We simply believe that if we leave these questions unanswered, enlargement will fail.[45]

The applicant countries were also becoming frustrated with delays in the accession process and were growing concerned about a perceived "loss of enthusiasm" for enlargement among the member states. According to Estonia's EU ambassador, this concern stemmed not just from efforts to delay the beginning of negotiations but also from the lack of progress to date with "Agenda 2000" and the EU's internal reforms (see chapters 7 and 8). He argued that the EU, while urging the applicants to make difficult reforms, was failing to hold up its end of the bargain and do its own "homework." Regarding the prospects for enlargement, he claimed, "Unfortunately, some signals coming from member states are creating some doubts."[46]

The Czech government also expressed concern about delays in the accession process and called for "a real start to real negotiations" in November.[47] According to Prague's EU ambassador, the decision to begin concrete negotiations would be "the first test" of the EU's political will to move forward with enlargement.[48] Seeking to increase pressure on the EU, in late September the governments of the first-group countries issued a joint call for concrete negotiations to begin in November, with a target date for full accession of 2002, or 2003 at the latest.[49]

After much wrangling, the go-ahead for substantive negotiations was finally given by the Council at a meeting in Luxembourg on October 5. After a "political debate" on the implications of enlargement, which was requested by the French government, EU foreign ministers decided to begin concrete negotiations at the ministerial level with the first-group applicants on November 10. The Council also asked COREPER to begin preparing common positions on the first seven screened chapters of the *acquis communautaire,* for which the applicants had submitted negotiating positions. In its "Conclusions on Enlargement," the Council reemphasized that the pace of progress in the negotiations would depend on the individual situation of each applicant, and it recalled the principle that any agreements reached during the course of negotiations would not be considered final until an overall agreement on accession with a given applicant had been established.[50]

The decision to proceed with substantive negotiations was almost blocked by disagreement over Cyprus, however. The French government, in particular, voiced its concern about beginning negotiations with Cyprus as long as the island remained divided into separate Greek and Turkish administrations. In response, the Greek government threatened to block negotiations with other applicant countries unless Cyprus was included. In the end, the French government relented and voted to include Cyprus in the negotiations, while emphasizing, in the words of its European affairs minister, that this decision "does not commit us to anything. . . . There can be no automatic membership for a divided island." In its "Conclusions on Enlargement," the Council once again expressed the hope that beginning negotiations with Cyprus might promote a political settlement for the island.[51]

Substantive negotiations actually began on October 29, with a deputy-level meeting in Brussels between EU permanent representatives and the chief negotiators of each of the six applicants. At the meeting, the member states and the applicants exchanged their respective negotiating positions on the seven screened chapters. The EU also requested that the applicants provide more detailed information on some of the chapters, so that this information could be taken account of in the EU's final common positions.[52] On November 9, the EU's common positions were formally approved by the Council.[53] At this meeting, the Council also received the Commission's first regular reports on the progress of the applicant countries in preparing for accession (see below). In its reports, the Commission was particularly critical of two first-group applicants, the Czech Republic and Slovenia, for their slow progress in implementing the *acquis communautaire*, but it also warned all the applicants that they lacked the administrative capacity to effectively implement and enforce EU legislation.[54]

Despite the criticism expressed in the progress reports, substantive negotiations with the six first-group applicants were officially launched on November 10, at a meeting of foreign ministers in Brussels. The meeting took the form of successive EU ministerial sessions with each of the applicant countries, followed by a press conference. For each applicant, negotiations on a number of chapters on which there was no disagreement, or for which EU legislation had already been implemented, were declared "provisionally closed," pending conclusion of a final accession agreement. On other chapters, however, it was decided that further negotiation was necessary. At the meeting, Austria's Foreign Minister, Wolfgang Schüssel, the acting Council president, declared that the "actual negotiations" had begun. "Nothing," he claimed, "can stop the [EU enlargement] train."[55]

The accession negotiations continued to be marred by disagreement over Cyprus, however. On the eve of the Brussels ministerial meeting, the governments of France, Germany, Italy, and the Netherlands issued a joint statement questioning the wisdom of admitting Cyprus while it was still divided and urging more progress toward a political settlement for the island. This statement prompted the Greek government to renew its threat to block any enlargement if Cyprus was not included.[56] Thus, while concrete negotiations were now under way, the Cyprus issue loomed as a potential roadblock in the accession process.

NOTES

1. "Turkei bricht politischen Dialog mit der EU ab," *Süddeutsche Zeitung*, 15 December 1997, 1; Emma Tucker and John Barham, "Turkey Angered by EU Conference Conditions," *Financial Times*, 15 December 1997, 16; David Buchan, "US Praise for NATO Partners in Bosnia," *Financial Times*, 17 December 1997, 2; John Barham, "Turks Threaten to Break Links with the EU," *Financial Times*, 18 December 1997, 2.

2. "Yilmaz: Kohl discriminiert die Turkei," *Süddeutsche Zeitung*, 20 December 1997.

3. John Barham and Quentin Peel, "Kohl Accused of Trying to Block Turkey's Hopes of Joining EU," *Financial Times*, 6 March 1998, 22; "Yilmaz: Bonn setzt Lebensraum-Politik fort," *Süddeutsche Zeitung*, 7 March 1998; Peter Norman, John Barham, and Lionel Barber, "German Anger Over Turkish PM's 'Insult,'" *Financial Times*, 7–8 March 1998, 1.

4. John Barham, "Turkey Attacks Greece's EU Veto," *Financial Times*, 24 December 1997, 2.

5. Kelly Couturier, "Turks Step Up Cyprus Pressure," *Financial Times*, 15 January 1998, 3.

6. Lionel Barber, "EU Holds Out Olive Branch to Turkey Over Cyprus Talks," *Financial Times*, 5 March 1998, 14.

7. Lionel Barber and David Buchan, "EU Increases Efforts to Avoid Cyprus Hitch in Expansion Plans," *Financial Times*, 13 March 1998, 22.

8. European Commission, "Agenda 2000: For a Stronger and Wider Union," *Bulletin of the European Union*, supp. 5/97, 52–54 and 79–89.

9. Agence Europe, *Europe Daily Bulletin*, no. 7188, 26 March 1998, 6. See also European Commission, MEMO/98/21, Brussels, 27 March 1998.

10. European Commission, MEMO/98/21. The full texts of the individual Accession Partnerships and annexes are available on the Internet, at the EU's official Website at http://europa.eu.int/comm/dg1a/enlarge/access_partnership/index.htm.

11. European Commission, MEMO/98/21.

12. European Commission, MEMO/98/21.

13. Accession Partnerships (see note 10).

14. Christopher Bobinski, "EU Conditions For Aid Under Attack," *Financial Times*, 22 December 1997, 2.

15. European Commission, "Agenda 2000," 53 and 85–86.

16. "Luxembourg Presidency Conclusions," para. 17, available on the Internet at http://europa.eu.int/council/off/conclu/dec97.htm#intro.

17. For details of the legislative proposals, see Agence Europe, *Europe Daily Bulletin*, no. 7189, 27 March 1998, 7–8. The proposals are available on the Internet, at the EU's official Website. For SAPARD: http://europa.eu.int/en/comm/dg06/index.htm; for ISPA: http://europa.eu.int/comm/dg16/document/doc1g_en.htm. For the Commission's indicative breakdown between the candidate countries of aid from these two instruments, see Agence Europe, *Europe Daily Bulletin*, no. 7513, 23 June 1999, 14.

18. Agence Europe, *Europe Daily Bulletin*, no. 7339, 9–10 November 1998. On the debate within the Council on the pre-accession aid instruments, see Agence Europe, *Europe Daily Bulletin*, no. 7330, 26-27 October 1998, 13–14.

19. Lionel Barber and David Buchan, "EU Reaches Compromise Deal Over Cyprus," *Financial Times*, 16 March 1998, 2.

20. Agence Europe, *Europe Daily Bulletin*, no. 7191, 30–31 March 1998, 4 and 10. Quote is on page 4.

21. Agence Europe, *Europe Daily Bulletin*, no. 7192, 1 April 1998, 2. For a listing of the specific points of the *acquis communautaire* that new members must accept, see Agence Europe, *Europe Daily Bulletin*, no. 7191, 30–31 March 1998, 10.

22. Central and Eastern Europe Barometer, no. 8, available on the Internet at http://europa.eu.int/comm/dg10/epo/ceeb.html. The percentage change in those voting "yes" in each country was Slovakia, +17; Hungary, +15; Estonia, +9; Bulgaria, +8; Slovenia, +7; Latvia, +6; the Czech Republic, +4; Lithuania, -2; Poland, -6; and Romania, -13. Despite the drop in support for EU membership in Romania, this country had the highest percentage of voters who would vote in favor of accession, 71 percent. Survey results also reported in Agence Europe, *Europe Daily Bulletin*, no. 7229, 27 May 1998, 15.

23. "Poles Likely to Back Membership," *Financial Times*, 17 March 1998, 3. The Polish survey was conducted by the Institute of Public Affairs, a nonpartisan think tank.

24. In most CEECs, after being high in the early 1990s, support for EU membership declined somewhat in the middle of the decade, as disillusionment with the EU's response to the CEECs and the slow pace of enlargement set in, only to rebound again after 1997 with the Luxembourg decisions and the formal launching of the accession process. On public opinion on EU accession in the CEECs, see Heather Grabbe and Kirsty Hughes, "Central and Eastern European Views on EU Enlargement: Political Debates and Public Opinion," in *Back to Europe: Central and Eastern Europe and the European Union*, ed. Karen Henderson (London: UCL Press, 1999), 185–202.

25. These chapters are (1) free movement of goods; (2) freedom of movement for persons; (3) freedom to provide services; (4) free movement of capital; (5) company law; (6) competition policy; (7) agriculture; (8) fisheries; (9) transport policy; (10) taxation; (11) EMU; (12) statistics; (13) social policy and employment; (14) energy; (15) industrial policy; (16) small and medium-sized business; (17) science and research; (18) education and training; (19) telecommunications and information technologies; (20) culture and audiovisual policy; (21) regional policy and coordination of structural instruments; (22) environment; (23) consumer and health protection; (24) JHA; (25) customs union; (26) external relations; (27) CFSP; (28) financial control; (29) financial and budgetary provisions; (30) institutions; and (31) other.

26. On the organization of the screening process, see Agence Europe, *Europe Daily Bulletin*, no. 7197, 8 April 1998, 8–9; and Agence Europe, *Europe Daily Bulletin*, no. 7193, 2 April 1998, 10.

27. European Commission, enlargement Website, available on the Internet at http://europa.eu.int/comm/enlargement/negotiations/ach_en.html#2.

28. This department technically no longer exists. In September 1999, the new Commission President, Romano Prodi, announced a reorganization of the Commission's DGs and administrative services, including the creation of a new enlargement directorate-general, which essentially replaced DG IA. By this point, however, the screening of the second-group countries was largely completed.

29. Agence Europe, *Europe Daily Bulletin*, no. 7210, 29 April 1998, 7.

30. Agence Europe, *Europe Daily Bulletin*, no. 7270, 25 July 1998, 4–5; Agence Europe, *Europe Daily Bulletin*, no. 7306, 23 September 1998, 9. For an interim assessment of the screening for the first group, see Agence Europe, *Europe Daily Bulletin*, no. 7235, 5 June 1998, 11.

31. Agence Europe, *Europe Daily Bulletin*, no. 7335, 3–4 November 1998, 9; Agence Europe, *Europe Daily Bulletin*, no. 7356, 4 December 1998, 11–12; European Commission, enlargement Website.

32. Agence Europe, *Europe Daily Bulletin*, no. 7356, 4 December 1998, 11–12.

33. Agence Europe, *Europe Daily Bulletin*, no. 7413, 26 February 1999, 10; European Commission, enlargement Website.

34. Agence Europe, *Europe Daily Bulletin*, no. 7388, 22 January 1999, 12–13. For an interim assessment of the screening for the second group, see Agence Europe, *Europe Daily Bulletin*, no. 7240, 12 June 1998, 6-7. On the progress of screening for the second group, see also Agence Europe, *Europe Daily Bulletin*, no. 7274, 31 July 1998, 4.

35. Agence Europe, *Europe Daily Bulletin*, no. 7388, 22 January 1999, 12–13. Lamoureux headed up the screening process for the second-group applicants.

36. Agence Europe, *Europe Daily Bulletin*, no. 7415, 1–2 March 1999, 11; European Commission, enlargement Website.

37. Christopher Bobinski, "Poland Itching to Begin EU Accession Talks," *Financial Times*, 24 June 1998, 3.

38. Bobinski, "Poland Itching to Begin EU Accession Talks," 3. The "Presidency Conclusions" of the Cardiff European Council are reprinted in Agence Europe, *Europe Documents*, no. 2094–2095, 18 June 1998, 1–13.

39. Agence Europe, *Europe Daily Bulletin*, no. 7249, 25 June 1998, 6.

40. Agence Europe, *Europe Daily Bulletin*, no. 7262, 13-14 July 1998, 8.

41. Christopher Bobinski, "EU Applicants Agree Deadline," *Financial Times*, 17 July 1998, 2.

42. Agence Europe, *Europe Daily Bulletin*, no. 7291, 2 September 1998, 7; Agence Europe, *Europe Daily Bulletin*, no. 7292, 3 September 1998, 8; Agence Europe, *Europe Daily Bulletin*, no. 7295, 7–8 September 1998, 10; Agence Europe, *Europe Daily Bulletin*, no. 7297, 10 September 1998, 8; Agence Europe, *Europe Daily Bulletin*, no. 7301, 16 September 1998, 7; Agence Europe, *Europe Daily Bulletin*, no. 7302, 17 September 1998, 13.

43. Quentin Peel, "EU States 'Try to Slow Enlargement,'" *Financial Times*, 30 September 1998, 3. Moscovici is quoted in Agence Europe, *Europe Daily Bulletin*, no. 7290, 31 August–1 September 1998, 4.

44. Peel, "EU States 'Try to Slow Enlargement,'" 3.

45. Quentin Peel and Stefan Wagstyl, "Journey into the Unknown," *Financial Times*, 9 November 1998, 15. On the French government's pique at being accused of seeking to delay enlargement, see Agence Europe, *Europe Daily Bulletin*, no. 7315, 5–6 October 1998, 4.

46. Agence Europe, *Europe Daily Bulletin*, no. 7304, 19 September 1998, 9.

47. Peel, "EU States 'Try to Slow Enlargement,'" 3.

48. Agence Europe, *Europe Daily Bulletin*, no. 7304, 19 September 1998, 10.

49. Christopher Bobinski and Stefan Wagstyl, "EU Applicants Urge Action on Entry Timetable," *Financial Times*, 1 October 1998, 4.

50. Agence Europe, *Europe Daily Bulletin*, no. 7314, 3 October 1998, 5–6; Agence Europe, *Europe Daily Bulletin*, no. 7315, 5–6 October 1998, 5; Quentin Peel, "Cyprus Fears Fail to Stop Membership Negotiations," *Financial Times*, 5 October 1998, 4; Quentin Peel, "Talks on EU Entry for Cyprus Agreed," *Financial Times*, 6 October 1998, 2. For the text of the "Council Conclusions on Enlargement," see Agence Europe, *Europe Documents*, no. 2100, 14 October 1998, 1–2.

51. Agence Europe, *Europe Daily Bulletin*, no. 7314, 3 October 1998, 5-6; Agence Europe, *Europe Daily Bulletin*, no. 7315, 5–6 October 1998, 5; Peel, "Cyprus Fears Fail to Stop Membership Negotiations," 4; "Council Conclusions on Enlargement," 2. The quotes of France's European affairs minister are in Peel, "Talks on EU Entry for Cyprus Agreed," 2.

52. Agence Europe, *Europe Daily Bulletin*, no. 7333, 30 October 1998, 6.

53. Agence Europe, *Europe Daily Bulletin*, no. 7338, 7 November 1998, 7; Agence Europe, *Europe Daily Bulletin*, no. 7339, 9-10 November 1998, 7.

54. Agence Europe, *Europe Daily Bulletin*, no. 7336, 5 November 1998, 6–7; Agence Europe, *Europe Daily Bulletin*, no. 7339, 9-10 November 1998, 7; Quentin Peel, "EU Warns Applicants on Slow Preparations," *Financial Times*, 5 November 1998, 3; European Commission, "Reports on Progress Towards Accession by Each of the Candidate Countries." The Commission's progress reports for each of the applicants, and its "Composite Paper" on the accession process, are available on the Internet, at the EU's official Website at http://europa.eu.int/comm/dg1a/enlarge/report_11_98_en/index.htm.

55. Michael Smith, "EU Warns Cyprus Split May Slow Talks," *Financial Times*, 11 November 1998, 2; Agence Europe, *Europe Daily Bulletin*, no. 7340, 11 November 1998, 8.

56. Smith, "EU Warns Cyprus Split May Slow Talks," 2; Agence Europe, *Europe Daily Bulletin*, no. 7339, 9–10 November 1998, 7–8; Agence Europe, *Europe Daily Bulletin*, no. 7340, 11 November 1998, 9.

6

To the Helsinki Summit

At the Luxembourg summit, the EU assured the five second-group countries that they would have the opportunity to join the accession negotiations at a later date. To determine whether they were prepared for this, the Commission would make annual reports on the progress of each applicant toward meeting the accession criteria. On the basis of these reports, the Commission could recommend, and the European Council could decide, to open negotiations with additional applicants. With the first such reports due in November 1998, after Luxembourg the second-group countries launched a furious campaign to accelerate their reforms and convince the EU of their preparedness for negotiations. As a result of these efforts, and of the rethinking of enlargement strategy motivated by the Kosovo war, the EU made the historic decision at its December 1999 Helsinki summit to expand the negotiations to include all of the applicant countries. In Helsinki, the EU also adopted a major change of policy toward Turkey, declaring it an official candidate for EU membership. At the Helsinki summit, therefore, the EU adopted a broader and more ambitious enlargement strategy in response to the challenge of a wider Europe.

EXPANDING THE NEGOTIATIONS?

After the announcement of the Commission's "Agenda 2000" recommendations on enlargement strategy, the five applicants not selected for the first group argued that they should also be allowed to begin accession negotiations. The governments of Latvia and Lithuania argued that the Commission's recommendations were based on outdated information, and that in any case it would be a serious mistake to split the Baltic states. The Romanian and Bulgarian governments argued that the double-rejection shock of exclusion from the first wave of both EU and NATO expansion would consign them to a geopolitical "grey zone" between Western Europe and Russia while undermining domestic support for difficult economic and political reforms. The Slovakian government also promised political reforms to enable it to quickly join the first group.[1]

Nevertheless, at the Luxembourg summit, the European Council maintained the two-tier approach recommended by the Commission as well as the composition of the two groups. However, it also decided upon an inclusive "single-framework" accession process that would give the second-group countries the opportunity to catch up with the first-group applicants and join them in negotiations. The main elements of this process were the multilateral screening of the *acquis communautaire* (to be followed by bilateral screening sessions), and the Accession Partnerships and enhanced pre-accession aid. The Luxembourg European Council also agreed to create a special "catch-up" fund for the second-group countries. Most importantly, it called upon the Commission to prepare annual progress reports on the individual applicants. Based upon the findings of these reports, in the fall of each year the Commission could recommend, and the European Council could decide, to allow additional applicants to begin accession negotiations.[2]

After the Luxembourg summit and the formal launching of the accession process in March 1998, therefore, considerable attention focused on the Commission's first regular progress reports. According to Deputy Director-General Lamoureux, these reports would essentially update the Commission's Opinions regarding the progress of individual applicants toward meeting the accession criteria. They would also take account of each country's progress toward meeting the short-term priorities and objectives identified in its Accession Partnership. In essence, the reports would provide a "photograph" of the situation in each country as of November 1, 1998. After being formally adopted by the Commission in early November, the completed reports would be ready by the end of the month, together with a "Composite Paper" containing the Commission's recommendations to the Council on the next steps of the accession process. The reports would then be submitted to the European Council in December, with the heads of state and government making the final decision on whether to allow additional applicants to begin accession negotiations.[3]

As the Commission began preparing its evaluations in the first half of 1998, the second-group countries launched a furious campaign to be included in the accession negotiations. The government of Lithuania promised to move quickly with its economic reforms so that Lithuania could join the negotiating group. According to Prime Minister Gediminas Vagnorius, "[Lithuania] will move so quickly that the European Commission will find it very uncomfortable not to invite us to join."[4] Vagnorius also claimed that Lithuania would soon overtake several of the first-group countries in its preparations for membership, assuming, he added, that the EU applied the same criteria to all the applicant countries.[5] At a meeting with

Commission President Santer in April, Lithuania's president also expressed confidence that his country would be ready to begin accession negotiations soon, "perhaps as soon as the end of this year."[6]

Also pressing its case was the Slovakian government. According to Foreign Minister Zdenka Kramplova, "[Slovakia's] priority is rapidly to obtain a positive opinion to be admitted to the accession negotiations as such."[7] In early July, Slovakia's deputy prime minister, Jozef Kalman, claimed that his country had made good progress, especially economically, and that "in many fields, Slovakia is more advanced than some countries already permitted to negotiate." According to Kalman, "If the Republic of Slovakia is judged on the basis of objective criteria, then it will join the first group. We are well prepared for that."[8] Nevertheless, Slovakia's bid to join the EU continued to be undermined by questions about its democracy and by a dispute with Austria over the start-up of a Soviet-era nuclear reactor in Mochovce.[9]

In the summer of 1998, Commissioner van den Broek visited each of the five second-group countries, using the opportunity to both encourage and pressure them to continue with their reforms. In June, van den Broek visited Slovakia, where he appealed for free and fair parliamentary elections (upcoming in September). He also expressed the EU's concerns about nuclear safety and the Mochovce plant.[10] In late July, van den Broek visited Latvia and Lithuania. Although on these visits he praised the progress each country had made over the past year, van den Broek nevertheless declared that he could not prejudge the Commission's upcoming report. While in Lithuania, the commissioner also stressed the EU's concern about the lack of a decommissioning plan for the Ignalina nuclear plant.[11] Van den Broek visited Romania and Bulgaria in September. In Bucharest, he called upon the Romanian government to make greater efforts to fight international crime and strengthen its controls over immigration.[12]

The lobbying efforts of the second-group countries continued into the fall, as government leaders from these countries visited Brussels. After a meeting with Commission officials in early October, Prime Minister Vagnorious warned that a decision not to admit Lithuania to accession negotiations could have negative consequences for the stability of his country. He also warned that it could negatively affect public opinion in Lithuania, causing it to become more "Europessimistic." Vagnorious claimed that while his government was aware that negotiations would take a long time, the government needed an early political decision on beginning them, and he expressed his hope that the "Commission will be our advocate."[13]

Latvia's president, Guntis Ulmanis, visited Brussels later in the month, on the heels of a national referendum supporting changes to Latvia's citizenship laws that made it easier for ethnic Russians to become citizens. Following the vote, the Riga government declared that Latvia now met all conditions for joining the accession talks. According to Latvia's EU ambassador, "There remain no more obstacles to the opening of accession negotiations." The Latvian government claimed that it could quickly catch up with the other countries in the bilateral screening process and indicated that it had already drafted position papers for the seven chapters on which the first-group countries were to begin negotiations in November.[14] During Ulmanis's visit, the Commission praised the new citizenship law and promised that its report would take account of the "considerable progress" that Latvia had made in the past year.[15]

Also visiting Brussels in October were government leaders from Bulgaria and Romania. While the governments of both countries understood that they had little chance of joining the accession negotiations anytime soon, they nevertheless hoped, in the words of Bulgaria's prime minister, for a "positive assessment" from the Commission in November.[16]

The visit of government leaders from Slovakia, however, was delayed by the outcome of legislative elections in late September; these elections resulted in a parliamentary majority for political parties opposed to the government of Prime Minister Meciar. By the end of October, a new four-party coalition government had been formed that included a party representing the country's Hungarian minority. The new government pledged to fulfill the political criteria for EU membership, including the passage of a new minority language law to protect speakers of Hungarian. It also asked the Commission to delay its report on Slovakia until closer to the December Vienna summit to give the EU a chance to more fully consider the changes that were taking place.[17]

While the EU welcomed the election results in Slovakia and the Commission expressed its hope that "measures will be taken to improve the political climate and solve problems related to political criteria for EU accession which so far have kept Slovakia out of the negotiating process," the Commission also insisted that it was "premature to speculate, at this stage, on speeding up Slovakia's accession process." Instead, it declared that the EU must await further political and legislative decisions by the new government before reviewing its evaluation of Slovakia's internal situation.[18]

There was considerable pressure on the Commission to reconsider Slovakia's application, however. Following the September elections, the EP's Foreign Affairs Committee called upon the Commission to postpone the adoption of its report on Slovakia for several months to give the new government time to adopt reforms.[19] The Commission promised, however, only that it would wait "as late as possible" to make its assessment of Slovakia.[20] Also supporting Slovakia's bid was Czech President Václav Havel, who claimed that Slovakia would now rapidly catch up with the more advanced applicants, and urged the speedy acceptance of Slovakia into the first group of countries negotiating accession.[21]

Another development in September was Malta's decision to reactivate its application for membership. In announcing this decision, Malta's newly elected Nationalist government stated its desire to join the first group of countries negotiating accession. The EU welcomed Malta's renewed application, and the Council instructed the Commission to reassess Malta's preparedness for membership. The Commission responded that it would examine the economic and political situation in Malta in order to determine whether its earlier (1993) Opinion needed to be updated. It would also examine how to fit Malta into the accession process and would include its thoughts on this matter in its report to the Council in November. However, the Commission stressed that the EU's decisions on Malta would not affect the negotiations with other countries, and it reaffirmed that each applicant must be considered "according to its own merits." Thus, the Commission addressed the possibility that some member states might demand a price for allowing Malta to join the accession negotiations; for instance, Sweden might insist that Latvia and Lithuania be allowed to join the negotiations as well.[22]

THE FIRST PROGRESS REPORTS

The hopes of the second-group countries to quickly begin accession negotiations were disappointed, however. In its first regular progress reports issued on November 4, 1998, the Commission praised the reform efforts made by the second-group countries yet nevertheless restated its view that none was ready to begin accession negotiations.[23]

All was not bleak, however. In its reports, the Commission singled out Latvia for special praise, concluding that there was "sufficient progress to consider the possibility of making a positive recommendation on the opening of negotiations at the end of 1999." It also praised the progress made by Lithuania and Slovakia, expressing the hope that, for these countries, it could "recommend the opening of accession negotiations within a reasonable length of time." The Commission also encouraged the continuation of political reform in Slovakia, noting that the new political situation in that country "enables us to consider the opening of accession negotiations, provided the regular, stable, and democratic working of the institutions is confirmed."[24]

At the same time, however, the Commission declared that, while all five second-group applicants had made considerable progress in their economic reforms, they all had further work to do. In particular, it noted that Bulgaria and Romania fell far short of meeting the necessary economic criteria for membership, but that while Bulgaria had made significant improvements over the past year, the situation in Romania had actually deteriorated. Regarding Malta, the Commission reaffirmed the need to update its 1993 Opinion and expressed the hope that it could do so by February of the next year.[25]

Reactions to the Commission's reports varied widely among the applicant countries. The Lithuanian government was particularly unhappy, with President Vagnorius claiming that his country's bid to join the EU was being unfairly held up by concerns about the safety of the Ignalina nuclear plant. The Lithuanian government was also upset that Latvia had been singled out for praise by the Commission and told that it might join accession talks in 1999. With Estonia already having begun concrete negotiations, the Lithuanian government feared that it was falling behind its two Baltic neighbors in its bid for EU membership.[26]

The reaction of the Slovakian government was more positive. Two days after the Commission issued its reports, the new Slovak prime minister, Mikudas Dzurinda, met in Brussels with van den Broek and Santer. At a press conference after the meeting, Dzurinda expressed disappointment that the Commission's report did not offer any concrete prospects for beginning negotiations. He claimed, however, that this was because the report was "exclusively based on Slovakia's past," and he promised that the new government would do everything possible to ensure that next year's evaluation would be more favorable. For the Commission's part, van den Broek praised the ambitious reform program of the Slovak government, and he expressed confidence that the new government was heading in the right direction with its policies. The Commission also announced the creation of a special high-level Working Group to assist Slovakia's integration with the EU, a step that the prime minister greeted as a "positive signal" to the Slovak people.[27]

The Commission presented its progress reports to the Council on November 9. At this meeting, the member states generally refrained from criticizing the reports, while praising the Commission for its objectivity and realism. The French government, however, along with Italy and Greece, warned against the risk to stability in Southeastern Europe if the EU isolated too markedly Romania and Bulgaria.[28]

The warning about isolating Romania and Bulgaria was repeated at a Council meeting in early December. Also at this meeting, the Nordic member states (Denmark, Sweden, and Finland) voiced their preference for a "more positive and encouraging treatment" of Latvia and Lithuania, while others declared that the EU should send a more positive signal to Slovakia to reward it for changes made since the September elections. However, a majority of the member states agreed that the EU should not give precise dates or perspectives on negotiations to any of the second-group countries at this point, fearing that to do so would only further divide the applicant countries, with possibly dangerous results for regional stability. As a consequence, while noting the particular progress of Latvia and Lithuania and the new political situation in Slovakia, as well as the Commission's intentions to propose opening negotiations with Latvia at the end of 1999 and its views on the prospect of opening negotiations with Lithuania and Slovakia, the Council decided that "at this stage" it would "not make any recommendations to the European Council to extend the accession negotiations."[29]

The Council's conclusions were endorsed by EU leaders at the Vienna summit on December 11–12. In its "Presidency Conclusions" for the summit, the European Council welcomed the progress made by the second-group countries in preparing for negotiations, and it expressed the hope that the transition from the multilateral to bilateral screening of the *acquis communautaire* beginning early in the next year "will confer new dynamism to the [accession] process and thus foster preparation for negotiations." The European Council also invited the Commission to present its further progress reports next fall, in time for consideration by the December 1999 summit in Helsinki.[30]

Following the Vienna summit, the Commission indicated that it was not disappointed that the member states had chosen not to follow its recommendation to give Latvia, and also Lithuania and Slovakia, more precise dates for beginning negotiations. Instead, the Commission pointed to its next round of progress reports (due in October) and the political decisions on enlargement to be taken by the European Council in Helsinki.[31] The governments of Latvia, Lithuania, and Slovakia did express some frustration, however, and all three indicated that they expected to be invited by the Helsinki summit to begin accession negotiations in 2000.[32]

TOWARD A NEW STRATEGY

After the Vienna summit, the five second-group applicants and Malta continued their campaign to join the accession negotiations. Slovakia's hopes were significantly bolstered in April 1999 when, on a visit to Bratislava, Commissioner van den Broek praised the democratic reform progress of the new Slovak government. He also declared that if Slovakia continued with its political and economic reforms, the Commission should be able to recommend in October that the member states begin accession negotiations with Slovakia in early 2000.[33] In May, Slovakia took another step toward fulfilling the political conditions of EU membership when it held direct popular elections for its president, thus filling a post that had been vacant for more than a year because of the authoritarian policies of former Prime Minister Meciar.[34]

Slovakia's chances of joining the accession negotiations were also bolstered by the strong support of several first-group applicants. In particular, the Czech Republic, which feared the disruption of close bilateral ties if the two countries did not join the EU together, gave strong backing to Slovakia's bid to join the negotiations. Also supporting Bratislava was Hungary, because of the large Hungarian minority in Slovakia. In May 1999, a summit meeting of the revived Visegrad group (Poland, Hungary, the Czech Republic, and Slovakia) declared that Slovakia should be allowed to begin accession negotiations as soon as possible.[35]

Latvia's chances were also improving. At an April meeting in Brussels, Commission President Santer told the Latvian prime minister, Vilas Kristopans, that if his country continued with its economic and structural reforms, the Commission should be able to recommend to the member states in October that they begin accession negotiations with Latvia. Santer also welcomed Latvia's (April 1999) decision to abolish the death penalty—thereby aligning its laws and human rights standards with those of the EU—as an important step toward membership.[36] Latvia's bid to join the negotiations was also strongly supported by Sweden and the other Nordic member states.

Lithuania's situation was a bit more problematic, mainly because of the Lithuanian government's reluctance to provide a firm plan for closing the Ignalina nuclear plant, a condition set by the Commission for beginning accession negotiations. However, the Swedish government—a strong supporter of Lithuania's membership bid—argued that a schedule for closing the plant should not be a precondition for beginning negotiations, although it also insisted that Lithuania must produce such a plan before it could join the EU.[37] In addition to the backing of Sweden and the other Nordic member states, Lithuania's inclusion in the accession negotiations was also supported by Poland, a neighboring country with close historical and political ties to Lithuania. Also supporting Lithuania's inclusion was the idea of Baltic solidarity, as well as concern about the negative consequences for political and economic reform in Lithuania if it was isolated from its Baltic neighbors and left behind in the accession process.

Also in a strong position was Malta. The Commission completed its review of Malta's reactivated application in February 1999, concluding that Malta was advanced enough economically and politically to begin accession negotiations. In March, the Commission received permission from the Council to begin bilateral screening of the *acquis communautaire* with Malta.[38] Despite its late entry into the accession process, Malta's application was considered relatively unproblematic. The main difficulty was presented by the island's small size, which required the EU to reform its institutions to accommodate the membership of another microstate. There were also concerns about the anti-EU views of Malta's main opposition party, the Labor Party. However, Malta's membership bid was strongly supported by the Italian government and by those (including the EP) who argued that Malta's accession would give substance to the EU's new Mediterranean strategy.

While Slovakia, Latvia, Lithuania, and Malta were all making considerable progress with their reforms and moving toward beginning accession negotiations, Romania and Bulgaria appeared to be falling further behind the other applicants. The Commission's first progress report was the most critical of these two countries, although it did offer some praise for reform efforts made by Bulgaria. In particular, the Commission was critical of Romania, where it said the economic situation had actually deteriorated over the past year. The Commission also criticized both the Romanian and Bulgarian governments for lax border controls, while it criticized the former government for its insufficient efforts to combat organized crime.[39] On the positive side, both countries had their own advocates within the EU and among the other applicants: Greece for Bulgaria (because of security concerns), and France and Hungary for Romania (the former because of long-standing cultural ties; the latter because of the large ethnic Hungarian minority in Romania). Concern about isolating Romania and Bulgaria was also voiced by several member states in response to the Commission's first progress reports in November 1998 (see above).

Nevertheless, there appeared to be a growing differentiation among the six applicants of the second tier. While the EU prospects of Slovakia, Latvia, Lithuania, and Malta appeared fairly good, those of Bulgaria and Romania were fairly dim. It appeared that only the first four applicants had a good chance of beginning accession negotiations any time soon.

The outbreak of war in Kosovo in March 1999 changed all of this, however, and led to a rethinking of enlargement strategy by the EU. As the EU's focus shifted to Southeastern Europe and broader security concerns as a result of the Kosovo war, support grew for the idea of including Romania and Bulgaria in the accession negotiations. Many in the EU felt that leaving these countries outside the negotiations could send them the wrong message, thus undermining their efforts at political and economic reform and having disastrous consequences for stability and security in Southeastern Europe. Including these countries in the negotiations, on the other hand, could bolster their reforms and assist them in becoming pillars of stability in the region. It was also felt that Romania and Bulgaria should be rewarded for their (domestically unpopular) support for NATO's bombing campaign against Serbia, a fellow Orthodox country. The EU also recognized the economic hardship for these countries caused by the Kosovo conflict and agreed that this situation deserved special consideration in the EU's decisions on enlargement strategy.[40] Emblematic of this shift in sentiment, in May 1999 British Prime Minister Blair visited Romania and Bulgaria and promised both governments that he would work for their early inclusion in the accession negotiations.[41]

Nevertheless, the June 3–4 Cologne summit did not make any major decisions on enlargement. In its "Presidency Conclusions" for the summit, the European Council merely welcomed "the fact that the analytical examination of the *acquis* with [the five second-group applicants] has now moved on from the multilateral phase to the crucial bilateral phase, which will allow those countries to speed up their preparations for membership." It also reaffirmed that "the Helsinki Council will examine the progress made by the accession candidates and draw the necessary conclusions." However, the European Council also invited the Commission, "in its next progress reports, to consider measures which can help crystallize [the prospect of accession] for all applicant countries." It also asked the Commission to submit a report on Malta's preparations for accession in time for the Helsinki summit, opening the possibility that a decision to begin negotiations with Malta could be made then as well.[42]

At the post-summit press conference, Austrian Foreign Minister Schüssel announced that there was "clear agreement" among the member states on a decision, at Helsinki, to include Latvia, Lithuania, and Slovakia in the negotiations. The status of Romania and Bulgaria, he indicated, was not yet clear.[43]

By September, however, support seemed to be growing for a more inclusive strategy that would include all of the second-group applicants in the accession negotiations. The Kosovo war was clearly the major catalyst in this shift of sentiment, since this led to increased support for Romania and Bulgaria within the EU and underlined the importance of enlargement for bringing stability and security to Southeastern Europe. Certain member states, especially Britain and Germany, were strongly advocating a change of strategy. Each of the second-group applicants also had its own champions among the member states, creating broad political support for a more inclusive strategy. Also favoring a broader strategy was the new Commission, including President-designate Romano Prodi and the incoming enlargement commissioner, Günter Verheugen. According to Prodi, a broader strategy was necessary to ensure stability and security in Eastern and Southeastern Europe. EU enlargement, he argued, must be guided by a "political vision, not a technocratic one."[44]

By the fall of 1999, therefore, the EU appeared ready for a major revision of its enlargement strategy. Before making this decision, however, the member states awaited the Commission's second set of progress reports and its new recommendations on the accession process. Several of the second-group countries also had major problems to settle before the EU would agree to admit them into the negotiations.

THE SECOND PROGRESS REPORTS

A major hurdle for several of the second-group applicants to overcome before they could begin accession negotiations was the issue of nuclear safety. The EU required that applicants develop comprehensive energy plans that respected Western nuclear safety standards and included plans for the closure of unsafe Soviet-era nuclear plants. Some applicants balked at this latter demand, however, because of the importance of nuclear power for their domestic energy supply (the Ignalina plant produces 80 percent of Lithuania's electricity, for instance) and the considerable cost of closing these plants. Particular points of conflict have been Ignalina, the Kozloduy plant in Bulgaria, and the Bohunice and Mochovce reactors in Slovakia.[45]

However, while recognizing that the closure of these plants posed "complex questions," the Commission declared that on the issue of nuclear safety the EU "cannot be flexible."[46] In the "Presidency Conclusions" of the June 1999 Cologne summit, the European Council stressed the importance of nuclear safety standards "in the context of the Union's enlargement" and called on the Commission to examine this issue thoroughly in its next regular progress reports on the applicant countries.[47] And in confirmation hearings before the EP in early September 1999, Commissioner-designate Verheugen vowed that no applicant would be allowed to join the EU as long as it operated unsafe nuclear power plants. Before Bulgaria, Lithuania, and Slovakia could begin accession negotiations, Verheugen declared, they must pledge to close their unsafe nuclear facilities.[48]

Lithuania was the first of these countries to announce a firm plan to decommission its unsafe reactors, declaring in early September that it would shut down the first of two Ignalina reactors by 2005 and review in 2004 the conditions under which the second could be closed by 2009 (the deadline set by the Commission).[49] Later that month, Slovakia announced that it would decommission the two oldest reactors at Bohunice in 2006 and 2008. This plan was greeted by the Commission "as an important step in [Slovakia's] European integration efforts." However, it was rejected as inadequate by the Austrian government, which threatened to block Slovakia's admission to accession talks unless the closure date was brought forward. The Slovakian government responded that acceding to Austria's demand would have serious negative economic consequences, since the two reactors accounted for 20 percent of Slovakia's total power supply, and Bratislava had recently invested $190 million in modernizing the reactors as well.[50]

Also attracting the EU's attention in the fall of 1999 was a proposed new language law in Latvia that would protect the preeminence of Latvian (and possibly discriminate against minority languages, especially Russian), and the decision of a local government in the Czech Republic to build a wall separating Roma families from other residents.[51]

On October 13, the Commission issued its Second Regular Reports on the progress toward accession of each of the applicant countries, along with a "Composite Paper" detailing its recommendations on the accession process. In its "Composite Paper," the Commission recommended doubling (to twelve) the number of applicant countries negotiating accession, by including all five of the second-group countries and Malta in the accession negotiations. However, the Commission attached certain preconditions for beginning negotiations with Romania and Bulgaria. Romania, the Commission declared, must first take steps to deal with its weak economy and budgetary position and implement structural reform of its child-care institutions. Negotiations with Bulgaria, on the other hand, were conditional upon the Bulgarian government's submission of an acceptable closure plan for the first four units of the Kozloduy nuclear power plant and further confirmation of economic progress.[52]

In its report, the Commission stressed that the "principle of differentiation" would be applied in the expanded negotiations, giving the newcomers the possibility of catching up with the already negotiating countries. In this new "regatta" approach, the finishing time of accession negotiations would be different for individual applicants, determined only by their preparedness for EU membership. The Commission also recommended that Turkey be given official candidate status by the EU (see the next section), and it proposed new procedures for conducting accession negotiations and a new policy on transition periods for new member states (see chapter 9).[53]

The Commission's report also evaluated the progress of each of the applicants toward meeting the political and economic criteria for EU membership. While generally praising the progress made by all of the applicants (except Turkey) toward "building stable and robust democracies" and "respecting the rule of law," the Commission expressed concern about "the treatment of minorities and the Roma, and the situation of children in care in Romania." It also expressed concern about the rights of linguistic minorities in Latvia and Estonia. The Commission also found that most of the applicants either already fulfilled (Cyprus and Malta), were close to fulfilling (Hungary, Poland, Slovenia, Estonia, and the Czech Republic), or were making progress toward fulfilling (Latvia, Slovakia, and Lithuania) the economic criteria for membership, although the Czech Republic "needs to make serious progress." Bulgaria and Romania were the economic laggards among the applicants, although the Commission noted that the former "continues to make significant progress and shows sustained efforts in the economic reform process," although from a very low starting point. In Romania, on the other hand, the Commission concluded that the economic situation had, "at best, stabilized compared with last year." The Commission also singled out Poland and the Czech Republic for criticism regarding progress with legal and institutional preparations for membership, declaring that in these countries "the pace of transposition [of the *acquis communautaire*] remains sluggish." According to the Commission, "The slow pace and piecemeal approach to [legislative and institutional] alignment in these two countries is not consistent with their political aspirations for rapid accession to the EU."[54]

The analysis of the second regular progress reports provided the basis for the Commission's revision of the Accession Partnerships for each of the CEECs. The revised Accession Partnerships, which included short-term priorities to be realized in 2000 as well as medium-term measures for each applicant, were formally adopted by the Commission in December 1999.[55]

In justifying the Commission's new regatta approach for accession negotiations, Prodi declared that it would be wrong to insist that all applicants fully meet the EU's economic criteria before beginning accession negotiations. The risk in taking such a "hard line approach," he argued, was that countries like Romania and Bulgaria, "having already made great efforts and sacrifices, will become disillusioned and turn their backs on us." If this happens, he declared, "an historic opportunity [to unite Europe] will have been lost perhaps forever." To prevent this from happening, a "bold step forward" needed to be taken. Thus, according to Prodi, the Commission was recommending to the European Council that it open accession negotiations in 2000 with all applicants that have met the Copenhagen political criteria, "and have proved ready to take the necessary measures to comply with the economic [criteria]."[56]

The Commission's new recommendations on accession strategy were greeted enthusiastically by the second-group countries, especially Romania and Bulgaria, whose governments pledged to meet the conditions set by the Commission for beginning negotiations. While the first-group countries also welcomed the expansion of accession negotiations, they insisted that this should not slow down their own timetable for completing negotiations and joining the EU.[57]

At an extraordinary meeting in Tampere, Finland, several days after the Commission issued its report, the European Council largely endorsed the Commission's new strategy. A broad consensus among the member states in favor of the Commission's plan to expand the accession negotiations was reported, thus paving the way for a formal decision at Helsinki.[58]

THE HELSINKI SUMMIT

In the run-up to Helsinki, several CEECs took measures to ensure a positive decision by the European Council on their applications. In late November, the

Romanian government announced that it was creating a new "National Agency for the Protection of Children," in an effort to satisfy one of the conditions imposed by the Commission for beginning accession negotiations.[59] Also in late November, the Bulgarian government announced plans for the early closure of units one through four of the Kozloduy plant (units one and two before 2003, units three and four likely by 2006), thus satisfying one of the Commission's conditions for opening negotiations.[60] In doing so, Bulgaria followed Lithuania and Slovakia in addressing the EU's concerns about nuclear safety. Although the Austrian government still objected to Slovakia's closure plans for the Bohunice plant, it had agreed not to block the beginning of accession talks with that country. It continued to insist, however, that Slovakia would not be allowed to join the EU unless it decommissioned its unsafe nuclear reactors.[61]

Also acting to satisfy EU concerns was the Latvian government. On the eve of the Helsinki summit, the Latvian parliament passed an amended language law that was less restrictive of minority languages than a previous version and that met with EU approval.[62] Although its place in the accession negotiations was not in danger, the Czech government made certain that the controversial wall separating Roma and other residents in Usti nad Lebem was torn down before the Helsinki summit.[63]

The Helsinki European Council on December 10–11, 1999, was the "enlargement summit." In its "Presidency Conclusions" for the summit, the European Council "[confirmed] the importance of the enlargement process launched in Luxembourg in December 1997 for the stability and prosperity for the entire European continent." For this reason, it declared, "an efficient and credible enlargement process must be sustained."[64]

In Helsinki, the European Council formally decided to begin accession negotiations with Romania, Slovakia, Latvia, Lithuania, Bulgaria, and Malta in February 2000. It also announced that in the accession negotiations, "each candidate will be judged on its own merits," and that the applicants just beginning negotiations would have the possibility of catching up with those already in negotiations. The European Council also declared that "progress in negotiations must go hand in hand with progress in incorporating the *acquis* into legislation and actually enforcing and implementing it."[65]

With the Helsinki decisions of the European Council, therefore, the EU formally abandoned the strategy of enlargement in groups or "waves" that it had adopted in Luxembourg and adopted instead the regatta approach to accession negotiations. In explaining this change, Commissioner Verheugen argued that the EU did not commit an error two years before in deciding on the two-group strategy; instead, the political situation in Europe had completely changed in the meantime, making it necessary to adopt a more inclusive strategy in order to ensure stability and security in Eastern and Southeastern Europe.[66]

Verheugen called the summit's decision to open accession negotiations with all candidates "an historic step towards the unification of Europe," declaring that "the iron curtain has been definitively removed." The reactions of the six countries newly admitted to the negotiations were equally enthusiastic, with most declaring their wish to catch up as quickly as possible with the already negotiating countries. While the first-group countries welcomed the European Council's decision, they also expressed concern that expanding the negotiations could delay their own accession because the Commission's resources would be stretched too thin in conducting parallel negotiations with twelve countries. Responding to this concern, Verheugen declared that the extension of negotiations to additional countries "in no case means that the first [group] applicants should fear any delay in the accession process." "Enlargement is a top priority for the Commission," he said. "If we [the Commission] need more support we will get it."[67]

The Helsinki summit also addressed the issue of a timetable for enlargement. Since the beginning of substantive negotiations in November 1998, the governments of the more advanced applicants had pressed the EU to set concrete dates for completing the negotiations and for accession, arguing that firm dates were needed to maintain public support for accession and to encourage difficult reforms in their countries. Both the Commission and the member states were opposed to setting dates, however, arguing that the negotiations were not yet far enough along to consider doing so (although in April 1999 the EP urged that such dates be set). The EU also believed, against the arguments of the applicants, that setting firm dates would be counterproductive, leading to complacency in the candidate countries and reducing their willingness to make necessary reforms. Arguing against setting dates, Commissioner van den Broek declared that the EU "should never give the impression that the 'time' factor could become more important than the 'conditionality' factor."[68] As a result, neither the Vienna nor Cologne summits considered setting target dates for the next accessions.[69]

The debate about target dates for accession was reignited in September 1999, however, when Commission President-designate Prodi, in a speech before the EP, urged the European Council "to give serious consideration in Helsinki to setting a firm date for the accession of those countries which are best prepared [for membership], even if this means granting lengthy transition periods to deal with their social and economic problems."[70] Prodi's bold statement contradicted the more cautious view of his designated enlargement commissioner, who declared that he opposed setting deadlines because "this risks creating disappointment if they are subsequently not met." Verheugen was only willing to say that by the middle of 2000 it might be possible to set deadlines for ending the negotiations for individual applicants, but not for actual accession.[71]

Prodi's intervention caused considerable unease among the member states, most of whom remained reluctant to talk about firm dates for accession. As a result, Prodi was forced to retreat from his statement. At a press conference in Helsinki at the end of September, he said only that the applicants should be given a "precise pathway" for accession. According to Prodi, the applicants have a right to know how long the accession process will take, "even if we don't go into the details of the dates."[72]

The Commission's Second Regular Report also avoided the mention of specific dates for accession, saying only that the EU should be "ready to decide from 2002 on the accession of candidates that fulfil all necessary criteria." This meant, primarily, conclusion of the planned IGC on institutional reform and full ratification of the resulting treaty. By that time (2002), the Commission considered it possible that negotiations with the most advanced candidates would be concluded.[73] Meeting in Tallin, Estonia, two days before the Commission issued its report, the foreign ministers of the six negotiating countries had proposed a slightly accelerated timetable, urging the EU to conclude negotiations by the end of 2001 at the very latest and to be ready to admit new members in 2002.[74]

Heading into the Helsinki summit, therefore, there was little support among the member states for setting a firm timetable or target dates for the next accessions,[75] and at Helsinki the European Council did not do so. Instead, following the Commission's recommendation, it merely declared that "after ratification of the results of [the IGC] the Union should be in a position to welcome new Member States from the end of 2002 as soon as they have demonstrated their ability to assume the obligations of membership and once the negotiating process has been successfully completed."[76] According to Commissioner Verheugen, ratification of the new accession treaties (by both the member states and candidates) would only begin after 2002, with the process taking at least another year, making 2004 the earliest likely date for the next accessions.[77]

In response to the Helsinki conclusions, Poland, Hungary, and the other first-group countries insisted on sticking with their goal of accession in 2003. According to the Polish government, negotiations could be concluded in the first half of 2001, leaving eighteen months for ratification of the entry agreement. Together with the other first-group applicants, the Polish and Hungarian governments claimed that ratification of the IGC and accession treaties could take place in parallel and need not be successive.[78]

A NEW POLICY ON TURKEY

The Helsinki summit also represented a major turning point in EU relations with Turkey. After being excluded from the accession process by the Luxembourg summit, the Turkish government adopted a harsh stance toward the EU that led to a deterioration of relations in early 1998. Turkey boycotted the March 12 European Conference in London, whose main purpose was to integrate Turkey, and it harshly criticized the subsequent beginning of accession negotiations with Cyprus. In May, the British EU presidency launched a diplomatic effort to improve relations with Ankara, including pressure on Greece to remove its veto on EU funds promised to Turkey as part of the 1995 Customs Union agreement. The British government also sought to renew the EU's political dialogue with Ankara by convincing it to attend a meeting of the EU–Turkey Association Council in Brussels in late May; in the end, however, the Turkish government decided to boycott this meeting as well.[79]

Soon thereafter, however, the EU's relations with Turkey appeared to be on the mend. In late May, the governments of Germany and Turkey decided to normalize political relations, ending several months of tension.[80] At the Cardiff summit in June, the European Council sought to send a positive signal to Turkey by reaffirming its eligibility for EU membership and endorsing the Commission's proposals to widen and enhance the EU-Turkey Customs Union Agreement.[81] Another step forward came in the fall, when Germany's new chancellor, Gerhard Schröder, pledged to work "emphatically" toward Turkey's membership in the EU.[82] The Turkish government also welcomed, as a positive sign, that the Commission's first progress reports in November included a section on Turkey, along with its evaluations of the other applicant countries. Even though the Commission was critical of "persistent violations of human rights and important deficiencies in the treatment of civilians" in Turkey, Ankara claimed that Turkey's inclusion in the Commission's report implicitly recognized it as a candidate for EU membership.[83]

In late 1998, however, EU-Turkish relations suffered another setback when the Italian government refused to extradite jailed Kurdish guerrilla leader Abdullah Öcalan. As a result, in March 1999 a top official of Turkey's Foreign Ministry painted a gloomy picture of bilateral relations, declaring that Turkey's relations with the EU were in a "sick period," and that the Turkish public had lost all interest in joining the EU.[84]

In the summer of 1999, however, there were new signs of a shift in EU policy toward Turkey. At the June Cologne summit, Chancellor Schröder was unsuccessful in his attempt, backed by most other member states, to get the European Council to agree to treat Turkey as a "candidate country" for EU membership.[85] While the Turkish government welcomed Schröder's efforts (and criticized the EU for allowing one member state, Greece, to determine its policy), it nevertheless declared that the summit's disappointing results were not enough to change its approach to relations with the EU. Therefore, Turkey declined an invitation to attend the second European Conference in late July.[86]

In early July, however, Commissioner-designate Verheugen stated that Turkey had a good chance of being named an official candidate at Helsinki, as long as it met two key conditions: it did not execute Öcalan (now convicted and in a Turkish prison); and it implemented in-depth political and legal reform, including making progress in human rights.[87] Also in July, the Greek and Turkish governments resumed discussions on low-key issues such as trade, the environment, and cultural cooperation.[88] Bilateral relations further improved after the massive Turkish earthquake in August, as a result of Greek sympathy and support for the quake victims.

At the end of August, the Greek government announced that it was ready to lift its long-standing veto on a portion of the EU financial aid promised to Turkey as part of the 1995 Customs Union deal, citing the need to help Turkey recover from the devastating earthquake. However, Athens added that it was still not ready to allow the EU to name Turkey an official candidate for membership, on a par with the other applicants.[89]

Soon thereafter, Commissioner-designate Verheugen declared, at confirmation hearings before the EP, that he favored naming Turkey a candidate country at Helsinki, since this would bolster its democratic reform movement and strengthen its ties to the West. However, he emphasized that Turkey did not presently meet the EU's conditions for membership, or even for beginning accession negotiations, because of problems with its democracy, rule of law, human rights, and protection of minorities.[90]

By the end of the summer, therefore, there appeared to be growing support for a change of EU policy toward Turkey. This shift in sentiment stemmed not only from the disastrous earthquake and the widespread sympathy for Turkey it evoked but also from the Kosovo conflict and increased appreciation of Turkey's role in any EU strategy aimed at stabilizing the Balkans and Southeastern Europe. Also pushing hard for Turkey's inclusion in the EU was the U.S. government, which valued Turkey's strategic role as a bridge to the Middle East/Islamic world and a key partner country in NATO. While touring the earthquake zone in early September, U.S. Secretary of State Madeleine Albright declared it "essential that Turkey become a . . . candidate [for EU membership]."[91] Another important factor enabling a change of EU policy on Turkey was the Greek government's more sympathetic view of its neighbor and traditional enemy.

Responding to this improved atmosphere in EU-Turkish relations, Ankara requested the EU to settle the issue of its candidacy at Helsinki, warning that it would try only once more to gain candidate status before abandoning the attempt.[92]

A major breakthrough came at an informal meeting of EU foreign ministers on September 5, where the Greek government announced that it was ready "in principle" to accept Turkey as an official candidate for EU membership. According to Greece's Foreign Minister George Papandreou, "It is in Greece's interest to see a European Turkey, a Turkey that is closer to the EU and in the final analysis a member of the EU." However, at the meeting it was still clear that there was no consensus on how to frame EU policy on Turkey.[93]

The outlines of a new EU policy on Turkey were contained in the Commission's October progress report. While the Commission proposed giving Turkey candidate status, it also declared that accession negotiations must await Turkey's fulfilling the Copenhagen political criteria. The Commission also proposed an "enhanced political dialogue" with Turkey focusing on human rights issues, and the adoption of an Accession Partnership that would detail the steps Turkey needed to take to prepare for accession.[94]

At the extraordinary Tampere summit on October 18, EU leaders agreed on their desire to make a positive decision on Turkey in Helsinki. The Greek government in particular, however, stressed the need for "genuine negotiations" on Cyprus as a precondition for such a decision.[95] Thus, Turkey's candidacy prospects received a boost in November from the agreement of Greek and Turkish Cypriot leaders to new UN-sponsored talks (the "proximity talks") in New York on

December 3. Also boosting Turkey's hopes was U.S. President Clinton's call, while on a November state visit to Turkey, for the EU to admit Turkey because of its importance to European peace and security.[96]

Before the EU's new policy could be confirmed in Helsinki, however, the Greek government insisted on a couple of conditions for lifting its veto of Turkey's candidacy. One was its insistence that Turkey agree to international arbitration of its territorial disputes with Greece in the Aegean; the other was that the EU must agree to admitting a divided Cyprus in the event that a political settlement for the island could not be reached before the prospective date of accession. On the latter question, in particular, there was disagreement, with the Netherlands and several other member states resisting any promise to admit a divided Cyprus.[97] Working against a Greek veto on Turkey, however, was Athens' desire to join EMU as soon as possible, with several member states (including France and the Netherlands) making it clear that they saw a linkage between these two issues.[98]

In Helsinki, the European Council announced that "Turkey is a candidate State destined to join the Union on the basis of the same criteria as applied to the other candidate States." It also approved a list of pre-accession measures for Turkey that included the "enhanced political dialogue" and an Accession Partnership. However, the European Council also agreed to a carefully phrased set of conditions for Turkey's candidacy that was imposed by Greece. These conditions included the statement that candidate states should bring any "outstanding border disputes and other related issues" they cannot resolve themselves to the International Court of Justice, and that the European Council would "review the situation relating to any outstanding disputes . . . at the latest by the end of 2004." The European Council also declared that a political settlement for Cyprus was not a "precondition" for Cyprus's membership in the EU.[99]

The wording of these conditions caused the Turkish government to balk, and a last-minute mission to Ankara by Verheugen and EU foreign policy spokesman Javier Solana was required (as well as a phone call to Turkey's prime minister by President Clinton) before the Turkish government could be persuaded to accept them. In particular, Ankara worried that by agreeing to the EU's candidacy offer it would be forced to accept the accession of a divided Cyprus; it also worried that the 2004 date was a rigid deadline for submitting its territorial disputes with Greece to the International Court of Justice, but the EU assured Ankara that it was not.[100]

Thus, after putting out its own statement expressing reservations on the Cyprus and Aegean issues, a delighted Turkish government accepted the EU's Helsinki conditions. According to Prime Minister Bulent Ecevit, the EU's decision to grant it candidacy opens "new horizons" for Turkey. He added that Turkey would meet the EU's accession criteria faster than anyone expected. After deciding to accept the EU's conditions for candidacy, Ecevit joined the heads of state and government of the other twelve candidate countries at the closing session of the Helsinki summit.[101]

Also welcoming the Helsinki decisions on Turkey was the Greek government. According to Greek Prime Minister Costas Simitis, Turkey's candidacy marks a "historic shift toward peace, security and development in our region [of Europe]."[102] The Greek government also insisted that it wants a "real" candidacy for Turkey, not merely a symbolic one, with a detailed "road map" for accession. According to the Greek government, this will give Turkey sufficient incentive to make democratic and human rights reforms and to accept settlements for territorial disputes with Greece in the Aegean and in Cyprus.[103]

In early 2000, relations between the EU and Turkey (and between Greece and Turkey) continued to improve. The EU also worked on developing its Accession Partnership for Turkey, with the Commission promising to have this ready by October. Nevertheless, as the arrest of three reformist Kurdish mayors in February demonstrated (an act that the EU condemned), Turkey's bid for EU membership is still highly problematic, and many questions about its proper place in Europe remain.[104]

With the Helsinki summit decisions to open accession negotiations with all twelve applicants and name Turkey as an official candidate for membership, the EU adopted a broader and more ambitious enlargement strategy. Before it could admit new member states, however, the EU first had to prepare itself for enlargement by conducting difficult internal policy, budgetary, and institutional reforms. This internal reform process is the subject of the next two chapters. The progress of accession negotiations after November 1998 and their future prospects are then examined in chapter 9.

NOTES

1. John Thornhill, "Lithuania Presses the EU for Accession," *Financial Times*, 18 July 1997, 3; Thomas Urban, "Die Balten wollen mehr als warme Worte," *Frankfurter Rundschau*, 16 October 1997; Hannes Gamillscheg, "Lettland und Litauen wollen nicht abgehängt werden," *Frankfurter Rundschau*, 21 October 1997; Kevin Done, "Promise to East Rings Hollow," *Financial Times*, 17 July 1997, 3; Anatol Lieven, "Romania Presses its Case," *Financial Times*, 30 September 1997, 3; "EU Urged to Introduce Progress Reports," *Financial Times*, 10 November 1997, 3; Robert Anderson and Kevin Done, "Slovakia Struggles to Rebut EU Criticism," *Financial Times*, 16 October 1997, 3.

2. "Luxembourg Presidency Conclusions," paras. 10–30, available on the Internet at http://europa.eu.int/council/off/conclu/dec97.htm#intro.

3. See the interview with Lamoureux in Agence Europe, *Europe Daily Bulletin*, no. 7240, 12 June 1998, 7.

4. John Thornhill and Matej Vipotnik, "Reformed Lithuania Now Ready to Join, Says PM," *Financial Times*, 23 February 1998, 2.

5. Hannes Gamillscheg, "Adamkus peilt EU und NATO an," *Frankfurter Rundschau*, 27 February 1998.

6. Agence Europe, *Europe Daily Bulletin*, no. 7207, 24 April 1998, 7.

7. Agence Europe, *Europe Daily Bulletin*, no. 7210, 29 April 1998, 7.

8. Agence Europe, *Europe Daily Bulletin*, no. 7261, 11 July 1998, 6.

9. The Austrian government opposed the start-up of the Mochovce reactor, which it felt was unsafe and which was only 120 kilometers from its border. After start-up of the reactor in early June, the Austrian government threatened to take a more hostile stance toward Slovakia's EU application. See "Slovakia Warned over N-Plant," *Financial Times,* 20 May 1998, 2; Robert Anderson and Eric Frey, "Vienna Anger Grows Over Nuclear Plant," *Financial Times,* 25 May 1998, 2; and Eric Frey, "Protests as Slovak Reactor Starts Up," *Financial Times,* 9 June 1998, 2.

10. Agence Europe, *Europe Daily Bulletin,* no. 7245, 19 June 1998, 13; and Agence Europe, *Europe Daily Bulletin,* no. 7246, 20 June 1998, 8.

11. Agence Europe, *Europe Daily Bulletin,* no. 7267, 20–21 July 1998, 9–9a; Agence Europe, *Europe Daily Bulletin,* no. 7268, 23 July 1998, 11.

12. Agence Europe, *Europe Daily Bulletin,* no. 7296, 9 September 1998, 3; Agence Europe, *Europe Daily Bulletin,* no. 7300, 14–15 September 1998, 14.

13. Agence Europe, *Europe Daily Bulletin,* no. 7313, 2 October 1998, 7.

14. Matej Vipotnik, "Latvia's Key Vote on Russians," *Financial Times,* 3–4 October 1998, 2. On the Commission's positive response to the Latvian vote, see Agence Europe, *Europe Daily Bulletin,* no. 7316, 7 October 1998, 7. On the Council's response, see Agence Europe, *Europe Daily Bulletin,* no. 7318, 9 October 1998, 5.

15. Agence Europe, *Europe Daily Bulletin,* no. 7326, 21 October 1998, 8.

16. Agence Europe, *Europe Daily Bulletin,* no. 7318, 9 October 1998, 9; Agence Europe, *Europe Daily Bulletin,* no. 7326, 21 October 1998, 8.

17. Robert Anderson, "Slovakia Asks EU, NATO to Reconsider Membership," *Financial Times,* 30 October 1998, 3.

18. Agence Europe, *Europe Daily Bulletin,* no. 7310, 28–29 September 1998, 3. For the response of the Austrian EU presidency to the elections in Slovakia, see Agence Europe, *Europe Daily Bulletin,* no. 7313, 2 October 1998, 3.

19. Agence Europe, *Europe Daily Bulletin,* no. 7312, 1 October 1998, 3.

20. The quote is from Commissioner João de Deus Pinheiro, speaking during an emergency debate on Slovakia in the EP, cited in Agence Europe, *Europe Daily Bulletin,* no. 7319, 10 October 1998, 3.

21. Robert Anderson, "Slovak EU Entry Urged by Havel," *Financial Times,* 19 October 1998, 2.

22. Michael Smith, "Malta to Push for EU Entry," *Financial Times,* 8 September 1998, 2; Agence Europe, *Europe Daily Bulletin,* no. 7296, 9 September 1998, 3; Agence Europe, *Europe Daily Bulletin,* 10 September 1998, no. 7297, 8; Michael Smith, "Malta Knocks at EU Door Again," *Financial Times,* 17 September 1998, 2; Peel, "Talks on EU Entry for Cyprus Agreed," 2; Agence Europe, *Europe Daily Bulletin,* no. 7315, 5–6 October 1998, 5. The EP also welcomed Malta's decision, declaring in a resolution that Malta's membership would strengthen the EU's "Mediterranean dimension." See Agence Europe, *Europe Daily Bulletin,* no. 7318, 9 October 1998, 3–4.

23. European Commission, "Reports on Progress Towards Accession by Each of the Candidate Countries: Composite Paper" (November 4, 1998), available on the Internet at http://europa.eu.int/comm/dg1a/enlarge/report_11_98_en/ index.htm. See also Peel, "EU Warns Applicants on Slow Preparations," 3.

24. European Commission, "Reports on Progress Towards Accession by Each of the Candidate Countries: Composite Paper," 28. The quotes are from Commissioner van den

Broek's presentation of the Commission's progress reports to the EP on November 4, cited in Agence Europe, *Europe Daily Bulletin,* no. 7336, 5 November 1998, 6–7.

25. European Commission, "Reports on Progress Towards Accession by Each of the Candidate Countries: Composite Paper," 28–29 and 20–21 (on Malta).

26. Stefan Wagstyl and Matej Vipotnik, "Lithuania Angered by EU Demands," *Financial Times,* 12 November 1998.

27. Agence Europe, *Europe Daily Bulletin,* no. 7338, 7 November 1998, 4.

28. Agence Europe, *Europe Daily Bulletin,* no. 7339, 9–10 November 1998, 7.

29. Agence Europe, *Europe Daily Bulletin,* no. 7358, 7–8 December 1998, 5–6. For the text of the Council's conclusions on enlargement, see Agence Europe, *Europe Daily Bulletin,* no. 7359, 9 December 1998, 8–9.

30. "Presidency Conclusions" of the Vienna European Council, 11–12 December 1998, reprinted in Agence Europe, *Europe Daily Bulletin,* no. 7363 (special edition), 13 December 1998, 14. See also Peter Norman and Michael Smith, "EU Leaders Put Off Enlargement Decisions," *Financial Times,* 14 December 1998, 2.

31. Interview with DG IA Deputy Director-General Lamoureux, in Agence Europe, *Europe Daily Bulletin,* no. 7388, 22 January 1999, 13.

32. Kevin Done, "Slovakia Seeks UK Support for EU Entry," *Financial Times,* 28 January 1999, 3; Agence Europe, *Europe Daily Bulletin,* no. 7410, 22–23 February 1999, 10; Agence Europe, *Europe Daily Bulletin,* no. 7411, 24 February 1999, 10–11.

33. Agence Europe, *Europe Daily Bulletin,* no. 7447, 17 April 1999, 7. Also see van den Broek's comments at the EU-Slovakia Association Council meeting on April 24 in Luxembourg, cited in Agence Europe, *Europe Daily Bulletin,* no. 7455, 29 April 1999, 9; and Agence Europe, *Europe Daily Bulletin,* no. 7451, 23 April 1999, 8.

34. Robert Anderson, "Slovakia's EU Hopes Boosted," *Financial Times,* 1 June 1999, 2; Agence Europe, *Europe Daily Bulletin,* no. 7477, 3 June 1999, 4. A further step was taken by Slovakia in July 1999 when it passed a new law on the protection of minority languages. Afterward, Commissioner van den Broek declared that Slovakia now met the political criteria for beginning accession negotiations. See Agence Europe, *Europe Daily Bulletin,* no. 7508, 15 July 1999, 7. In September, the High-Level Working Group set up by the Commission in November 1998 to help Slovakia prepare for membership was dissolved, since the Commission considered that the Working Group had successfully completed its mission. See Agence Europe, *Europe Daily Bulletin,* no. 7551, 15 September 1999, 11–12.

35. Robert Anderson, "East European States Resume Co-Operation," *Financial Times,* 17 May 1999, 2.

36. Agence Europe, *Europe Daily Bulletin,* no. 7453, 26–27 April 1999, 12. On Latvia's abolition of the death penalty, see "Latvia Abolishes Death Penalty," *Financial Times,* 16 April 1999, 3; and Agence Europe, *Europe Daily Bulletin,* no. 7451, 23 April 1999, 5.

37. "Backing for Lithuania on EU," *Financial Times,* 5 April 1999, 5.

38. "Brussels Recommends Talks," *Financial Times,* 18 February 1999, 2; Agence Europe, *Europe Daily Bulletin,* no. 7407, 18 February 1999, 6–7; Agence Europe, no. 7432, *Europe Daily Bulletin,* 25 March 1999, 9.

39. European Commission, "Reports on Progress Towards Accession by Each of the Candidate Countries: Composite Paper"; on the Romanian economic situation, see 7, 9, and 28; on the issue of border controls, see 12 and 17; on praise for Bulgaria, see 28.

40. On the EU's recognition of the special hardships imposed on these countries by the Kosovo conflict, see Agence Europe, *Europe Daily Bulletin,* no. 7454, 28 April 1999, 10. See also the "Council Declaration on Romania and Bulgaria," in the "Council Conclusions" of the April 26, 1999 meeting of the General Affairs Council in Luxembourg; reprinted in Agence Europe, *Europe Documents,* no. 2136, 29 April 1999, 3–4. On the growth of anti-Western sentiment in these countries as a result of the NATO campaign against Serbia, see Stefan Wagstyl, "Romania Still Looks West in the Long Term," *Financial Times,* 14 May 1999, 2; and Stefan Wagstyl and Theodor Troev, "Bulgarians Start to Ponder Hidden Costs of the Conflict," *Financial Times,* 18 May 1999, 2.

41. "Blair Declares Support for Sofia's Early Accession to EU and NATO," *Financial Times,* 18 May 1999, 2; Agence Europe, *Uniting Europe,* no. 52, 10 May 1999, 1; Agence Europe, *Uniting Europe,* no. 54, 24 May 1999, 6.

42. "Cologne European Council, 3–4 June 1999: Presidency Conclusions" ("Cologne Presidency Conclusions"), reprinted in Agence Europe, *Europe Daily Bulletin,* no. 7480, 6 June 1999, 16.

43. Agence Europe, *Europe Daily Bulletin,* no. 7480, 6 June 1999, 6.

44. Speech by Romano Prodi, president-designate of the European Commission, to the EP, 14 September 1999, reprinted in Agence Europe, *Europe Documents,* no. 2155, 22 September 1999, 3. On Verheugen's views, see "Verheugen Pledges to Guard Standards on EU Entry," *Financial Times,* 13 September 1999, 3. On the support of Britain and Germany for a more inclusive enlargement strategy, see Stefan Wagstyl, "EU Set to Double Number in Accession Talks," *Financial Times,* 22 September 1999, 3. On discussion of enlargement strategy among the member states, see Agence Europe, *Europe Daily Bulletin,* no. 7545, 6–7 September 1999, 7.

45. The figure for the Ignalina plant is cited in Wagstyl and Vipotnik, "Lithuania Angered by EU Demands." On the EU's demands for energy plans and the closure of unsafe nuclear plants, see the Accession Partnerships for the individual applicants, available on the Internet at http://europa.eu.int/comm/dg1a/enlarge/access_partnership/index.htm; see also the Commission's November 1998 and October 1999 Regular Progress Reports.

46. See the comments of External Affairs Commissioner van den Broek, cited in Agence Europe, *Europe Daily Bulletin,* no. 7426, 17 March 1999, 9.

47. "Cologne Presidency Conclusions," 16.

48. "EU Entry Bar on Those with Unsafe Nuclear Stations," *Financial Times,* 2 September 1999, 2. See also Agence Europe, *Europe Daily Bulletin,* no. 7542, 2 September 1999, 12.

49. "Lithuania to Close Two Reactors at Ignalina," *Financial Times,* 9 September 1999, 2. See also Agence Europe, *Europe Daily Bulletin,* no. 7549, 11 September 1999, 8. The decision was formally approved by the Lithuanian parliament on October 5. See Agence Europe, *Europe Daily Bulletin,* no. 7569, 9 October 1999, 13.

50. "Austria Threatens to Block Slovakia's Entry to EU," *Financial Times,* 24 September 1999, 2. On the Slovak government's announcement, see Agence Europe, *Europe Daily Bulletin,* no. 7555, 21–22 September 1999, 10; and for Austria's response, see Agence Europe, *Europe Daily Bulletin,* no. 7563, 1 October 1999, 6. For the Commission's response, see Agence Europe, *Europe Daily Bulletin,* no. 7562, 30 September 1999, 11.

51. In Latvia, an initial law passed by the parliament in July that would have required the use of Latvian in public affairs and private business was vetoed by the president; this, after the EU indicated that the new law violated EU human rights standards and could hurt Latvia's membership bid. See Matej Vipotnik, "Latvians Give New President Baptism of Fire," *Financial Times,* 9 July 1999, 3; "Call to Latvia on Language Law," *Financial Times,* 15

July 1999, 2; and Agence Europe, *Europe Daily Bulletin,* no. 7509, 6. The Czech wall was constructed in Usti nad Lebem, in northern Bohemia, on the very day the Commission issued its progress reports. The action drew strong EU condemnation, with Commission President Prodi declaring that "Europe will never again accept new walls separating European citizens from one another. We have had enough walls in the past." See Agence Europe, *Europe Daily Bulletin,* no. 7573, 15 October 1999, 8.

52. European Commission, "Regular Report from the Commission on the Progress Towards Accession by Each of the Candidate Countries: Composite Paper," 13 October 1999, IV.2.2; available on the Internet at http://europa.eu.int/comm/enlargement/report_ 10_99/composite/index.htm. See also the Commission's Introductory Memo for the report (IP/99/751) at http://europa.eu. int/comm/enlargement/report_10_99/intro/index.htm. See also Peter Norman, "Brussels Moves to Double Number of Countries in Talks to Join EU," *Financial Times,* 14 October 1999, 14; Peter Norman, "New Flexible Finishing Line for Entrants," *Financial Times,* 14 October 1999, 2; and Agence Europe, *Europe Daily Bulletin,* no. 7572, 14 October 1999, 6.

53. European Commission, "Regular Report: Composite Paper," iv.

54. European Commission, "Regular Report: Composite Paper," iii.

55. Agence Europe, *Europe Daily Bulletin,* no. 7625, 3–4 January 2000, 9–10. The 1999 versions of the Accession Partnerships for each of the ten CEECs are published in the EU's *Official Journal,* no. L/335, 28 December 1999. They are also available on the Internet at http://europa.eu.int/comm/enlargement/docs/index.htm.

56. Prodi's remarks were made in presenting the Commission's progress reports to the EP. See Agence Europe, *Europe Daily Bulletin,* no. 7572, 14 October 1999, 6–7.

57. "E. Europe Joy as EU Door Opens Wider," *Financial Times,* 15 October 1999, 2.

58. Agence Europe, *Europe Daily Bulletin,* no. 7575, 18–19 October 1999, 10–11.

59. Agence Europe, *Europe Daily Bulletin,* no. 7597, 20 November 1999, 12.

60. Agence Europe, *Europe Daily Bulletin,* no. 7604, 1 December 1999, 13–14; "Bulgaria to Close N-Plants," *Financial Times,* 1 December 1999, 2.

61. Radio Free Europe, *RFE/RL Newsline,* vol. 3, no. 223, 16 November 1999, pt. 2; Radio Free Europe, *RFE/RL Newsline,* vol. 3, no. 229, 24 November 1999, pt. 2.

62. "Language Law is Passed," *Financial Times,* 10 December 1999, 3; Agence Europe, *Europe Daily Bulletin,* no. 7612, 11 December 1999, 8.

63. "Romany Wall Demolished," *Financial Times,* 25 November 1999, 3.

64. "Helsinki Presidency Conclusions," I.3, available on the Internet at http://europa. eu.int/council/off/conclu/dec99/dec99_en.htm.

65. "Helsinki European Council," I.10 and I.11.

66. Agence Europe, *Europe Daily Bulletin,* no. 7612, 11 December 1999, 4.

67. Verheugen quotes are cited in Agence Europe, *Europe Daily Bulletin,* no. 7612, 11 December 1999, 3–4; and Michael Smith, "EU Paves the Way for Another Six," *Financial Times,* 11–12 December 1999, 2. For reaction of the six newly admitted applicants, see Agence Europe, *Europe Daily Bulletin,* no. 7614, 13–14 December 1999, 9–10.

68. Agence Europe, *Europe Daily Bulletin,* no. 7426, 17 March 1999, 8–9.

69. "Presidency Conclusions" of the Vienna and Cologne European Councils. For the EP, see Agence Europe, *Europe Daily Bulletin,* no. 7447, 17 April 1999, 11.

70. Speech by Romano Prodi, president-designate of the European Commission, to the EP, 14 September 1999, reprinted in Agence Europe, *Europe Documents,* no. 2155, 22 September 1999, 3.

71. "Verheugen Pledges to Guard Standards on EU Entry," *Financial Times,* 13 September 1999, 3.

72. Peter Norman, "Prodi Retreats Over Firm EU Entry Dates," *Financial Times,* 29 September 1999, 2.

73. European Commission, "Regular Report: Composite Paper," IV.4.

74. Vijai Maheshwari and Stefan Wagstyl, "EU Applicant Countries Urge Speedier Enlargement," *Financial Times,* 12 October 1999, 2.

75. Although on a late September visit to Prague, Germany's Chancellor Schröder declared that the EU should be ready to admit new members as early as 2003. See Robert Anderson, "Schröder Speaks Out on EU Expansion," *Financial Times,* 1 October 1999, 2.

76. "Helsinki Presidency Conclusions," I.5.

77. Smith, "EU Paves the Way for Another Six Members," 2; Agence Europe, *Europe Daily Bulletin,* no. 7612, 11 December 1999, 3–4.

78. Michael Smith, "Candidates Target 2003 for Entry," *Financial Times,* 13 December 1999, 4; "Early End to Talks Sought," *Financial Times,* 16 December 1999, 2; Agence Europe, *Europe Daily Bulletin,* no. 7614, 13–14 December 1999, 9–10.

79. David Buchan, "Cook Tries to Mend Turkish Fences," *Financial Times,* 19 May 1998, 2; David Buchan, "Turks Wary on Brussels Talks," *Financial Times,* 20 May 1998, 2; David Buchan and Lionel Barber, "Greece Pressed on Turkey Veto," *Financial Times,* 21 May 1998, 3; "Turkey to Boycott Meeting," *Financial Times,* 22 May 1998, 2; "Turkey May Lift Talks Boycott," *Financial Times,* 27 May 1998, 2.

80. "Relations with Bonn Renewed," *Financial Times,* 29 May 1998, 2.

81. "Presidency Conclusions" of the Cardiff European Council; reprinted in Agence Europe, *Europe Documents,* no. 2094–2095, 18 June 1998, 9. See also "Ankara Urged to Match Moves for Closer Links," *Financial Times,* 26 June 1998, 2.

82. Christopher de Bellaigue and Ralph Atkins, "Turks Honour Ataturk's Secular State," *Financial Times,* 30 October 1998.

83. Christopher de Bellaigue, "Turkey Says EU Recognizes Candidacy," *Financial Times,* 6 November 1998, 2. The Commission's progress report on Turkey is available on the Internet, at the EU's official Website at http://europa.eu.int/comm/dg1a/enlarge/report_11_98_en/index.htm. For quotes, see European Commission, "Reports on Progress Towards Accession by Each of the Candidate Countries: Composite Paper," 19. The Commission's decision to include Turkey in the progress report enraged the Greek government; see Agence Europe, *Europe Daily Bulletin,* no. 7333, 30 October 1998, 4.

84. Leyla Boulton, "Ties with EU Worsening Says Turkey," *Financial Times,* 18 March 1999, 2.

85. Agence Europe, *Europe Daily Bulletin,* no. 7479, 5 June 1999, 4; Agence Europe, *Europe Daily Bulletin,* no. 7480, 6 June 1999, 3.

86. Agence Europe, *Europe Daily Bulletin,* no. 7481, 7–8 June 1999, 3; Agence Europe, *Europe Daily Bulletin,* no. 7495, 26 June 1999, 7.

87. Agence Europe, *Europe Daily Bulletin,* no. 7505, 10 July 1999, 10.

88. Kerin Hope, "Greece Rebuilds Ties with Turkey," *Financial Times,* 31 July–1 August 1999, 3; Agence Europe, *Europe Daily Bulletin,* no. 7535, 23–24 August 1999, 1.

89. David Buchan, "Greece Ready to Lift Veto on EU Aid to Turkey," *Financial Times,* 1 September 1999, 3.

90. David Buchan, "Turkey Warns Over EU Membership," *Financial Times,* 2 September 1999, 2; Agence Europe, *Europe Daily Bulletin,* no. 7542, 2 September 1999, 12.

91. Peter Norman and Leyla Boulton, "Greece Backs EU Cash Aid to Turkey," *Financial Times,* 6 September 1999, 1.

92. Buchan, "Turkey Warns Over EU Membership," 2.

93. Norman and Boulton, "Greece Backs EU Cash Aid to Turkey," 1; Agence Europe, *Europe Daily Bulletin,* no. 7545, 6–7 September 1999, 5–6.

94. European Commission, "Regular Report: Composite Paper," IV.5. See also Agence Europe, *Europe Daily Bulletin,* no. 7572, 14 October 1999, 6–7.

95. Agence Europe, *Europe Daily Bulletin,* no. 7575, 18–19 October 1999, 10–11.

96. Leyla Boulton, "Turkey, Greece Urged to Continue Talking," *Financial Times,* 16 November 1999, 2.

97. Leyla Boulton, "Call for Halt to Cyprus Accession Talks," *Financial Times,* 2 December 1999, 2; "Greek PM in Veto Talks," *Financial Times,* 9 December 1999, 2; Leyla Boulton and Peter Norman, "Better Ties at Risk, Turkey Warns Greece," *Financial Times,* 10 December 1999, 2. See also Agence Europe, *Europe Daily Bulletin,* no. 7608, 6–7 December 1999, 5.

98. Quentin Peel and Kerin Hope, "Greeks Press for Accession 'Road Map' for Turkey," *Financial Times,* 15 December 1999, 3.

99. "Helsinki Presidency Conclusions," I.12 (Turkey candidacy), I.4 (settlement of international disputes), and I.9(b) (Cyprus).

100. Peel and Hope, "Greeks Press for Accession 'Road Map' for Turkey," 3; Peter Norman, Quentin Peel, and Leyla Boulton, "Solana Tries to Clear Turkey's Path to EU Candidacy," *Financial Times,* 11–12 December 1999, 1; Quentin Peel and Leyla Boulton, "Little is Left to Chance in Turkey's Bid for Europe," *Financial Times,* 13 December 1999, 10. See also Agence Europe, *Europe Daily Bulletin,* no. 7612, 11 December 1999, 4.

101. Peel and Boulton, "Little is Left to Chance in Turkey's Bid for Europe," 10; Leyla Boulton, "Delighted Turks Face Some Big Adjustments," *Financial Times,* 13 December 1999, 4.

102. Boulton, "Delighted Turks Face Some Big Adjustments," 4.

103. Peel and Hope, "Greeks Press for Accession 'Road Map' for Turkey," 3.

104. Leyla Boulton, "Çem's Visit Set to Bolster Growing Links with Athens," *Financial Times,* 4 February 2000, 3; Leyla Boulton, "Kurds' Arrest Dents Turkey's EU Hopes," *Financial Times,* 21 February 2000, 2; Agence Europe, *Europe Daily Bulletin,* no. 7646, 2 February 2000, 6–7; Agence Europe, *Europe Daily Bulletin,* no. 7666, 1 March 2000, 9.

7

Preparing the EU for Enlargement (I): "Agenda 2000"

In previous enlargements, the burden of adjustment fell mainly on the applicant countries. The current enlargement, however, also requires substantial adjustment by the EU, including the reform of key common policies and EU decision-making institutions. These changes are necessary because of the number of countries attempting to join in the current enlargement and their relatively poor economic status. Without these reforms, enlargement into Central and Eastern Europe would be too costly, and it would threaten the EU's institutional cohesion and effectiveness. Concern about the institutional and distributive consequences of enlargement has also led some member states to make such reforms a precondition for the admission of new member states.

The internal reforms required by enlargement are of two main types: changes to the EU's decision-making institutions and procedures, so that a larger and more diverse EU can function effectively and democratically; and the reform of key common policies and the EU's financing system, so that a larger EU will be affordable within the fiscal limits established by the current member states. The issue of institutional reform will be examined more closely in the next chapter, while this chapter will explore the issue of policy and financing reform.

The issue of policy and financing reform itself consists of two separate but related issues: (1) the reform of two major policies, the CAP and the Structural and Cohesion Funds, which together consume more than 80 percent of the EU budget and whose extension to the candidate countries in their current form would be too costly; and (2) changes to the EU's financing system, including the system of national contributions and EU "own resources," within the context of agreement on a medium-term financial perspective for the years 2000–2006 that includes the first new accessions. These two issues are closely linked, with agreement on the overall budget and financing system being an essential precondition for final agreement on policy reform, while the details of policy reform necessarily affect the final budgetary settlement.

The issues of policy reform and the EU's future budget and financing system were a key focus of the "Agenda 2000" report issued by the Commission in July 1997. Since agreement on these issues and a new medium-term financial perspective were considered an important precondition for further enlargement, the failure to agree on "Agenda 2000" could have caused significant delays in the accession process and perhaps even threatened enlargement altogether. The EU did not fail in this regard, however, and after almost two years of intensive debate and intergovernmental negotiations, final agreement on "Agenda 2000" was reached at the Berlin summit in March 1999, thus enabling enlargement to go forward.

The "Agenda 2000" agreement is also significant for enlargement because it will affect the substance of the accession negotiations and the terms of membership for the candidate countries. The new financial perspective also includes funding for pre-accession aid to the CEECs. For all of these reasons, the "Agenda 2000" reforms are an integral part of the enlargement process.

THE HISTORY OF "AGENDA 2000"

EU leaders were aware from the beginning that major internal reforms would be necessary as a precondition for eastern enlargement. This awareness, plus the knowledge that these reforms would be politically painful and difficult to negotiate, contributed to the EU's initial reluctance to discuss the possibility of eastern enlargement. The EU also delayed any serious discussion of internal policy and budgetary reforms related to enlargement. In its 1992 report to the European Council, "Europe and the Challenge of Enlargement," the Commission emphasized that enlargement must not be allowed to weaken the EU and mentioned the need to reform decision-making institutions so that a larger Union would function effectively; however, there was no reference to the impact of enlargement on common policies and the budget.[1]

Similarly, in the "Presidency Conclusions" for the Copenhagen European Council, EU leaders referred only to the "Union's capacity to absorb new members, while maintaining the momentum of European integration," a rather oblique reference to the need for internal reforms as a precondition for enlargement.[2]

The EU only began to seriously confront the issue of internal reform in the second half of 1994, as it debated the pre-accession strategy for the CEECs. With widespread estimates that enlargement could lead to the doubling of expenditures on current agricultural and structural policies, concerns grew among the member states about the potential financial cost of enlargement. Especially concerned were large net contributors to the EU budget, including Germany, the Netherlands, and Great Britain. As a consequence, at the Essen summit the European Council asked the Commission to prepare a detailed analysis of the "effects of enlargement in the context of the Union's current policies and their future development," and to submit this report in the second half of 1995.[3]

In November of the following year, the Commission submitted separate papers on the impact of enlargement on the CAP and the Structural Funds. The conclusions of its summary report foreshadowed those of "Agenda 2000": the Commission argued that it would be too costly to extend the EU's current policies to new member states from Central and Eastern Europe. However, while reform of the CAP and the Structural Funds was necessary for enlargement, this would not entail a wholesale dismantling or dramatic revision of current policies. The Commission also argued that the impact on common policies and the budget should be softened by long transitional periods for the new member states, so that they would be phased into these policies only gradually.[4]

At the December 1995 Madrid summit, the European Council considered the Commission's report and called upon the Commission to "take its evaluation of the effects of enlargement on Community policies further, particularly with regard to agricultural and structural policies." It also asked the Commission to "undertake a detailed analysis as soon as possible of the EU's financing system in order to submit, immediately after the conclusion of the [1996–97] IGC, a communication on the future financial framework of the Union as from 31 December 1999, having regard to the prospect of enlargement." The European Council requested that these reports, together with the Commission's Opinions on the CEEC applications and its paper on enlargement strategy, be ready soon after conclusion of the IGC, expected to be sometime in the first half of 1997.[5]

These various reports formed the basis of the Commission's "Agenda 2000" document that was officially presented on July 16, 1997. In addition to the ten Opinions and the Commission's recommendations on enlargement strategy, "Agenda 2000" contained proposals for reforming the CAP and the Structural Funds as well as a proposed new financial framework for the years 2000–2006 in the perspective of enlargement.[6]

The "Agenda 2000" proposals initially drew only a muted response from the member states, since their immediate focus was on the Commission's recommendations on enlargement strategy and the question of differentiation among the candidate countries. This remained the situation in the run-up to the Luxembourg summit, at which the European Council was due to make its formal decisions on beginning the accession process. Serious debate also awaited the Commission's tabling of formal legislative proposals for the "Agenda 2000" reforms in March 1998. Even after this point, however, negotiations on "Agenda 2000" were stalled by the approach of German federal elections in September 1998. Facing an uphill electoral battle, the Kohl government let it be known that it was not in a position to make any decisions on politically sensitive policy and budgetary issues until after the elections (which in any case it lost). Without the full engagement and cooperation of Germany—the EU's largest net contributor and its most populous and influential member state—progress on policy and budgetary reform was impossible. Thus, the real negotiations over "Agenda 2000" did not begin until late 1998.

The following three sections examine the Commission's "Agenda 2000" proposals for reforming the CAP and the Structural Funds, its proposed financial perspective for 2000–2006, and the views on these issues of the member states and other interests. The focus then turns to the intense intergovernmental bargaining that led to the final agreement on "Agenda 2000" in March 1999.

THE CAP

In the EU budget and politics, the CAP has an importance that is greatly disproportionate to the role of agriculture in the EU economy; while agriculture accounts for only 2.4 percent of the EU's GDP and 5.3 percent of employment, the CAP consumes nearly half of the EU budget.[7] The reasons for this have to do with the historical, political, and cultural importance of agriculture in Europe— including the postwar desire for food self-sufficiency—that has led to traditionally high levels of protection and support for this sector. The CAP's importance also stems from its role as part of the EEC's "founding bargain," with France accepting a common market for industrial products in return for Germany's agreement to help subsidize French agriculture.[8]

Originally created in the 1960s, the CAP consisted of three main elements: external protection for European agriculture through high import duties on non-EU products, price subsidies for EU agricultural products, and export subsidies. Together these measures guaranteed high prices and incomes for EU farmers, while also encouraging tremendous overproduction and waste. In the early 1970s, the CAP alone consumed nearly 90 percent of the EU budget. However, by the 1980s, growing pressure for reform was coming from EU consumers and the governments of some member states as well as from the United States and other major agricultural producing countries within the framework of global trade negotiations. Pressure to reduce agricultural spending also resulted from the creation and expansion of other EU programs that competed with the CAP for a share of the limited EU budget. A first major effort at reform came in 1992 with the so-called MacSharry reforms, which began the shift from price supports to direct income payments to farmers, thus decoupling EU financial support from production. However, CAP reform has been inhibited over the years by the power of well-organized farmers, especially in such key member states as France and Germany (where the intricacies of coalition politics have also played a role), and by the continued near-mythical status of the CAP within the EU.

Eastern enlargement poses a problem for the CAP because of the much greater role of agriculture in the economies of most CEECs. In the ten CEECs, agriculture accounted for 8.6 percent of GDP in 1995, ranging from a high of 20.5 percent in Romania to a low of 5 percent in Slovenia. Agriculture is also important for employment in these countries, accounting for 22.5 percent of employment in the CEEC ten, ranging from 34.4 percent in Romania to an EU-like low of 6.3 percent in the Czech Republic. The accession of all ten CEECs would roughly double the size of the EU's agricultural labor force and increase its agricultural area by almost half. A particular problem is posed by Poland, by far the most populous of the CEECs (38.6 million) and likely to be one of the first to enter the EU, since in Poland agriculture accounts for nearly 27 percent of total employment.[9]

As the high percentage of the labor force engaged in agriculture implies, farming in Central and Eastern Europe is also highly inefficient. Nor has greater efficiency been much promoted by the restrictive provisions for agricultural trade of the Europe Agreements. The EU has given PHARE aid to promote agricultural modernization and restructuring, and in "Agenda 2000" the Commission proposed an additional ECU 500 million per year for agricultural structural reform in the CEECs for the years 2000–2006.[10] This is a relatively small amount considering the size of the agricultural modernization task faced by these countries, however.

The challenge for eastern enlargement posed by the CAP and the agricultural situation in the CEECs stems from the greatly increased expenditures, and hence budgetary problems, that would result if the current policies were extended to new member states. The Commission's 1995 report estimated these increased expenditures at ECU 12 billion per year, about a one-third increase in the current level of expenditures.[11] Other estimates by academic and policy experts were considerably higher, ranging all the way to a 50-percent increase.[12]

In other words, without substantial reform of the CAP, the budgetary impact of extending the CAP to new CEEC member states would be much too severe. One strategy might be to grant EU membership to the CEECs without the right to full benefits from the CAP. This strategy would mean exclusion of the CEECs from a core EU policy and central element of the *acquis communautaire,* however, and hence a form of second-class membership; not only would this be politically unacceptable for the CEECs, but it would also violate the key EU principles of solidarity and cohesion. For these reasons, and because there were other pressures for agricultural policy reform stemming from budgetary considerations and future rounds of global trade talks, CAP reform became a major element of the Commission's "Agenda 2000" report.

In "Agenda 2000," the Commission proposed reducing support prices paid to farmers for grain, beef, dairy, and other products by up to a third, thereby forcing European farmers to be more competitive in world markets. As compensation, and continuing with the thrust of the 1992 MacSharry reforms, it also proposed further shifting EU assistance from price subsidies to direct income payments, with a limit on the amount of aid that individual farmers could receive. The Commission also proposed incorporating agriculture policy into a more coherent rural aid policy, by integrating it with environmental and structural policies, and allowing member states greater freedom in deciding how to allocate aid, in keeping with the principle of subsidiarity. Although in the Commission's plan, CAP spending—

excluding the costs of enlargement—would rise in absolute terms to ECU 50 billion in 2006 (from ECU 43.3 billion in 1999), it would decline slightly as a percentage of the total budget (from 44.3 to 43.7 percent).[13] Moreover, this increase in spending was justified by the Commission with the argument that the reformed CAP would eventually be less expensive. The Commission also argued that increased payments, especially under existing and new rural development accompanying measures, were necessary to reward farmers for their role in preserving the rural environment.

In "Agenda 2000," the Commission also argued that new member states from Central and Eastern Europe would require a lengthy transitional period before they could be fully integrated into the CAP. After entry, new member states would receive assistance from CAP market organization and rural development accompanying measures (to help with agricultural modernization), but they would not receive direct compensatory payments, which would make up the great bulk of CAP expenditures. As a result, in the Commission's plan, enlargement (assuming the accession of five CEECs in 2002 and including pre-accession aid) would cost only ECU 3.9 billion per year in the framework period, with agricultural expenditures for new member states and those still receiving pre-accession aid totaling ECU 4.5 billion in 2006.[14] Thus, by largely excluding new member states from CAP benefits for a lengthy transitional period, the Commission was able to argue that enlargement would not lead to a sizable increase in agricultural expenditures.

Despite the basically cautious approach to CAP reform adopted by the Commission, its "Agenda 2000" proposals were harshly criticized by the EU farm lobby, which claimed that the proposals would cost farmers ECU 6.5 billion a year.[15] The Commission's proposals were also criticized by some member states. Germany was a particularly strong critic, with the Kohl government calling the Commission's proposed reforms "unnecessary" and charging that they would reduce the competitiveness and incomes of EU farmers. Also critical of the Commission's proposals, for various reasons, were the governments of Belgium, the Netherlands, and Austria. On the other hand, the pro-reform governments of Britain and Sweden complained that the Commission's proposals did not go far enough, and they argued instead for more substantial cuts in price supports and compensatory payments. However, indicating the complexity of the issue and interests involved, the British government also joined with Bonn in opposing the Commission's plan to limit income payments to individual farmers.[16] Also, while the member states generally approved the Commission's idea of giving them more discretion in allocating CAP assistance, such "renationalization" was opposed by many farmers because they feared it would lead to unequal treatment and subsidies in different member states.[17]

These criticisms were addressed somewhat by the Commission in its formal legislative proposals that were published in March 1998.[18] Still, the proposals were widely criticized by national farm ministers after they were released. Germany's Agriculture Minister, Jochen Borchert, complained that the proposed reforms would reduce the income of German farmers while leading to increased German payments into the CAP. Ireland's farm minister complained that his country would be a big loser in the Commission's plans to allocate increased milk quotas, while the Spanish and Greek governments criticized the proposals to limit support to the olive oil sectors of individual member states. The French government argued that the Commission's proposals would be more expensive yet would not guarantee farmer incomes. It also criticized as too complicated and impractical plans to give member states more discretion over the allocation of farm aid. Even those member states that were broadly supportive of the Commission's proposals, such as Britain and Denmark, criticized specific elements of the plan. While national agriculture ministers savaged the Commission's proposals, EU farmers mounted large-scale demonstrations against the reforms.[19]

The Commission's proposals also drew criticism at the June 1998 Cardiff summit, where it was decided to postpone serious negotiations on CAP reform and other aspects of "Agenda 2000" until after the September German elections.[20] In October, negotiations among EU farm ministers resumed. By this point, the debate over CAP reform was affected by depressed agricultural markets, which made it more difficult for the Commission to claim that its planned price cuts would be fully compensated by direct income payments, and by the broader debate over the EU budget and financing system. A key focus of attention was the new Commission proposal that national governments "co-finance" a portion—perhaps as much as 25 percent—of direct payments to farmers as a means of reducing budgetary imbalances among the member states. This idea was strongly opposed by some member states, especially France, Spain, and Ireland—all major beneficiaries of the CAP—which claimed that they would suffer financially in this scheme.[21] It was also becoming increasingly clear that a deal on CAP reform was closely linked to agreements on the Structural Funds and the EU budget and financing system.

THE STRUCTURAL AND COHESION FUNDS

Since the 1980s, the Structural and Cohesion Funds have become the second major element of the EU budget, accounting in 1999 for about 40 percent of EU spending.[22] Although the Structural Funds trace their roots to the very beginning of the EEC, they gained increased importance with the creation of the ERDF in 1975. This was a program to distribute developmental aid to the EU's poorest regions, although another motive behind its creation was to compensate Britain for budgetary imbalances resulting from its lack of receipts from the CAP, which at that time consumed nearly three-quarters of the EU's budget. The Structural Funds became a more important component of the budget in the mid-1980s, when the EU decided to double structural spending in connection with the Single Market project and the accession of poorer Mediterranean countries (Greece, Spain, and Portugal). As a result of this increase and the corresponding cuts in CAP spending, the proportion of the EU budget absorbed by the Structural Funds grew to 25 percent in 1992. Further increases to the Structural Funds were agreed to in 1993. At this time, the EU also created a new "Cohesion Fund" to assist the economic convergence of the four poorest member states (Greece, Spain, Portugal, and Ireland) and to prepare them for EMU.[23]

In addition to the Cohesion Fund, the Structural Funds are comprised of four separate funds: the ERDF, the Social Fund, the Agricultural Guidance and Guarantee Fund, and the Fisheries Guidance Fund. Since 1988, money from these funds has been allocated to meet seven main "Objectives":

Objective 1: developing economically backward regions, defined as having a per capita GDP less than 75 percent of the EU average;

Objective 2: restructuring regions suffering from industrial decline;

Objective 3: combating long-term and youth unemployment;

Objective 4: adapting the workforce to industrial change and new technologies;

Objective 5a: accelerating structural change in agriculture and fisheries;

Objective 5b: developing and assisting the structural adjustment of rural areas;

Objective 6: assisting peripheral northern areas with a population density of less than eight persons per square kilometer (a new objective added with the EFTA enlargement).

Of these, objective 1 is by far the most significant, absorbing close to 70 percent of the Structural Funds. One reason for the high level of spending on this objective is that the GDP per capita criteria has not always been strictly observed, with political pressures leading to regions that are well above the 75-percent limit receiving assistance.

From the perspective of enlargement, the problem presented by the Structural and Cohesion Funds is the potential budgetary impact of the accession of relatively poor CEECs. As a group, in 1997 the ten CEECs had a per capita GDP that was only 40 percent of the EU average (calculated at purchasing power parity). Even the wealthiest CEEC applicant, Slovenia, had a per capita GDP that was only 68 percent of the EU average, less than that of Greece, which at 69 percent is the poorest current member state.[24] Even assuming that the CEECs grow at a much faster rate than the EU, it will be many years before they approach the EU average in terms of per capita income. Thus, the new member states would easily qualify for EU assistance under objective 1 of the Structural Funds. They would also qualify for Cohesion Fund aid, which is given to member states with a per capita GDP less than 90 percent of the EU average. According to 1995 Commission estimates, extending the current Structural Funds to all ten CEECs would add another ECU 38 billion to the EU budget, more than doubling present structural policy expenditures.[25]

Because of the unwillingness of most member states, especially net contributors such as Germany and the Netherlands, to accept an increase of the EU budget, reform of the Structural Funds is an important precondition for enlargement. Another option—denying new member states structural aid—is not possible because it would contradict the EU's basic principles of solidarity and cohesion, and because gross economic disparities could hinder the effective functioning of the Single Market. Reforming the Structural Funds is politically difficult, however, because it threatens the benefits that all member states receive from the current policies. In particular, the poorest member states, for whom structural spending has the biggest relative economic impact, are concerned about the loss of financial benefits and are opposed to any reductions of structural spending. Even without reform, however, enlargement could reduce the amount of structural assistance received by current member states: Because the accession of all ten CEECs and Cyprus would lower the average per capita GDP of the EU by some 16 percent, many regions and member states that currently receive structural aid would no longer be eligible, since they would be above the 75-percent threshold for objective 1.[26]

In "Agenda 2000," the Commission declared that "economic and social cohesion must remain a political priority" for an enlarged EU. Therefore, it proposed maintaining the upper limit for structural spending at 0.46 percent of EU GNP—the limit set by the European Council in 1992—until 2006. This amounted to a total expenditure for the seven-year period of ECU 275 billion (at 1997 prices), of which ECU 45 billion would be earmarked for the new member states.[27]

To meet the structural policy goals of an enlarged EU within this budgetary limit, the Commission proposed consolidating structural operations by reducing the present seven objectives for Structural Funds spending to three and tightening up the eligibility requirements for assistance. While objective 1 would be retained as a high priority (with a stricter enforcement of the 75-percent threshold), objective 2 would be redefined to include all regions facing economic and social restructuring, and a new objective 3 would assist member states in developing human resources to fight unemployment. Altogether, the Commission's plan would reduce the proportion of the EU population receiving structural assistance under objectives 1 and 2 from its current level of 51 percent to between 35 and 40 percent and would result in a slight decrease in the level of annual funding for the current member states (from ECU 31.4 billion in 1999 to ECU 27.3 billion in 2006). Regions and member states losing structural aid would benefit from (unspecified) transitional arrangements. As with the CAP, national governments would also be given more control over the use of Structural Funds. The Commission also recommended maintaining Cohesion Fund assistance to the poorest member states in its present form, with an eligibility review to be carried out in 2003. However, current recipients would have to share the same amount of aid (about ECU 3 billion per year) with the new member states after 2002. As with its CAP proposals, the Commission sought to prevent unhappiness with structural policy reform from generating opposition to enlargement by arguing that the reforms were not necessitated only by the accession of new member states but would have been required in any case for budgetary reasons.[28]

According to the Commission's plan, the level of Structural and Cohesion Fund aid for new member states would grow only gradually and would not exceed the general limit of 4 percent of national GDP. The Commission argued that this was necessary in order to avoid problems caused by the limited capacity of the new member states to absorb the funds, but capping structural spending in this manner would also help keep the cost of enlargement manageable. The Commission estimated that by 2006, the amount of structural assistance going to new member states would grow to around ECU 12.6 billion, or about one-third of the EU total. The Commission's plan also included a small amount (ECU 1 billion) for pre-accession aid, in addition to already-existing PHARE aid, to be used for infrastructure improvements in the CEECs.[29]

The Commission's proposals were cautiously received by the member states. While most of them generally agreed that reform was necessary, there was a strong difference of views between wealthier net contributors to the EU budget, especially Germany and the Netherlands, and poorer member states, such as Spain, who received the bulk of structural assistance. While the former opposed further increases in EU spending to pay for enlargement—as part of their demands for a reduction in net contributions and out of fear that they would pay the lion's share of the costs of enlargement—the latter argued that it would be unfair to pay for enlargement by reducing the amount of structural assistance given to the poorest member states. Spain led the latter group in questioning whether enlargement could be accomplished without an increase in EU spending, declaring that the poorer member states were not prepared to "foot the bill" for enlargement. The Spanish government also strongly rejected German-backed suggestions that member states joining the euro-zone should forfeit their rights to receive Cohesion Fund assistance.[30]

Among nearly all the member states, there was concern about the loss of structural aid for specific regions as a result of the Commission's proposals, especially the tightened requirements for objective 1. Under the Commission's plan, regions as diverse as Northern Ireland and the Scottish Highlands and Islands (Britain), Lisbon (Portugal), Valencia (Spain), the island of Corsica (France), Sardinia and Puglia (Italy), Fletvoland (the Netherlands), the Franco-Belgian border regions of Valenciennois and Hainault, and the entire Republic of Ireland were threatened with a loss of objective 1 aid.[31] The German government expressed concern about the loss of aid for eastern Berlin, while the British government complained about the reconfiguration of objective 2 for declining industrial and rural regions, fearing that the new criteria for aid, together with the tightening of criteria for objective 1, could lead to a loss of benefits for many British regions.[32] The intensity of national lobbying indicated the difficulty of reforming a program that benefited more than half of the EU's population and all of its member states, giving it a broad and diverse constituency.

These concerns were not much allayed by the Commission's formal legislative proposals, which were released in March 1998. However, the Commission did respond to member state pressures by abandoning the goal of reducing the proportion of the EU population receiving structural assistance to 35 percent, settling instead for the somewhat less ambitious target of 38 percent. The Commission's legislative blueprint also provided more details on the transition arrangements for areas losing assistance, specifying a gradual six-year phasing-out period for regions losing objective 1 aid, and a similar four-year period for those losing objective 2 support. The proposals also included a "safety net" that would limit the loss of structural assistance for individual member states, largely in response to British concerns about the redefinition of objective 2.[33]

Little progress in negotiations on Structural Funds reform was achieved at subsequent ministerial meetings or the Cardiff summit in June 1998. While member states voiced unanimous support for the broad principles of greater concentration and efficiency advanced by the Commission's proposals, they also sought to limit reductions in their own support and pled nationally specific "special cases."[34] As was the case with CAP reform, no forward movement on structural policy reform would occur until after the September 1998 German elections. It was also clear that a final deal on reforming the Structural and Cohesion Funds was linked to an agreement on the overall EU budget and financing regime.

THE BUDGET AND FINANCING SYSTEM

Budgetary matters, including the relative contributions of the individual member states, are a major issue related to eastern enlargement. Concern about the impact of enlargement on the EU budget and finances stems mainly from three factors. First, there is fear that the accession of relatively poor and heavily agricultural CEECs will lead to dramatically increased expenditures via the CAP and Structural Funds; hence the emphasis on reforming these policies in advance of enlargement. Second, it is recognized that the new member states will not be major contributors to the EU budget and in fact will remain major net recipients for quite some time. Third, as a consequence of the first two factors, there is concern among the current member states about the impact of enlargement on their own net budgetary positions.

To elaborate on this final point, member states that are major net contributors to the EU budget (principally Germany, the Netherlands, Austria, and Sweden) do not want to pay more for enlargement; in fact, some are calling for a reduction of their net contributions as the budgetary constraints of EMU and slower economic growth make national contributions to the EU a bigger issue in domestic politics. Also politicizing the issue of net contributions is the increasingly redistributive effects and goals of the EU budget, especially with the growing relative importance of the Structural and Cohesion Funds. On the other hand, member states that are major net recipients (Spain, Portugal, Greece, and Ireland) oppose a reduction in their EU benefits because of enlargement.

Since 1975, the EU budget has consisted soley of Community "own resources"—the term for "sources of revenue that the Member States have agreed should belong to the Union rather than the Member States—what a Commission publication on the Union budget defines as 'tax revenue allocated once and for all to the Union.'"[35] These own resources consist of customs duties and agricultural levies, a percentage of national value-added tax (VAT), and GNP-related national contributions. For 1999, it was estimated that 35.5 percent of EU revenues came from the VAT resource and 45.9 percent from the GNP-based resource, indicating a high level of reliance by the EU on contributions from the member states for its revenues.[36] The amount of these revenues and the overall size of the budget are limited by the member states. In 1992, the Edinburgh European Council agreed to a budgetary ceiling of 1.27 percent of EU GNP for the period until 1999. As a consequence, while the size of the EU budget appears large in absolute terms—about EUR 97 billion in 1999—it is actually quite small in relation to overall public spending in the EU, which exceeds 50 percent of GNP in many member states.[37]

Until recently, public discussion of national net contributions was frowned upon, being viewed as anti-*communautaire* and not in the interest of European integration. The one major exception to this silence was the vocal campaign of Prime Minister Thatcher for an adjustment to the British contribution in the early 1980s. Since Britain's small and relatively efficient farm sector received only limited payments from the CAP, which at the time consumed over two-thirds of EU expenditures, after accession in 1973 Britain became a large net contributor to the EU budget. The creation of the ERDF in 1975, with much of its spending going to underdeveloped and declining industrial regions in Britain, was in part an effort to redress this budgetary imbalance, but it had only a limited effect. As a consequence, after her election in 1979, Thatcher launched a public campaign to get "our money back" from Brussels. Thatcher's "handbag diplomacy," including the threat to block agreements on Mediterranean enlargement and further deepening, led to the 1984 Fontainebleau Agreement on a "rebate" for Britain that would reduce the amount of its net contribution. No ending date for this annual rebate was determined.[38]

By the mid-1990s, in the context of slow economic growth and the budgetary constraints imposed by the EMU convergence criteria, and with the EU now facing the prospect of a potentially expensive eastern enlargement, the issue of net contributions (payments into the EU budget minus receipts, or share of EU expenditures) became more visible and politically salient. In 1997, the largest net contributors to the EU budget were relatively wealthy northern member states: Germany accounted for about 62 percent of total net contributions, the Netherlands 13 percent, Britain (even after the rebate) 10 percent, Sweden 6.4 percent, and Austria 4 percent. While France contributed 4.4 percent of the total, this amount accounted for only 0.06 percent of national GNP, compared to 0.7 and 0.6 percent for the Netherlands and Germany, respectively. The largest net recipients were relatively poor, southern member states: Spain was the main beneficiary, with 34 percent of total net receipts, followed by Greece at 24 percent, and Portugal and Ireland at 15 percent each. Belgium and Luxembourg were also notable net beneficiaries, at 6 and 4 percent respectively. For Luxembourg, its net receipts accounted for almost 5 percent of national GNP! The budgetary positions of the remaining member states (Denmark, Italy, and Finland) were pretty much in balance.[39] Because of these divergent budgetary positions, with net contributors demanding a reduction of their payments and net recipients seeking to defend their benefits, by the end of the 1990s the debate over EU finances was generating a growing north-south divide among the member states that threatened both policy reform and enlargement.[40]

At the 1995 Madrid summit, the European Council charged the Commission with preparing a new financial perspective for 2000–2006, including an analysis of the budgetary impact of enlargement. This report was subsequently released as part of "Agenda 2000." Because of the known opposition of such net contributors as Germany and the Netherlands to increased expenditures, the Commission began with the assumption that any upward revision of the existing own resources ceiling (1.27 percent of GNP) was not possible. Therefore, in "Agenda 2000" the Commission argued that the challenges of policy reform and enlargement could be met without exceeding the established spending limit. In fact, the Commission estimated that actual budgetary appropriations for 2006 would amount to only 1.22 percent of GNP, well under this ceiling.[41]

In "Agenda 2000," the Commission proposed total spending of ECU 114.5 billion for 2006, a slight increase in absolute terms from the projected total of ECU 97.8 billion for 1999. It also called for retaining the present financing system during this period, arguing that, while the next enlargement would "inevitably provoke a deterioration in the budgetary positions of all the current Member States, reducing the positive balances of net beneficiaries and increasing the negative ones of the others," it should not "lead to major changes in [their] relative budgetary positions." Nevertheless, the Commission warned that further enlargement, beyond the first wave of six, would probably require a raise of the EU spending ceiling and fundamental reform of the financing system, including a reconsideration of the British rebate. As a contribution to this looming debate, the Commission reaffirmed that it would present, in the course of 1998, a report on the functioning of the own resources system.[42]

The Commission's "Agenda 2000" proposals did little to assuage the concerns of the member states, however. After the release of "Agenda 2000," the German and Dutch governments renewed their demands for a reduction in their EU payments and a rebalancing of national contributions. The German government was particularly vocal in demanding a fairer distribution of budgetary burdens. Arguing that it would no longer be the "paymaster" of Europe, Bonn pointed out that, because of unification with the poorer eastern states (Länder), Germany had slipped down the EU list in terms of per capita GDP and now ranked in the middle of the pack (fifth in 1997, behind Luxembourg, Denmark, Austria, and Belgium). It also claimed that it was unfair for Germany to continue paying 0.6 percent of its national income to the EU, or more than half the total net contributions, when its GDP made up only 25 percent of the EU total. Instead, Bonn argued for linking contributions more closely to the wealth of member states, by capping them at something like 0.4 percent of GDP.[43]

On the other hand, member states that were net recipients, led by Spain, opposed any reduction of their benefits and countered the Commission's proposals by arguing that it would be difficult to pay for enlargement within the existing budgetary ceiling (without, that is, "unjust" reductions in transfers to poorer current member states). Spain also rejected German government suggestions that it and other poorer member states that join the euro-zone should give up their rights to Cohesion Fund assistance. The "cohesion countries" also pointed out that it was the wealthier (mainly northern European) net contributors, after all, that were more likely to benefit economically from eastern enlargement, while they were unlikely to benefit much at all because of geography and the lack of historical ties to the applicant countries. Instead, enlargement would only bring them problems in the form of increased economic competition from low-cost countries and reduced shares of EU assistance. Among the other member states, Britain rejected calls to eliminate its special rebate, while such relatively wealthy net recipients as Denmark, Luxembourg, and Belgium strongly defended their privileged budgetary positions.[44]

There was little progress made on budgetary issues at either the Luxembourg or Cardiff summits. As with the other "Agenda 2000" items, hard bargaining and tough decisions would follow the German elections and take place under the pressure of the March 1999 deadline for an agreement on "Agenda 2000" that was set at Cardiff.[45] In anticipation of this intergovernmental bargaining, Commission President Santer admonished the member states to avoid "falling into the trap of a purely national, penny pinching approach," arguing that squabbling over money should not be allowed to paralyze the EU's historic enlargement into Central and Eastern Europe.[46]

In October 1998, the Commission provided additional fuel to the debate over the EU's budget and finances by releasing its promised own resources report. The report was historically significant because in it the Commission admitted, for the first time ever in a public EU document, the existence of "budgetary imbalances" for certain member states, with some receiving less from the EU budget than they put in. As a means of addressing these imbalances, the Commission proposed several options, including simplification of the own resources system through greater reliance on GNP-based contributions. However, the Commission opposed introducing greater progressivity into the system, as advocated by Spain and other poorer member states, since this would be contrary to the EU principle of solidarity and to the current policy of practicing solidarity through the expenditure side of the budget. The Commission also expressed skepticism about the idea of a "generalized correction mechanism" for net contributors on the model of the

British rebate. Instead, its favored ideas for dealing with budgetary imbalances included the partial renationalization of the CAP ("co-financing"), with national governments becoming responsible for a proportion (25 percent) of direct income payments to farmers. It also favored elimination of the British rebate, which the Commission argued was no longer justified because of changing circumstances since 1984 (especially the decreased budgetary share of the CAP) and the anticipated impact of enlargement on Britain's relative prosperity in the EU. However, the Commission repeated its "Agenda 2000" claim that early reform of the own resources system was not necessary, and that this could await the accession of new member states.[47]

THE VIENNA SUMMIT

With the Commission's report on own resources in hand and the election of a new Social Democratic–led government in Germany, the stage was set by the late fall of 1998 for serious intergovernmental bargaining on "Agenda 2000." By this point, however, member state positions seemed to be hardening. The French government immediately rejected the Commission's proposal for co-financing a portion of CAP subsidies. As the largest recipient of EU farm aid, France would be particularly negatively affected by co-financing, which would shift some of the spending burden back to national budgets. At a meeting of EU finance ministers in October, France's Dominique Strauss-Kahn argued against the idea by claiming that it was "not in the spirit of community action." The British government also rejected any attempt to eliminate its rebate. On the other hand, Germany's outgoing finance minister, Theo Waigel, argued that a combination of co-financing, a reduction of the British rebate, and a generalized correction mechanism for net contributors was the only viable solution to the problem of budgetary imbalances.[48] Also pressing for change was the Dutch government, which objected to its status as the EU's largest net contributor in proportional terms (0.76 percent of GDP) and threatened a first-ever use of its veto to block a financing deal that did not treat the Netherlands more fairly. Specifically, the Dutch government argued for a generalized correction mechanism, including a "net limiter," that would prevent excessive burdens on particular member states from arising.[49]

The rigidity of member state positions indicated that achieving a compromise would be difficult. As a result, interest grew in the idea of "freezing" the EU budget for 2000–2006 at 1999 levels, thus eliminating the small increase in spending contained in the Commission's financial perspective. The budget freeze (or "stabilization") idea was supported by the large net contributors and by the French and British governments, who saw it as a means of reducing pressure for actions (co-financing and reducing the British rebate, respectively) that would be more harmful to their interests. It was strongly opposed, however, by the net recipients and by the Commission, which argued that a budget freeze would hurt its plans for

reforming the CAP and the Structural Funds. On the eve of the December summit in Vienna, the EU's north-south divide on budgetary and spending issues
appeared to be growing deeper.[50]

Further complicating matters was the demand of the new German government
that an agreement on greater tax harmonization within the EU, including the use
of majority voting on tax issues, should be part of the EU reforms in advance of
enlargement. Greater tax harmonization was necessary, according to Bonn, because
unfairly low tax levels in other member states (such as Luxembourg) were distort-
ing economic activity and penalizing higher-tax countries such as Germany. A
major source of this problem was the existence of different national rates for indi-
rect taxes, such as the VAT. German Finance Minister Oskar Lafontaine linked the
tax issue to the budget and financing issue by declaring that the EU cannot "expect
Germany to pay the highest net contribution, but at the same time it does nothing against unfair tax competition." This was a situation, he argued, that "is incompatible with the thought of solidarity."[51]

Meeting in Vienna on December 11–12, EU leaders made little headway on
"Agenda 2000." Instead, they agreed to disagree, while emphasizing the need to
reach a final decision on the budget and policy reforms at the special summit
scheduled for March 1999. While the meeting was amicable, national leaders held
fast to their previously declared positions. After the summit, Belgian Prime Minister Jean-Luc Dehaene summed up the EU's dilemma: "Nobody wants to pay more,
some want to pay less, nobody wants to get less and we have to spend more for
enlargement." Nevertheless, in the summit's "Presidency Conclusions," EU leaders
declared their "firm commitment to reach overall agreement on Agenda 2000 at
the European Council on 24–25 March 1999." The statement also stressed the
need for compromise by inviting "all Member States to make their full contribution to achieving a fair, balanced and acceptable outcome on the basis of budgetary rigour."[52]

The prospects for an agreement were bolstered by the German government's
announcement that achieving a deal on "Agenda 2000" would be the main goal of
its EU presidency in the first half of 1999. The failure to reach an agreement,
according to German Foreign Minister Joschka Fischer, would create a "logjam of
problems" that would endanger the EU's "historic" enlargement into Central and
Eastern Europe.[53]

ACHIEVING A DEAL

At the beginning of 1999, therefore, the stakes for the EU were quite high. The
failure to reach an agreement on "Agenda 2000" would almost certainly mean a
new period of crisis and uncertainty for the EU. Not only would failure endanger
enlargement, but it would also make impossible medium-term budgetary planning,
lead to heightened acrimony among the member states, and result in increased

public disaffection with the EU. All of the member states were aware of these high stakes, and none wanted to be seen as responsible for failure of the talks and the ensuing problems. Thus, behind the façade of formal national positions was evidence of a willingness to compromise, or so it was claimed by Germany's Fischer, who returned from a pre-Christmas tour of EU capitals expressing "cautious optimism" about the prospect of reaching a deal. Nonetheless, Fischer agreed that the "Agenda 2000" negotiations would be a "tough nut to crack," and he admitted that much hard bargaining remained.[54]

After a slow beginning under the German presidency, the pace of negotiations intensified with a meeting of EU foreign ministers (General Affairs Council) in late January. This was followed by a meeting of economics and finance ministers (Ecofin) on February 8. Neither meeting produced any major breakthroughs, although the foreign ministers agreed on creating a "performance reserve," amounting to 4 percent of the money allocated for the Structural Funds, which the Commission would use to finance projects of special merit in poorer regions of the EU. Even though it had originally proposed a 10-percent fund, this decision was welcomed by the Commission as an "important step" toward raising the overall quality of Structural Funds projects. On the other hand, the foreign ministers failed to agree on a German proposal for a "top-down" system of financial control with strict limits on farm spending.[55] At the Ecofin meeting, national ministers simply restated the well-known positions of their governments, and the debate on EU finances revealed continued widespread differences. After the meeting, Dutch Finance Minister Gerrit Zalm claimed that it "would need a small miracle" to achieve agreement on "Agenda 2000" in March.[56]

There was some movement on the CAP, however, with the French government's announcement in January that it now supported progressively cutting direct aid payments to farmers after these payments peaked early in the next decade. This action would allow a freeze in CAP spending and would put an end to the tradition of ever-expanding CAP budgets. However, the French government still opposed cuts in milk prices, and it continued to reject the idea of co-financing.[57]

At the end of February, there was a series of meetings aimed at generating progress toward a final deal. On February 22, the German presidency organized a "conclave" of foreign ministers in Luxembourg to discuss "Agenda 2000" and prepare for an informal summit in Bonn later that week. The meeting produced no real breakthroughs, however, and widely divergent interpretations of its results; while Germany's Fischer spoke of "very useful and constructive discussions" revealing "possible means of drawing positions closer together," France's European Affairs Minister, Pierre Moscovici, referred to the conclave as a "day of useful but unproductive discussion."[58]

On the same day, EU farm ministers met in Brussels to begin a "marathon" session on CAP reform. As they gathered, an estimated thirty thousand European farmers staged massive protests in the city against cuts in agricultural support. The marathon session proved fruitless, however, ending without agreement after four days of intense negotiations; this, despite the Commission's offer of a compromise package that would reduce its proposed cuts in beef prices (from 30 to 25 percent) and milk prices (from 15 to 10 percent), along with other concessionary changes to its "Agenda 2000" proposals. The meeting revealed that serious disagreements among national governments remained over specific items, such as changes to pro-duction-limiting quotas for milk, cereals prices, and options for cutting direct aid payments to farmers. France and other member states also insisted that there could be no final agreement on the CAP until a broader deal on EU finances and the Structural Funds was reached.[59]

As the meeting of farm ministers in Brussels broke up, EU leaders convened an informal summit at the historic Petersberg hotel near Bonn. Before the meeting, the German government had announced that its purpose was not to reach any final decisions but rather to serve as an opportunity for EU leaders to exchange views in preparation for later negotiations. Given the still widely divergent positions of the member states, some observers claimed that the summit could be counted as a success merely if it avoided acrimonious discussion and kept the "Agenda 2000" negotiations from being derailed.[60]

However, while the Petersberg summit did not produce any final decisions, it did generate some movement toward a final agreement. At the meeting, Chancel-lor Schröder backed away from German insistence on co-financing of the CAP, and support appeared to be building for the German idea of replacing the VAT own resource with one based on GNP. There was also broad agreement that some stabilization of EU spending was required, although there remained widely differ-ing views on what this meant, ranging from the opposition of the "cohesion coun-tries" (Spain, Portugal, Greece, and Ireland) and other member states (Belgium and Luxembourg) to an actual freeze of current spending, to the view of net contrib-utors (such as the Netherlands) that existing stabilization proposals did not go far enough. The summit was also united in criticizing the farm ministers for failing to reach an accord at their Brussels meeting. According to Chancellor Schröder, the Agricultural Council did "not fulfil its mission" of reaching an acceptable agree-ment. EU leaders criticized the Council's interim report for exceeding the EUR 40.5 billion per year spending limit on the CAP, which had been set by the Euro-pean Council, and they asked the farm ministers to, in the words of French Presi-dent Chirac, "reframe" their negotiations in view of the signals sent by the Peters-berg discussions. At Petersberg, EU leaders reaffirmed their intention to reach an agreement on "Agenda 2000" at the Berlin summit in March. Chancellor Schröder also revealed his plans to make a tour of EU capitals in mid-March in the effort to secure a deal.[61]

Negotiations among EU farm ministers were due to resume several days after the Petersberg meeting. However, the French government requested a brief pause in the negotiations to allow the French and German governments to reconcile their conflicting views, and this was reluctantly agreed to by the other member states. On March 4, after direct bilateral discussions between representatives of Paris and Bonn, the German government announced that it was dropping its proposal for co-financing of the CAP.[62]

Bonn's surprising decision not only improved relations between the French and German governments, which had been noticeably soured by the dispute over the CAP and EU finances, but also cleared the way for an agreement on farm spending. On March 4, the agriculture ministers reconvened their negotiations in Brussels. The following day, the German government presented new proposals that diluted proposed reforms even further, including decreasing price cuts for beef and cereals and leaving the EU's milk quota regime untouched until 2006. The German government claimed that these proposals would reduce the need for increased direct payments to farmers—thus making unnecessary a politically difficult decision to progressively reduce, or "degress," these as well—and thereby keep the yearly CAP budget within the EUR 40.5 billion limit set by the European Council. Member states favoring more radical reform, such as Britain, Sweden, and Denmark, were greatly upset with the German proposals, as was the Commission, which pointed to the high costs of extending an unreformed CAP to agriculturally intensive CEECs such as Poland.[63]

After further discussion, on March 10 the German presidency presented a "final compromise," which served as the basis for an agreement. This compromise accepted the Commission's 20-percent cut in cereals prices while proposing cuts of 15 and 20 percent for milk and beef prices, respectively. It also proposed raising the production quotas for milk by 1.5 percent for most countries, with additional allowances for Italy, Britain, Greece, Spain, and Ireland, and a review in 2003 to discuss letting the present quota arrangements expire after 2006. There was no co-financing, and there were no provisions for cutting direct aid to farmers in the proposal.[64]

At 3:30 A.M. on March 11, a final agreement was reached that followed closely the German compromise proposal. Its total cost for seven years exceeded by more than EUR 6 billion (about 2 percent) the budget limit set by the European Council. This amount was deemed insignificant by the German presidency and the Commission, however, and justified by the benefits the deal would bring EU consumers and farmers. Speaking at a joint press conference after conclusion of the negotiations, the German agriculture minister, Karl-Heinz Funke, and EU agricultural commissioner, Franz Fischler, termed the agreement the most important reform in the history of the CAP. More reform-minded member states were less happy with the deal, however. In particular, the British, Swedish, and Dutch governments criticized the agreement for not going far enough—it did not provide for the gradual reduction of direct payments to farmers, for instance—and for exceeding the expenditure limits set by the European Council. The deal reached by the farm ministers, they argued, did not represent a real freeze of spending, as desired by the European Council. Also unhappy were farmer's organizations, which attacked the agreement as too onerous.[65]

In any event, the CAP agreement would not be final until overall agreement was reached on "Agenda 2000" in Berlin. At an informal meeting in Germany on

March 14, EU foreign ministers decided that they would not reopen the complex farm deal, leaving intact its decisions on prices and marketing arrangements, but instead talked of "fine tuning" to reduce the overall cost of the package, perhaps through reductions in direct payments to farmers. After the meeting, Germany's Fischer also reported progress in the Structural Funds negotiations, indicating that special arrangements would be made to help Portugal and Ireland, both of whom would lose heavily under the Commission's reform proposals. The Lisbon government had previously (in February) announced that it would block an "Agenda 2000" agreement unless a way was found to spare Portugal sharp cuts in regional aid. Fischer indicated no progress, however, on the issue of reducing Germany's budgetary contributions and the related question of the British rebate.[66]

These and other issues were the subject of discussions between Chancellor Schröder and other national leaders during his five-day tour of EU capitals in mid-March. In the meantime, a new crisis had emerged with the surprise resignation of the entire Commission on March 16, following the release of a special independent committee report accusing some commissioners of fraud, nepotism, and mismanagement.[67] While the Commission's resignation caused an institutional crisis for the EU, the German presidency denied that it would negatively impact the "Agenda 2000" negotiations. According to Fischer, the Commission's preparatory work for an agreement was already largely completed, and the remaining issues to be resolved were political decisions for the EU heads of state and government.[68] If anything, the Commission's resignation gave the member states greater incentive to reach a deal to avoid compounding the EU's institutional crisis with a failure on "Agenda 2000."

Heading into the Berlin summit, the main outstanding issue was the EU's financing system, including the matter of national contributions. At a foreign ministers' conclave on March 21, the German government proposed a compromise plan whereby Britain would be allowed to keep its rebate, although with some modifications, and the EU's VAT resource would be gradually replaced by one based on GNP. The German plan also included a "safety net" that would provide a partial correction for member states with a net budgetary imbalance in excess of a certain percentage of GNP (for example, 0.6 percent). Another outstanding issue was the level of Structural and Cohesion Funds spending, with Germany and other net contributors favoring a seven-year limit of less than EUR 200 billion—well below the Commission's original proposal—while Spain and other poor member states defended a ceiling of EUR 239 billion or above. In the German plan, a compromise level would be found somewhere between EUR 190.5 and 216 billion. Decisions also had to be made on the allocation of Structural Funds spending, including the nature of transitional arrangements for regions losing support. No agreements on these and other issues were reached at the conclave, however, meaning that final decisions would have to await Berlin. Nevertheless, after the meeting, the German government claimed that the prospects of reaching a final agreement were "clearly improved."[69]

THE BERLIN SUMMIT

On the eve of the Berlin summit, the basis of a deal on Structural Funds spending began to emerge. The Spanish government announced that it could accept an overall ceiling for structural spending of between EUR 210 billion and 220 billion. Also, the German government had previously agreed that Spain and other poorer member states could continue receiving Cohesion Fund assistance even if they belonged to the euro-zone, provided their GNPs remained less than 90 percent of the EU average. However, Bonn also insisted upon regular reviews of Cohesion Fund eligibility beginning in 2002. The rapprochement between Spain and Germany, together with Italy's willingness to shift EU financing from a VAT-based to a GNP-based resource (a move that would hurt Italy in particular), put increased pressure on other member states, especially France and Britain, to also show flexibility. In a letter to fellow leaders just before the summit, Chancellor Schröder appealed for all member states to show flexibility and a readiness to compromise, declaring that an adequate agreement, "based on the principles of strict budgetary discipline, solidarity, fair burden sharing and balance," was necessary to open the door for enlargement.[70]

Despite Schröder's appeal, the Berlin summit quickly bogged down in disputes over the expected issues. There was disagreement over how, and whether, to trim EUR 6 billion from the CAP package agreed to by the Agricultural Council in order to reduce farm spending to the level previously set by the European Council. President Chirac—under strong pressure at home from French farmers—sought improvements in the agriculture deal and proposed reopening the entire CAP package, a move that was rejected by other leaders. Spain and other poor member states rejected the German proposal to set a ceiling of EUR 210 billion on Structural and Cohesion Funds spending, while the Netherlands and other wealthy net contributors called for a ceiling of EUR 190 billion. The British government also refused to accept any changes to its budget rebate, leading France's European affairs minister to warn that British intransigence could poison relations between the two countries. An exasperated Chancellor Schröder warned that he would allow the negotiations to lapse for the remainder of the German presidency if there was no agreement in Berlin, implying that Germany would be a much tougher bargaining partner in negotiations to reduce its budgetary contribution once its presidency term was over.[71]

Finally, at dawn of the summit's third day, and after twenty hours of difficult negotiations, EU leaders reached an agreement. Because of pressure from Chirac, the CAP reform package agreed to in early March was "redesigned" (Chirac's description) and substantially diluted. Reform of the milk quota regime was delayed, and price cuts for cereals were reduced from 20 to 15 percent. There was no agreement on reducing direct payments to farmers, mainly because EU leaders could not agree on a model for doing so. However, since higher price subsidies would reduce the need for direct payments, the cost of the total farm package was right around, or only slightly above, the freeze target of EUR 40.5 billion per year. EU leaders also agreed to a seven-year total of EUR 213 billion for Structural and Cohesion Funds spending. Because of the consolidation of structural operations, the proportion of the EU population receiving regional aid would drop from 51 to 42 percent. Generous transitional arrangements and special packages were agreed for regions losing aid, and a British-proposed "safety net" limiting the loss of objective 2 aid to one-third of the 1999 amount was approved. The four poorest member states won the right to continue receiving Cohesion Fund assistance, and the total amount of the Cohesion Fund for 2000–2006 was actually increased to EUR 18 billion (from the EUR 15 billion proposed by the German presidency).

Regarding the financing system, in Berlin the British government successfully defended its budget rebate, although it agreed to forfeit "windfall gains" that would result from the implementation of financing reforms agreed at the summit; this would reduce Britain's total rebate by only about EUR 220 million by 2006. EU leaders agreed to reduce the role in EU financing of the VAT resource and to increase the amount paid on the basis of GNP. Other changes to the financing system included agreement to allow member states to retain 25 percent of "traditional own resources"—customs duties and agricultural levies—to cover collection costs, a move that would benefit the Netherlands particularly, and agreement that the four biggest net contributors (Austria, Germany, the Netherlands, and Sweden) would contribute less in the future to Britain's rebate, with the other member states making up the difference. There would be no safety net or generalized correction measure to prevent excessive net contributions, however. Because of these and other changes to the financing system, the German net contribution would be somewhat reduced below its current EUR 11 billion, although no figures for this reduction were given by the German government.

The financial framework agreed to by EU leaders in Berlin also included money for enlargement, including EUR 3.12 billion per year for pre-accession aid to the applicant countries. It also included funding, beginning with EUR 4.14 billion in 2002 and rising to EUR 14.22 billion by 2006, that was designated specifically for the new member states to cover payments resulting from accession. It was agreed that the pre-accession aid and money for "accession-related expenditure" would be "ring-fenced" to prevent misappropriation by the member states for other purposes.[72]

Despite these agreements, the Berlin deal on "Agenda 2000" was criticized as insufficient by many commentators. Drawing particular criticism was the summit's dilution of the CAP reforms. While the Berlin deal stabilized agricultural spending for the near future, by reducing price cuts and failing to agree on a plan for reducing direct payments to farmers it would also make the full extension of CAP benefits to new member states too expensive. Therefore, unless the new member states were to be excluded from full participation in the CAP indefinitely, something that would be politically and morally unsustainable, additional and more radical reforms of the CAP would be necessary in the future. Pressure for further reforms was also certain to come from the United States and other agricultural exporting countries in future rounds of global trade talks. Thus, the Berlin deal simply postponed difficult reforms of the CAP until a later date.[73]

EU leaders viewed the Berlin agreement more positively, however. While acknowledging that the compromise deal was "not ideal," Chancellor Schröder nevertheless declared that he was "a bit proud" of the agreement, which represented a "reasonable combination of budgetary discipline and social justice," of "solidarity by the strongest with the weakest." He also called attention to the fact that this was the first time ever the EU had undertaken simultaneous negotiations on changes to its finances, the CAP, and the Structural Funds. These positive sentiments were echoed by the Commission. Most national government leaders were also able to declare victory for having won concessions on issues that were of particular importance to them and their domestic constituencies.[74]

Because of the Berlin deal on "Agenda 2000," the EU avoided another crisis on top of its ongoing institutional one. The Berlin agreement also enabled the EU to appear united and to focus more of its attention on the mounting crisis in Kosovo and the Western Balkans. Perhaps most importantly, however, by giving the EU a financial framework for the next seven years and by allowing it to focus on other necessary internal reforms, the Berlin agreement on "Agenda 2000" allowed the EU to move forward with enlargement. In the summit's "Presidency Conclusions," the European Council sought to signal the anxious applicants that enlargement was on track, declaring:

> In the light of the outcome on Agenda 2000 on 24/25 March, the European Council wishes to send a message of reassurance to the countries negotiating for accession. Enlargement remains a historic priority for the European Union. The accession negotiations will continue each in accordance with its own rhythm and as rapidly as possible. It calls on the Council and the Commission to ensure that the pace of the negotiations is maintained accordingly.[75]

The Berlin "Agenda 2000" package still faced some hurdles, however. The EP had to give its Opinion on the CAP agreement, and its approval ("assent") was needed for the changes to the Structural and Cohesion Funds and for the budgetary Interinstitutional Agreement required for the financial perspective. In late February, the EP's President, José María Gil-Robles, had threatened to block an "Agenda 2000" agreement that was "very imbalanced"; he also pointed out the short amount of time (twenty-five working days) between the Berlin summit and the EP's last plenary session in early May before June elections for a new Parliament. Failure to gain the EP's approval would mean beginning the new financial year (in July 1999) without a budget and could delay enlargement and other EU business.[76] Working against time, the Council gave final approval to the legal texts ("Regulations") for the Structural and Cohesion Funds on April 12, so that these could be presented to the EP. After negotiations between the Council, the EP, and the Commission to resolve remaining differences, the "Agenda 2000" package was formally approved by the EP on May 6.[77] With "Agenda 2000" approved, the EU could now turn its attention to the other major task of internal reform in preparation for enlargement: the reform of its decision-making institutions and procedures.

NOTES

1. European Commission, "Europe and the Challenge of Enlargement," annexed to "Lisbon Presidency Conclusions," in *The European Councils: Conclusions of the Presidency 1992–1994* (Brussels: European Commission, Directorate-General for Information, 1995), 24–29.

2. "European Council in Copenhagen, 21–22 June 1993: Presidency Conclusions" ("Copenhagen Presidency Conclusions"), in *European Councils* (1992–94), 86.

3. "European Council in Essen, 9–10 December 1994: Presidency Conclusions" ("Essen Presidency Conclusions"), in *European Councils* (1992–94), 146 and 158. On estimates of the potential cost of eastern enlargement, see Lionel Barber, "EU's Outstretched Hand to East Begins to Waver," *Financial Times,* 23 November 1994, 3.

4. European Commission, "Interim Report from the Commission to the European Council on the Effects on the Policies of the European Union of Enlargement to the Associated Countries of Central and Eastern Europe," CSE (95) 605, 5 December 1995; Lionel Barber, "Larger EU at Any Price," *Financial Times,* 30 November 1995, 2.

5. "Madrid European Council, 15–16 December 1995: Presidency Conclusions" ("Madrid Presidency Conclusions"), in *The European Councils: Conclusions of the Presidency 1995* (Brussels: European Commission, 1995), 47–48.

6. European Commission, "Agenda 2000: For a Stronger and Wider Union," *Bulletin of the European Union,* supp. 5/97.

7. European Commission, "Agenda 2000," 138; GDP and employment figures are for 1994 and 1995, respectively. In the EU's 1999 budget, the CAP accounted for 42.2 percent of expenditures (appropriations for commitments); see European Commission, "General Budget of the European Union for the Financial Year 1999: The Figures," SEC (99) EN, January 1999, 7.

8. On the origins and development of the CAP, see Desmond Dinan, *Ever Closer Union: An Introduction to European Integration* (Boulder: Lynne Rienner, 1999), 333–46.

9. European Commission, "Agenda 2000," 113 and 138.

10. European Commission, "Agenda 2000," 53.

11. European Commission, "Interim Report From the Commission." See also European Commission, "Agricultural Strategy Paper," CSE (95) 607, 1995, 196.

12. On these estimates, see Heather Grabbe and Kirsty Hughes, *Enlarging the EU Eastwards* (London: Royal Institute of International Affairs, 1998), 97; and Alan Mayhew, *Recreating Europe* (Cambridge: Cambridge University Press, 1998), 273–74.

13. European Commission, "Agenda 2000," 29–33 and 73. Figures are for "appropriation for commitments" and are in 1997 prices.

14. European Commission, "Agenda 2000," 62–63 and 73.

15. Michael Smith, "The Great Survivor," *Financial Times,* 3 November 1997, 16.

16. Michael Smith, "Bonn Attacks 'Unnecessary' CAP Reforms," *Financial Times,* 9 September 1997, 4; Michael Smith, "Reform of CAP Divides Ministers," *Financial Times,*

23 September 1997, 2; Maggie Urry, "Softer Stance on Farm Subsidies," *Financial Times,* 22 January 1998, 24.

17. Michael Smith, "Farmers Uneasy at CAP Reform Plan," *Financial Times,* 19 February 1998, 2.

18. Michael Smith and Maggie Urry, "Fischler Prepares to Turn Farmers into Entrepreneurs," *Financial Times,* 17 March 1998, 2; Lionel Barber, "EU Puts Itself to the Test with Proposals to Overhaul CAP and Regional Spending," *Financial Times,* 19 March 1998, 2; Knut Pries, "Kampf um knappere EU-Hilfen eröffnet," *Frankfurter Rundschau,* 19 March 1998; "EU-Kommission stellt Details der 'Agenda 2000' vor," *Süddeutsche Zeitung,* 19 March 1998. The Commission's legislative proposals for reforming the CAP are available on the Internet at the EU's official Website at http://europa.eu.int/en/comm/dg06/ag2000/reg-prop/index_en.htm. For a summary and explanation of the CAP proposals, see European Commission, "Explanatory Memorandum: The Future of European Agriculture" at http://europa.eu.int/en/comm/dg06/ag2000/agprop/mot_en.htm.

19. Michael Smith, "Ministers Denounce Farm Blueprint," *Financial Times,* 1 April 1998, 2; "Farmers Protest Over Reforms," *Financial Times,* 25 March 1998, 2; Agence Europe, *Europe Daily Bulletin,* no. 7192, 1 April 1998, 8 bis; Agence Europe, *Europe Daily Bulletin,* no. 7196, 6–7 April 1998, 12–13; Agence Europe, *Europe Daily Bulletin,* no. 7227, 23 May 1998, 8–9.

20. Lionel Barber and Robert Peston, "EU Sets Tough Deadline For CAP Reform," *Financial Times,* 17 June 1998, 2. For the formal conclusions of the Cardiff summit, see "Presidency Conclusions, Cardiff European Council, 15–16 June 1998" ("Cardiff Presidency Conclusions"), reprinted in Agence Europe, *Europe Documents,* no. 2094–2095, 18 June 1998, 1–13.

21. Michael Smith, "Fischler Faces Fight to Reform EU Common Agricultural Policy," *Financial Times,* 19 October 1998, 2; and Michael Smith, "EU Seeks Farm Accord Soon," *Financial Times,* 21 October 1998, 2. The Commission's co-financing proposal was part of its report on the EU's financing system and own resources. See European Commission, *Financing the European Union: Commission Report on the Operation of the Own Resources System* (Brussels: European Commission, 1998); available on the Internet at the EU's official Website at http://europa.eu.int. On the announcement of the report and reactions to it, see Agence Europe, *Europe Daily Bulletin,* no. 7317, 8 October 1998, 7–8; Agence Europe, *Europe Daily Bulletin,* no. 7318, 9 October 1998, 7; and Agence Europe, *Europe Daily Bulletin,* no. 7320, 12–13 October 1998, 8.

22. Spending on "structural operations" in the EU's 1999 budget was EUR 39.26 billion (appropriations for commitments); European Commission, "General Budget of the European Union for the Financial Year 1999," 7.

23. On the origins and development of the Structural and Cohesion Funds, see Ian Bache, *The Politics of European Union Regional Policy: Multi-Level Governance or Flexible Gatekeeping?* (Sheffield, Eng.: Sheffield Academic Press, 1998), 31–92. The specific target areas for Cohesion Fund aid are transportation infrastructure and the environment.

24. Source of GDP figures is EUROSTAT; published in Agence Europe, *Europe Weekly Selected Statistics,* no. 1068, 21 September 1998, 1.

25. Lionel Barber, "EU Warned Budget Cannot Grow to Pay for Expansion," *Financial Times,* 23 October 1995, 1. See also Bache, *Politics of European Regional Policy,* 121.

26. Calculation of the change in per capita GDP in an enlarged EU is based on 1995 data; European Commission, "Agenda 2000," 110.

27. European Commission, "Agenda 2000," 21.

28. European Commission, "Agenda 2000," 21–26 and 74. According to Regional Affairs Commissioner Monika Wulf-Mathies, "The rationalization [of the Structural Funds] has nothing to do with enlargement. We would have to do it anyway." Quoted in Lionel Barber, "No Turning Back From Brave New Europe," *Financial Times,* 17 July 1997, 3.

29. European Commission, "Agenda 2000," 21–26 and 74. The Commission's proposed 4 percent of GDP limit for Structural and Cohesion Funds receipts applied to both current and new member states.

30. Lionel Barber and Michael Smith, "EU States in Revolt Over Cost of Admitting Poorer Members," *Financial Times,* 16 September 1997, 16; Lionel Barber, "Spa Town May Not Soothe EU Nerves," *Financial Times,* 24 October 1997, 2; David White, "Spain Prepares to Fight for EU Grants," *Financial Times,* 18 November 1997, 4.

31. Brian Groom, "Brussels May Strip 11 EU Regions of Top Aid Facility," *Financial Times,* 1 December 1997, 16; Lionel Barber, "EU Regions Must Kick the Aid Habit," *Financial Times,* 20 February 1998, 2.

32. Barber, "Spa Town May Not Soothe EU Nerves," 2; Brian Groom and Lionel Barber, "Clash Over EU Regional Aid Plans," *Financial Times,* 26 February 1998, 9.

33. Lionel Barber, "Countries Aim to Cling on to Brussels Hand-Outs," *Financial Times,* 17 March 1998, 2; Barber, "EU Puts Itself to the Test," 2; Knut Pries, "Rückzug statt großer Sprünge," *Frankfurter Rundschau,* 19 March 1998; Pries, "Kampf um knappere EU-Hilfe eröffnet"; and "EU-Kommission stellt Details der 'Agenda 2000' vor." The full texts of the Commission's legislative proposals for the Structural and Cohesion Funds are available on the Internet, at the EU's official Website at http://europa.eu. int/comm/dg16/document/doc1g_en.htm. For a summary of the Structural Funds proposals, see European Commission, "Reform of the Structural Funds" (Explanatory Memorandum), COM (1998) 131 final, Brussels, 18 March 1998.

34. Lionel Barber and Brian Groom, "Aid Rows 'Threat to Enlargement,'" *Financial Times,* 8 June 1998, 3; Brian Groom, "EU Moves Towards Regional Aid Accord," *Financial Times,* 10 June 1998, 3; Barber and Peston, "EU Sets Tough Deadline for CAP Reform." On the ministerial negotiations, see Agence Europe, *Europe Daily Bulletin,* no. 7239, 11 June 1998, 11.

35. Iain Begg and Nigel Grimwade, *Paying for Europe* (Sheffield, Eng.: Sheffield Academic Press, 1998), 37; the cited Commission document is *The Community Budget: The Facts in Figures* (Luxembourg: Office for Official Publications of the European Communities, 1997).

36. European Commission, "General Budget of the European Union for the Financial Year 1999," 15.

37. The 1999 budget figure is for "appropriations for commitments"; see European Commission, "General Budget of the European Union for the Financial Year 1999," 5.

38. On the issue of net contributions and the British rebate, see Begg and Grimwade, *Paying for Europe,* 86–98.

39. Figures calculated from data contained in European Commission, *Financing the European Union.* The full text of the report is available on the Internet, at the EU's official Website at http://europa.eu.int. The report's key statistical tables are reprinted in Agence Europe, *Europe Selected Statistics,* no. 1072, 19 October 1998, 1–3. On the net contributions issue and debate, also see Dick Leonard, "The Price That Must be Paid for Friendship," *Financial Times,* 17 September 1998, 14. Leonard's article also contains an unofficial calculation (in ECU billions) of national net budgetary positions, done by the Center for European Policy Studies in Brussels.

40. On the EU's north-south divide and its implications for decision making, see Quentin Peel, "The EU's Real Split," *Financial Times,* 25 February 1999, 14.

41. European Commission, "Agenda 2000," 61–69 and 73.

42. European Commission, "Agenda 2000," 61–69 and 73; quotes are on page 68. The Commission's report was mandated by the 1994 own resources decision. This decision modified the February 1988 Brussels Agreement, which established the parameters of the current own resources system, including the upper limits and relative proportion of the various revenue sources making up the budget; see Begg and Grimwade, *Paying for Europe,* 45–48.

43. Peter Norman, "Bonn to Seek Reduction in EU Contributions," *Financial Times,* 21 July 1997, 2; Lionel Barber, "Foreign Ministers Divided on Cost of EU Enlargement," *Financial Times,* 23 July 1997, 14; "Waigel Wants Payments Cut," *Financial Times,* 11 August 1997, 2; Barber, "Row Threatens EU Enlargement Plans," 2; Barber, "Spa Town May Not Soothe EU Nerves," 2; Knut Pries, "Bundesregierung will für geringeren EU-Beitrag kämpfen," *Frankfurter Rundschau,* 14 October 1997; "Europas Zahlmeister steht allein," *Süddeutsche Zeitung,* 14 October 1997.

44. Barber, "Row Threatens EU Enlargement Plans," 2; Barber, "EU States in Revolt Over Costs of Admitting Poorer Members," 16; White, "Spain Prepares to Fight for EU Grants," 4; "EU Streitet vor dem Gipfeltreffen über Finanzierung der Ost- Erweiterung," *Süddeutsche Zeitung,* 8 December 1997, 21.

45. "Cardiff Presidency Conclusions," 8.

46. "EU Told Not to Penny Pinch," *Financial Times,* 23 October 1997, 3.

47. European Commission, *Financing the European Union.* For a summary of the Commission's report, see Agence Europe, *Europe Daily Bulletin,* no. 7317, 8 October 1998, 7–8. Also see Quentin Peel, "Way Paved for EU Funds Shift," *Financial Times,* 8 October 1998, 2; and Quentin Peel, "Santer Dares to Confront Taboo," *Financial Times,* 8 October 1998, 2.

48. Quentin Peel, "French Squash Hopes of EU Finance Deal," *Financial Times,* 13 October 1998, 2; Agence Europe, *Europe Daily Bulletin,* no. 7320, 12–13 October 1998, 7–8.

49. Gordon Cramb, "Dutch Anger Over EU Payment," *Financial Times,* 16 October 1998, 2. On national positions in the budget debate, see Quentin Peel, "Europe's Hard Sums," *Financial Times,* 20 October 1998, 16.

50. Michael Smith, "Support Grows for Budget Freeze," *Financial Times,* 20 November 1998, 2; Neil Buckley, "EU North and South Split on Spending Freeze," *Financial Times,* 7 December 1998, 3; Michael Smith, "Santer Warns Spending Cuts Could Freeze Reforms," *Financial Times,* 10 December 1998, 2; Peter Norman, "Budget Squabble Looms at the Vienna Summit," *Financial Times,* 10 December 1998, 2; Agence Europe, *Europe Daily Bulletin,* no. 7348, 23–24 November 1998, 9; Agence Europe, *Europe Daily Bulletin,* no. 7354, 2 December 1998, 8; Agence Europe, *Europe Daily Bulletin,* no. 7355, 3 December 1998, 6–7; Agence Europe, *Europe Daily Bulletin,* no. 7357, 5 December 1998, 7; Agence Europe, *Europe Daily Bulletin,* no. 7358, 7–8 December 1998, 7–8.

51. "Germany to Push Plans for Tax Harmonisation," *Financial Times,* 28 December 1998, 2; Peter Norman, Ralph Atkins, and Robert Peston, "Schröder Backs Lafontaine on EU Tax Decision-Making," *Financial Times,* 3 December 1998, 16; Ralph Atkins, "Lafontaine Links Tax Issue to EU Budget," *Financial Times,* 17 December 1998, 3.

52. "Presidency Conclusions," Vienna European Council, 11–12 December 1998; reprinted in Agence Europe, *Europe Daily Bulletin,* no. 7363, 13 December 1998, 7–21 (quotes on page 13); Peter Norman, Michael Smith, and David Wighton, "North-South Split on Financing EU Expansion Plans, *Financial Times,* 12–13 December 1998, 2; Peter

Norman and Michael Smith, "EU Leaders Put Off Enlargement Decisions," *Financial Times,* 14 December 1998, 2; Peter Norman, "Europe's Spoils Up for Grab," *Financial Times,* 14 December 1998, 13. The Dehaene quote is in Norman.

53. Peter Norman, "Bonn Says Failure to Secure Deal Will Create Logjam," *Financial Times,* 15 December 1998, 2; Agence Europe, *Europe Daily Bulletin,* no. 7364, 14–15 December 1998, 5. See also "Preview of the European Council in Vienna on 11 and 12 December 1998 and of the German Presidency in the First Half of 1999," Policy Statement by Gerhard Schröder, Chancellor of the Federal Republic of Germany, in the Bundestag on 10 December 1998, available on the Internet, at the Website of the German Information Center at http://www.germany-info.org/govern/schroeder _12_10_98.htm.

54. Peter Norman, "Bonn Keen to Rein in EU Farm Spending," *Financial Times,* 2–3 January 1999, 3. See also Quentin Peel, "Fischer Says Goal is Political Union," *Financial Times,* 13 January 1999, 2; and Agence Europe, *Europe Daily Bulletin,* no. 7381, 13 January 1999, 7.

55. Peter Norman, "EU Takes Step to Reform of Finances," *Financial Times,* 26 January 1999, 2; Agence Europe, *Europe Daily Bulletin,* no. 7390, 25–26 January 1999, 7.

56. Peter Norman, "Details of EU Reforms in Dispute," *Financial Times,* 9 February 1999, 2; Agence Europe, *Europe Daily Bulletin,* no. 7400, 8–9 February 1999, 9–10. For the text of the German government's "Presidency Conclusions" for the meeting, see Agence Europe, *Europe Daily Bulletin,* no. 7401, 10 February 1999, 4–5.

57. Michael Smith, "Farmers in EU Face Cuts in Subsidies," *Financial Times,* 19 January 1999, 3; Michael Smith, "EU Edges Closer to Cuts on Farm Subsidies," *Financial Times,* 8 February 1999, 2; Michael Smith, "CAP Cuts Aimed at Richer Farmers," *Financial Times,* 10 February 1999, 3.

58. Agence Europe, *Europe Daily Bulletin,* no. 7410, 22–23 February 1999, 7-8.

59. Michael Smith, "Tear Gas Used on Protesting Farmers," *Financial Times,* 23 February 1999, 2; Michael Smith, "Commission Unveils First Concessions," *Financial Times,* 23 February 1999, 2; Michael Smith, "EU Farm Ministers Close to Radical CAP Plan," *Financial Times,* 23 February 1999, 26; Michael Smith, "Brussels Offers Compromise Package," *Financial Times,* 26 February 1999, 2; Michael Smith, "Farm Deal Eludes EU Ministers," *Financial Times,* 27–28 February 1999, 2; Agence Europe, *Europe Daily Bulletin,* no. 7411, 24 February 1999, 12–13; Agence Europe, *Europe Daily Bulletin,* no. 7412, 25 February 1999, 8; Agence Europe, *Europe Daily Bulletin,* no. 7413, 26 February 1999, 9; Agence Europe, *Europe Daily Bulletin,* no. 7414, 27 February 1999, 8.

60. Peter Norman, "Fischer Out on a Limb as EU States Agree to Differ on Agenda 2000," *Financial Times,* 26 February 1999, 2; Agence Europe, *Europe Daily Bulletin,* no. 7413, 26 February 1999, 3.

61. On the Petersberg results, see Peter Norman, Andrew Parker, and Ralph Atkins, "European Leaders Fail to Reach Agreement on Reform Plans," *Financial Times,* 27–28 February 1999, 1; Agence Europe, *Europe Daily Bulletin,* no. 7414, 27 February 1999, 3–4; and Agence Europe, *Europe Daily Bulletin,* no. 7415, 1–2 March 1999, 3–5. Schröder's and Chirac's remarks are quoted in the latter citation.

62. On the French request for a pause, see Robert Graham, "France Seeks Pause in Talks on EU Reforms," *Financial Times,* 1 March 1999, 2; and Robert Graham, "Delay on Farm Policy Reform Talks Agreed," *Financial Times,* 2 March 1999, 3. On the impact of the dispute over the CAP and "Agenda 2000" on Franco-German relations, see Robert Graham, "Barnyard Noises," *Financial Times,* 3 March 1999, 13; and Ralph Atkins, "Germany Bites Back," *Financial Times,* 3 March 1999, 13. On the Franco-German negotiations and the Ger-

man decision on co-financing, see "French and Germans in Talks," *Financial Times,* 4 March 1999, 2; and Haig Simonian, "Bonn Offers Concession on EU Reform," *Financial Times,* 5 March 1999, 2.

63. For details of the negotiations and proposals, see Agence Europe, *Europe Daily Bulletin,* no. 7418, 5 March 1999, 8; Agence Europe, *Europe Daily Bulletin,* no. 7419, 6 March 1999, 5; Agence Europe, *Europe Daily Bulletin,* no. 7420, 8–9 March 1999, 9–10; Agence Europe, *Europe Daily Bulletin,* no. 7421, 10 March 1999, 13; and Michael Smith, "Germany's Change of Heart Over CAP Reform Leaves Brussels Baffled," *Financial Times,* 9 March 1999, 2.

64. Agence Europe, *Europe Daily Bulletin,* no. 7422, 11 March 1999, 10; Michael Smith, "Brussels on Course to Win Farm Reforms," *Financial Times,* 11 March 1999, 2.

65. Agence Europe, *Europe Daily Bulletin,* no. 7423, 12 March 1999, 6; Michael Smith and Tim Burt, "UK to Seek Tougher Terms on Farm Deal," *Financial Times,* 12 March 1999, 3; Michael Smith, "Brussels in Triumphal Mood After Deal on Farm Aid Regime," *Financial Times,* 12 March 1999, 2. For a summary of the Agricultural Council's CAP agreement, see Agence Europe, *Europe Daily Bulletin,* no. 7427, 18 March 1999, 11–12.

66. Peter Norman, "'Fine Tuning' for EU Farm Reform Deal," *Financial Times,* 15 March 1999, 2; Agence Europe, *Europe Daily Bulletin,* no. 7425, 15–16 March 1999, 3–5. On the Portuguese government's threat to block an agreement, see Peter Wise, "Portugal May Block EU Aid Reforms," *Financial Times,* 10 February 1999, 2.

67. The independent committee was established in December 1998 by the EP, with the agreement of the Commission, following a move by some MEPs to censure the Commission for its conduct. For the text of the committee's Conclusions, see Agence Europe, *Europe Documents,* no. 2128, 19 March 1999, 1–7.

68. Haig Simonian, "Reform Plan Still on Course," *Financial Times,* 17 March 1999, 2.

69. Peter Norman, "Bonn Offers Compromise Reform Plan," *Financial Times,* 22 March 1999, 3; Agence Europe, *Europe Daily Bulletin,* no. 7430, 22–23 March 1999, 9–11. The quotes are from Hans-Friedrich von Ploetz, Germany's under-secretary of state for foreign affairs, cited in the above. For details of the German plan, see Agence Europe, *Europe Daily Bulletin,* no. 7429, 20 March 1999, 3–4. On the Spanish position on Structural Funds spending, see David White, "Madrid Leads the Fight to Keep its Share of EU's Pot of Money," *Financial Times,* 11 March 1999, 2.

70. David White and Peter Norman, "Signs of EU Regional Funding Deal Emerge," *Financial Times,* 24 March 1999, 3. Bonn's views on the Cohesion Fund were contained in the compromise plan it submitted to the foreign ministers' conclave on March 21; for details, see Agence Europe, *Europe Daily Bulletin,* no. 7429, 20 March 1999, 4. For discussion of the pre-summit atmosphere, see Peter Norman, "Fit for Enlargement," *Financial Times,* 24 March 1999, 15; and Haig Simonian, "Schröder Faces Test of Leadership," *Financial Times,* 24 March 1999, 3. The text of Schröder's letter is reprinted in Agence Europe, *Europe Daily Bulletin,* no. 7431, 24 March 1999, 9–10.

71. For details of the negotiations in Berlin, see Peter Norman, Michael Smith, and Haig Simonian, "Talks on Farm Reform Hit Rough Ground," *Financial Times,* 26 March 1999, 3; Agence Europe, *Europe Daily Bulletin,* no. 7432, 25 March 1999, 7–8; and Agence Europe, *Europe Daily Bulletin,* no. 7433, 26 March 1999, 3–4.

72. On the results of the Berlin summit, see Peter Norman, Michael Smith, and Stefan Wagstyl, "Europe's Leaders Compromise on EU Reforms," *Financial Times,* 27–28 March 1999, 1; Peter Norman, "Twenty-Hour Talk Marathon Ends in Compromise," *Financial*

Times, 27–28 March 1999, 2; Michael Smith, "Defeat for Champions of Market Liberalisation," *Financial Times,* 27–28 March 1999, 2; Michael Smith, "UK and Spain are Big Winners," *Financial Times,* 27–28 March 1999, 2; Quentin Peel, "Blair Pays a Small Price to Keep Budget Rebate," *Financial Times,* 27–28 March 1999, 2; and Agence Europe, *Europe Daily Bulletin,* no. 7434, 27 March 1999, 4–7. The full text of the "Agenda 2000" agreement is contained in the Berlin summit "Presidency Conclusions," reprinted in Agence Europe, *Europe Documents,* no. 2131/2132, 27 March 1999, 2–15.

73. For criticism that the Berlin deal is insufficient, especially in the area of CAP reform, see "A Feeble Deal For Europe" (editorial), *Financial Times,* 29 March 1999, 15; and Michael Smith, "Diluted Farm Reforms Sap EU Stance," *Financial Times,* 30 March 1999, 3.

74. For Schröder's comments and the reactions of other EU leaders, see Norman, Smith, and Wagstyl, "Europe's Leaders Compromise on EU Reforms," 1; and Agence Europe, *Europe Daily Bulletin,* no. 7434, 27 March 1999, 4–7. For the Commission's assessment of the Berlin agreement, see Agence Europe, *Europe Daily Bulletin,* no. 7438, 2 April 1999, 6–7.

75. "Berlin Presidency Conclusions," 17.

76. On Gil-Robles's statement and the need for the EP's approval, see Peter Norman, "Leaders Warned Against Imbalance," *Financial Times,* 27–28 February 1999, 2; and Agence Europe, *Europe Daily Bulletin,* no. 7414, 27 February 1999, 4–5.

77. On preparation of the legal texts and interinstitutional negotiations, see Agence Europe, *Europe Daily Bulletin,* no. 7443, 12–13 April 1999, 8; Agence Europe, *Europe Daily Bulletin,* no. 7452, 24 April 1999, 12; and Agence Europe, *Europe Daily Bulletin,* no. 7454, 28 April 1999, 7. On final approval of the "Agenda 2000" package, see Agence Europe, *Europe Daily Bulletin,* no. 7460, 7 May 1999, 8–10.

8

✛

Preparing the EU for Enlargement (II): Institutional Reform

In addition to "Agenda 2000," the EU also needs to reform its decision-making institutions and procedures before it can further enlarge. With some modifications, the EU has been operating with essentially the same decision-making system since the 1950s. This system was originally created for a Community of only six member states and has become increasingly strained as the EU has grown in both size and complexity. The addition of new member states over the years has increased not only the number of governmental actors in the EU but also the range and diversity of interests that need to be accommodated. At the same time, the expansion of EU activities and policy competencies has increased the amount of EU business and the number of decisions that have to be made. As a consequence, the EU's decision-making system has become increasingly overburdened and inefficient.

In this context, the prospect of further enlargement poses an enormous challenge. The addition of twelve or more new member states, each with its own distinctive interests and views, would further burden the EU's decision-making system and could lead to paralysis. If the EU is to maintain its coherence and effectiveness, therefore, at the same time that it strives to become more open and democratic, institutional reform becomes a necessary precondition of further enlargement. As is the case with policy and financing reform, however, any effort to reform the EU's institutions must overcome the divergent interests and views of its member states. These interests vary according to such factors as size and basic attitudes toward integration. Also, specific EU institutions, such as the Commission and the EP, have their own interests and views that they have sought to interject into the debate on institutional reform.

When it comes to the question of institutional reform, therefore, the stakes are high, and achieving agreement will not be easy. Without adequate institutional reform, however, further enlargement could lead to a less coherent and effective EU. At the same time, the failure to achieve institutional reform could be another factor delaying enlargement, as some member states have made such reform a precondition for their agreement to admit new member states.

THE EU'S DECISION-MAKING INSTITUTIONS

The EU's basic institutional system was established by the 1957 Rome Treaty, and amended by key agreements and treaties in each of the following decades.[1] The EU's executive arm is the Commission, which is headquartered in Brussels. The Commission is headed by the college of commissioners, which is currently comprised of twenty members (commissioners) that are appointed by the member states. The number of commissioners is determined by a formula that gives each of the five large member states (Germany, France, Britain, Italy, and Spain) the right to appoint two commissioners, while each of the other member states appoints one. The basic rule is that every member state, no matter how small, has the right to appoint at least one commissioner. One of the commissioners serves as president, with this individual chosen by consensus among the member states. Both the Commission president and the entire Commission must be approved by the EP. The Commission serves a five-year term that is concurrent with that of the EP.

Each of the commissioners has management responsibilities for specific policy areas and oversees one or more of the Commission's twenty-four Directorate-Generals (DGs) and specialized services. The DGs are the administrative departments that run day-to-day policy in particular areas, such as agriculture, regional policy, environment, and transport. While it is the responsibility of the Commission president to assign policy portfolios, member states have traditionally lobbied for specific portfolios that are of particular interest to them to be given to their own appointees. However, commissioners are expected to perform their duties with the interests of the EU in mind and not those of their home country or government. The college of commissioners is the peak level of a multinational bureaucracy comprised of some fifteen thousand "Eurocrats," who work primarily in Brussels and Luxembourg.

The Commission's main power is its sole right to initiate new legislative proposals, although other EU institutions can make policy recommendations and requests for new initiatives. In particular, the European Council—the regular summits of EU heads of state and government that began in the mid-1970s—has played an increasingly important role in suggesting new policy initiatives. Beyond formulating and submitting policy proposals and participating in the legislative process, the Commission is also charged with monitoring the implementation of EU legislation by the member states and overseeing their compliance with EU laws. In cases of noncompliance, the Commission can take national governments to the ECJ and in some instances levy fines. The Commission also drafts and submits the annual EU budget, manages EU finances, and serves as the EU's main external representative in dealing with other governments and international organizations. It is also regarded as the "conscience" of the EU and the "keeper of the flame" of the ideal of European integration.

Although the Commission proposes, the primary legislative body of the EU is the Council of Ministers. This institution is comprised of national government ministers with responsibility for specific policy areas. Its composition varies, therefore, according to the policy matter under discussion. The most important and frequent Councils are those bringing together member state foreign ministers (General Affairs Council), economics and finance ministers (Ecofin), and agriculture ministers (Agricultural Council). While major policy decisions are made by the ministers when they get together, much of the preparatory work for their meetings is done in weekly meetings of the Committee of Permanent Representatives (COREPER) of the member states in Brussels.

Leadership and direction for the Council is provided by the government of an individual member state, which occupies the office of the EU presidency for a six-month period (January–June or July–December). The EU presidency is rotated among the member states according to a schedule that maintains a balance between large and small member states and ensures every member state an equal opportunity to hold this position. The government holding the EU presidency chairs meetings of the Council and hosts the end-of-term meeting of the European Council in either June or December, as well as any special summits that might be necessary. It also oversees EU foreign policy for six months. Before enactment of the Amsterdam Treaty in May 1999, the government holding the presidency also served as the EU's main voice in the global arena, a role that is now performed by the head of the Council secretariat.[2] While the EU presidency imposes significant administrative burdens on the member state holding it—especially if this is a smaller country—it also allows this government to set the agenda and exercise a major influence over EU policy for a certain period of time.

Since it is the EU's primary legislative body, voting procedures in the Council are of crucial importance. Increasingly, voting in the Council is done on a qualified-majority basis. The Rome Treaty had called for a shift from unanimity to QMV for most policy decisions by a certain date. This plan was frustrated, however, by the "empty-chair" tactics of French President Charles DeGaulle in 1965 and the resulting Luxembourg Compromise of January 1966, which preserved the right of member states to veto EC decisions that negatively affected vital national interests. The national veto was only partially revoked by the 1986 Single European Act, which specified majority voting procedures for legislation to implement the Single Market. The use of QMV was then expanded to additional policy decisions by the Maastricht and Amsterdam Treaties. As a result, QMV now applies to most policy decisions made within the EU's first pillar. Unanimity voting still applies, however, to policy decisions within EU pillars two and three (CFSP and JHA, respectively) as well as to treaty reform and the accession of new member states.[3]

There also remains some question about the continued validity of the national veto in other policy areas. While it is widely regarded as necessary to ensure the effectiveness of EU decision making, the increased use of QMV is also highly controversial and is opposed by some member states and political groups who view it as an infringement on national sovereignty and authority. Even when QMV procedures apply, however, the normal practice is for the Council to attempt to make decisions on the basis of consensus.

When QMV procedures are used, each member state is allocated a weighted vote that is roughly proportional to its population. Currently, the four largest member states (Germany, Britain, France, and Italy) have ten votes each, followed by Spain with eight. The Netherlands, Greece, Belgium, and Portugal have five votes apiece, while Sweden and Austria have four. Denmark, Finland, and Ireland cast three votes each, while the smallest member state, Luxembourg, has two. The voting weights are skewed to favor the smallest member states. As an example, Germany, the largest member state, has one vote for about every eight million citizens while Luxembourg, the smallest, has one vote for every 120,000 citizens. To achieve a qualified majority, and hence be approved, a proposal must win sixty-two votes out of the total of eighty-seven, or 71 percent. This means that twenty-six votes constitutes a "blocking minority." However, under a March 1994 agreement (the Ioannina Agreement) that was forced by Britain and Spain in an effort to preserve the power of the larger member states, when a minority of twenty-three votes exists (the old blocking minority, before the last enlargement) there is a delay of "a reasonable time" to allow the Council to do "all within its power" to reach a compromise so that a blocking minority of twenty-six is unnecessary.[4]

While the Council, which represents the interests of the member states and national governments, remains the EU's primary legislative body, it has increasingly had to share its decision-making power with the EP. The EP consists of 626 Members of the European Parliament (MEPs), which are elected as national delegations that are roughly proportional in size to the populations of the member states. Since 1979, these delegations have been directly elected every five years, according to national electoral laws and procedures. In the EP, there are a number of transnational party groups that cover the usual left–right ideological spectrum, with the two largest being the Party of European Socialists and the European Peoples Party (Christian Democrats and moderate Conservatives). These party groups bring together MEPs from national parties of similar persuasion and are the primary organizational basis for the EP's legislative activities. They also develop common programs and mount transnational campaigns for EP elections. The EP is required to hold monthly plenary sessions in Strasbourg, yet most of its administrative offices are located in Luxembourg and Brussels and most of its committee meetings, as well as additional sessions, take place in Brussels.

Once the poor relation of EU institutions, the EP has gained steadily in power and influence since the 1980s. The 1986 SEA granted the EP a second reading of legislative proposals and the right to amend proposals submitted under QMV procedures. A further enhancement of power came with the Maastricht Treaty, which gave the EP real powers of "codecision" for the first time. Under the new codecision procedures, for some legislative proposals the EP was granted a third reading and the right of veto. The Amsterdam Treaty extended the EP's codecision powers even further, to an additional twenty-three areas of policy competence within pillar one, making the EP an effective codecider with the Council of Ministers in many areas and a more powerful (and potentially problematic) partner of the Commission.[5] As a result of these treaty changes, in many areas of EU legislation the Council no longer has the final word. The increased powers of the EP are justified by the EP and its supporters as an important means of democratizing the EU by giving more power to directly elected institutions, as opposed to those that are appointed (the Commission) or once-removed from the control of national voters and parliaments (the Council).

In addition to its powers of codecision, the EP also approves the annual EU budget and exerts influence over noncompulsory spending (that is, basically everything other than the CAP). However, it has no powers to raise revenues. EU approval—the power of "assent"—is also required for international treaties and agreements, including the accession of new member states. The EP also exercises control over the Commission through its approval of the president and the entire Commission and its right to remove the entire Commission through a motion of censure (requiring a two-thirds majority of votes cast, representing a majority of all MEPs). The EP cannot reject or remove individual commissioners, although this is a power that it has asked for and would dearly love to have.

The EP's influence was further enhanced by the resignation of the entire Commission in March 1999 because of the damaging findings of a special committee investigating corruption and mismanagement in the Commission. The investigative committee was established by the EP in December, with the Commission's agreement, following a move by some MEPs to censure the Commission for its conduct. Although the Commission's resignation was not due, in a direct sense, to EP actions, it signified the growing role of the EP as a democratic watchdog over the EU's appointed institutions.[6]

INSTITUTIONAL REFORM AND ENLARGEMENT

From the beginning of discussions about EU widening in the early 1990s, there was awareness that enlargement would require institutional reform. In its 1992 report, "Europe and the Challenge of Enlargement," the Commission declared:

> The impact of future enlargement on the capacity of the Community to take decisions merits the most careful reflection and evaluation. Non-members apply to join because the Community is attractive; the Community is attractive because it is seen to be effective; to proceed to enlargement in a way which reduces its effectiveness would be an error.[7]

For the Commission, therefore, a key question was how the EU could enlarge while preserving its operational effectiveness—or, in the Commission's words, how to ensure that "'more' does not lead to 'less.'" With the prospective EFTA enlargement in mind, the Commission expressed the view that only limited institutional changes were necessary for the admission of a few new member states. However, "with the prospect of a Union of 20 or 30 members, fundamental questions of decision-making and the institutional framework cannot be evaded."[8]

Concern about the impact of enlargement on the EU's institutional effectiveness was also evident in the European Council's June 1993 Copenhagen decisions. Among the conditions for membership announced by EU leaders at Copenhagen was the "Union's capacity to absorb new members while maintaining the momentum of European integration."[9] The European Council thus implicitly linked further enlargement to the EU's ability to carry out necessary internal reforms, including the reform of its decision-making institutions.

The issue of institutional reform was more specifically addressed in the "Presidency Conclusions" of the December 1993 European Council in Brussels and the Ioannina Agreement of March 1994. These documents elaborated a list of institutional questions that would have to be dealt with in advance of further enlargement, including the weighting of votes in the Council of Ministers, the threshold for qualified majority decisions, the number of members of the Commission, and any other measures deemed necessary to guarantee the effective operation of an enlarged EU.[10]

The focus of institutional reform efforts became the IGC that was mandated by article N of the Maastricht Treaty and that was scheduled to begin in 1996. The IGC's original purpose was to review the functioning of the EU's two intergovernmental pillars—CFSP and JHA—and investigate the possibility of incorporating them into the supranational structures that governed decision making in pillar one, or "communitizing" them. The IGC was also supposed to examine the possibility of giving additional power to the EP, in order to close the EU's "democratic deficit" and thus improve its popular and democratic legitimacy. As the EU's focus turned toward enlargement, however, the IGC also became the logical forum for discussing changes to the EU's decision-making system to accommodate a much larger membership.

Thus, at the June 1994 Corfu summit, the European Council declared that "the institutional conditions for ensuring the proper functioning of the Union must be created at the 1996 Intergovernmental Conference, which for that reason must take place before accession negotiations begin." To prepare for the IGC, the European Council established a "Reflection Group" consisting of representatives of the member states and the Commission president, as well as two representatives from the EP. It charged the Reflection Group with reviewing the operation of the TEU and examining ways to make the EU more open and democratic. In addition, the European Council asked the Reflection Group to "elaborate options in the perspective of the future enlargement of the Union on the institutional questions set out in the conclusions of the European Council in Brussels and in the Ioannina agreement." The Reflection Group was asked to report in time for the meeting of the European Council at the end of 1995.[11]

The importance for enlargement of achieving an agreement on institutional reform at the IGC was reaffirmed by the Essen (December 1994) and Cannes (June 1995) summits. At the latter meeting, the European Council also promised to keep the associated CEECs "fully informed of developments at the Intergovernmental Conference, bearing in mind their status as future members of the Union."[12] The CEECs, however, argued that they should be allowed to participate in the IGC since institutional decisions made by the conference would affect them as future members. This request was viewed with sympathy by some EU officials, including Commissioner Leon Brittan, who urged that the CEECs be given nonvoting "observer status" at the IGC.[13] In the end, however, the Madrid European Council agreed only that the governments of the associated countries would "be briefed regularly on the progress of discussions and [would] be able to put their points of view at meetings with the Presidency of the European Union to be held, in principle, every two months."[14]

In December 1995, the Reflection Group published its final report. This document outlined a number of options for institutional reform to improve the EU's efficiency and democracy in preparation for enlargement. Among the possible reforms addressed in the report were extending the use of QMV in the Council, reweighting votes in the Council to take better account of member state population, making changes to the system of rotating the EU presidency, and reducing the number of commissioners. The report also hinted vaguely at the possibility of "flexible solutions" that respected the EU's single institutional framework and the *acquis communautaire,* suggesting the increased use of a multi-speed or variable geometry approach to decision making that would allow some member states to take action without the full participation of others. However, the report was also couched with numerous references to the divergent views of the member states on institutional questions, particularly the issue of QMV, thus indicating how difficult it would be to achieve a consensus on institutional reform and presaging hard bargaining at the IGC.[15]

At the Madrid summit, the European Council announced that the accession process for the CEECs would begin soon after conclusion of the IGC, which it decided to launch in March 1996.[16] After beginning under the Italian presidency, the IGC would eventually conclude fifteen months later, at the Amsterdam summit. In the end, however, the aspirations of the Corfu summit—that "the institutional conditions for ensuring the proper functioning of the Union . . . be created at the 1996 Intergovernmental Conference"—were not met, since very little institutional reform was actually achieved by the IGC. Instead, the accession process would begin in March 1998 without the institutional conditions for enlargement having yet been created.

THE 1996–97 IGC

The IGC opened, as planned, at a special summit in Turin on March 29, 1996. In the summit's "Presidency Conclusions," the European Council declared that, in the perspective of future enlargement, the EU's "institutions, as well as their functioning and procedures have to be improved in order to preserve its capacity for action, while maintaining the *acquis communautaire* and developing it and also respecting the balance between the institutions."[17] After the opening meeting, the conference proceeded on the basis of monthly meetings at the foreign minister level and weekly sessions of a Working Group made up of representatives of each member state and the Commission.

After a slow start, the negotiations received a boost from the Irish EU presidency in early December 1996, when it presented a general outline for a draft revision of the EU treaties to be discussed at the December 13–14 Dublin summit.[18] However, further progress was impeded by the domestic political situation in several member states and by the intransigent position on EU reform of the British Conservative government of Prime Minister John Major. As a result, progress on many issues awaited the outcome of British parliamentary elections that were due in the spring of 1997, with many European leaders hoping for a victory by the more EU-friendly Labor Party. Nevertheless, EU leaders were determined to stick to their June 1997 deadline for concluding the IGC, fearing that failure to do so would disrupt plans for enlargement and the launching of EMU. Pessimism about reaching agreement on some controversial issues by this deadline, however, particularly on institutional changes related to enlargement, generated discussion (as early as fall 1996) about the need for yet another IGC in the future; there would need to be a "Maastricht III" if the current "Maastricht II" conference did not achieve the necessary reforms.[19]

The 1996–97 IGC focused on a number of themes besides institutional reform, including enhancing cooperation in JHA; improving the EU's capacity for external action through changes to the CFSP; and making the EU more democratic, open, and transparent, and hence closer to its citizens. The inclusion in the EU treaties of a chapter on employment policy also became a major issue, especially after the surprise election of a Socialist government in France just before the Amsterdam summit. With regard to the institutional changes necessary for enlargement, however, there were four key issues: (1) extending the use of QMV; (2) reweighting votes in the Council; (3) improving the efficiency of the Commission, perhaps by reducing its size and changing the way in which commissioners are selected; and (4) introducing greater "flexibility" in decision making by allowing some member states to proceed with further integration without the participation of all.

Greater use of majority voting, as opposed to unanimity, was generally considered necessary to prevent the paralysis of decision making in an enlarged EU.[20] Already, in an EU of fifteen member states, the diversity of member state views and interests made achieving a consensus difficult on an ever-expanding agenda of policies and decisions. In an EU of twenty-seven or more member states, unanimity might well become impossible. Despite seemingly widespread support for extending QMV, however, an agreement to do so was impeded by the opposition of governments who viewed the increased use of majority voting as unnecessary and posing a threat to national sovereignty. The precise identification of member state positions on this issue is difficult.[21] While only Britain openly and systematically opposed the extension of QMV, other governments were reluctant to accept it as well and often hid their true views on this issue behind a façade of Europeanist rhetoric. In fact, at the Amsterdam summit, it was the government of one of the EU's traditionally most integrationist member states—Germany—that for domestic political reasons blocked the extension of QMV to a number of new policy areas (see below). Also hindering the extension of QMV was the resistance of national bureaucracies to surrendering power in specific policy areas, as evidenced by the "bureaucratic no" of fall 1996.[22]

The British government remained the focal point of opposition to more QMV, however. British intransigence, in turn, led other member states, principally Germany and France, to promote arrangements that permitted greater flexibility in EU decision making. In October 1996, the French and German governments launched a joint initiative for flexibility that would allow "strengthened cooperation" between some member states on issues currently decided by unanimity. According to the proposal, such cooperation would take place within certain limits, including respect for the *acquis communautaire* and the Commission's right to initiate and monitor EU laws. Within these limits, however, no member state would be allowed to veto the planned action of a group of member states, and all member states willing and able to take part in any initiative should be allowed to do so. In announcing this initiative, a top German government official, Werner Hoyer, used the prospect of further enlargement as a justification for greater flexibility in EU decision making. According to Hoyer, "If things are not working with 15 member states, they are certainly not going to work any better with 20 or more members."[23]

The Franco-German proposal drew support from the more federalist Benelux countries yet met with considerable opposition from the British government, which demanded a veto over any new form of cooperation. The proposal was also greeted suspiciously by the more sovereignty-conscious Scandinavian countries and the poor southern member states, which feared the emergence of an elite core, centered on Germany and France, that would press forward with integration based on their own interests and leave others behind in an increasingly two-tiered EU. In response to such criticism, German Foreign Minister Kinkel defended the proposal for enhanced cooperation, insisting that "flexibility is the recipe for reconciling the apparent contradiction between 'deepening' and 'widening' [the EU]."[24]

The IGC also considered the reweighting of votes in the Council and the size and effectiveness of the Commission. Regarding the former, the larger (more populous) member states complained that voting weights were skewed too much in favor of the smaller countries, and they demanded for the sake of democratic representation that votes be reweighted to more accurately reflect the populations of the member states. Such a reweighting was considered particularly important given the possible extended use of QMV so that larger member states could not be easily outvoted by coalitions of smaller countries. Under the existing system, for instance, Germany, Britain, and the Netherlands could not block a qualified majority decision even though they accounted for 42 percent of the EU's population, while a combination of Greece, Belgium, Portugal, Denmark, Finland, Ireland, and Luxembourg could prevent a qualified majority even though their combined population was only about 12 percent of the EU total.[25]

A reweighting of votes in the Council was also necessitated by enlargement, not only because of the likely greater use of QMV in an enlarged EU, but also because many of the prospective new member states are relatively small, making the issue of proportionality even more acute. Without a reweighting of votes, the possibility existed that in an enlarged EU a qualified majority could be achieved by a group of small member states representing only half of the EU's total population.[26] For the larger member states, this possibility was clearly not acceptable. Another idea for protecting the interests of the larger member states was "double majority" voting. Under proposals favored by the governments of Germany and other larger member states, decisions would have to receive the backing of a combination of member states representing a specified majority of both votes in the Council and the EU population in order to pass.

As for reform of the Commission, there was concern that the college of commissioners was already too large and unwieldy, with some commissioners not having sufficient real responsibilities or duties. This problem of size and efficiency would only grow with the addition of new member states, presuming that the rule was preserved that each member state had the right to name a commissioner, along with the customary practice of larger member states being able to name a second commissioner. There was thus broad support for the idea of limiting the size of the Commission, perhaps by eliminating the second commissioner for larger member states or even abandoning the right of every member state to have a commissioner. There was also discussion of selecting commissioners according to more general procedures, on the basis of objective qualifications and commitment to the EU, as well as enhancing their independence from national governments.[27] The French government, in particular, favored a drastic reduction in the size of the Commission to ten to twelve commissioners, having regard only to regional balance. However, the smaller member states, which traditionally viewed the Commission as a key ally and defender of their interests, were strongly opposed to surrendering their right to have a representative on the Commission, especially in view of the possible reweighting of votes in the Council to the advantage of the larger member states.[28]

Thus, the debate on these two institutional questions largely divided the member states according to size. The smaller member states opposed the reweighting of votes in the Council and insisted on keeping their right to name a commissioner. They also opposed proposals for reforming the EU presidency by changing the rotation to favor larger member states or by creating collective presidencies among groups of smaller countries. The larger member states, on the other hand, demanded a reweighting of votes in the Council. But while they also wanted to hold on to their second commissioner, they were ready to deal this away in order to achieve their more important goal of a reweighting of votes in the Council. Within these two broad camps, however, there were many variations in national positions and views on these issues.

The deadlock in negotiations continued into 1997, as the Dutch government took over the reins of the EU presidency. The real bargaining only began after the election of a Labor government in Britain on May 1. The new prime minister, Tony Blair, pledged to restore Britain to the center of European affairs and promised that his government would be a constructive force in the EU, rather than an obstructive one. The new British policy of "constructive engagement" raised hopes within the EU that real progress on institutional reform could now be made.[29] Attention focused on a special summit in Noordwijk on May 23. The Dutch "non-paper" for the meeting, however, failed to include any concrete proposals for extending the use of QMV or reweighting votes in the Council. At the meeting, Chancellor Kohl, with grudging French acquiescence, advocated that the institutional status quo be maintained for the time being, arguing that this would be preferable to an open quarrel between large and small member states that might endanger EMU and the opening of accession negotiations. On May 30, the Dutch government presented a consolidated draft treaty that left many institutional questions open for decision at the Amsterdam summit.[30]

THE AMSTERDAM SUMMIT

The Amsterdam summit of June 16–17, 1997, brought the IGC to a somewhat disappointing conclusion. The resulting Amsterdam Treaty did contain some significant agreements. Much of the EU's third pillar, including common policies on immigration, asylum, and visas, was "communitized," or moved into the first pillar. Also, the Schengen Agreement on the removal of internal border controls was incorporated into the EU treaties. Under pressure from the French Socialist-Communist government, an employment chapter was added to the EU treaties, thus balancing the agreement on a Stability Pact governing national budgetary and fiscal policies for the euro-zone countries. In the area of CFSP, a new common unit for foreign policy analysis and planning was created, and new responsibilities for representing EU foreign policy to the outside world were given to the Council's secretary-general. Perhaps the main beneficiary of the Amsterdam Treaty was the EP, which gained an extension of codecision rights to a significant number of additional policy areas.[31]

Regarding the institutional changes necessary for enlargement, however, very little was accomplished. One of the biggest disappointments was the very limited extension of QMV. Although at the beginning of the IGC there seemed to be widespread agreement that a generalization of QMV was necessary for an enlarged EU to function effectively, by the conference's end it was clear that any extension of QMV would be much more limited. Nevertheless, going into the Amsterdam summit, there was considerable support for extending QMV to a number of policies traditionally subject to unanimity. The Dutch draft treaty proposed retaining unanimity for decisions on constitutional issues (such as treaty revisions), EU financing (own resources), the Structural Funds, and taxation, but extending QMV to most other areas. Among the member states supporting a significant extension of QMV were Belgium, Italy, France, Austria, Finland, and Portugal, with even Britain's new Labor government willing to consider more majority voting for policies related to the internal market. Surprisingly, however, the German government of Chancellor Kohl, under pressure from the governments of Germany's sixteen federal states (Länder) and facing new elections in September, did an about-face at Amsterdam, abandoning its traditional integrationist position and blocking the extension of QMV to many new areas.[32]

As a result, the Amsterdam Treaty extends QMV to only a handful of new policy areas, including the following: equal pay for, and treatment of, men and women; research and development framework programs; access to official documents; combating fraud; and customs cooperation. Especially problematic is the fact that QMV was not extended to many areas where codecision now applies, including freedom of movement and residence for EU citizens, social security for migrant workers, recognition of professional qualifications, and cultural policy. Altogether, after the Amsterdam Treaty there remain, by one account, fifty-seven cases of policy decisions requiring unanimity.[33]

The Amsterdam Treaty also contains only weak provisions for flexibility. The Franco-German proposals for enhanced cooperation evoked a suspicious response from many member states, who expressed concerns about the workability of such arrangements and the possible negative consequences for the EU and its institutions. As a result, the flexibility clauses approved at Amsterdam were highly qualified. The flexibility clause for pillar one enables the Council to grant authorization for closer cooperation between groups of member states within clearly defined limits. However, although Council authorization is to be granted on the basis of QMV, any member state can block this vote—and hence veto authorization—"for important and stated reasons of national policy."[34] A similar clause governs flexibility in pillar three, while decision-making procedures for pillar two (CFSP) specify that any member state can veto the use of QMV to adopt joint actions or common positions.[35] In other words, the flexibility clauses of the Amsterdam Treaty are constructed in a manner that makes their use against the wishes of any member state virtually impossible. According to one analysis, this introduction of the "veto safeguard" is the first formal recognition in the EU treaties of the French interpretation of the Luxembourg Compromise, that is, the right of any member state to block decisions affecting vital national interests.[36]

Even less progress was achieved on other institutional issues. In Amsterdam, the Dutch presidency proposed a draft protocol that linked the reweighting of votes in the Council to a reduction in the size of the Commission. According to the Dutch proposal, the institutional status quo would remain until two new member states joined the EU; at this point, the large countries would give up their second commissioner in exchange for a reweighting of Council votes in their favor. Under the proposed system, Germany, France, Britain, and Italy would each have twenty-five votes in the Council; Spain, twenty-one; the Netherlands, twelve; Belgium, Greece, and Portugal, ten; Sweden and Austria, eight; Denmark, Finland, and Ireland, six; and Luxembourg, three. The draft protocol also proposed a system of dual-majority voting.[37]

This attempted compromise failed, however, due to the objections of several member states. The Belgian government resented the fact that the Dutch proposal gave the Netherlands a greater voting weight in the Council than its own weight. Belgium also linked its approval of a reweighting of votes in the Council to agreement on the extension of QMV, fearing that otherwise it would lose a vital bargaining chip in its struggle for a more efficient EU. The Spanish government, which would lose its second commissioner under the Dutch proposal, insisted on equality with the largest member states in the weighting of its Council vote, something that other member states were reluctant to grant. The proposal for dual-majority voting was opposed by the French government—although it was favored by most other member states—because the new system would give the more populous Germany a greater weight in Council voting than France had, thus eliminating an important symbol of formal equality between these two countries.[38]

Unable to reach agreement, EU leaders decided to accept Chancellor Kohl's earlier advice and postpone any major decisions on institutional reform. Instead, at Amsterdam they agreed to a Protocol on the institutions and enlargement, which declared that "at the date of the first enlargement of the Union . . . the Commission shall comprise one national of each of the Member States, provided that, by that date, the weighting of the votes in the Council has been modified, whether by reweighting of the votes or by dual majority, in a manner acceptable to all Member States, taking into account all relevant elements, notably compensating those Member States which give up the possibility of nominating a second member of the Commission." The Protocol went on to specify that "at least one year before the membership of the European Union exceeds twenty," an IGC shall be convened "in order to carry out a comprehensive review of the provisions of the Treaties on the composition and functioning of the institutions."[39] Furthermore, in a Declaration attached to the treaty, the member states agreed that the Ioannina Agreement of March 1994 would be extended until the time of the next accessions, thus preserving the present system of QMV.[40]

The failure on institutional reform was perhaps the most disappointing outcome of the 1996–97 IGC and the Amsterdam summit. Not only was there no substantial reform of decision-making institutions, but decisions on this matter were put off for the future. The Protocol on institutions specified only that another IGC be held at least one year before EU membership exceeds twenty, meaning that a smaller first wave of accessions (with five or fewer new member states) could occur without any institutional changes being made, in the event that agreement on the reweighting of votes in the Council had not been achieved. This outcome was not satisfactory for many member states nor for the Commission (see below), and it may have played a role in the Commission's decision to recommend a first wave of six in its "Agenda 2000" report (issued one month after Amsterdam), thereby increasing pressure on the member states to agree on institutional reform.

A number of factors contributed to the Amsterdam failure on institutional reform. One was the division of interests between large and small member states, an intra-EU cleavage that is bound to grow with further enlargement and the addition of mainly smaller new member states. Another was Malta's decision in November 1996 to freeze its application, thus reducing pressure on the EU to reform its institutions to cope with the accession of another microstate. Perhaps the main factor influencing the Amsterdam results, however, was that in June 1997 further enlargement still seemed only a distant prospect, being too far off in the future to warrant making difficult decisions and changes now. It was much less painful to maintain the status quo for yet a while longer and put off difficult changes until the next accessions were more imminent. Although the momentum for institutional reform had seemed strong at the beginning of the 1996–97 IGC, by the time of the Amsterdam summit it had greatly dissipated. At Amsterdam, therefore, EU leaders simply made the easy choice.

REACTIONS TO AMSTERDAM

The results of the Amsterdam summit were extremely disappointing to many within the EU. Commission President Santer judged the outcome "mediocre" and claimed that it did not augur well for enlargement.[41] This assessment was rejected by Dutch Foreign Minister Hans van Mierlo, however, who argued that the Amsterdam Treaty's negative impact on enlargement was "scandalously exaggerated." Instead, he asserted that the EU had "plenty of time" ("years") to resolve its institutional questions.[42]

In its "Agenda 2000" document, the Commission was highly critical of the Amsterdam results. It declared that the institutional reforms achieved at Amsterdam "were only partial and need to be completed before the forthcoming enlargements." "Any delay in this respect," it argued, "would only serve to compromise the Union's effective enlargement." The Commission therefore urged that the reforms agreed to in the Protocol regarding the reweighting of Council votes and the composition of the Commission be implemented immediately, not postponed until the date of the next enlargement. The Commission also declared that this step alone would not prepare the EU for further enlargement. It proposed, therefore, that "a new IGC be convened as soon as possible after 2000 to produce a thorough reform of [the EU's institutions]." According to the Commission, such a reform "would, in any event, have to involve the introduction of qualified majority voting across the board."[43]

The Commission's view of the Amsterdam Treaty was basically shared by the EP. In a resolution backing the treaty, the EP nevertheless declared that "the institutional framework which has emerged from the Amsterdam Treaty does not meet the necessary conditions for achieving enlargement without endangering the operation of the Union and the effectiveness of its actions." Together with the Commission, it called for the generalization of QMV, arguing that unanimity voting should be restricted to decisions of a constitutional nature (treaty revisions, own resources, accessions, and so on). The EP also opposed postponing an IGC on institutional reform until just before the number of member states exceeded twenty, arguing that this only reinforced the idea that the first accession wave would be limited to a small, "privileged group of candidates."[44]

Also critical of the Amsterdam results were several member state governments. In a Declaration attached to the final version of the Amsterdam Treaty, the governments of Belgium, France, and Italy asserted that the treaty's provisions on institutional reform were insufficient, and that further institutional reform was "an indispensable condition for the conclusion of the first accession negotiations." In other words, no enlargement without institutional reform. The Declaration went on to state that the three governments "are determined to give the fullest effect appropriate to the Protocol as regards the composition of the Commission and the weighting of votes and consider that a significant extension of recourse to qualified majority voting forms part of the relevant factors which should be taken into account."[45]

Despite their agreement on the need for institutional reform, the institutional interests of these three member states were not necessarily the same. France wanted a reduction in the size of the Commission and a reweighting of Council votes to favor the larger member states. Italy, another large member state, also favored a reweighting of votes in the Council. Belgium, on the other hand, was most concerned about gaining an extension of QMV. The Belgian government, like most other smaller member states, also sought to prevent the Commission from losing too much power to other EU institutions, such as the Council, that were more intergovernmental and dominated by the larger member states. The three governments were unified, however, in agreeing that institutional reform was necessary before further enlargement. Implicit in the Belgian/French/Italian Declaration and other statements by these governments, therefore, was the threat that enlargement could be held hostage to an acceptable agreement on institutional reform.[46]

The prospect that a prolonged process of institutional reform could delay enlargement clearly worried the applicant countries. For this reason, the Polish government suggested in the fall of 1998 that institutional reform should not be viewed as a prerequisite for enlargement, arguing instead that decisions on institutional reform could be made after the first new accessions. This scenario would also be appropriate, Polish authorities claimed, because the new member states will be affected by these decisions and thus should be involved in making them.[47] Such arguments received little support within the EU, however.

TOWARD A NEW IGC

The debate over institutional reform subsided somewhat after the formal signing of the Amsterdam Treaty in October 1997, as EU attention shifted to the beginning of accession negotiations and the "Agenda 2000" reforms. Further debate also awaited final ratification of the Amsterdam Treaty, which would take more than a year. At the December Luxembourg summit, where the decision was made to begin the accession process for the ten CEECs and Cyprus, the European Council merely proclaimed that "as a prerequisite for enlargement of the Union, the operation of the institutions must be strengthened and improved in keeping with the institutional provisions of the Amsterdam Treaty."[48]

It was not until the following year, in the run-up to the June 1998 Cardiff summit, that the British EU presidency sought to relaunch the discussion of institutional reform. The British government proposed the idea of a brief constitutional conference in early 1999, to be held under the German Presidency, to negotiate necessary institutional reforms—what it termed the "unfinished business" of the Amsterdam Treaty—in advance of enlargement. This idea did not receive much support from the German government, however, and the pre-summit Franco-German letter to the EU presidency merely called for a "more profound" debate on institutional questions at the December 1998 summit in Vienna.[49] The British government also proposed the creation of a high-level group, made up of personal representatives of member state heads of government, to study the future shape of the EU. This proposal was intended to counter French President Chirac's call for the creation of a group of "Wise Men," headed by former Commission President Delors, which would have a similar mandate. By making this proposal, Prime Minister Blair sought to keep the debate over the EU's future firmly in the hands of national governments, and out of the hands of an independent group with federalist leanings. For the British government, Chirac's idea suggested unhappy memories of the Delors-led committee that launched the EMU process with its final report in 1989.[50]

At the Cardiff summit, the focus of discussions was on actualizing the principle of subsidiarity and creating an EU "closer to the people." This meant, among other things, curtailing the power of the Commission and ensuring the prerogatives of national and subnational governments against encroachment by Brussels. The primary instigator of this discussion was Chancellor Kohl, who, facing new elections in September, was seeking to portray himself as a defender of German national interests. Nevertheless, the Cardiff European Council agreed that following ratification of the Amsterdam Treaty, "an early decision would be required on how and when to tackle the institutional issues not resolved at Amsterdam." The Cardiff summit also decided against creating a special group of experts to consider the EU's future. Instead, EU leaders decided that on this issue they were the experts, thus making such a committee unnecessary. EU leaders also agreed to pursue their discussion of institutional issues further at an informal summit in the fall held under the Austrian presidency.[51]

At the informal Pörtschach summit on October 25, there was general agreement that further discussion of a new IGC on institutional reform should await final ratification and enactment of the Amsterdam Treaty, now expected sometime in the first half of 1999. Moreover, following the Pörtschach summit Germany's new chancellor, Gerhard Schröder, indicated that the focus of his government's EU presidency beginning in January would be "Agenda 2000," and that he did not want to "overload" the German presidency by pushing for a deal on institutional reform before June.[52] This strategy was then backed by the European Council at its December 11–12 meeting in Vienna. As part of the "Vienna Strategy for Europe" agreed to at the summit, the European Council proclaimed the goal of achieving agreement on "Agenda 2000" by the end of March 1999 and called for a decision at the June European Council in Cologne on "how and when to tackle the institutional issues not resolved at Amsterdam."[53]

Early the next year, German Foreign Minister Joschka Fischer announced that his government would present its ideas on institutional reform at the June summit in Cologne. The focus of the German paper, he declared, would be on the "Amsterdam leftovers": extending the use of QMV, the reweighting of votes in the Council, and the size and composition of the Commission. According to Fischer, the Cologne summit would launch a discussion of institutional reform that would culminate in an IGC in 2001.[54] Shortly afterward, the Finnish government announced that it would use its EU presidency in the second half of 1999 to focus on institutional reform and enlargement and prepare for a new IGC. Emphasizing the same institutional issues stressed by the German government, Finnish Prime Minister Paavo Lipponen declared that "the Union must get its own house in order" before it enlarges. "Prolonging the process or delaying the reforms will not benefit anyone," he said.[55]

Heading into the Cologne summit, while there was general agreement on the need to convene a new IGC on institutional reform, there remained considerable debate over the mandate for this conference. While some member states favored a narrowly focused IGC that concentrated only on the three Amsterdam issues, others wanted a broader "constitutional" conference to consider the EU's long-range institutional future. Also favoring a broader conference were the Commission and the EP. There was also debate over the method of preparing for the conference. Generally speaking, those favoring a broader conference wanted to see it prepared by a "group of the wise"—prominent persons who were independent of national governments and who could develop a visionary approach to EU reform—while those favoring a more limited or minimalist IGC favored preparation by a committee of national government representatives. There was little debate about the timetable for the IGC, however, with most member states favoring a conference that began and ended in 2000.[56]

At the Cologne summit, EU leaders decided to convene a new IGC on institutional reform in early 2000, agreeing that this conference would conclude by the end of the year, under the French EU presidency. The European Council also decided that the IGC would have only a limited mandate, focusing on the three "Amsterdam leftovers." These issues were described in the summit's "Presidency Conclusions" as the "size and composition of the Commission; weighting of votes in the Council (reweighting, introduction of a dual-majority and threshold for qualified majority decision making); possible extension of qualified majority voting in the Council." The European Council also decided on an "intergovernmental method" for preparing for this conference, rejecting calls for a broader constitutional conference that would solicit the input of a "committee of the wise."[57]

The Cologne summit also decided that the final decisions on launching a new IGC would be made at the December 1999 summit in Helsinki. In the meantime, it asked the incoming Finnish presidency to draw up a report on institutional issues to be settled at the conference and invited other member states, the Commission, and the EP to submit proposals as well. By doing so, and by declaring that "other necessary amendments to the Treaties [beyond the Amsterdam leftovers] . . . could be discussed" at the IGC, the European Council appeared to leave the door open somewhat for a broader conference.[58] Nevertheless, it was clear that support for this among the member states was limited.

THE DEHAENE REPORT

After Cologne, therefore, it seemed fairly certain that the IGC on institutional reform would have a narrow or minimalist agenda. By the fall, however, pressure for a broader conference was building. One reason for this was fallout from the Kosovo war, which generated growing support within the EU for a broader enlargement strategy that would help spread stability in Eastern and Southeastern Europe. As a result, support grew for admitting all five of the second-group applicants to the accession negotiations at the upcoming Helsinki summit, in order to send them encouraging signals and prevent the emergence of new divisions in Europe. The move to a broader enlargement strategy, together with pressure from the negotiating countries to ensure that their accession dates would not be postponed as a result, convinced many within the EU that a large-scale enlargement was more imminent than they had previously thought, and that the institutional changes necessary for an EU of twenty-seven or more member states to function effectively must be addressed sooner rather than later.

Also promoting a broader IGC was the new Commission president, Romano Prodi. In a speech to the EP on July 21, the president-designate announced that he disagreed with those who viewed the IGC as a "simple tidying up exercise after the Amsterdam summit." It was instead, he argued, the EU's "opportunity— perhaps our last opportunity—to prepare for the potential doubling of the number of members of the Union." According to Prodi, "an IGC with only limited objectives would not . . . respond to this challenge." "Tinkering at the edges will not do the trick," he stated. "A full institutional overhaul is needed for enlargement to work."[59]

Prodi went on to announce that he was setting up a "small, high-level group to prepare . . . a report on the issues which the IGC should address," and that this report would be a contribution to preparation of the Commission's official position on the IGC. Prodi declared that he was "determined to at least put the options [for a broader conference and more far-reaching institutional reforms] on the table," claiming that it would "be a mistake of historic proportions for the European Union to launch a limited IGC in Helsinki by default, simply because of a collective fear of looking the real challenges of future enlargement squarely in the face."[60]

In late August, Prodi announced that his high-level group would be chaired by former Belgian Prime Minister Jean-Luc Dehaene. The other two members of the "wise man" group were Lord David Simon, former chairman of British Petroleum, and former German President Richard von Weizsäcker. Much of the actual drafting of the group's report would be done by Philippe de Schoutheete, former EU permanent representative for Belgium. In giving the group its mandate, Prodi instructed it to "consider whether the limited agenda so far identified for the IGC is adequate [to the challenge of future enlargement]."[61]

The Dehaene committee began its work in mid-September.[62] One month later, on October 18, it handed its report to the Commission president. As expected, the brief (fifteen-page) report, entitled "The Institutional Implications of Enlargement," called for a broader and more ambitious approach to institutional reform than envisaged by the Cologne summit.[63] In presenting the committee's report, Dehaene argued that the recent acceleration of the accession process meant that the approach adopted in the Amsterdam Treaty Protocol—of putting off comprehensive institutional reform until the EU's membership exceeded twenty—was no longer valid. According to Dehaene, comprehensive reform was "necessary and urgent if one wants successful enlargement."[64]

In its content, the Dehaene report addressed the three Amsterdam issues. It accepted that the Commission's size could not be reduced substantially because of the opposition of the member states to giving up their right to nominate a commissioner; however, it argued that the Commission could be made more effective by strengthening the powers of the Commission president to select and dismiss individual commissioners and to organize and guide the Commission's work. The report also recommended the generalization of QMV, including for decisions in pillars two and three, and it recommended giving the EP codecision rights in all pillar one issues decided by QMV, both to simplify EU decision making and to make it more democratic. The Dehaene report also advocated reweighting votes in the Council to ensure greater proportionality. It also called attention to the implications of enlargement for the size and efficiency of other EU institutions, including the EP, ECJ, and Court of Auditors.[65]

The most controversial recommendations of the Dehaene report, however, concerned the issues of "enhanced cooperation" and reorganization of the EU treaties. Regarding the former, the report recommended that the IGC revisit the flexibility clauses agreed to at Amsterdam, with the goal of making them less complex and more workable. Specifically, it argued that the initiation of enhanced cooperation should not be subject to veto by any single member state. The Dehaene report also recommended dividing the EU treaties into two parts: a basic treaty (dealing with the EU's aims, principles and general policy orientations, citizens' rights, and the institutional framework) that could be altered only through an IGC and by unanimous vote, with the ratification of each member state; and a separate text (or texts) containing the remaining treaty clauses, including those dealing with specific policies, which could be modified by a Council decision on the basis of QMV or unanimity. Such a reorganization, the report argued, would simplify the treaties and make them more understandable to the public but would also avoid the need for continuous treaty revision and ongoing IGCs. It would also address the difficult prospect of securing full ratification of even relatively minor treaty changes in an expanding EU of twenty-seven or more member states.[66]

As to the IGC's method of procedure, the Dehaene report recommended that the Commission submit a comprehensive and concrete set of proposals on institutional reform questions, in the form of a draft treaty, at the very beginning of the IGC. To give the conference enough time to conclude its work by the end of the year, the report also recommended that the IGC should begin as early as possible in 2000 (rather than the March launching planned by the member states).[67]

The conclusions of the Dehaene report, and its IGC strategy of "Amsterdam plus," were welcomed by the Commission as it prepared its official contribution to the institutional reform debate.[68] In commenting on the Dehaene report, Prodi reiterated his view that "we must undertake serious institutional reforms to prepare [the EU] for enlargement." However, he also endorsed the goal of completing the IGC by the end of 2000 so as not to delay enlargement. According to Prodi, "The necessary changes [meaning full ratification and enactment of a new treaty] must be completed by the end of 2002, because negotiations with the most advanced candidate countries will by then be reaching their conclusions."[69] In early November, the Commission formally presented its views on the IGC, largely endorsing the recommendations of the Dehaene report.[70]

Also welcoming the Dehaene report and favoring a broader IGC was the EP. In a resolution approved on November 18, the EP called for a more ambitious institutional reform agenda that would include the generalization of QMV and codecision but also go beyond the Amsterdam issues to include further debate on flexibility and the "constitutionalization" of the EU treaties, including a division of the treaty texts as suggested by the Dehaene report.[71] A broader IGC was also supported by various European political parties and NGOs.[72]

The response of the member states to the Dehaene report was largely skeptical, however. France's European affairs minister, Pierre Moscovici, rejected the report's suggestion of splitting the EU treaties into two parts, which he argued was an attempt by the committee to constitutionalize the IGC. According to Moscovici, "If this idea of constitutionalization, which is premature at the present time, were accepted as the objective of the future IGC, it would lead to a resounding failure, because the Member States are not ready for it." Instead, he favored limiting the IGC to "the three matters left unsettled at Amsterdam, trying to go as far as possible on related issues."[73]

Also warning against an over-full IGC agenda that could delay enlargement was the Finnish EU presidency, while the British government was highly critical of the report's suggestions on flexibility and division of the treaties.[74] These reactions echoed what seemed to be the general response of the member states, most of whom opposed radical changes and favored keeping the IGC's focus narrow.[75] An important exception to this rule was the three Benelux states, who expressed support for a broader IGC that dealt with the issue of enhanced cooperation.[76]

Also critical of certain aspects of the Dehaene report were the applicant countries. According to Poland's chief EU negotiator, Jan Kulakowski, the report's proposal for broadening the IGC to include constitutional issues could lead to a more protracted and inconclusive conference, which in turn could threaten the timetable for enlargement. Instead, Kulakowski (whose views reflected those of the applicant states more generally) favored a narrow IGC limited to the Amsterdam issues, which could be safely concluded within a year. Kulakowski also criticized the report's suggestion of reopening the flexibility discussion, claiming that enhanced cooperation could lead to a two-tiered EU that would discriminate against new member states.[77]

THE HELSINKI SUMMIT AND 2000 IGC

With the majority of the member states opposing a broader IGC, the Helsinki summit appeared set to approve a minimalist agenda for the conference. In their pre-summit meeting on November 30, the French and German governments agreed that the IGC should focus narrowly on the Amsterdam issues.[78] The following day, the Finnish presidency published its agenda for the Helsinki summit, which excluded from discussion the more controversial issues of reorganizing the EU treaties and enhanced cooperation. In justifying this decision, the Finnish government declared that "there was not enough support for either" among the member states.[79]

At the summit, the Finnish presidency presented its report on the IGC, proposing a narrow conference agenda that was limited to the three Amsterdam issues on the grounds that a broader IGC would be difficult to conclude before the end of 2000. However, the governments of Belgium, the Netherlands, and Luxembourg lobbied hard for a broader agenda that would also include the issues of treaty reorganization and flexibility. Supporting the Benelux states in this effort were the governments of Austria and Italy, as well as the Commission.[80]

In the end, a compromise was reached that, in the words of Austrian Prime Minister Viktor Klima, "opened the door beyond the Amsterdam leftovers by a small amount." It was agreed that while the IGC would begin with a limited agenda—extension of QMV, the reweighting of votes in the Council, the size and composition of the Commission—in its progress report to the European Council in June 2000 the incoming Portuguese presidency could propose additional issues for the negotiations. In order to accommodate the possibility of a broader IGC, it was also decided to begin the negotiations in February rather than late March, as had originally been planned. The goal remained to complete the negotiations and conclude the IGC by December 2000.[81]

Thus, the Helsinki European Council left open the possibility of expanding the IGC's agenda to include more far-reaching reforms. This outcome was welcomed by Prodi, who declared himself "well satisfied with the overall results" of the summit. According to Prodi, "We are all just beginning to realize what it will mean to have a Europe of more than 25 Member States, and it would certainly have been imprudent to close the agenda at this early stage."[82]

The IGC formally opened on February 14, 2000, with a meeting of EU foreign ministers in Brussels. A subministerial preparatory group, consisting largely of member state permanent representatives to the EU, began work the following day. Also participating in both the ministerial and preparatory group meetings were representatives of the Commission and the EP. According to the IGC schedule announced by the Portuguese presidency, in addition to more regular meetings of the preparatory group, there would be at least five ministerial meetings before the June summit in Santa Maria da Feira. The Portuguese presidency also indicated that, in consultation with the other member states, it would seriously explore the possibility of expanding the IGC's agenda, especially to include discussion of enhanced cooperation. However, it emphasized that any expansion of the IGC's agenda should not be at the expense of slowing down the enlargement process.[83] For the applicant states this was precisely the fear, that an expanded IGC agenda could lead to a protracted debate on institutional reform that would further delay the next accessions. On the other hand, a minimal or inadequate IGC outcome could result in an ineffective EU after enlargement and thus necessitate further institutional reform in the future.

NOTES

1. There are a number of excellent books on the history, structure, and functioning of EU institutions, including Neill Nugent, *The Government and Politics of the European Union,* 4th ed. (Durham: Duke University Press, 1999); John McCormick, *The European Union: Politics and Policies,* 2nd ed. (Boulder: Westview, 1999); Desmond Dinan, *Ever Closer Union? An Introduction to the European Union,* 2nd ed. (Boulder: Lynne Rienner, 1999); and John Peterson and Elizabeth Bomberg, *Decision-Making in the European Union* (New York: St. Martin's, 1999).

2. The first "Mr. CFSP" (or "Mr. PESC" to use the French initials), is Spain's Javier Solana, the former NATO secretary-general, who was named to this position at the June 1999 Cologne summit.

3. Although the Amsterdam Treaty shifted much of pillar three into pillar one, or "communitized" it. As a result, after a five-year transitional period, if this is approved by a unanimous vote of the member states, decision making on immigration and asylum policy will be done by QMV.

4. The Ioannina Agreement came after the failed British attempt to raise the threshold for QMV from 71 to 78 percent. British and Spanish intransigence on this issue threatened to block the conclusion of entry agreements with the four EFTA candidates, thus causing a small crisis for the EU. The Ioannina Agreement takes its name from the site of the Council meeting in March 1994 where the agreement was reached.

5. As a result of the Amsterdam Treaty, the EP now has codecision powers in thirty-eight different areas of legislation, as compared to fifteen previously.

6. For the text of the investigating committee's report, see Agence Europe, *Europe Documents,* no. 2128, 19 March 1999, 1–7.

7. European Commission, "Europe and the Challenge of Enlargement"; annexed to the "Presidency Conclusions of the European Council in Lisbon, 26–27 June 1992," in *The European Councils: Conclusions of the Presidency 1992–1994* (Brussels: European Commission, Directorate-General for Information, 1995), 26.

8. European Commission, "Europe and the Challenge of Enlargement," 26–27.

9. "European Council in Copenhagen, 21–22 June 1993: Presidency Conclusions," in *European Councils* (1992–94), 86.

10. "European Council in Brussels, 10–11 December 1993: Presidency Conclusions," in *European Councils* (1992–94), 110–117.

11. "European Council at Corfu, 24–25 June 1994: Presidency Conclusions," in *European Councils* (1992–94), 136.

12. "European Council at Essen, 9–10 December 1994: Presidency Conclusions," 145; "Cannes European Council, 26–27 June 1995: Presidency Conclusions," in *The European Councils: Conclusions of the Presidency 1995* (Brussels: European Commission, Directorate-General for Information, 1995), 13–14.

13. Caroline Southey, "Brittan Urges IGC Status for East," *Financial Times,* 12 September 1995, 2; and *Financial Times,* 27 September 1995, 3.

14. "Madrid European Council, 15–16 December 1995: Presidency Conclusions" ("Madrid Presidency Conclusions"), in *European Councils* (1995), 55.

15. The Reflection Group's report, "The Intergovernmental Conference: A Strategy for Europe," is annexed to the "Madrid Presidency Conclusions" (annex 15), 96–103. The section entitled "Enabling the Union to Work Better and Preparing it for Enlargement" is on pages 100–101. See also Lionel Barber, "EU Reforms Urged Before Enlargement," *Financial Times,* 5 December 1995, 18.

16. "Madrid Presidency Conclusions," 54.

17. "Turin European Council, 29 March 1996: Presidency Conclusions," in *The European Councils: Conclusions of the Presidency 1996* (Brussels: European Commission, Directorate-General for Information, 1997), 6.

18. "The European Union Today and Tomorrow. Adapting the European Union for the Benefit of Its Peoples and Preparing for the Future. A General Outline for a Draft Revision of the Treaties. Dublin II" (presented to the Conference of the Representatives of the Governments of the Member States, Brussels, 5 December 1996), CONF 2500/96.

19. Lionel Barber, "Paris and Bonn Scale Down EU Reform Plans," *Financial Times,* 5–6 October 1996, 1; Lionel Barber, "EU Keeps to Deadline for Reforming Maastricht," *Financial Times,* 7 October 1996, 1. See also "Dublin European Council, 13–14 December 1996: Presidency Conclusions," in *European Councils* (1996), 28 and 31. For a discussion of the 1996–97 IGC, see Youri Devuyst, "Treaty Reform in the European Union: The Amsterdam Process," *Journal of European Public Policy* 5, no. 4 (December 1998): 615–31.

20. See, for instance, European Commission, *Reinforcing Political Union and Preparing for Enlargement: Opinion for the Intergovernmental Conference 1996* (Luxembourg: Office for Official Publications of the EU, 1996), 21.

21. However, for a discussion of national positions on this and other issues at the IGC, see European Parliament, "White Paper on the 1996 Intergovernmental Conference: Summary of Positions of the Member States of the European Union With a View to the 1996 Intergovernmental Conference" (EP Intergovernmental Task Force); available on the Internet, at the EU's official Website at http://europa.eu.int/en/agenda/igc-home/ms-doc/state-it/pos.htm.

22. In September 1996, the Irish presidency presented national delegations with a list of EU treaty articles governed by unanimity and asked them to indicate, in each instance, whether a move to QMV would be acceptable. In most cases, this list was then transmitted to national administrations. In a disappointing result, even those member states most in favor of extending the use of majority voting produced lengthy lists of exceptions, reflecting the opposition of national bureaucracies to the loss of their powers. On the "bureaucratic no," see Devuyst, "Treaty Reform in the European Union," 626.

23. Caroline Southey, "Germany and France Seek More Flexibility," *Financial Times,* 23 October 1996, 3. For the text of the initiative, see "Verstärkte Zusammenarbeit im Hinblick auf die weitere Vertiefung des europäischen Einigungswerks" (Joint Franco-German Discussion Paper for the IGC), in *Bulletin,* no. 84, 23 October 1996 (Bonn: Presse- und Informationsamt der Bundesregierung), 918–20.

24. Lionel Barber, "EU Finds Flexibility Bends Both Ways," *Financial Times,* 28 October 1996, 2; Lionel Barber, "Paris, Bonn Sidestep Divisions," *Financial Times,* 21 January 1997, 16.

25. This example is borrowed from "Weighty Matters for Europe's Union," *Economist,* 1 February 1997, 54.

26. Stuart Croft, John Redmond, G. Wyn Rees, and Mark Webber, *The Enlargement of Europe* (Manchester: Manchester University Press, 1999), 70–72.

27. See, for instance, "The Intergovernmental Conference: A Strategy for Europe" (Reflection Group report), 101.

28. For a discussion of national government positions on this and other institutional questions, see Andrew Duff, ed., *The Treaty of Amsterdam: Text and Commentary* (London: Federal Trust, 1997), 132–33.

29. Lionel Barber, "New Labour, New Europe," *Financial Times,* 6 May 1997, 15.

30. Devuyst, "Treaty Reform in the EU," 620–21; Lionel Barber, "The Second Coming," *Financial Times,* 13 May 1998, 10.

31. *Treaty of Amsterdam* (Luxembourg: Office for Official Publications of the European Communities, 1997). The treaty was formally signed in Amsterdam on October 2, 1997. For analysis of the treaty's various provisions, see Duff, ed., *Treaty of Amsterdam: Text and Commentary.* The Schengen Agreement, originally signed by some member states in 1985, calls for the gradual abolition of checks on common (that is, internal EU) frontiers, thereby providing for the free movement of people within the Union.

32. Devuyst, "Treaty Reform in the EU," 626–27. The Länder governments opposed the extension of majority voting because it would undermine their prerogatives in a number of policy areas, especially immigration and asylum, residency rights for foreigners, environment, urban and rural planning, the media, and culture. On the role of the Länder at the IGC and Amsterdam summit, see Michael J. Baun, "The Länder and German European Policy: The 1996 IGC and Amsterdam Treaty," *German Studies Review* 21, no. 2 (May 1998): 329–46.

33. This is according to the "Bourlanges Report," adopted by the EP's Committee on Institutional Affairs in January 1999. The report's conclusions are summarized in Agence Europe, *Europe Daily Bulletin,* no. 7389, 23 January 1999, 4–5.

34. *Treaty of Amsterdam,* article 2(5), 25–26; article 11 of the "Consolidated Version of the Treaty Establishing the European Community," *European Union Consolidated Treaties* (Luxembourg: Office for Official Publications of the European Communities, 1997), 46.

35. *Treaty of Amsterdam,* article K.12, 21, and article J.13(2), 14–15; articles 40 and 23 of the "Consolidated Version of the TEU," *European Union Consolidated Treaties,* 27–28 and 20–21.

36. Devuyst, "Treaty Reform in the EU," 624. For a more detailed discussion of flexibility in the Amsterdam Treaty, see Alexander C-G. Stubb, "The Amsterdam Treaty and Flexible Integration," *ECSA Review* 11, no. 2 (Spring 1998): 1–5. On the Amsterdam Treaty's flexibility provisions, see Duff, ed., *Treaty of Amsterdam: Text and Commentary,* 181–97; and Josef Janning and Claus Giering, "Differenzierung als Integrationskonzept der künftigen Europäischen Union," in *Systemwandel in Europa—Demokratie, Subsidiarität, Differenzierung,* ed. Bertelsmann Stiftung Forschungsgruppe (Gütersloh: Verlag Bertelsmann Stiftung, 1998), 44–46.

37. Devuyst, "Treaty Reform in the EU," 627.

38. Devuyst, "Treaty Reform in the EU," 627–28; and Duff, ed., *Treaty of Amsterdam: Text and Commentary,* 133.

39. *Treaty of Amsterdam,* "Protocol on the Institutions with the Prospect of Enlargement of the European Union," 111.

40. *Treaty of Amsterdam,* "Declaration Relating to the Protocol on the Institutions with the Prospect of Enlargement of the European Union," 142.

41. Lionel Barber, "Santer Gloomy About Summit," *Financial Times,* 27 June 1997, 2.

42. Lionel Barber and Gordon Cramb, "Luxembourg Back in the EU's Hot Seat," *Financial Times,* 1 July 1997, 2.

43. European Commission, "Agenda 2000: For a Stronger and Wider Union," *Bulletin of the European Union,* supp. 5/97, 12–13.

44. European Parliament, "Resolution on the Communication from the Commission 'Agenda 2000: For a Stronger and Wider Union' (COM(97)2000–C4–0371/97)," PE 264.945, 4 December 1997, 8–9.

45. *Treaty of Amsterdam,* "Declaration by Belgium, France and Italy on the Protocol on the Institutions with the Prospect of Enlargement of the European Union," 144.

46. This intention was apparently signaled by the Belgian government at an EU foreign minister meeting in September 1997. See Lionel Barber and Michael Smith, "EU States in Revolt over Cost of Admitting Poorer Members," *Financial Times,* 16 September 1997, 16.

47. See the comments of Polish government officials, cited in Agence Europe, *Europe Daily Bulletin,* no. 7300, 14–15 September 1998, 4 and 16; Agence Europe, *Europe Daily Bulletin,* no. 7315, 5–6 October 1998, 3; and Agence Europe, *Europe Daily Bulletin,* no. 7321, 14 October 1998, 8.

48. "Luxembourg Presidency Conclusions," para. 3, available on the Internet at http://europa. eu.int/council/off/conclu/dec97.htm#intro.

49. Lionel Barber, "France and Germany Move to Reshape EU's Future," *Financial Times,* 9 June 1998, 2. For the text of the Franco-German letter, see *Bulletin,* no. 41, 15 June 1998 (Bonn: Presse- und Informationsamt der Bundesregierung), 537–38.

50. "Chirac Likely to Suggest Delors Heads Study," *Financial Times,* 6 May 1998, 2; Lionel Barber and Neil Buckley, "UK Wants New Body to Study EU's Future," *Financial Times,* 13–14 June 1998, 2; Barber, "The Second Coming," 10.

51. Ralph Atkins, "Kohl Warns Against EU Centralization," *Financial Times,* 19 June 1998, 3; Lionel Barber, "Long on Words and Short on Action," *Financial Times,* 17 June 1998, 2; "Cardiff Presidency Conclusions," reprinted in Agence Europe, *Europe Documents,* no. 2094–2095, 18 June 1998, 8.

52. Peter Norman, "Schröder Warns on EU Enlargement," *Financial Times,* 27 November 1998, 3. For a summary of discussions at the Pörtschach summit, see Agence Europe, *Europe Daily Bulletin,* no. 7330, 26/27 October 1998, 3–8.

53. "Vienna Presidency Conclusions," in Agence Europe, *Europe Daily Bulletin,* no. 7363, 13 December 1998, 7.

54. Ralph Atkins and Frederick Stüdemann, "Green Outlook on the World" (interview with Joschka Fischer), *Financial Times,* 28 January 1999, 12.

55. Tim Burt, "Finland Outlines Its EU Strategy," *Financial Times,* 3 February 1999, 3.

56. On the debate over the IGC mandate and method of preparation, see Agence Europe, *Europe Daily Bulletin,* no. 7466, 17–18 May 1999, 5; Agence Europe, *Europe Daily Bulletin,* no. 7474, 29 May 1999, 4; and Agence Europe, *Europe Daily Bulletin,* no. 7475, 31 May-1 June 1999, 6.

57. "Presidency Conclusions" of the Cologne European Council, 3–4 June 1999," reprinted in Agence Europe, *Europe Daily Bulletin,* no. 7480, 6 June 1999 (special edition), 15.

58. "Cologne Presidency Conclusions," 15.

59. Agence Europe, *Europe Daily Bulletin,* no. 7513, 23 July 1999, 4. The full text of Prodi's speech is available on the Internet at http://europa.eu.int/comm/commissioners/prodi/speeches/designate/210799_en.htm.

60. Prodi speech; see note 59.

61. Peter Norman, "Prodi Names Group to Spur Wide-Ranging EU Reforms," *Financial Times,* 28–29 August 1999, 2.

62. Agence Europe, *Europe Daily Bulletin,* no. 7552, 16 September 1999, 10.

63. "The Institutional Implications of Enlargement" (report to the European Commission, Brussels, 18 October 1999). The Dehaene report is available on the Internet, at the EU's official Website at http://europa.eu.int; it is also reprinted in Agence Europe, *Europe Documents,* no. 2159, 22 October 1999.

64. Peter Norman and Andrew Parker, "'Wise Men' Urge Reforms Ahead of EU Expansion," *Financial Times,* 19 October 1999, 2; and Agence Europe, *Europe Daily Bulletin,* no. 7575, 18/19 October 1999, 3–4. Dehaene's quote is on page 3 of the latter reference.

65. "The Institutional Implications of Enlargement," 7–10.

66. "The Institutional Implications of Enlargement," 10–12.

67. "The Institutional Implications of Enlargement," 10–11 and 15.

68. Agence Europe, *Europe Daily Bulletin,* no. 7577, 21 October 1999, 5.

69. Peter Norman, "Prodi Gives Strong Backing to Call for Serious EU Reform," *Financial Times,* 21 October 1999, 3.

70. "Adapting the Institutions to Make a Success of Enlargement: Contribution by the European Commission to Preparations for the Intergovernmental Conference on Institutional Issues," available on the Internet, at the EU's official Website at http://europa.eu.int/igc2000/index_en.htm. See also Agence Europe, *Europe Daily Bulletin,* no. 7591, 11 November 1999, 3–4. The Commission's formal Opinion on the IGC followed in January. See European Commission, "Adapting the Institutions to Make a Success of Enlargement," COM (2000) 34, 26 January 2000.

71. The full text of the EP resolution is reprinted in Agence Europe, *Europe Documents,* no. 2163, 26 November 1999, 1–6. For the EP debate on this resolution, see Agence Europe, *Europe Daily Bulletin,* no. 7596, 19 November 1999, 3–5.

72. On the political parties, see Agence Europe, *Europe Daily Bulletin,* no. 7611, 10 December 1999, 3.

73. Agence Europe, *Europe Daily Bulletin,* no. 7582, 28 October 1999, 7.

74. For the Finnish government, see Agence Europe, *Europe Daily Bulletin,* no. 7586, 4 November 1999, 4. For the British government's response, see Agence Europe, *Europe Daily Bulletin,* no. 7586, 4 November 1999, 4.

75. For a critical summary of the member states' response to the Dehaene report, see the editorial in Agence Europe, *Europe Daily Bulletin,* no. 7585, 2/3 November 1999, 3.

76. On the position of the Benelux states regarding the IGC agenda, see Agence Europe, *Europe Daily Bulletin,* no. 7608, 6–7 December 1999, 4. For the views of Luxembourg Prime Minister Jean-Claude Juncker, see Agence Europe, *Europe Daily Bulletin,* no. 7589, 8/9 November 1999, 4.

77. "The Dangers of a Two-Tier Europe," *Financial Times,* 28 October 1998, 17.

78. Agence Europe, *Europe Daily Bulletin,* no. 7604, 1 December 1999, 5.

79. Peter Norman, Michael Smith, and Andrew Parker, "Radical Plan to Split EU Treaties Rejected," *Financial Times,* 2 December 1999, 2.

80. On the Finnish presidency's report on the IGC, entitled "Effective Institutions after Enlargement: Suggestions for the Intergovernmental Conference," see Agence Europe, *Europe Daily Bulletin,* no. 7611, 10 December 1999, 3–4. On the bargaining in Helsinki, see Peter Norman, "Door Left Ajar for Reforms," *Financial Times,* 13 December 1999, 4.

81. "Presidency Conclusions" of the Helsinki European Council, 10–11 December 1999, points 15 and 16, available on the Internet at http://europa.eu.int/council/off/conclu/dec99/dec99_en.htm. Klima is quoted in Norman, "Door Left Ajar for Reforms," 4.

82. "Statement by Romano Prodi, President of the European Commission, on the Results of the European Council in Helsinki," European Parliament, Strasbourg, 14 December 1999 (Speech/99/210).

83. Agence Europe, *Europe Daily Bulletin,* no. 7628, 7 January 2000, 3–4; Agence Europe, *Europe Daily Bulletin,* no. 7640, 24–25 January 2000, 6; Agence Europe, *Europe Daily Bulletin,* no. 7655, 14–15 February 2000, 5–6; Agence Europe, *Europe Daily Bulletin,* no. 7657, 17 February 2000, 3; Agence Europe, *Europe Daily Bulletin,* no. 7671, 8 March 2000, 3–4; "Majority Voting Proposal," *Financial Times,* 8–9 January 2000, 4; Peter Norman, "Commission Wants Wider IGC Agenda," *Financial Times,* 24 January 2000, 3; Peter Norman, "Reformers Out to Transform Europe," *Financial Times,* 14 February 2000, 2.

9

✛

The Accession Negotiations

The beginning of accession negotiations between the EU and the six first-group applicants in 1998 was only the start of a long and difficult process. For even the best-prepared applicants, the negotiations will take several years, with plenty of hard bargaining and the likelihood of occasional setbacks. As the negotiations advance to the more difficult chapters of the *acquis communautaire,* they will also inevitably become more politicized, with domestic politics and pressure from sectoral and other organized interests becoming a more important factor influencing the bargaining of both the applicants and the member states. Domestic politics, and the level of public support for enlargement or accession, will also become more important as the negotiations enter their crucial final phase and thereafter. Because it will ultimately have to give its assent to the Accession Treaties before they can be ratified by the member states and acceding countries, the EP's views on the accession process become increasingly important as well.

THE NEGOTIATIONS CONTINUE

After getting under way in November 1998, substantive negotiations with the first-group countries continued into the next year. In early January, the German EU presidency announced its agenda for the negotiations in the first half of 1999. It scheduled two meetings at the "deputy level"—member state EU ambassadors (permanent representatives) with the chief negotiators of the six applicants—for April 19 and May 19, and meetings at the ministerial (foreign ministers) level for June 22. The goal for its six-month presidency, the German government declared, would be to conclude negotiations on all of the first seven chapters and to open concrete negotiations on eight additional screened chapters: company law, free movement of goods, consumer protection, fisheries, statistics, external economic relations, customs union, and competition policy. According to Bonn, negotiations on some of the least difficult of these chapters could be provisionally concluded the very day they were opened. The Council endorsed this schedule for the negotiations on January 26.[1]

The six applicants also prepared for further negotiations. At a coordination meeting in Budapest in December 1998, the governments of the first-group countries agreed to submit negotiating positions for each of the next eight chapters by early February 1999. In contrast to the first seven chapters, these position papers contained numerous requests for derogations. For the chapter on external economic relations, several applicants sought permission to maintain, for a certain period after accession, free trade or Customs Union agreements with neighboring countries: the Czech Republic with Slovakia; Estonia with Latvia, Lithuania, and Ukraine; and Slovenia with Croatia, Bosnia, and Macedonia. For the chapter on competition policy, Poland and the Czech Republic requested permission to maintain state aid schemes for economically disadvantaged regions. For the chapter on external economic relations, Hungary and the Czech Republic requested permission to maintain, for a period after accession, special import tariffs and quotas on "sensitive" products from non-EU countries. And for the chapter on free movement of goods, Poland and Slovenia requested transitional periods before having to fully apply EU rules on the marketing of certain products, such as pharmaceuticals. Poland and Estonia also requested derogations for the sensitive fisheries chapter. The only country making no derogation requests was Cyprus.[2]

Upon receiving the new batch of position papers from the six applicants, the Council asked the Commission to begin drafting the EU's common positions for negotiations on these eight chapters. On April 19, the member state permanent representatives met with the chief negotiators of the applicants to begin negotiations on four of these chapters: fisheries, consumer protection, company law, and statistics. They also continued discussions on the industrial policy and telecommunications chapters, on which negotiations had been launched in November but were not yet provisionally closed. After this session, while most of the applicants expressed satisfaction with the way negotiations were proceeding, the Polish delegation, unhappy that negotiations on several chapters were not provisionally closed that day, voiced disappointment with the slow pace of enlargement. According to Poland's chief negotiator, Jan Kulakowski, there was a "discrepancy" between the March 27 Berlin summit declaration, in which the European Council pledged to speed up the enlargement process after agreement on "Agenda 2000," and the actual progress of the negotiations.[3]

One reason for this slow progress was that the accession negotiations were entering a more difficult phase. In March, the Commission announced that it would begin taking a more differentiated approach to the applicants in the negotiations. According to Commissioner van den Broek, "As negotiations intensify and enter increasingly complex and difficult sectors, we shall be able to note that some will be capable of responding more effectively than others to EU demands." He declared that, as a consequence, "negotiations will not necessarily be over on the same chapters of the *acquis* with the same applicants at the same time . . . with each candidate being able to join the EU when they are ready." In other words, the applicants would be increasingly treated individually, rather than as members of a group. This was in keeping, van den Broek said, with the EU's original declaration, made at the beginning of the accession process, that it would judge each candidate for membership on its own merits.[4]

The negotiations were also becoming more difficult because they were now dealing with chapters that were not self-contained but were interdependent with other chapters or areas of the negotiations. As a result, it was likely that fewer chapters would be declared provisionally closed after specific negotiating rounds; instead, they would remain open until a more comprehensive compromise embracing other chapters of the negotiations could be found. This trend toward "horizontal" negotiations was evident at the May 19 deputy-level meeting, which failed to reach closure on many of the newly opened chapters.[5]

By the end of May, the six applicants had submitted position papers on several additional chapters, including the free movement of capital, EMU, energy, and social policy and employment. The most notable derogation requests contained in these position papers were the requests of both Hungary and Estonia (concerning the free movement of capital chapter) to be allowed to maintain restrictions on the purchase of farming land and real estate for a period after accession.[6]

On June 21–22, EU foreign ministers held their second set of meetings with counterparts from the six negotiating countries. These successive bilateral ("15 + 1") meetings essentially confirmed the results of the two negotiating sessions in April and May. As a result, by the end of the German presidency, Poland and Estonia had provisionally concluded negotiations with the EU on seven chapters; Hungary, the Czech Republic, and Slovenia on eight; and Cyprus on ten. Altogether, a total of fifteen of the thirty-one chapters of the *acquis communautaire* were officially opened for negotiations.[7]

At the June ministerial meeting, the EU generally praised the progress made by the applicants, although Commissioner van den Broek recalled that EU legislation must be actually implemented before accession, and he reemphasized the importance of creating administrative structures and capacities to ensure the effective application of the *acquis communautaire*. Poland's foreign minister, Bronislaw Geremek, urged the member states to be more flexible in the negotiations, declaring that they should more rapidly close negotiations on chapters that were "very close to conclusion," even though some details remained open. All of the applicants pressed the EU to set dates for concluding the negotiations, with Hungary declaring that January 2002 was its target date for accession, while Poland, Estonia, and Slovenia set their sights on January 2003.[8]

For the second half of 1999, the incoming Finnish presidency pledged to maintain the pace of accession negotiations, promising to conclude as many chapters as possible and to open several new ones.[9] On September 30, the first deputy-level meeting under the Finnish presidency took place. At this meeting, three new chapters—EMU, free movement of capital, and social policy and employment—were opened for negotiation. However, the scheduled opening of a fourth chapter (energy policy) was blocked by the Austrian government, with the backing of Germany, when these two member states refused to approve the EU's draft common position on this chapter. For the Austrian government, the draft common position was unacceptable because it did not take a firm enough stance on the issue of nuclear safety in the applicant countries; before it would agree to the common position, Austria wanted the insertion of a paragraph demanding that nuclear power stations in the applicant countries must meet the highest possible safety standards. Thus, to the dismay of the six first-group countries, negotiations on the energy chapter were delayed because of Austria's concern about the safety of nuclear power plants across its border in Slovakia, a country that was not even a part of the negotiations.[10]

At the next deputy-level meeting on November 12, the Austrian government agreed to lift its reservation on energy policy, allowing the opening of negotiations on this chapter. Also opened for negotiation at this meeting were the chapters on transport and free movement of services. Negotiations on a fourth chapter, taxation, were opened with only five of the six applicants, since Poland was unable to provide its position paper on this chapter in time. However, at this meeting Poland was able to provisionally close its negotiations with the EU on the external relations chapter.[11]

At the December 7 ministerial meeting, negotiations on the difficult environment chapter were opened with all six applicants. Reflecting the difficult nature of this chapter, in their position papers each of the applicants requested several transitional periods of varying length, declaring that they needed more time to make the tremendous investments required for adopting EU legislation in such areas as water purification and waste treatment. In its position paper, the Polish government announced that it was planning to spend EUR 30 billion over the next fifteen years on environmental projects in order to bring Poland up to EU standards. At the meeting, the EU provisionally concluded negotiations on the EMU chapter with all six applicants, and the chapter on free movement of goods with the Czech Republic. As a result, by the end of the Finnish Presidency, negotiations on twenty-three of the thirty-one chapters of the *acquis communautaire* were opened. Estonia had provisionally concluded negotiations with the EU on eight chapters; Poland, Hungary, and Slovenia on nine; the Czech Republic on ten; and Cyprus on eleven.[12]

In the "Presidency Conclusions" of the Helsinki summit, held three days later, the European Council noted "with satisfaction" the progress in substantive negotiations with the six applicants.[13] Following the summit, the incoming Portuguese presidency declared its intention to maintain the pace of the negotiations and to open as many of the remaining chapters of the *acquis communautaire* to negotiation as possible by the end of its term in June 2000.[14] These would include such difficult chapters as agriculture, free movement of persons, JHA, and regional policy. The chapter on institutions, however, could only be negotiated after completion of the 2000 IGC on institutional reform. Once all thirty-one chapters were opened, for the first time a complete overview of the "hard core" negotiating issues to be resolved with each of the applicants would be possible. Also during the Portuguese presidency, because of the Helsinki summit decisions, substantive negotiations would also begin with the five second-group applicants and Malta, with unpredictable consequences for the accession negotiations with the first-group countries.

EXPANDED NEGOTIATIONS, NEW PROCEDURES

When negotiations resumed in 2000 with all twelve applicants, they did so using new procedures. These procedures were first announced by the Commission in its October 1999 Regular Report, which declared that the expanded negotiations would be increasingly governed by the principle of "differentiation." The Commission announced that this principle would now be applied by the EU when deciding "which and how many chapters" of the *acquis communautaire* would be opened for negotiation with each applicant. No longer would an equal number of chapters be simultaneously opened for negotiation with all applicants; instead, for each applicant the EU would base its decision on the number and subject of chapters to open on the state of preparedness of the country concerned.[15]

The Commission also announced new procedures for the provisional closure of chapters. According to the Commission, the existing procedure of provisionally closing chapters once certain criteria (full acceptance of the *acquis communautaire*, absence of requests for transitional periods, satisfactory answers to EU questions, and so on) had been met was counterproductive. It had resulted in increased political pressure by the applicants—stemming from their need to show progress toward accession—to have chapters declared provisionally closed, with identified difficulties put aside to be dealt with in a final "global negotiating package." However, the Commission warned that this emphasis on provisionally closing chapters ran the risk of overshadowing adequate preparations for accession. "Ideally," the Commission declared, "negotiations should inject increased momentum into the candidate's preparations for membership." However, "the procedure for provisional closure of chapters not directly linked with the state of preparatory progress, as applied until now, may have the contrary effect."[16]

The Commission thus proposed a new procedure. Recalling its previously announced plans to reopen all provisionally closed chapters from the beginning of 2000 ("in order to allow newly adopted *acquis,* not yet addressed in the negotiations, to be included"), the Commission now proposed using "this occasion to establish a strong link between the negotiations and the preparatory process." In the future, according to the Commission, "no chapter would . . . be provisionally closed (or closed again after re-opening) unless the EU is satisfied that the candidates' preparations are in line with their commitments in terms of preparation for accession."[17]

To examine these preparations, the Commission promised a more effective monitoring system using the tools already in place (screening reports, the Europe Agreements, the annual progress reports, and the Accession Partnerships and National Programs for the Adoption of the *Acquis Communautaire*). Moreover, on the basis of its monitoring and the comparison of "progress with commitments," the Commission also indicated that it could decide to reopen chapters that had been provisionally closed.[18]

According to the Commission, this new procedure offered a number of advantages. First, by "presenting an objective picture of actual overall progress achieved," it would create "a strong incentive for the candidates to intensify their preparations for membership," and it would stimulate "objective public debate in these countries about priorities for reform and assistance." Second, by applying the principle of differentiation objectively to all applicants, it would make the accession negotiations more fair, allowing them to proceed "on merit," and would thus allow the countries beginning negotiations in 2000 the opportunity to catch up with the already negotiating countries. Finally, the new procedure would ensure "parallelism between negotiating and preparatory progress, reducing the risk that accession treaties may not be approved."[19]

The Commission's report also proposed new rules for defining what constituted a "reasonable" transition period for the application of EU legislation. Declaring that, what made this enlargement different from previous enlargements is that "following the completion of the Single Market the EU operates without [internal] border restrictions," the Commission proposed distinguishing between two cases of transitional requests: (1) For policy areas linked to the extension of the Single Market, EU regulations should "be implemented quickly," with any transitional periods being "few and short." However, (2) "for those areas of the *acquis* where considerable adaptations are necessary and which require substantial effort, including important financial outlays (in areas such as the environment, energy, infrastructure), transition arrangements could be spread over a definite period of time provided candidates can demonstrate that the alignment is underway and that they are committed to detailed and realistic plans for alignment, including the necessary investments."[20] This new distinction posed potential problems for the requests of some applicants for derogations concerning free trade arrangements with neighboring nonmember countries and restrictions on the purchase of real estate by foreigners (see below).

In announcing these new procedures, Commission President Prodi declared that the expanded negotiations would not proceed uniformly but would instead constitute a "fully flexible, multi-speed accession process."[21]

The Commission's proposals for revising the procedures of the accession negotiations were essentially endorsed by the Helsinki European Council, which stressed in its "Presidency Conclusions" that the pace of negotiations for the individual applicants would henceforth vary, based on the objective preparedness of each country. The European Council also emphasized the principle of parallelism, declaring that "progress in negotiations must go hand in hand with progress in incorporating the *acquis* into legislation and actually implementing it."[22]

THE NEGOTIATIONS IN EARLY 2000

In January, the Portuguese presidency announced its plans for accession negotiations during its six-month term in office. It announced that accession negotiations with the five second-group applicants and Malta would be formally launched on February 15, at a ceremonial meeting of EU foreign ministers and their counterparts from the six applicant states. The actual negotiations would begin at deputy level in late March, once the Commission had decided how many and which chapters should be opened for negotiation with each applicant. (Unlike with the first group, the Commission had declared that negotiations on the same chapters would not be opened simultaneously with all of the newly negotiating applicants.) A second deputy-level meeting was scheduled for May. For the first-group applicants, deputy-level meetings would take place in April and May, with the possibility left open for additional meetings. A meeting at ministers' level with all twelve applicants would take place in June.[23]

For the first-group countries, the Portuguese presidency reiterated its intention to open all remaining chapters for negotiation by the end of its term, with the exception of the chapters on institutions and "miscellaneous" matters. Based on the Commission's estimates of when its draft common positions would be ready for submission to the Council, it appeared that the difficult agriculture chapter could be opened for negotiation in May, the six first-group applicants having already submitted their own position papers on this chapter in December 1999. The Portuguese government also declared its wish to pursue negotiations on the "left-over" chapters (those previously opened but not yet provisionally closed), and to provisionally close as many of these as possible before the end of June.[24]

On February 15, as planned, accession negotiations with the five second-group CEECs and Malta were formally opened. At the ceremonial meeting in Brussels, Commissioner Verheugen asserted the EU's determination to give the six "Helsinki group" countries a real chance to catch up with the applicants of the "Luxembourg group," declaring that for this reason the newly negotiating countries might expect that "many more" chapters would be opened for negotiations with them over the next ten months than was the case in the first year of negotiations with the first group. At the meeting, each of the six applicants expressed their desire to rapidly catch up in the negotiations and join the EU as quickly as possible, with Malta and Latvia setting the most ambitious target date for entry (January 2003). For the others, the announced target dates were January 2004 for Lithuania and Slovakia, January 2006 for Bulgaria, and January 2007 for Romania. At the meeting, it was also announced that actual negotiations would begin with a deputy-level meeting on March 28. Before this point, the Commission would submit its draft common positions for the first chapters and its recommendations for which chapters negotiations should be opened with each applicant.[25]

On March 8, the Commission announced its recommendation that negotiations be opened with Malta, Latvia, Lithuania, and Slovakia on eight chapters, with Bulgaria on six, and with Romania on only five. This announcement disappointed some of the applicants, who had declared that they were ready to begin negotiations on many more chapters (up to fifteen, in the cases of several countries). Nevertheless, all six governments were generally pleased that concrete negotiations were about to begin.[26]

The Commission also worked in early 2000 to prepare its draft common positions for the remaining chapters to be negotiated with the first-group countries. It also launched a renewed screening process for all twelve applicants to review new EU legislation since the opening of accession negotiations on March 31, 1998, on the basis of which it could decide to reopen for negotiation already provisionally closed chapters.[27]

Among the first-group applicants, however, signs of growing impatience were emerging. In early February, Hungary's EU ambassador, Endre Juhasz, called for the EU to table as soon as possible "precise, complete and substantial" negotiating positions for all chapters, including a clearer stance on requests for transitional arrangements. Arguing that the EU and candidate countries were now beyond the stage of making declarations, he declared that it was time to "confront the real controversial issues," including those touching on the most sensitive chapters, such as agriculture, the free movement of people, and the environment. According to Juhasz, "If there is a problem, let's face it now. If there is a risk of tensions, let the tensions come. If there is a crisis, the crisis must come now, not later." In other words, he argued, let's finally get down to business and let the real negotiations begin.[28]

These more precise negotiation positions were coming, responded the Commission.[29] In an effort to assuage the concerns of the first-group countries as well, Commissioner Verheugen repeated his contention that the expansion of accession negotiations would not slow down the enlargement process for the Luxembourg six. He also held out the possibility that as early as the fall of 2000, when the Commission published its next annual progress reports, it might be possible to set a timetable for concluding negotiations with the most advanced applicants, and possibly set dates for the first accessions as well. However, he reemphasized that the ratification process for the first accession treaties could not begin until after the ratification process for the IGC treaty on institutional reform was completed. The two ratification processes, he declared, could not occur in parallel.[30]

PROBLEM AREAS

As the (now expanded) accession negotiations moved into their second year, the EU and the applicant states prepared to tackle some of the more difficult chapters of the *acquis communautaire*; these included the chapters on agriculture, the environment, regional policy (Structural Funds), JHA, and the free movement of people. As a result, the negotiations would likely become much more intense, and their pace considerably slower.

Agriculture promises to be a particularly difficult chapter to negotiate. In "Agenda 2000," the Commission proposed only gradually integrating the CEECs into the CAP, with lengthy transition periods after accession before they become fully eligible for EU subsidies. In particular, the EU is reluctant to provide direct compensatory payments to farmers in new member states, arguing that these are not necessary since CEEC farmers will benefit from higher EU prices for their products, and that they did not need to be compensated for the loss of price subsidies they had never received. This intention was reaffirmed by the Commission's October 1998 report on the agricultural situation in the CEECs; this report noted encouraging developments in the agricultural sectors of these countries since the Commission's previous (1995) report, yet argued that major problems remain.[31]

However, the applicant countries insist that they should be fully integrated into the CAP immediately upon accession and that their farmers should enjoy full CAP benefits. This is a particularly sensitive issue for heavily agricultural Poland, where the government's efforts to modernize agriculture have met with fierce resistance from farmers, and where demonstrating farmers have demanded full CAP benefits upon accession.[32] In its position paper on agriculture submitted to the Commission in December 1999, the Polish government declared that it would not request any exemptions from CAP rules and legislation, but in return it insisted on full CAP benefits for Polish farmers, including direct compensatory payments. Similar demands were made in the position papers of the other five applicants.[33]

In early 2000, there were some signs of compromise. In February, the Commission announced that it was studying the possibility of extending some direct aid payments to CEEC farmers after accession.[34] Early the next month, Agriculture Commissioner Fischler suggested that CEEC farmers could receive direct payments upon accession, but only on a phased-in basis, with eligibility for full CAP benefits only after a transition period lasting five to seven years. These direct payments would be linked to production limits. The money to fund the payments would come from savings in the EU budget stemming from the first new members not joining in 2002, as projected by the Commission in its "Agenda 2000" calculations, but rather in 2003 or (more likely) in 2004. However, the member states would have to agree to use this money, originally allocated in the 2000–2006 financial perspective for enlargement costs, to fund payments to CEEC farmers. Fischler emphasized, however, that the Commission's position on this matter was not yet final, and that its draft common position on agriculture was still being revised.[35] While the proposal fell short of what was desired by the CEECs, it nonetheless represented a significant move away from the EU's original position of no direct payments.

In the meantime, agriculture continues to be a problem area in trade relations between the EU and the CEECs. Under the Europe Agreements, which call for the gradual liberalization of agricultural trade, heavily subsidized EU farm exports have swamped the markets of the CEECs, generating bitter complaints of unfair competition from CEEC farmers. This has led the CEECs to impose ad hoc import duties on some EU farm products (including, notably, the Czech Republic on EU apples in January 1999). In late June 1999, the EU proposed a new farm trade regime to the CEECs; this would be a system of quotas for goods to be traded free of subsidy and free of import duties (the "double-zero" option: exports that were not subsidized would attract no duty). While this proposal drew the suspicion and ire of EU farmers (because of the cuts in subsidies), the Commission hoped that it would reduce problems in farm trade relations with the CEECs.[36] In September, however, Warsaw angered the EU by proposing a plan to raise import duties on farm products, combined with quotas for duty-free or reduced-duty imports from the EU. This move was intended to placate Poland's restive farmers while also creating leverage for the Polish government in its upcoming negotiations with the EU on the agriculture chapter.[37]

Another difficult issue for accession negotiations is the environment. After more than four decades of Communist rule and economic mismanagement, most of the CEECs suffer from serious environmental problems. For these countries, meeting the EU's stiff environmental standards and regulations will prove difficult as they also seek to maximize economic growth and attract foreign investment. It will also be hugely expensive, with the cost of meeting EU standards for Poland alone estimated by the World Bank to be around $40 billion.[38] Nevertheless, the EU insists upon full adoption of the environmental *acquis communautaire* by the applicants, pointing to the threat to EU environmental standards and conditions if not adopted, as well as the competitive problem for EU industry posed by "environmental dumping."[39]

The Commission recognized the special challenge to the CEECs posed by EU environmental standards in a May 1998 Communication in which it estimated the total cost of transposing the environmental *acquis communautaire* for the ten CEECs at ECU 100–120 billion. To help the CEECs meet this challenge, the Commission proposed a special pre-accession strategy for the environment that would identify priority actions in each country, especially in the key areas of air and water quality and waste treatment. The Commission's strategy did not include any new EU funding but sought to coordinate the use of existing aid instruments—including PHARE and the Instrument for Structural Policies for Pre-accession (ISPA)—to help the applicants meet their environmental goals. It also sought to mobilize funding from other sources, including local government authorities in the candidate countries and foreign private investment. For Cyprus, the Commission promised to prepare a separate document outlining an environmental strategy geared to this country's special economic and historical situation.[40]

In September 1998, the Commission and Council presidency began a series of informal meetings with the environment ministers of each of the eleven applicants to discuss the environmental pre-accession strategy. At the September meeting, EU representatives once again stressed the importance of fully integrating the environmental *acquis communautaire* as a condition for membership. The EU also presented the applicant countries with a detailed manual to help them with the practical implementation of EU legislation in this field.[41] At the fifth such meeting, in November 1999, the first attended by representatives from Malta, the EU called upon the applicants to redouble their efforts to apply the environmental *acquis communautaire,* and it launched a new common environment investment strategy (called Priority Environmental Investment Program for Accession, or PEPA) to help them do so.[42]

Despite such special assistance, however, the environment promises to be a particularly difficult issue for the accession negotiations, as indicated by the numerous requests for transitional arrangements made by the first-group applicants in their position papers on this chapter (see above). In its position paper, the Polish government asked for transitional periods in fourteen different areas, including gas emissions, solid waste, and sewage disposal. Poland's chief negotiator, Jan Kulakowski, has stated that the environment chapter will be, along with agriculture, the most difficult for his country to negotiate.[43]

Another potential problem area is JHA, which includes policies on immigration and asylum and the fight against international organized crime. The EU is greatly concerned about the ability of new member states to control their external borders. This is because, under the Schengen Agreement, persons are free to move throughout the EU once inside its borderless zone. As a counterpoint to internal freedom of movement, however, the EU places considerable importance on the control of its external borders. Because, upon accession, the external borders of the new member states will become the external borders of the EU, helping these countries to better manage their borders with nonmembers has become a key goal of the pre-accession process. Unless confident of an applicant's ability to secure its external borders and block illegal immigration and smuggling, the EU is unlikely to admit that country or permit the free movement of its citizens within the Schengen zone after accession. The EU has been particularly critical of the border management policies of Romania and Bulgaria, and because of this kept these two countries on its common list of countries whose citizens require a visa to enter the Union until January 2000.[44]

The EU insists, therefore, that the applicant countries adopt and effectively implement the Schengen *acquis* before accession. In September 1998, at a meeting of the Schengen member states (all EU member states except Britain and Ireland) with the applicant countries, Germany's interior minister, Manfred Kanther, declared that "only those countries effectively able to meet all the necessary con-

ditions will be able to join and be a part of this zone of free movement and security that is the Schengen area."[45] To help them meet this requirement, the Schengen member states established a special "Standing Committee" to monitor the
adaptation process in the applicant countries and their compliance with EU rules,
and they have scheduled regular information meetings with the applicants at various government levels. The EU has also invited the interior ministers of the applicant countries to meet with the JHA Council, with the first such meeting occurring in September 1998.[46]

The EU is also helping the applicant countries improve their efforts at combating international organized crime. The EU's assistance in this area began in September 1994, with a conference in Berlin on drugs and organized crime that
brought together EU JHA ministers and their counterparts from the CEECs. Since
the Essen summit and approval of the pre-accession strategy, the EU has permitted
the use of PHARE aid for assisting the CEECs on JHA issues, and there also has
been cooperation in JHA within the parameters of the structured dialogue. The
pre-accession strategy also allowed the participation of the CEECs in EU-funded
programs for justice and police cooperation.[47] Cooperation in the fight against
organized crime was a key theme of the first European Conference in March 1998
as well as of the second one in July 1999.[48] In May 1998, the EU member states
and the eleven applicants adopted a "Pre-Accession Pact on Organized Crime," the
purpose of which was to help the applicants in approximating EU legislation in
the area of JHA and to assist their efforts in fighting organized crime. To this end,
the pact called for the signatory countries to develop and implement common
projects to combat organized crime. The EU also promised to provide technical
and financial assistance to help prepare the applicants for accession in this area.[49] In
October 1999, the Commission launched a new (EUR 4.5 million) program to
help the CEECs improve their police training and combat international organized
crime.[50]

Concern about the capacity of the applicants to effectively police their borders
and combat organized crime, joined with domestic labor-market concerns and
anti-foreigner sentiment in such member states as Germany and Austria (see
below), could lead the EU to insist in accession negotiations on lengthy transitional
periods before allowing the free movement of persons from new member states.
This is something that the applicants generally reject, however, and the governments of these countries are likely to come under considerable domestic pressure
to win the right for their nationals to freely travel and work in the EU soon after
membership.[51] In addition to its economic benefits, the right to free movement
would also have tremendous symbolic value for the new member states, signifying
their full acceptance into the Western community of nations. Presaging difficult
negotiations on this issue, after a meeting with the Commission in October 1998,
Poland's prime minister, Jerzy Buzek, insisted that any transitional period for the
free movement of persons be kept to a minimum. Buzek claimed that, by the time
of accession, Poland's economy would be so stable and its unemployment rate so

low that the EU should have no difficulty in agreeing to allow the free movement of workers without much delay.[52] In the EU, however, concern about the labor market and political consequences of enlargement have led the Commission to consider the possibility of flexible transition quotas for particular labor sectors for acceding countries.[53]

A related issue for some applicants is the control of borders and relations with neighboring (nonmember) countries. For some applicants, the EU's demand for tougher border restrictions will cause problems because of special ties and existing agreements with neighboring countries. The Polish government, for example, has balked at the EU's insistence that it tighten control of its border with Ukraine, since it currently has visa-free travel agreements with Kiev and earns an estimated $7 billion annually in cross-border trade with its large eastern neighbor. The EU's demand for tougher border controls also causes a problem for first-wave applicants who may join the EU before neighboring CEECs with which they have close relations. Hungary worries that tougher border restrictions will inhibit ties with the large Hungarian minorities residing in Romania and Slovakia as well as in the Vojvodina region of Serbia. And the Czech Republic is keen to maintain an open border with Slovakia, in the event that it enters the EU before its neighbor and former partner country in the Czech and Slovak Federation. Even after the 1993 "velvet divorce," close economic and social ties between these two countries remain; in 1998, mutual trade accounted for more than one-fifth of their total trade turnover. The EU, however, insists that the Czech-Slovak customs union must be ended before either country can be considered for membership. Aside from the economic costs of doing so, the CEECs also argue that closing their borders with neighboring nonmember countries will only create new divisions in Europe.[54]

Finding a way to maintain the special external ties of the new member states while at the same time meeting the legitimate security and immigration concerns of the EU's current member states will no doubt be a difficult issue to resolve in the accession negotiations. While the applicants may ask for special waivers or transitional arrangements in this area, they do not want such concessions to be at the cost of postponed accession, delayed free movement for their own citizens, or a second-class EU membership.

Another problem for accession negotiations (under the free movement of capital chapter) is the restrictions on land and real estate purchases by foreigners that are imposed by many of the applicant countries. Such rules violate the EU's Single Market legislation and principles and will have to be changed upon accession. This is a particularly sensitive issue for some of the applicant countries, however, especially Poland, which fears a rush by wealthier Germans to purchase relatively cheap Polish property, particularly the families of Germans who were expelled from the western regions of Poland after World War II. As a result, the Polish government has asked for special exemptions from EU rules in this area, including an eighteen-year ban on the sale of farm and building land to foreigners and a six-year ban on purchases of land for industrial purposes. The Hungarian government has also requested a derogation in this area, allowing it to maintain restrictions on the purchase of agricultural land by foreigners for ten years after accession and to impose a five-year ban on the sale of land for industrial purposes. Budapest claims that, otherwise, relatively inexpensive Hungarian land will be bought up by foreigners, leading to a bidding up of land prices that will make ownership too expensive for Hungarians.[55] The issue of land purchases by foreigners is also a sensitive one for the Czech Republic and Slovenia.

The land-purchase issue is also a sensitive one for many Germans, however, especially the Polish and Sudeten (Czech) expellees and their descendants. In July 1998, the organization representing Polish expellees (the Bund der Vertriebenen) argued that Poland's restrictions on the purchase of real estate by foreigners indicated that it was not yet ready for EU membership.[56] Because of the sensitivity of this issue on both sides, it is certain to be a difficult subject for accession negotiations.

DOMESTIC POLITICS AND PUBLIC OPINION

As the accession negotiations focus on more difficult and politically sensitive chapters, the role of domestic politics and public opinion will become increasingly important. Because of pressure from organized interests and public opinion, the governments of both the member states and the applicant countries will be compelled to take tougher stances in the negotiations on certain issues. Much of the hard bargaining will be over the length and nature of transitional arrangements, concerning such issues as the free movement of labor, the CAP, environmental legislation, and the purchase of land by foreigners. As the accession process advances, disputes over these and other issues could temporarily paralyze negotiations between the EU and particular applicants.

Domestic politics and pressure from sectoral interests already play an important role in the accession negotiations. The Polish government, for instance, has come under heavy pressure to win full CAP subsidies for Polish farmers. In March 1998, just before the official start of accession negotiations, this demand was underscored by demonstrating farmers and industrial workers dependent on the farm sector. And in September 1999, as the Polish government prepared its negotiating position on the agriculture chapter, some fifty thousand farmers and workers demonstrated over EU and government policies in Warsaw.[57] In Poland and other applicant countries, full access to EU labor markets and lengthy transitional restrictions on the purchase of land by foreigners are among the demands that are strongly supported by public opinion.[58]

Domestic politics and public opinion are also becoming more of a factor in the member states, particularly in countries that share borders with potential new member states and thus will be the most directly affected by enlargement. In both Germany and Austria, already-high levels of unemployment and rising antiforeigner sentiment have raised fears about the influx of low-wage workers from

Poland and other poorer new member states. In both countries, a major concern is that commuting Polish, Czech, and Slovak workers will cause higher levels of unemployment in already-depressed border regions. Such concerns have led even mainstream German and Austrian politicians to talk of the need for lengthy transitional periods after accession—in some cases fifteen to twenty years—before the EU's rules on the free movement of labor are fully applied to Poland and other new member states. In both countries, concerns about enlargement and the influx of foreign workers were a campaign issue in national and regional elections in 1998.[59] In Austria, enlargement fear was a major factor accounting for the rise to power of far-right politician Jörg Haider and the Freedom Party after national elections in October 1999. Concern about the possible influx of Eastern European (especially Polish) workers is also strong in Sweden.

In Germany, expellee organizations have pressured their government to oppose the restrictions on land purchases by foreigners after accession requested by the Polish and Czech governments (see above). Pressure from expellee groups also led the German parliament (Bundestag) to adopt a declaration, in May 1998, linking Polish and Czech accession to the settlement of outstanding issues between these countries and Germany, such as the restitution of confiscated property. Expellee groups in both Germany and Austria have also urged their governments to insist on revocation of the 1945 "Benes decrees"—under which Germans, Hungarians, and other "enemies of the Czechoslovak peoples" were expelled from Czechoslovakia and their property confiscated—as a precondition of EU membership for the Czech Republic and Slovakia.[60] While the governments of both countries have thus far refused such a linkage, the leadership of Austria's Freedom Party, which entered the federal government as a coalition partner in February 2000, has expressed sympathy with this demand, setting off alarm bells in the Czech Republic and Slovakia as well as in Slovenia, from which ethnic Germans (Austrians) were also expelled.[61]

Because of domestic politics and pressure from sectoral and organized interests, individual applicants could experience problems in the accession negotiations with particular member states. In May 1999, for instance, the Swedish government briefly threatened to delay Poland's membership talks if it did not agree to liberalize its telecommunications sector, thus giving a Swedish company (Ericsson) access to the Polish market for telecommunications equipment.[62] The Austrian government, faced with a strong domestic antinuclear movement, has also threatened to block accession negotiations with Slovakia because of concerns about the safety of the nuclear reactors of its neighbor (see above). As another example of potential bilateral problems, Austria's governing Freedom Party, based in the southern border state of Carintha, has expressed concerns about the safety of the Slovenian nuclear plant in Krško, and stressed the issues of property restitution and rights for German-speakers, all issues that could hold up accession talks with Slovenia.[63]

Domestic politics and public opinion will also become more important as the negotiations enter their closing phase and thereafter. Once the Accession Treaties are signed and the EP gives its assent, the treaties must be ratified by each of the fifteen member states as well as the applicant countries before they can take effect and new member states are allowed to join. Regardless of national ratification procedures—whether requiring legislative approval or (more rarely) a positive vote in a direct referendum—in all countries the prospects for ratification will be greatly affected by domestic politics and popular views on enlargement or accession. In the EU, member state governments will be reluctant to sign Accession Treaties unless they are confident of public support for enlargement, thus avoiding the possibility of a ratification debacle. In the candidate countries, the possibility exists that Accession Treaties could be rejected due to rising anti-EU sentiment or a nationalist-populist backlash.

For this reason, opinion surveys indicating only limited public support for enlargement in the EU indicate potential problems for ratification. According to a *Eurobarometer* survey conducted by the Commission and issued in July 1999, on average only 42 percent of EU citizens are in favor of enlargement, with the lowest levels of support existing in Austria (29 percent), France (33 percent), Germany and Portugal (38 percent), Belgium (39 percent), and Britain (40 percent). By contrast, the highest levels of support were found in Denmark (62 percent), Greece (58 percent), Sweden (56 percent), and the Netherlands (55 percent).[64]

The same survey also found that only 27 percent in the EU regard enlargement as a priority for the EU, compared with 90 percent who consider both fighting unemployment and maintaining peace and security in Europe priorities for EU action. Other higher priorities for EU citizens were the fighting of poverty and social exclusion and combating organized crime and drug trafficking (both 88 percent), protecting the environment (83 percent), and guaranteeing individual rights and respect for democratic principles in Europe (81 percent).[65]

The *Eurobarometer* survey also found that support for the membership of individual applicants was low. Only for tiny Malta was there close to majority support (50 percent) for membership among EU citizens. For the other applicant countries, the percentage favoring accession measured the following: Hungary (46 percent), Poland (43 percent), Cyprus (42 percent), the Czech Republic (40 percent), Estonia (36 percent), Latvia, Lithuania, Slovakia, and Bulgaria (35 percent), Romania (33 percent), and Slovenia (32 percent). Only 29 percent of EU citizens favored the accession of Turkey, which at that time was not yet an official candidate for EU membership. By contrast, 70 percent favored membership for Switzerland and Norway, two more highly developed Western European democracies.[66]

The survey also found that support levels for the individual applicants varied considerably among the member states. While Hungary enjoyed the highest level of support among the CEEC applicants overall, support levels ranged from a high of 68 percent in Denmark to a low of 33 percent in France. For Poland, support ranged from 71 percent in Denmark to only 17 percent in Austria. And for Cyprus, support ranged from 82 percent in Greece to 27 percent in Austria.[67]

In Germany, because of its size and location arguably the most important member state when it comes to enlargement, not a single applicant country garnered majority support. Hungary and the Czech Republic had the most support among Germans (49 and 38 percent, respectively), and Romania (20 percent), Slovenia (25 percent), and Bulgaria (27 percent) the lowest. Interestingly, or perhaps ominously, only 33 percent of Germans favored EU membership for neighboring Poland.[68]

These survey results should perhaps not be taken too seriously, since they are based on a general lack of knowledge about enlargement and the accession process. Within the EU, public discussion of enlargement has thus far (until early 2000) been rare, and this issue is generally "off the radar screen" as far as public issues are concerned. The main exception to this rule has been Austria since 1999, where the rise to power of the Haider's Freedom Party has focused considerable (although largely negative) attention on the issue of enlargement. This situation of public apathy and neglect will undoubtedly change, however, as the accession negotiations focus on more difficult and politically sensitive issues, and as they near their concluding phase, thus serving to concentrate minds and mobilize organized interests.

Nevertheless, the survey results are notable in that they show a sizeable gap between official government positions in favor of enlargement and public disinterest or opposition. A similar gap caused major problems in securing ratification of the Maastricht Treaty in 1992, as member state governments no doubt remember.[69]

Declining public support for EU membership could also cause problems for treaty ratification in the applicant countries. In most of the CEECs, initial enthusiasm for "joining Europe" was replaced in the mid-1990s by "Euro-fatigue" and declining levels of public support for membership, in many cases just as the Europe Agreements were beginning to take full effect. Support for EU membership rebounded somewhat just before the official beginning of accession negotiations in early 1998 (see chapter 5). However, the level of public support has dropped considerably since, as the negotiations have advanced and as intensified preparations for membership have imposed hardships and clarified the financial and social costs of accession.[70]

In perhaps no applicant country has disillusionment with the EU been greater than in Poland, in part the result of numerous disputes with the EU over Polish government policies and preparations for membership since the beginning of accession process. In late May 1998, after previously having criticized Poland's Solidarity-led government for not providing more specific details of projects to be financed by PHARE aid and warning that the disbursal of allocated aid was in jeopardy as a result, the Commission announced that it was cutting Poland's aid allocation for the year by some ECU 34 million. In doing so, the Commission claimed that Warsaw was too late in presenting suitable projects for funding, and that its proposed spending plans failed to comply with the terms of its Accession Partnership.[71] The Commission has also expressed unhappiness with the manner in which the Polish government handles EU aid funds and with the internal organization of its team negotiating accession. The EU has also tussled with Warsaw over its plans to restructure Poland's steel industry and tariffs on imported steel as well as Polish duties and quotas on EU farm products. Because of these and other problems, the Commission has warned Poland that its membership bid could suffer and its EU entry be delayed.[72]

These disputes, together with concerns about the politically sensitive issues of agriculture, the purchase of farmland by foreigners, and the free movement of labor, as well as the fear expressed by some church leaders and nationalist politicians that EU integration could threaten Poland's Catholic identity and lead to an unacceptable loss of sovereignty, have led to declining public support in Poland for EU membership. In a survey released in June 1999, only 55 percent of all Poles said they favored joining the EU, down from 60 percent in May 1998 and a peak of 80 percent in 1994.[73] Survey results reported in October 1999 showed support for EU membership in Poland declining even further, to 46 percent.[74]

The low or declining levels of public support for EU enlargement (in the member states) or accession (in the applicant countries) create a major "public relations problem" for the EU and the acceding states. Before the final Accession Treaties are signed and submitted for ratification, both the EU and national governments must launch major information campaigns to convince their publics of the importance of enlargement or accession and to ensure them that the overall benefits are well worth the undeniable costs for the budget or to certain economic and social sectors. Otherwise, painfully negotiated treaties could fail to win approval. The precedent for such failure exists on the applicants' side, with Norway's rejection of EU membership in national referendums in 1972 and 1994.

The challenge of public opinion was recognized by the Commission in its "Agenda 2000" report as a particularly important one for the success of further enlargement. According to the Commission,

> the consent and support of European public opinion to enlargement is a clear prerequisite for the realization of the project. This will require, during the pre-accession period, a substantial public information effort in both the present and the acceding Member States.[75]

In February 2000, clearly concerned by the lack of public enthusiasm in the EU for enlargement and by the possibility that enlargement fears could generate a political backlash in some member states replicating the Haider phenomenon in Austria, the Commission announced that it was planning a major public relations campaign to convince Europeans of the merits of enlargement. To fund this information and persuasion campaign, the Commission confirmed that the Enlargement DG was preparing a submission for the 2001 budget.[76]

A strong indication of the impact of public opinion and domestic politics (and the Haider phenomenon) on enlargement came in early March 2000, when Commission President Prodi announced that the EU would henceforth take a harder line in accession negotiations with the CEECs. According to Prodi, unless the EU held the applicants to strict conditions for entry on such issues as agriculture and free movement of people, opposition to enlargement could grow, and the Austrian situation could be repeated in other member states. Because of the need for this tougher approach, said Prodi, "I am prepared to disappoint countries and ourselves too."[77] These remarks were quickly criticized by the Polish government, whose foreign minister, Bronislaw Geremek, called on the EU to do more to promote awareness of the benefits of enlargement rather than allowing fear of the consequences and the success of a right-wing party in one member state to hinder the enlargement process.[78]

In Poland itself, the beginnings of an informational effort are evident. In response to the October 1999 survey results, which he termed "alarming," Polish Foreign Minister Geremek called for a government campaign of "information and persuasion," and the Foreign Affairs Commission of the Polish parliament proposed spending $9 million on "goals related to integration."[79] It has been suggested, however, given the low level of popular support for enlargement in the EU, that the individual applicant countries will also need to expend some effort on "lobbying their case" or marketing themselves to the EU public in order to succeed in their bid for accession.[80]

THE EUROPEAN PARLIAMENT

The role of the EP will also increase in importance as the accession negotiations enter their final phase. Since the 1986 Single European Act, the EP must give its assent, by an absolute majority, to any new accessions. This step is required before the Accession Treaties can be ratified by the parliaments (or citizens, in a direct referendum) of the member states and the acceding state.

According to one inside observer, however, even before the moment when its assent to new accession treaties is required, the EP's role in the enlargement process has already been prolonged and extensive:

> If . . . one considers the enlargement of the European Union as a process which has been going on for most of the 1990s, it is clear that the European Parliament does have a substantial and influential role to play in this process. The European Parliament is involved in the process of enlargement partly in a formal capacity, partly in an informal capacity, but in due course this will certainly be in a decisive capacity.[81]

The EP's involvement in the enlargement process began in the early 1990s. In 1992, pressure from the EP, making use of its budgetary powers, was responsible for creation of the PHARE Democracy Program, which designated the promotion of democracy, human rights, and civil society as key goals of the PHARE aid program.

The EP also has sought to influence the EU's strategy for enlargement and the accession negotiations. Principally, it has argued against the division of the applicant countries into distinctive groups, and in favor of the principle of equal treatment. In a 1996 resolution, the EP declared that there should be "no first and second-class candidates" for EU membership.[82] The EP was also highly critical of the

Commission's "Agenda 2000" recommendations on enlargement strategy, arguing that all the applicant countries that met the Copenhagen political criteria "have the right to . . . open the reinforced accession and negotiating process at the same time," even though it also recognized that "intensive negotiations should begin with the countries which have made the most progress."[83] In the end, this view was essentially adopted by the Luxembourg European Council with its decision to launch a "non-discriminatory," single-framework accession process for all applicants.

After the formal beginning of accession negotiations in 1998, the EP continued exerting pressure for a more inclusive enlargement strategy that brought all second-tier applicants into the negotiations. The EP has also supported setting firm target dates for concluding the negotiations and the next accessions.[84]

While it favors a broader and more ambitious enlargement strategy, the EP has also made it clear that it will not accept further enlargement unless the EU's institutions are adequately reformed to allow for greater efficiency and democracy in an enlarged Union. The EP was highly critical of the Amsterdam results on institutional reform, and it has pressed for a broader agenda for the 2000 IGC that goes beyond the "Amsterdam leftovers"; in particular, it favors the constitutionalization of the EU treaties and the addition of a charter of fundamental rights for EU citizens and member states.[85]

The EP also plays a role in the enlargement process through the Joint Parliamentary Committees. These are standing bodies established under the Europe Agreements with each of the CEECs as well as with Cyprus, Malta, and Turkey, which have given the EP a role in the EU's structured dialogue with the candidate countries. Each of the Joint Parliamentary Committees is comprised of delegations from the EP and the national parliaments of individual candidate countries. Also attending the biannual meetings of the Joint Parliamentary Committees are representatives of the Commission and the EU presidency as well as high-level representatives of the government of the candidate country concerned. At the end of each meeting, the Committees can adopt recommendations and reports to the Association Councils, which are then dealt with in follow-up discussions at subsequent meetings.

According to an EU official who has been closely involved with their work, the Joint Parliamentary Committees perform several important functions. First, they "provide an opportunity for members of each parliament to share information and enter into an exercise of joint parliamentary control," including the opportunity to question EU and national government officials present at the meetings. Second, the longer and more wide-ranging meetings of the Joint Parliamentary Committees provide "a convenient opportunity for the Commission and EU Presidency to pass messages directly into the heart of the political system of a [candidate] country," something that briefer and more formal meetings at the diplomatic and ministerial level do not always allow. Thus, the publicly held "parliamentary dialogue . . . fills an important gap in terms of exchanging ideas and encouraging debate, both at parliamentary level and within public opinion, both in the candidate countries and within the European Union itself." Finally, the Joint Parliamentary Committees promote mutual knowledge and understanding. According to the EU official, "One could summarize the work of the Joint Parliamentary Committees as a 'vast getting to know you' exercise, given that in reality the Members of the European Parliament and the members of the parliaments of the candidate countries do not know much about each other."[86]

In addition to the bilateral Joint Parliamentary Committees, there are also regular multilateral parliamentary meetings that began in April 1995, involving the presidents of the EP and the national parliaments of the candidate countries, that have made their own significant contribution to the structured dialogue between the EU and the applicant states.[87]

Ultimately, of course, the principle leverage the EP exerts over the accession process is the requirement for its assent to the Accession Treaties at the end of the negotiations. In its debates and resolutions thus far, and in its work through the Joint Parliamentary Committees, the EP has stressed the issues of democracy and civil society, and it is certain that these issues will also figure prominently in its final decisions on the Accession Treaties. The EP has also strongly emphasized the importance of nuclear safety in the candidate countries.[88] Through the public discussion, debate, and exchange of information that they encourage, the EP and the Joint Parliamentary Committees will also undoubtedly play a key role in securing public acceptance of the Accession Treaties once these are put forward for ratification.[89]

NOTES

1. Agence Europe, *Europe Daily Bulletin,* no. 7377, 7 January 1999, 10; Agence Europe, *Europe Daily Bulletin,* no. 7391, 27 January 1999, 6.

2. Agence Europe, *Europe Daily Bulletin,* no. 7394, 30 January 1999, 7; Agence Europe, *Europe Daily Bulletin,* no. 7400, 8–9 February 1999, 11. In February, Hungary angered the EU by announcing it was planning to sign a free trade agreement with neighboring Croatia, with which the EU has no free trade relations. This agreement, Budapest announced, would end once Hungary joined the EU. See Robert Wright, "Hungary Plans Annoy Brussels," *Financial Times,* 3 February 1999, 9.

3. Agence Europe, *Europe Daily Bulletin,* no. 7447, 17 April 1999, 7. For details of the negotiating sessions with each applicant on April 19, and for Kulakowski's comment, see Agence Europe, *Europe Daily Bulletin,* no. 7449, 21 April 1999, 9–10.

4. Agence Europe, *Europe Daily Bulletin,* no. 7426, 17 March 1999, 8–9.

5. For details of the May 19 deputy-level meeting and an overview of the status of negotiations for each applicant after this meeting, see Agence Europe, *Uniting Europe,* no. 54, 24 May 1999, 1–5. See also Agence Europe, *Europe Daily Bulletin,* no. 7469, 21 May 1999, 6.

6. Agence Europe, *Europe Daily Bulletin,* no. 7481, 7–8 June 1999, 11; Agence Europe, *Uniting Europe,* no. 56, 7 June 1999, 1–4.

7. Agence Europe, *Europe Daily Bulletin,* no. 7490, 19 June 1999, 7; Agence Europe, *Europe Daily Bulletin,* no. 7492, 23 June 1999, 8–10. For all six applicants, negotiations on the following chapters were provisionally closed: science and research, telecommunications, education and training, industrial policy, small and medium-sized business, consumers and health protection, and statistics. For Hungary, the Czech Republic, and Slovenia, the chapter on fisheries was also provisionally closed. For Cyprus, the chapters on culture and audiovisual policy, external economic relations, and customs union were also closed.

8. Agence Europe, *Europe Daily Bulletin,* no. 7492, 23 June 1999, 8–10. See also Peter Norman, "Bonn Upbeat About EU Enlargement," *Financial Times,* 23 June 1999, 2.

9. Agence Europe, *Europe Daily Bulletin,* no. 7484, 11 June 1999, 8; Agence Europe, *Europe Daily Bulletin,* no. 7496, 28–29 June 1999, 3–4.

10. Agence Europe, *Europe Daily Bulletin,* no. 7563, 1 October 1999, 6.

11. Agence Europe, *Europe Daily Bulletin,* no. 7592, 13 November 1999, 12.

12. Agence Europe, *Europe Daily Bulletin,* no. 7609, 8 December 1999, 9. On Poland's environmental position paper, see "Polish Plans for Environment," *Financial Times,* 8 October 1999, 3.

13. "Helsinki European Council, 10–11 December 1999: Presidency Conclusions" ("Helsinki Presidency Conclusions"), I.8, available on the Internet at http://europa.eu.int/council/off/conclu/dec99/dec99_en.htm.

14. Portuguese EU Presidency Website, at http://www.portugal.ue-2000.pt/.

15. European Commission, "Regular Report from the Commission on Progress Towards Accession by Each of the Candidate Countries: Composite Paper," 13 October 1999, IV.2.2; available on the Internet at http://europa.eu.int/comm/enlargement/report_10_99/composite/index.htm.

16. European Commission, "Regular Report: Composite Paper," IV.3.1–2.

17. European Commission, "Regular Report: Composite Paper," IV.3.2.

18. European Commission, "Regular Report: Composite Paper," IV.3.2.

19. European Commission, "Regular Report: Composite Paper," IV.3.3.

20. European Commission, "Regular Report: Composite Paper," IV.3.4.

21. Peter Norman, "New Flexible Finishing Line for Entrants," *Financial Times,* 14 October 1999, 2.

22. "Helsinki Presidency Conclusions," I.11.

23. Agence Europe, *Europe Daily Bulletin,* no. 7639, 22 January 2000, 3; Agence Europe, *Europe Daily Bulletin,* no. 7641, 26 January 2000, 8–9. On the Commission's statement that not all second-group applicants would begin negotiations on the same chapters, see Agence Europe, *Europe Daily Bulletin,* no. 7631, 12 January 2000, 8.

24. Agence Europe, *Europe Daily Bulletin,* no. 7639, 22 January 2000, 3; Agence Europe, *Europe Daily Bulletin,* no. 7641, 26 January 2000, 8–9.

25. Agence Europe, *Europe Daily Bulletin,* no. 7656, 16 February 2000, 5–6; Michael Smith and Stefan Wagstyl, "Late Starters Strain to Catch Favourites for EU," *Financial Times,* 14 February 2000, 2.

26. For all six applicants, the Commission recommended opening talks on the following chapters: small and medium enterprises, science, education, external relations, and CFSP. For Bulgaria, it also recommended opening negotiations on culture. For Malta, the Commission recommended also opening talks on culture, industry, and telecommunications. For Latvia, Lithuania, and Slovakia, the Commission recommended also opening negotiations on cul-

ture, competition, and statistics. Michael Smith, "Brussels Plots Course of EU Entry," *Financial Times,* 9 March 2000, 2. On the views of Latvia and Bulgaria that they were ready for negotiations on fifteen chapters, see Smith and Wagstyl, "Late Starters Strain to Catch Favourites for EU," 2.

27. Agence Europe, *Europe Daily Bulletin,* no. 7631, 12 January 2000, 8.

28. Agence Europe, *Europe Daily Bulletin,* no. 7650, 7–8 February 2000, 9.

29. See comments of Günter Verheugen, cited in Agence Europe, *Europe Daily Bulletin,* no. 7663, 25 February 2000, 9.

30. Agence Europe, *Europe Daily Bulletin,* no. 7651, 9 February 2000, 7–8.

31. Agence Europe, *Europe Daily Bulletin,* no. 7314, 3 October 1998, 9. The Commission's individual reports on the agricultural sectors of the applicant countries and its general summary are available on the Internet, at the EU's official Website at http://europa.eu.int/eu/comm/dg06/ew/peco/index_en.htm.

32. "Call For Equal EU Support," *Financial Times,* 17 February 1998, 2; "Farmers Demand EU Subsidies," *Financial Times,* 5 March 1998, 3; Edith Heller, "Klagen über verschüttete Milch," *Frankfurter Rundschau,* 13 March 1998; Christopher Bobinski, "Polish Workers Demand Action to Protect Jobs," *Financial Times,* 20 March 1998, 2; Stefan Wagstyl, "Poland's 'Peasants' Set the Pace as They Prepare to Enter EU Market," *Financial Times,* 8 July 1998, 2; Stefan Wagstyl, "Poland's Farmers Dig in for Change," *Financial Times,* 9 September 1999, 3; "Poles Protest over Economy," *Financial Times,* 26 September 1999, 3; Christopher Bobinski, "Poles Split on Joining EU by Farms Dispute," *Financial Times,* 3 December 1999, 3; Christopher Bobinski, "Poland Slows Farm Reforms," *Financial Times,* 14 December 1999, 2.

33. Agence Europe, *Europe Daily Bulletin,* no. 7620, 22 December 1999, 11; Michael Smith and Stefan Wagstyl, "Front-Runners Demand Farm Subsidies," *Financial Times,* 4 January 2000, 4.

34. Stefan Wagstyl and Michael Smith, "Brussels May Ease Line on Direct Farm Aid," *Financial Times,* 9 February 2000, 2.

35. Michael Smith and Rainer Koch, "EU May Phase CAP Payments to East Europe," *Financial Times,* 2 March 2000, 3; Agence Europe, *Europe Daily Bulletin,* no. 7668, 3 March 2000, 9.

36. Stefan Wagstyl, "EU Proposes Farm Quotas to Control Trade with East Europe," *Financial Times,* 5 July 1999, 14. Also see Agence Europe, *Europe Daily Bulletin,* no. 7503, 8 July 1999, 8–9. On the problems for Polish agriculture caused by subsidized EU exports, see Wagstyl, "Poland's Farmers Dig in For Change," 3.

37. Stefan Wagstyl and Christopher Bobinski, "Warsaw Heads for Clash with EU," *Financial Times,* 21 September 1999, 4; Agence Europe, *Europe Daily Bulletin,* no. 7558, 24 September 1999, 15.

38. Christopher Bobinski, "Poland to Seek Waiver From Some EU Rules," *Financial Times,* 9 March 1998, 2. For the environmental situation in Estonia, where the problem is dependence on relatively dirty open-cast oil shale mining for energy, see Leyla Boulton, "Estonia Counts the Cost of Cleaning Up for the EU," *Financial Times,* 3 March 1998, 3.

39. Environmental dumping is the unfair competitive (cost) advantage of goods produced in countries with less rigorous environmental standards.

40. European Commission, "Communication from the Commission to the Council, the European Parliament, the Economic and Social Committee, the Committee of the Regions

and the Candidate Countries in Central and Eastern Europe on Accession Strategies for Environment: Meeting the Challenge of Enlargement with the Candidate Countries of Central and Eastern Europe," COM (98) 294, 3 June 1998. Also see Agence Europe, *Europe Daily Bulletin,* no. 7228, 25–26 May 1998, 9–10.

41. Agence Europe, *Europe Daily Bulletin,* no. 7299, 12 September 1998, 5–6; Agence Europe, *Europe Daily Bulletin,* no. 7300, 14–15 September 1998, 11.

42. "Wallström Meets Environment Ministers of the Candidate Countries" (press release), IP/99/862, Brussels, 23 November 1999; Agence Europe, *Europe Daily Bulletin,* no. 7628, 7 January 2000, 14–15.

43. "Polish Plans for Environment," 3.

44. For EU criticism of Romania and Bulgaria, see the Accession Partnerships for these countries and the Commission's November 1998 progress reports. Until their removal in January 2000, Romania and Bulgaria were the only two of the CEEC candidates to be on the EU's common visa list, which was profoundly irritating and embarrassing for these countries. For the EU's discussions with Romania and Bulgaria on this issue, see Agence Europe, *Europe Daily Bulletin,* no. 7210, 29 April 1998, 8; Agence Europe, *Europe Daily Bulletin,* no. 7300, 14–15 September 1998, 14; and Agence Europe, *Europe Daily Bulletin,* no. 7324, 17 October 1998, 7–8. On their removal from the visa list, see Agence Europe, *Europe Daily Bulletin,* no. 7642, 27 January 2000, 7–8.

45. Agence Europe, *Europe Daily Bulletin,* no. 7308, 25 September 1998, 12. The German (Kohl) government was particularly concerned about the ability of the applicant countries to control their external borders. See the comments to this effect of an official of the German Federal Interior Ministry, in "Dritte Säule soll Festung Europa stützen," *Süddeutsche Zeitung,* 20 March 1998.

46. Agence Europe, *Europe Daily Bulletin,* no. 7250, 26 June 1998, 7; Agence Europe, *Europe Daily Bulletin,* No. 2307, 24 September 1998, 8; Agence Europe, *Europe Daily Bulletin,* no. 7308, 25 September 1998, 11–12.

47. On the pre-accession strategy and EU–CEEC cooperation in JHA, see Gerhard Eisl, "EU Enlargement and Cooperation in Justice and Home Affairs," in *Back to Europe: Central and Eastern Europe and the European Union,* ed. Karen Henderson (London: UCL Press, 1999), 175–81.

48. On the first European Conference, see "Kampf gegen Kriminalität vereinbart," *Süddeutsche Zeitung,* 13 March 1998. On the second Conference, see Agence Europe, *Europe Daily Bulletin,* no. 7512, 21 July 1999, 8.

49. On the pact, see Agence Europe, *Europe Daily Bulletin,* no. 7207, 24 April 1998, 6–7; and Agence Europe, *Europe Daily Bulletin,* no. 7232, 30 May 1998, 6–7.

50. Agence Europe, *Europe Daily Bulletin,* no. 7565, 4–5 October 1999, 10.

51. A June 1998 survey of Polish citizens indicated that a majority wanted their government to win this right in accession negotiations. Cited in Christopher Bobinski, "Poland to Woo EU with Better Image," *Financial Times,* 21 July 1998, 3.

52. Agence Europe, *Europe Daily Bulletin,* no. 7323, 16 October 1998, 6.

53. Such a transitional quota system might also, according to some Commission plans, be coupled with special aid programs for the regions of member states bordering on applicant countries. See Agence Europe, *Europe Daily Bulletin,* no. 7651, 9 February 2000, 7–8; and Michael Smith, "East European Workers May Face Curbs," *Financial Times,* 22 February 2000, 2.

54. "Poland to Fight EU Demand," *Financial Times,* 6 February 1998, 2; Anatol Lieven, "EU Accession Raises Visa Worry in East," *Financial Times,* 23 February 1998, 2; "Europe's

Divide" (editorial), *Financial Times*, 27 February 1998, 23; Joe Cook, "Czech-Slovak Customs Union 'Must End,'" *Financial Times*, 2 July 1999, 3.

55. On the Polish exemption request, see Lionel Barber, "Poles Seek Financial Aid for EU Entry," *Financial Times*, 1 April 1998, 2; and Christopher Bobinski, "Poland Seeks Land Sales Ban," *Financial Times*, 14 July 1999, 3. On the Hungarian request, see Agence Europe, *Uniting Europe*, no. 54, 24 May 1999, 5–6; see also "Exemption Sought Over Land," *Financial Times*, 21 January 1999, 2.

56. "Vertriebene: EU-Reife Polens fraglich," *Süddeutsche Zeitung*, 8 July 1998, 6.

57. Bobinski, "Polish Workers Demand Action to Protect Jobs," 2; "Poles Protest over Economy," 3. See also Wagstyl, "Poland's 'Peasants' Set the Pace as They Prepare to Enter EU Market," 2; and Wagstyl, "Poland's Farmers Dig in for Change," 3.

58. In Poland, a survey published in July 1999 by the Warsaw-based Institute of Public Affairs showed that 89 percent of Polish farmers, and 83 percent of the rural population, favored continued restrictions on land sales to foreigners (and not just Germans) after Poland joined the EU. See "Poles Oppose Land Sales," *Financial Times*, 15 July 1999, 2; and "The Poles Bargain with Europe," *Economist*, 31 July 1999. A June 1998 survey showed that a majority of Poles wanted their government to win the free movement of labor in accession negotiations. See Bobinski, "Poland to Woo EU with Better Image," 3.

59. Eric Frey, "Austrians Oppose EU Enlargement," *Financial Times*, 26 March 1998, 3; Quentin Peel and Frederick Stüdemann, "SPD Warns on EU Enlargement," *Financial Times*, 2 June 1998, 4; Lionel Barber, "Germany First," *Financial Times*, 3 June 1998, 12; Michael Smith, "Austria Plans Push for Tax Harmonisation," *Financial Times*, 2 July 1998, 2; "Größere EU macht Union Sorge," *Süddeutsche Zeitung*, 8 July 1998, 6; Ralph Atkins, "Kohl Sees the Economy as Vote Winner," *Financial Times*, 13 August 1998, 2.

60. After previously refusing to discuss the Benes decrees, the Czech and Slovak governments both indicated in December 1999 that they were ready to begin discussions on the decrees with Austria. See Radio Free Europe, *RFE/RL Newsline*, vol. 3, no. 244, 17 December 1999, pt. 2.

61. Radio Free Europe, *RFE/RL Newsline*, vol. 4, no. 30, 11 February 2000, pt. 2; Radio Free Europe, *RFE/RL Newsline*, vol. 4, no. 31, 14 February 2000, pt. 2; Robert Wright, "Austria Awakens Ghosts from the Post-War Settlements," *Financial Times*, 2 March 2000, 2.

62. "Swedes Press for Liberalisation," *Financial Times*, 14 May 1999, 3. In the end, the Swedish government lifted this threat, however; see "EU Negotiations on Track," *Financial Times*, 20 May 1999, 3.

63. Irena Brinar, "Slovenia: From Yugoslavia to the European Union," in *Back to Europe*, ed. Henderson, 248–49.

64. *Eurobarometer*, no. 51 (Brussels: European Commission, Directorate-General X, July 1999), 73. The figures for the remaining member states are Spain and Finland (51 percent), and Ireland, Italy, and Luxembourg (45 percent).

65. *Eurobarometer*, no. 51, 55–56.

66. *Eurobarometer*, no. 51, 72.

67. *Eurobarometer*, no. 51, 72; and annexes, table 4.8.

68. *Eurobarometer*, no. 51, annexes, table 4.8.

69. On mounting concern about public support for enlargement, see Quentin Peel, "Europe's Pressing Public Relations Problem," *Financial Times*, 16 December 1999, 15.

70. On the rise, decline, and rise of support for EU membership in Hungary and other CEECs between 1990 and 1997, see Attila Ágh, "Europeanization of Policy-Making in East Central Europe: The Hungarian Approach to EU Accession," *Journal of European Public Pol-*

icy 6:5 (December 1999): 846–47. On the similar pattern of public opinion on EU membership in Slovenia, see Irina Brinar and Marjan Svetličič, "Enlargement of the European Union: The Case of Slovenia," *Journal of European Public Policy* 6:5 (December 1999): 814. On public attitudes toward EU membership in the CEECs before 1998, also see Heather Grabbe and Kirsty Hughes, *Enlarging the EU Eastwards* (London: The Royal Institute of International Affairs, 1998), 81–88; and Heather Grabbe and Kirsty Hughes, "Central and East European Views on EU Enlargement: Political Debates and Public Opinion," in *Back to Europe,* ed. Henderson, 185–202.

71. Christopher Bobinski, "EU Tussles with Poland over Aid," *Financial Times,* 12 May 1998, 3; "Poland Promises Project Details," *Financial Times,* 14 May 1998, 2; "Poland Faces Cuts After Being Slow Off the Mark," *Financial Times,* 26 May 1998, 2; Agence Europe, *Europe Daily Bulletin,* no. 7219, 11–12 May 1998, 10–11; Agence Europe, *Europe Daily Bulletin,* no. 7229, 27 May 1998, 10.

72. Lionel Barber, "Poland Facing More EU Pressure Over Steel," *Financial Times,* 2 July 1998, 2; Lionel Barber, "Polish PM Takes Over Reins of EU Bid," *Financial Times,* 28 July 1998, 2; Lionel Barber, "The Pole's Position," *Financial Times,* 30 July 1998, 12. Many of Poland's problems in 1998–99 stemmed from disagreement within the governing three-party AWS (Solidarity Electoral Action) coalition, and in particular the role of the anti-reform Christian Nationalist Party. A member of the Christian Nationalists, Ryszard Czarnecki, headed the government's Committee for European Integration until being demoted in late July 1998. Problems for Poland's negotiating team continued into 1999. See "Reforms Face Political Turmoil," *Financial Times,* 21 December 1998, 2; "Move Weakens EU Approach," *Financial Times,* 3 March 1999, 2; and "Polish Negotiator on EU Quits," *Financial Times,* 24 March 1999, 2.

73. Survey results reported in "The Poles Bargain with Europe"; and "Public Less Keen to Join EU," *Financial Times,* 9 September 1999, 3. On the issue of Poland's Catholic identity and Euro-skepticism, see Christopher Bobinski, "Poland's Nationalists Seek to Win Clergy's Political Blessing," *Financial Times,* 22 April 1998, 4.

74. Survey conducted by the Institute for Public Affairs (Warsaw) and reported in "Fewer Poles Want to Join the EU," *Financial Times,* 20 October 1999, 2. See also Agence Europe, · *Europe Daily Bulletin,* no. 7576, 20 October 1999, 13. On increased economic nationalism in Poland and its implications for EU accession, see Stefan Wagstyl, "Voices of Economic Nationalism Raised Louder in Poland," *Financial Times,* 25 August 1999, 2. On opposition to EU membership in Poland, see Frances Millard, "Polish Domestic Politics and Accession to the European Union," in *Back to Europe,* ed. Henderson, 203–19.

75. European Commission, "Agenda 2000: For A Stronger and Wider Union," *Bulletin of the European Union,* supp. 5/97, 136.

76. Michael Smith, "EU Plans Campaign to Sell Expansion," *Financial Times,* 16 February 2000, 3. Also see the concern about public opinion on enlargement and the "Haider effect" expressed by Enlargement Commissioner Verheugen, in Agence Europe, *Europe Daily Bulletin,* no. 7651, 9 February 2000, 7–8.

77. Peter Norman and Thomas Klau, "EU to Get Tougher on Expansion," *Financial Times,* 3 March 2000, 16.

78. Christopher Bobinski, "Poland Takes Prodi to Task over EU Expansion," *Financial Times,* 7 March 2000, 4.

79. Radio Free Europe, *RFE/RL Newsline,* vol. 3, no. 205, 20 October 1999, pt. 2.

80. Danica Fink Hafner, "Dilemmas in Managing the Expanding EU: The EU and Applicant States' Points of View," *Journal of European Public Policy* 6:5 (December 1999): 798; Geoffrey Harris, "Enlargement of the European Union: The Democratic Dimension" (paper presented to the 6th Biennial Conference of the European Community Studies Association [USA], Pittsburgh, Penn., June 1999), 17.

81. Geoffrey Harris, "Enlargement of the European Union: The Parliamentary Dimension" (paper presented at the 3rd Pan-European International Relations Conference and joint meeting with the International Studies Association, Vienna, 16–19 September 1998), 14–15. Harris is with the EP Secretariat.

82. EP Resolution on the White Paper, "Preparing the Associated Countries of Central and Eastern Europe for Integration into the Internal Market," 17 April 1996, OJ No. 141, 13.5.1996, 135.

83. EP Resolution on the Communication from the Commission, "Agenda 2000: For a Stronger and Wider Union" (COM(97)2000-C4–0371/97), 4 December 1997, A4–0368/97, 6–7.

84. Agence Europe, *Europe Daily Bulletin,* no. 7447, 17 April 1999, 11.

85. EP Resolution on the Treaty of Amsterdam, 19 November 1997, A4–0347/97; and EP Resolution on the Preparation of the Reform of the Treaties and the Next Intergovernmental Conference, reprinted in Agence Europe, *Europe Documents,* no. 2163, 26 November 1999, 1–6.

86. Harris, "Enlargement of the European Union: The Parliamentary Dimension," 14–15.

87. Harris, "Enlargement of the European Union: The Parliamentary Dimension," 17. On the multilateral parliamentary dialogue, see also Geoffrey Harris, "Re-Inventing the Union: The European Parliament in a Wider Europe" (paper presented at the conference of the International Studies Association, San Diego, Calif., 16–12 April 1996), 16–17. At the eighth multilateral meeting on 30 November–1 December 1999, the parliamentary presidents expressed their desire to see the first new accessions in 2003. See Agence Europe, *Europe Daily Bulletin,* no. 7607, 4 December 1999, 5.

88. On the importance of nuclear safety for the EP, see Agence Europe, *Europe Daily Bulletin,* no. 7596, 19 November 1999, 12.

89. Harris, "Enlargement of the European Union: The Parliamentary Dimension," 22.

Conclusion

Toward a Wider Europe

As the EU enters the new millennium, the historic process of eastern enlargement is under way. The EU has begun formal accession negotiations with ten CEECs and Cyprus and Malta, and it has recognized Turkey as an official candidate for membership. It has also begun efforts to integrate the troubled countries of the Western Balkans more closely into the EU orbit (see below). Also, the EU has begun the process of internal policy, budgetary, and institutional reform necessary to prepare itself for the addition of new member states. While some limited reforms have already been achieved (such as the Berlin agreement on "Agenda 2000"), additional changes will have to be made to the EU's policies and institutions as it adapts to the requirements of a wider Europe.

While it is difficult to forecast the precise timetable for enlargement, it is likely that the first new member states will join the EU by 2005, possibly earlier. At the time of writing (early 2000), January 2004 was increasingly being suggested as the prospective date for the first new accessions. Among the first countries to join will likely be Hungary (because of its economic and political progress) and Poland (because of its size and political importance). The Czech Republic, Estonia, and Slovenia also stand a reasonably good chance to enter the EU with this first group or shortly thereafter, as do Cyprus and Malta. Not too far behind will be Latvia, Lithuania, and Slovakia. Because of close intraregional ties and political considerations, it may make sense to delay Czech and Estonian membership so that they can join together with their Slovak and Baltic neighbors. Accession for Bulgaria and Romania will only come toward the end of the decade, while a membership date for Turkey is not yet in sight. In the meantime, additional Western European countries, such as Norway and Switzerland, may decide to join the EU as well. Within ten years, therefore, an EU of twenty-seven or more member states is entirely possible. This will be an EU, however, that is different from today's Union in many important ways.

Enlargement is accepted by the EU and its member states as both a historic opportunity and a moral and political obligation. By enlarging, the EU can spread stability and prosperity to its east and southeast and advance toward the long-desired goal of a united, peaceful, and democratic Europe. While enlargement entails potential benefits for the EU and its member states in terms of improved security, increased economic opportunity, and enhanced political and diplomatic weight for Europe on the world stage, it is also driven by a sense of moral obligation to integrate the former Communist countries and finally end Europe's cold war division between East and West.

However, enlargement also poses an enormous challenge for the EU as well as certain risks. Because of the number of applicant countries and their relatively poor economic condition, further enlargement requires substantial internal reforms by the EU, including changes to key common policies (especially the CAP and the Structural Funds), and to the EU's financing system and its decision-making institutions and procedures. This adaptive process contrasts with previous enlargements, in which the burden of adjustment fell almost exclusively on the applicant countries. By adding more member states and increasing the EU's diversity and complexity, enlargement could also make the EU less cohesive and the achievement of consensus more difficult. An enlarged EU, therefore, could be a weaker Union without adequate accompanying institutional changes.

Because of the enormous challenge and risks that it poses, the enlargement process has moved slowly, painfully slowly for anxious CEECs, for whom EU membership and "returning to Europe" is a major political and security goal as well as the route to enhanced economic prosperity. The slow pace of enlargement is explained by a number of factors, including the difficult internal changes it requires and the uneven distribution of its costs and benefits (both economic and political) among the present member states, leading to different degrees of enthusiasm for enlargement among national governments. It is also explained by the EU's preoccupation with internal deepening in the 1990s, especially EMU; this internal agenda was largely set before the dramatic events of 1989 and was lent greater urgency by the end of the cold war and German unification. The slow pace of enlargement also reflects, however, the uniquely complex nature of the EU, an organization of fifteen member states that still makes major decisions on the basis of consensus, although within a supranational institutional framework. The EU is also based on an accumulation of rules and legislation (the *acquis communautaire*) and an institutional legacy that reflect past (often painfully achieved) compromises and agreements and are therefore extremely difficult to change or renegotiate. As a result, the EU is like an enormous ocean tanker, which changes direction and speed only with great difficulty and very slowly.

The slow pace of eastern enlargement has led some observers to accuse the EU of myopia and a lack of strategic vision. The EU has also been criticized for its preoccupation with internal deepening to the detriment of widening, as well as its technocratic approach to enlargement and overconcern with the financial and economic costs of adding new member states.[1] While some of this criticism may be justified, it also bears remembering that, for all the moral and strategic importance of eastern enlargement, the EU is itself a historic achievement that deserves to be preserved and protected. A precipitate or badly planned enlargement, or one that is not adequately based on intra-EU consensus, could easily undermine the Union rather than enhancing it and possibly even lead to its unraveling. Given the EU's importance for Europe's future security and prosperity, and for the preservation and extension of European democracy, this is a development that would not be in anyone's interest.

To a considerable extent, the frustration of the applicant countries over the slow pace of enlargement stems from a fundamental mismatch of perceptions. While the EU is concerned chiefly with the future effective management of an enlarged supranational polity, the CEECs view accession largely as an international relations issue, to be decided on political, moral, and strategic grounds.[2] Because of these different perceptions (inward looking and functional versus outward looking and strategic), the EU and the applicant states often seem to be talking past each other, or carrying on two very different conversations.

Nevertheless, EU enlargement is coming, even though not as quickly as some would have liked. It is not yet a "done deal," however, and a number of potential roadblocks remain. One is the possibility that the EU will be unable to reform itself sufficiently, meaning that an enlarged Union would be too ineffective and costly. To avoid this prospect, the EU must achieve adequate institutional reform at the 2000 IGC as well as further reform of its policies and finances. Another potential roadblock is limited public enthusiasm for enlargement in the EU, which could lead some member states to refuse to sign Accession Treaties or result in ratification failures. The Haider phenomenon in Austria is a particularly serious indicator of potential domestic political opposition to enlargement within the EU. In the applicant countries as well, declining public support for EU membership could create problems for treaty ratification. Finally, there is the problem of Cyprus. At the Helsinki summit, the European Council declared (as a concession to Greece, in exchange for its agreement to official EU candidacy for Turkey) that a political settlement for the island was not a precondition for Cyprus's accession. Nevertheless, some member states remain opposed to the idea of membership for a divided Cyprus, and the issue could reignite at a later date. In this event, the Greek government may carry through with its threat to block an enlargement that does not include Cyprus.

Moreover, beyond the timing and order of the next accessions, some other important questions remain. Principally, what are the geographical limits of enlargement, and how will the future borders of the EU be defined? Relatedly, how can the EU ensure that enlargement does not lead to new divisions and conflicts in Europe? And, what will an enlarged EU look like, in terms of its institutional architecture and internal political dynamics? These questions are examined in the remaining sections of this conclusion.

THE LIMITS OF ENLARGEMENT

Beyond the twelve candidate states currently negotiating accession and Turkey, what other countries might someday be allowed to join the EU? Clearly, the EU cannot continue to enlarge indefinitely. To do so would make the Union unworkable and destroy its cohesion and identity. However, setting limits to the EU's enlargement also entails risks, including the possibility of creating new political and economic divisions in Europe that could lead to insecurity and conflict in the future. A Europe divided into countries that are secure and prosperous members of the EU and other Western (or Euro-Atlantic) institutions and countries left outside of this institutional sphere that are economically troubled and politically unstable cannot ultimately be secure. In such a Europe, where the cold war's iron curtain is simply replaced by new economic and political divisions, the EU's own peace and prosperity will eventually be threatened. Whether and where these divisions might arise depend largely on where the EU decides to draw its future geographical boundaries. It also depends on how the EU enlarges and on the policies it adopts toward nonmember countries.

The issue of the EU's future external borders is bound up with the philosophical question of "What is Europe?"—a question that has attracted considerable attention since the end of the cold war. Definitions of "Europe" abound, based on such factors as geography, culture, religion, history, and politics. These definitions do not always coincide. A strictly geographical definition of Europe, for instance, would include Russia and Turkey, while these two countries might be excluded by definitions that focus on culture, religion, or geopolitics. Certainly, all of these various definitions of Europe play a role in the ongoing debate about the future limits of EU enlargement. What is clear, however, is that the EU's future borders will not be determined by any abstract definition of Europe but instead by the internal politics of the EU and the interests of its people and member states.

Debate over the limits of EU enlargement and the EU's role in a wider Europe has intensified since the Kosovo war. In a discussion paper presented to the Council in early September 1999, the Finnish presidency posed bold questions about the future prospects of integration and EU relations with the countries of the Western Balkans and Eastern Europe, especially Ukraine and Moldova.[3]

Later that month, in his investiture speech to the EP, Commission President Prodi posed the question of whether the EU "can rest content having achieved peace, stability and prosperity only for ourselves, the 15 Member States?" Answering in the negative, Prodi went on to ask whether the EU "has the courage, the vision and ambition to offer a genuine prospect of peace, stability and prosperity to an enlarged Union *and beyond, to the wider Europe?*" [my emphasis]. Prodi then asserted the need for a comprehensive strategy for "how, over the next 25 years, we are going to enlarge the European Union from 15 to 20 to 25 to 30 Member States." This strategy must take account not only of the staged accessions of the current candidate countries, he argued, but also of "the specific needs of those countries who face a longer wait for membership" (here he mentioned specifically the Western Balkans countries) and of "the way in which this process of enlargement affects our other neighbors, for whom membership itself is not an issue but with whom we want close and constructive relations" (here he mentioned Russia and Ukraine).[4]

On the eve of the Helsinki summit, Prodi once again called for a "very, very broad" debate on the nature and frontiers of Europe.[5] Making a similar call was the president of the EP, Nicole Fontaine. In her meeting with EU heads of state and government on the first day of the Helsinki summit, Fontaine declared that, while the EP supported a broader strategy for enlargement, "one of its fundamental concerns is to know how far the Union wishes to extend geographically and culturally."[6] In public statements made after the summit, several EU leaders also stressed the need to define the EU's future boundaries.[7]

The European countries not currently involved in the accession process (excluding such Western European nonmembers as Switzerland, Norway, and Iceland) fall mainly into one of two groups: the Western Balkans countries, and Russia and other successor states of the former Soviet Union, excluding the three Baltic republics. Even though it is now an official candidate for EU membership, Turkey also remains a special case.

The EU's relations with the countries of the Western Balkans—Croatia, Macedonia, Bosnia, Albania, and Yugoslavia (Serbia and Montenegro)—have undergone a transformation since the outbreak of the Kosovo war in March 1999. Since the breakup of the Yugoslav federation in the early 1990s, the Western Balkans has been a region of conflict and turmoil, experiencing war, economic collapse, political repression, and gross violations of human rights (such as "ethnic cleansing"). Although the EU has given economic and humanitarian aid to the countries of the Western Balkans since 1990 and it sent peace observers to Bosnia in 1994, its attention has been diverted from this region by its focus on internal deepening and enlargement into Central and Eastern Europe. Since the onset of the Kosovo war, however, the Western Balkans and Southeastern Europe have become a new priority area for the EU. This new focus was motivated, in part, by an increased surge of refugees from the Western Balkans into the EU but also by the shock of witnessing the most intensive warfare in Europe since 1945.

At the instigation of the German presidency in early April 1999, the EU announced its plans to draft a major regional Stability Pact for Southeastern Europe. The Stability Pact, which was eventually adopted at an international conference in June 1999, included increased financial aid for the countries of this region. Most importantly, however, it emphasized the prospect of EU (and NATO) membership for the Western Balkans countries. According to a statement by the

German government that was endorsed by other member states, long-term stabilization in the region required a "clear and repeated commitment on the part of the EU that the countries in the region have a prospect of acceding [to the EU], even if the time of accession cannot yet be determined."[8] At an emergency summit in Brussels on April 15, EU leaders declared that all countries in the region had a "prospect for an increasing rapprochement to the EU."[9]

In the near term, the Kosovo war and the EU's new focus on the Western Balkans have increased the prospects of association with the EU for the countries of the region. In particular Macedonia and Albania, two countries bordering on Kosovo that absorbed the majority of refugees and bore the economic brunt of the conflict, have sought to translate goodwill over their support for NATO's bombing campaign against Serbia into closer relations with the EU. In late April 1999, the German presidency announced that it might be possible to soon begin negotiations on association agreements with these two countries. One month later, the Commission presented the outlines of a new type of association agreement for the countries of the Western Balkans. The proposed "Stability and Association Agreements" were something in between the Europe Agreements and traditional association agreements. They would include provisions for increased trade and EU financial and economic assistance as well as plans to engage the associated countries in political dialogue and cooperation in the field of JHA. Most importantly, however, they held out the prospect of future membership for the associated countries. In presenting its proposal, the Commission suggested that negotiations on Stability and Association Agreements with Macedonia and Albania could begin as early as the fall of 1999.[10]

After further study, the Commission decided that of the five eligible countries (Macedonia, Albania, Croatia, Bosnia, and Yugoslavia) only Macedonia was ready to begin negotiations on a Stability and Association Agreement. It thus recommended to the Council in September 1999 that negotiations with Macedonia be opened "as soon as possible." These negotiations eventually began in March 2000. In late November, however, the Commission decided that, because of continued economic, political, and institutional deficiencies, Albania was not yet prepared to begin negotiations on an association agreement with the EU.[11]

While association with the EU may come soon, full membership remains in the distant future for Albania, Macedonia, and other countries of the Western Balkans. Even assuming that peace can be restored and democracy and market economies established, significant hurdles for all of these countries remain. Cultural and religious differences could hinder EU accession for Albania and Bosnia, both of which are predominantly Muslim. Yugoslavia will have to overcome the terrible legacy of its policies toward other states and ethnic groups since 1991 as well as the considerable resentment of the Serbian people toward the West after the NATO bombings. Macedonia has historical border and identity conflicts with Greece and Bulgaria. Because it is Roman Catholic and has close historical ties to Germany, Austria, and Hungary, Croatia is the country in this region that perhaps stands the best chance of someday joining the EU should it establish democratic institutions and take measures to protect the rights of its ethnic minorities. Some progress in this direction may be expected following the death of Croatian dictator Franjo Tudjman in December 1999. In fact, after the democratic election of a new government and president in early 2000, the EU moved quickly to build closer ties to Croatia, including offering the possibility of a rapid beginning to negotiations on a Stability and Association Agreement.[12] For its part, the EU insists that it will treat the Western Balkans countries as a group, requiring substantial cooperation among themselves before they can individually qualify for membership.

Despite the still-distant prospects of the Western Balkans countries for membership, the Kosovo war appears to have galvanized the EU into taking action and responsibility for this traditionally troubled region of Europe. It may also have prompted a rethinking of the EU's basic goals and purposes, including the nature of membership, with some EU leaders talking of a "Europe of values" rather than one that is mainly a technocratic and economic community.[13] The Kosovo crisis may also result in new and innovative approaches to EU membership. The Brussels-based Center for European Policy Studies (CEPS), for instance, has proposed the concept of "associate membership status" for countries like Albania and Macedonia. This would be a sort of "virtual membership" that would stop far short of full membership yet would be a means of quickly integrating the Western Balkans countries into the EU's institutional sphere and encouraging the reforms necessary for eventual full membership.[14] The idea of virtual membership for the countries of the Western Balkans, perhaps as a prelude to full membership, was also mentioned by Commission President Prodi in his September 1999 speech to the EP.[15] It is still too early to say for sure, however, what the results of this new thinking may be.

The second group of European countries not involved in the accession process consists of Russia and other successor states of the Soviet Union, excepting the Baltic states. Outside of Russia, of principal importance for the EU are Ukraine, Belarus, and Moldova. Among other things, these three countries are distinguished by their close political, cultural, and economic links to Russia. Russia is also clearly the dominant power and influence among these countries and in the CIS. Mainly because of their orientation toward Russia, Ukraine, Belarus, and Moldova are not viable candidates for EU membership in the foreseeable future, although both Ukraine and Moldova have voiced an interest in possibly joining the EU someday, as has the former Soviet republic of Georgia.[16] Russia itself is simply too large and culturally and politically distinctive to ever be a part of the EU, while Ukraine appears torn between its ties to Russia and its desire to join the West. Instead of enlargement, the EU has promoted the CIS as the best framework for economic integration and political cooperation in former-Soviet Europe. It has also sought to build economic and political links to Russia and the CIS, with the goal of liberalizing trade throughout the continent and constructing a pan-European system of economic and political cooperation.

The EU began differentiating between the CIS states and other CEECs in the early 1990s by establishing a separate aid program (TACIS) for Russia and the CIS states rather than including them in the PHARE program, and by developing a unique system of PCAs for these countries rather than offering them Europe Agreements and the prospect of future membership. However, the EU realizes that more must be done in the future to promote stability and democracy in Russia and the CIS states, and that new ways must be found of binding these countries to Europe. It has therefore developed new "Common Strategies" toward Russia and Ukraine, the two largest and most important CIS states.[17] After months of preparation, the EU's Common Strategy toward Russia was adopted by the European Council at the June 1999 Cologne summit.[18] A Common Strategy for Ukraine was adopted by the Helsinki European Council six months later.[19] Both Common Strategies focus on the development of long-term bilateral relationships across a range of foreign and economic policy areas. They also seek to promote the building of democratic institutions and legal structures in these countries. In the Common Strategy for Ukraine, the European Council also explicitly recognizes Ukraine's "European aspirations and welcomes Ukraine's pro-European choice," although it does not mention the possibility of eventual EU membership.[20]

Even though Turkey is now an official candidate for EU membership, this goal remains only a distant prospect. Even if Turkey does become more democratic and improve its human rights performance, because of its size (63 million people), its relative poverty and large agricultural sector, and its religious-cultural differences from Western Europe, it would remain a difficult country for the EU to absorb as a new member state. Many Europeans agree with German Christian-Democratic leader Wolfgang Schäuble, who has argued that EU membership for Turkey would be "too much for Europe."[21] Also standing in the way of Turkey's membership is its traditionally hostile relationship with Greece, which can utilize the requirement of unanimity to block decisions on Turkish accession. Despite the surprising reconciliation between Greece and Turkey in the second half of 1999, which allowed Turkey to be declared an official candidate at the Helsinki summit, many problems remain between these two countries that could inhibit Turkey's integration in the EU. However, in early 2000 they did appear to be making some progress in resolving key bilateral issues.[22] There is also some doubt that Turkey will ever be willing to make the kinds of internal changes and cessions of sovereignty that EU membership requires.[23]

Turkey remains a crucial country for the EU, however, and one that it cannot afford to alienate or turn away. For one thing, Turkey occupies a strategic position in Southeastern Europe. Not only is Turkey a key "bridge" between Europe and the Islamic world of the Middle East and Central Asia, but it is also a major player in the politics of Southeastern Europe and the Balkans (and the eastern Mediterranean) and therefore must be included in EU strategies to stabilize these regions. A greater appreciation for Turkey's strategic importance resulted from the Kosovo war as well as from increased U.S. pressure on behalf of its key NATO ally. According to Enlargement Commissioner Günter Verheugen in September 1999, "Turkey is strategically the most important of the [thirteen] applicant countries. . . . It is a top priority for Europe and the U.S. that Turkey is firmly anchored in the family of Western democracies." However, Verheugen added that Turkey must meet the same accession criteria as other applicants, declaring that "there is no rebate [special concession] for political and strategic importance."[24]

Turkey is, of course, also a key factor in efforts to resolve the troublesome Cyprus issue. In fact, since the EU granted Turkey official candidate status at the Helsinki summit, there has been substantial movement in efforts to resolve the island's political problems, with progress in the ongoing "proximity talks" between Greek and Turkish Cypriot authorities giving rise in early 2000 to hopes for a settlement.[25] For political and strategic reasons, therefore, the EU must keep the door open to Turkey and find ways of integrating it into Europe.

To conclude, EU enlargement must have limits. Because of this, however, the danger exists that enlargement could contribute to the emergence of new economic and political divisions in Europe, especially to the extent that it reinforces those created by NATO enlargement. Whether the EU can develop the kinds of policies necessary to prevent or overcome such divisions, therefore, is a key question for future European peace and security. Of course, the EU is not the only international institution with a role to play in uniting Europe; also important are more specifically pan-European organizations, such as the OSCE and the Council of Europe. NATO as well, through its Partnership for Peace program and special relations with Russia and Ukraine, can make a contribution to this goal. Because of its economic power and unique integrative capacity, however, the EU has a particularly important role to play in the effort to unify Europe.

To prevent the emergence of new divisions in Europe, an enlarged EU must remain open to nonmembers in at least two ways. First, it must hold open the possibility of future membership, however unlikely this may be, and not definitively slam the door on aspiring countries. To do so would only cause resentment and undermine the chances for economic and democratic reform in these countries. Second, it must be open to intensified economic and political links with nonmember countries and provide them with economic and social access to the EU. Of particular importance is the preservation of links between new member states and nonmember neighbors with which they have traditionally close ties, such as Poland with Ukraine and Belarus, the Baltic states with Russia, and Romania with Moldova. Perhaps the proposals for new categories of membership—such as associate membership status—that have been developed for Southeastern Europe in response to the Kosovo conflict could provide a model for future relations with nonaccession countries. In any event, an enlarged EU cannot become a "fortress Europe" and turn its back on nonmember countries. If it does so, instability and conflict on the EU's periphery will be the inevitable result, with negative consequences for the EU's own security and prosperity.

THE ARCHITECTURE AND POLITICS OF AN ENLARGED EU

What will an enlarged EU look like, in terms of its institutional architecture and internal political dynamics? One common prediction is that enlargement, by adding more member states and making the EU more politically, economically, and culturally diverse, will inevitably promote the trend toward a multi-speed or variable-geometry pattern of integration in the EU. As a result, an enlarged EU could be one that has multiple tiers, or is structured along core-periphery lines.

Discussion of a multi-speed or variable-geometry EU is not new, having begun in the 1970s following the first enlargement. In 1975, the final report of the Tindemans committee suggested the possibility of a two-speed approach to integration as a means of dealing with the varying abilities and wills of the member states to proceed with further deepening.[26] Since the 1970s, interest in a multi-speed approach for the EU has grown, as subsequent enlargements have added new member states with different interests, traditions, and views on integration. In September 1994, a strategy paper presented by the parliamentary group of Germany's governing Christian Democratic Union/Christian Social Union suggested the idea of a multi-speed EU centered on a "hard core" of member states, led by Germany and France, which would push ahead with further integration while leaving other member states to catch up later. The so-called Schäuble-Lamers paper generated considerable debate and received much criticism, especially from the governments of member states not included in the proposed "hard core." Nevertheless it, and similar proposals by former Commission President Delors in February 1995, indicated a high level of interest in a multi-speed or more flexible design for an enlarging EU.[27]

In actuality, multi-speed arrangements have been an important part of the EU's development since the 1970s. Not all member states joined the exchange-rate mechanism of the EMS that was created in 1979. Nor did all member states sign the 1985 Schengen Agreement to eliminate internal border controls, although eventually all but Britain and Ireland would adhere to it. Another example is the WEU, in which not all EU member states are full members. Each of these "parallel cooperation" arrangements were, initially at least, formally separate from the EU, thus allowing some member states to not participate in the efforts of others to achieve further integration.[28]

The Maastricht Treaty set a different sort of precedent by giving special opt outs to Britain on EMU and social policy. Special exemptions for EMU and other Maastricht chapters were also later granted to Denmark to ensure ratification of the treaty by popular referendum. EMU itself is also a multi-speed arrangement, with only those member states allowed to join that meet strict economic convergence standards on such matters as budget deficits, levels of public debt, and inflation. Britain and Ireland were also able to maintain special exemptions with regard to the Schengen rules on internal border controls when these were incorporated into the EU treaties at Amsterdam.[29]

Despite predictions to the contrary, these variable-speed arrangements have not led to a permanently multi-tiered EU or divided the EU into core and periphery, or into first-class and second-class members. In most cases, they have instead served as catalysts for further deepening, with all member states eventually joining so as not to be excluded or left behind. Also, most of the "parallel cooperation" arrangements initially set up outside of the EU, such as the EMS and Schengen, have eventually been incorporated into the EU treaty framework ("communitized") or, in the case of the WEU, there are plans to do so. As a result, a striking degree of uniformity in integration has been maintained, despite the dual processes of widening, which makes the EU more diverse, and deepening, which makes the terms of membership more demanding and complex.

Nevertheless, the special circumstances and problems of the current enlargement could push the EU toward a more permanent multi-speed or variable-geometry structure. This is mainly because of the large economic gap between the present member states and the applicant countries. Further enlargement will also greatly increase the EU's diversity in terms of political traditions and interests, making agreement on new policies and additional integration even more difficult. At the same time, however, certain areas of the *acquis communautaire*, such as the Single Market and Schengen, require uniform application or else they will not function properly. Also, the applicant countries are likely to strongly resist any suggestion that they are being given a second-class status or membership. Still, lengthy transitional periods for many areas of EU legislation and policy—such as the CAP, the environment, and free movement of people—which could in some cases border on permanent exemptions, could result in a multi-speed or variable-geometry design for an enlarging EU, without it necessarily being called as such.[30]

Enlargement is also likely to reinforce another trend within the EU: the increased use of flexible integration or enhanced cooperation arrangements. Such arrangements permit some member states to agree to further cooperation without being held back by unwilling member states; however, they operate within the EU's common institutional framework, thus preserving overall unity and preventing permanent multi-tiered structures from developing. It is this goal of preserving unity while permitting flexibility that is inevitably the most difficult aspect of differentiated integration arrangements to resolve.

Flexibility, or enhanced cooperation, was a key topic in the 1996–97 IGC, yet the flexibility provisions of the resulting Amsterdam Treaty were extremely limited and, in the view of many observers, inadequate.[31] The Commission's "Wise Man" group recommended in October 1999 that the next IGC on institutional reform revisit the issue of enhanced cooperation, an action that is supported by the EP as well as the governments of some member states. However, further discussion of this issue is thus far (March 2000) not on the IGC's limited agenda (see chapter 8). Nevertheless, it seems inevitable that further enlargement and the creation of a wider Union will generate greater interest in the concepts of flexibility and enhanced cooperation.

A move toward differentiated integration arrangements could also be spurred by the EU's decision, in the wake of the Kosovo war, to pursue a broader enlargement strategy that includes admitting Romania and Bulgaria to accession negotiations, giving official candidate status to Turkey, and giving the troubled countries of the Western Balkans a (albeit distant) perspective of membership. Because the Western Balkans countries are clearly not ready for full membership, it has been suggested that some sort of special membership status be created for them (and possibly for Turkey, Ukraine, and Moldova too). One such idea—for associate membership status—was proposed in May 1999 by the CEPS. Both the CEPS and Commission President Prodi have suggested the idea of some form of "virtual membership" for these countries. The Italian government has proposed creating a "Confederation of Europe" that would provide eligible countries with something in between full membership and association. Another interesting idea along these lines is the proposal of the EP's Liberal Group, made in early 2000, for an EU of two concentric parts, a federation and a confederation.[32] The decision to create such arrangements would mark a historical departure for the EU, of course, and would result in the creation of a semipermanent (or permanent) multi-tiered structure for the EU.

Further enlargement will also affect the EU by altering its internal political dynamics. Of course, the simple addition of new member states will make the EU's decision making more difficult and complex. Beyond this, however, enlargement could also accentuate existing divisions or cleavages within the EU, or even create new ones. These divisions include the economic division between wealthy and poor member states (net contributors to the EU budget versus net recipients); the institutional division between large and small member states; the ideological division between member states favoring more integration ("federalists") and those favoring less ("intergovernmentalists"); and the external defense and security division between neutral and non-neutral member states that are also members of NATO. Several of these divisions overlap to create a discernible north-south cleavage, which expresses itself geopolitically (Mediterranean versus eastern and northern focus), culturally (Latin/Catholic versus Protestant/Social-Democratic), and economically (wealthy net contributors versus poor net recipients).[33]

By adding new member states that are generally small and poor, with their own distinctive attitudes toward integration and views on defense and security policy, enlargement will likely accentuate many of these internal EU cleavages. The addition of countries that are located mainly in Central and (north) Eastern Europe will also accentuate the EU's geopolitical divide, possibly creating an east-west division that cuts across the existing north-south one. The growing importance of a Balkans or Southeastern Europe dimension, including possibly Turkey, could further complicate the EU's geopolitical orientation; it would also accentuate its cultural divisions through the addition of predominantly Orthodox and Islamic countries.

Many of the EU's internal cleavages are "cross-cutting" rather than mutually reinforcing, however, and this characteristic is likely to prevent them from becoming permanent divisions or ruptures. Because of this, however, intergovernmental bargaining in an enlarged EU is likely to become even more complex, with shifting coalitions and alliances among member state governments from issue to issue (not even taking into account internal divisions within member states and national governments, and the growing importance of transnational interest group lobbying and social movements in the EU). This picture becomes even more complicated when one considers the growing role of the EP as well as the increased importance of subnational or regional governments in European politics. Whether consensus can be achieved and efficiency in decision making preserved (and paralysis avoided) in an enlarged EU is thus a key question for the future. Increased flexibility may well be the answer. The 2000 IGC on institutional reform is another opportunity for the EU and its member states to grapple with this dilemma.

Enlargement will also affect the internal political dynamics of the EU through its impact on the vital Franco-German partnership. This partnership, which has traditionally served as the "motor" of European integration, has already been strained by German unification and the consequent growth of Germany's size and power relative to France. However, by shifting the EU's geopolitical center of gravity eastward and adding new member states with close historical, economic, and political ties to Germany, enlargement will probably further enhance Germany's influence within the EU. Thus, whether the Franco-German partnership can survive this growing disequilibrium in power and influence is an important question for the future development of the EU.

One option for France is to counter Germany's growing influence and eastward focus by promoting a southern or Mediterranean dimension for the EU, something that Paris has attempted to do through the EU's new Mediterranean policy since 1994 and its support for enlargement into Southeastern Europe. The French government could also seek to build closer ties to Britain. Here, as well, some preliminary steps have been taken, especially with growing Franco-British cooperation on defense and security policy issues since the end of 1998.[34]

Nevertheless, the Franco-German partnership remains indispensable for European integration, and any weakening of this special relationship would have important, yet unpredictable, consequences for the EU. One possible consequence could be a weakening impulse toward further deepening. Another could be the growth of more pronounced internal cleavages in the EU, since the partnership between these two countries bridges many of the Union's key geopolitical, cultural, and ideological divides. On the other hand, a weakening of the Franco-German partnership could lead to more flexible intergovernmental coalitions that push the EU in new and more innovative directions. It must be noted, finally, that the demise of the Franco-German partnership has been predicted many times before, and it would probably be foolish to prematurely bury it now.

In conclusion, all that can be said with any degree of certainty is that an enlarged EU will be a much more complex and multidimensional entity. With possibly thirty member states or more, the EU will assume dimensions that its founding members and earliest proponents could not have imagined, and that still remain unclear today.

NOTES

1. For examples of this criticism, see Timothy Garton Ash, "Europe's Endangered Liberal Order," *Foreign Affairs* 77:2 (March/April 1998): 51–65; Lionel Barber, "Europe's Myopia," *Financial Times,* 17 September 1997, 14; Thomas Friedman, "NATO or Tomato," *New York Times,* 22 January 1997, A19; and Kirsty Hughes, "A Most Exclusive Club" (personal view), *Financial Times,* 26 August 1998, 8.

2. For this argument, see Danica Fink Hafner, "Dilemmas in Managing the Expanding EU: The EU and Applicant States' Points of View," *Journal of European Public Policy* 6:5 (December 1999): 783–801.

3. "Relations of the EU with European States and the Longer-Term Prospects for Enlargement," (paper presented to the General Affairs Council on 7 September 1999), reprinted in Agence Europe, *Europe Documents,* no. 2154, 9 September 1999, 1–4.

4. Speech by Romano Prodi, president-designate of the European Commission to the EP, 14 September 1999; reprinted in Agence Europe, *Europe Documents,* no. 2155, 22 September 1999, 3–4.

5. Agence Europe, *Europe Daily Bulletin,* no. 7606, 3 December 1999, 3–4.

6. Agence Europe, *Europe Daily Bulletin,* no. 7612, 11 December 1999, 5.

7. Agence Europe, *Europe Daily Bulletin,* no. 7613, 13 December 1999, 1–5.

8. Emma Tucker, Stefan Wagstyl, and Robert Wright, "EU to Draft Regional Stability Plan," *Financial Times,* 9 April 1999, 2. See also Agence Europe, *Europe Daily Bulletin,* no. 7441, 9 April 1999, 3–4. For details of the German proposal, see Agence Europe, *Europe Daily Bulletin,* no. 7453, 26/27 April 1999, 6. The idea of a Stability Pact for Southeastern Europe was formally approved by the Council on May 17, 1999. See Agence Europe, *Europe Daily Bulletin,* no. 7467, 19 May 1999, 2. For an outline of the EU's Common Position on the conclusion of a Stability Pact for Southeastern Europe, see Agence Europe, *Europe Daily Bulletin,* no. 7468, 20 May 1999, 4.

9. Peter Norman, "EU Aims to Take Heat Off Ethnic Cauldron," *Financial Times,* 16 April 1999, 2; Agence Europe, *Europe Daily Bulletin,* no. 7446, 16 April 1999, 5–6. On the international conference in Cologne on June 11, 1999, which adopted the "Stability Pact," see Agence Europe, *Europe Daily Bulletin,* no. 7385, 12 June 1999, 6–7.

10. For the German government's statement on the possibility of beginning association negotiations, see Agence Europe, *Europe Daily Bulletin,* no. 7455, 29 April 1999, 4–5. On the Commission's work drafting the outlines for such agreements, see Agence Europe, *Europe Daily Bulletin,* no. 7463, 12 May 1999, 13. The outlines of the Stability and Association Agreements are provided in Agence Europe, *Europe Daily Bulletin,* no. 7471, 25–26 May 1999, 5–6. For Commissioner Hans van den Broek's comments in presenting the Commission's proposal for the agreements, see Agence Europe, *Europe Daily Bulletin,* no. 7472, 27 May 1999, 3–4.

11. Agence Europe, *Europe Daily Bulletin,* no. 7547, 9 September 1999, 11; Agence Europe, *Europe Daily Bulletin,* no. 7603, 29–30 November 1999, 13; Agence Europe, *Europe Daily Bulletin,* no. 7669, 4 March 2000, 3; Radio Free Europe, *RFE/FL Newsline,* vol. 4, no. 48, 8 March 2000, pt. 2.

12. Robert Wright, "EU Welcomes Croation Election Results," *Financial Times,* 5 January 2000, 2; Robert Wright, "Croatia's New Government: Looks to EU Accession," *Financial Times,* 7 January 2000, 2; Robert Wright, "Brussels Moves to Cement Ties with Croatia," *Financial Times,* 14 January 2000, 3; Stefan Wagstyl, "Croatia Aims to Join EU by 2005," *Financial Times,* 18 February 2000, 3; Robert Wright, "Croatia Seeks Rapid NATO Tie," *Financial Times,* 25 February 2000, 2; Agence Europe, *Europe Daily Bulletin,* no. 7641, 26 January 2000, 5; Agence Europe, *Europe Daily Bulletin,* no. 7669, 4 March 2000.

13. On the galvanizing effect of the Kosovo crisis, see Peter Norman, "Union Finds Unity of Purpose," *Financial Times,* 30 April 1999, 3.

14. "A System for Post-War South-East Europe: Plan for Reconstruction, Openness, Development, and Integration," working document no. 131 (Brussels: Center for European Policy Studies, May 1999). For discussion of the contents of this proposal by one of its authors, see Michael Emerson, "After the War is Over," *Financial Times,* 17 May 1999, 12. Also see Agence Europe, *Europe Daily Bulletin,* no. 7467, 19 May 1999, 8.

15. Speech by Romano Prodi to the EP, 14 September 1999, 3.

16. On Ukraine's interest in possible EU membership, see Agence Europe, *Europe Daily Bulletin,* no. 7333, 30 October 1998, 7; and Charles Clover and Stefan Wagstyl, "Kuchma Asks EU to 'Believe in Ukraine,'" *Financial Times,* 23 November 1999, 4. On Moldova, see Agence Europe, *Europe Daily Bulletin,* no. 7642, 27 January 2000, 9.

17. The provision for EU "common strategies" is contained in the 1997 Amsterdam Treaty, article J.3 (article 13 of the consolidated TEU). The Common Strategies for Russia and Ukraine were the first uses of this new CFSP instrument. The EU is also developing common strategies for the Mediterranean and Western Balkans regions.

18. Agence Europe, *Europe Daily Bulletin,* no. 7478, 4 June 1999, 9; "Presidency Conclusions" of the Cologne European Council; reprinted in Agence Europe, *Europe Daily Bulletin,* no. 7480, 6 June 1999 (special edition), 18. The full text of the Common Strategy toward Russia is reprinted in Agence Europe, *Europe Documents,* no. 2144-45, 16 June 1999, 1–12.

19. "Helsinki European Council, 10–11 December 1999: Presidency Conclusions" ("Helsinki Presidency Conclusions"), V.56 and annex 5 ("European Council Common Strategy on Ukraine"), available on the Internet at http://europa.eu.int/council/off/conclu/dec99/dec99_en.htm. The Common Strategy on Ukraine is also reprinted in Agence Europe, *Europe Documents,* no. 2168/2169, 16 December 1999, 1–12. See also Agence Europe, *Europe Daily Bulletin,* no. 7614, 13–14 December 1999, 10.

20. "Common Strategy on Ukraine," pt. I.6. At a meeting in early December 1999 with Ukrainian President Leonid Kuchma, Commission President Prodi stressed that, "for objective reasons," the EU was not yet ready to discuss the possibility of EU membership with Ukraine. See Agence Europe, *Europe Daily Bulletin,* no. 7608, 6–7 December 1999, 12.

21. "Turkish Membership 'Too Much for Europe,'" *Financial Times,* 21–22 March 1998, 2.

22. Kerin Hope, "Greece and Turkey Make a Start by Mending the Small Things That Have Kept Them Apart," *Financial Times,* 20 January 2000, 2; Kerin Hope, "Ankara and Athens Agree Defence Talks," *Financial Times,* 21 January 2000, 3; Leyla Boulton, "Çem's Visit Set to Bolster Growing Links with Athens," *Financial Times,* 4 February 2000, 2; Leyla Boulton and Quentin Peel, "Ecevit Upbeat over Accord on Territorial Dispute with Greece," *Financial Times,* 10 March 2000, 3.

23. On these doubts, as well as for the argument that Turkey is a "special case" for the EU, see the comments of Karl Lamers, foreign policy spokesman for Germany's CDU/CSU, reported in Agence Europe, *Europe Daily Bulletin,* no. 7601, 26 November 1999, 6.

24. Cited in "Verheugen Pledges to Guard Standards on EU Entry," *Financial Times,* 13 September 1999, 3.

25. "Hopes Rise for Cyprus Settlement This Year," *Financial Times,* 1 February 2000, 2; Agence Europe, *Europe Daily Bulletin,* no. 7669, 4 March 2000, 5; Simon Taylor, "Turkish Cypriots Urged to Join Entry Talks," *European Voice,* 9–15 March 2000, 8.

26. For the Tindemans committee report, see *Bulletin of the European Communities,* supp. 1/76. For a fuller exploration of multi-speed or variable-geometry integration concepts, see Helen Wallace, *Europe: The Challenge of Diversity* (Boston: Routledge, 1985), 29–49.

27. CDU/CSU Parliamentary Group, "Reflections on European Policy," 1 September 1994. The text of the Schäuble-Lamers paper is reprinted in *Blätter für deutsche und internationale Politik* 39, no. 16 (October 1994): 1271–80. Wolfgang Schäuble was the CDU's parliamentary group leader; Karl Lamers is a leading CDU policy strategist. On the critical response to the paper by other European governments and political leaders, see Michael J. Baun, *An Imperfect Union: The Maastricht Treaty and the New Politics of European Integration* (Boulder: Westview, 1996), 164–65. On Delors's comment that a core-periphery approach was needed to allow the EU to cope with further enlargement, see *Financial Times,* 24 February 1995, 2.

28. On these various multi-speed and parallel-cooperation arrangements, see Hugh Miall, *Shaping a New European Order* (London: Royal Institute of International Affairs, 1994), 88–89; see also Stuart Croft, John Redmond, G. Wyn Rees, and Mark Webber, *The Enlargement of Europe* (Manchester: Manchester University Press, 1999), 80–82.

29. On the Maastricht Treaty opt outs and Danish exemptions, and the terms of the EMU agreement, see Baun, *An Imperfect Union,* 59–128. On the Amsterdam Treaty and integration of the Schengen rules, see Andrew Duff, ed., *The Treaty of Amsterdam: Text and Commentary* (London: Federal Trust, 1997), 46–53.

30. Françoise de La Serre and Christian Lequesne, "Enlargement to the CEEC's: Which Differentiation?" in *Enlarging the European Union: Relations Between the EU and Central and Eastern Europe,* ed. Marc Maresceau (London: Longman, 1997), 357.

31. On the issue of flexibility and the flexibility provisions of the Amsterdam Treaty, see Duff, ed., *Treaty of Amsterdam: Text and Commentary,* 185–97; Alexander C.-G. Stubb, "The Amsterdam Treaty and Flexible Integration," *ECSA Review* 11, no. 2 (Spring 1998): 1–5; and Josef Janning and Claus Giering, "Differenzierung als Integrationskonzept der künftigen Europäischen Union," in *Systemwandel in Europa—Demokratie, Subsidiarität, Differenzierung,* ed. Bertelsmann Stiftung Forschungsgruppe Europa (Gütersloh: Verlag Bertelsmann Stiftung, 1998), 41–50.

32. On the CEPS and Prodi proposals, see the previous section of this conclusion; on the Italian government's confederation proposal, see "Italy Urges Enlargement Reform," *Financial Times,* 8 December 1999, 2. On the Liberal Group's federation/confederation proposal, see Agence Europe, *Europe Daily Bulletin,* no. 7635, 17–18 January 2000, 7.

33. On the EU's north-south cleavage, see Quentin Peel, "The EU's Real Split," *Financial Times,* 25 February 1999, 14. On the various EU cleavages, see Janning and Giering, "Differenzierung als Integrationskonzept der künftigen Europäischen Union," 41–42.

34. Most notably, the "Saint Malo accord" of December 1998, in which the French and British governments agreed to work together to promote a stronger EU defense and security capacity. See Agence Europe, *Europe Daily Bulletin,* no. 7358, 7–8 December 1998, 4.

Suggestions for Further Reading

BOOKS

Avery, Graham, and Fraser Cameron. *The Enlargement of the European Union* (Sheffield: Sheffield Academic Press, 1998).

Croft, Stuart, John Redmond, G. Wyn Rees, and Mark Webber, *The Enlargement of Europe* (Manchester: Manchester University Press, 1999).

Emerson, Michael. *Redrawing the Map of Europe* (London: Macmillan, 1998).

Enlarging the Union: The Intergovernmental Conference of the European Union (London: Federal Trust, 1996).

Grabbe, Heather, and Kirsty Hughes. *Enlarging the EU Eastwards* (London: Royal Institute of International Affairs, 1998).

Henderson, Karen, ed. *Back to Europe: Central and Eastern Europe and the European Union* (London: UCL Press, 1999).

Maresceau, Marc, ed. *Enlarging the European Union: Relations Between the EU and Central and Eastern Europe* (London: Longman, 1997).

Mayhew, Alan. *Recreating Europe: The European Union's Policy Towards Central and Eastern Europe* (Cambridge: Cambridge University Press, 1998).

Michalski, Anna, and Helen Wallace. *The European Community: The Challenge of Enlargement* (London: Royal Institute of International Affairs, 1992).

Pinder, John. *The European Community and Eastern Europe* (London: Pinter, 1991).

Preston, Christopher. *Enlargement and Integration in the European Union* (London: Routledge, 1997).

Redmond, John, and Glenda G. Rosenthal, eds. *The Expanding European Union: Past, Present, Future* (Boulder: Lynne Rienner, 1998).

Redmond, John, and Lee Miles. *Enlarging the European Union* (London: Macmillan, forthcoming).

243

Sperling, James, ed. *Two Tiers or Two Speeds? The European Security Order and the Enlargement of European Union and NATO* (Manchester: Manchester University Press, 2000).

OFFICIAL DOCUMENTS AND WEBSITES

European Commission. "Agenda 2000: For a Stronger and Wider Union." *Bulletin of the European Union*, supp. 5/97 (Luxembourg: Office for Official Publications of the European Communities, 1997).

"Agenda 2000," the Commission's opinions on the various applications for membership, the Accession Partnerships, the Regular Reports (progress reports), and other official EU documents related to enlargement are available through the Enlargement Website of the European Commission, Directorate-General for Enlargement at http://europa.eu.int/comm/enlargement/index.htm.

About the Author

Michael J. Baun is Marguerite Langdale Pizer Associate Professor of International Politics at Valdosta State University. He is the author of *An Imperfect Union: The Maastricht Treaty and the New Politics of European Integration* (Boulder, Colo.: Westview, 1996).

Index